CREDITS

Photo Editor: William Rosenthal

TITLE PAGE: Rubbing of "Serpent Negro" Surinam, South America, by Ann Parker and Avon Neal.

CONTENTS: Carving done after a rubbing of "The Fabulous Water Dog," Aztec, Mexico, by Ann Parker and Avon Neal.

PREFACE: Carving done after a rubbing of "Priest with Offering," Maya, Mexico, by Ann Parker and Avon Neal.

PART ONE   THE SCIENCE OF HUMANITY Rubbings of temple sculpture, West Lake, Hangchow, China, Sung Dynasty. Courtesy of the Seattle Art Museum   1

CHAPTER ONE   THE DISCOVERY OF CULTURE Rubbing of Mayan glyphs, Tikal, Guatemala, by Ann Parker and Avon Neal   5   Neal Graham, Editorial Photocolor Archives, Inc.   6 Georg Gerster, Rapho Guillumette   14

CHAPTER TWO   THE MODERN ANTHROPOLOGICAL ENTERPRISE   Carving after a rubbing of "The Enchanter," Maya, Mexico, by Ann Parker and Avon Neal   30 S. Beckerman, Editorial Photocolor Archives, Inc.   46   E. Hosking, Bruce Coleman Inc.   49   Drawing adapted from Vincent Sarich and Allan Wilson, "Immunological Time Scale for Hominid Evolution," *Science*, vol. 158, pp. 1200–1203, December 1967   52

PART TWO   THE EMERGENCE OF MAN   A detail of a rubbing from Angkor Wat, Cambodia. Courtesy of the Fogg Art Museum, Harvard University, Cambridge, Massachusetts 54

CHAPTER THREE   EVOLUTION OF THE CULTURAL CAPACITY   Rubbing of an early Scottish carving by Ann Parker and Avon Neal.   59   D. L. Breneman   66 Drawing adapted from C. Loring Brace, Harry Nelson, and Noel Korn, *Atlas of Fossil Man*, Holt, Rinehart and Winston, Inc., New York, 1971, p. 10   69   N. Myers, Bruce Coleman Inc.   78   Courtesy of the American Museum of Natural History   82

CHAPTER FOUR   TO THE ENDS OF THE EARTH: CULTURAL AND PHYSICAL VARIATION Rubbing of "The Fanged Man," Peru. Courtesy of the American Museum of Natural History 87   Drawing adapted from Betty J. Meggers, *Prehistoric America*, Aldine Atherton, Inc., Chicago, 1972, p. 8   90   Eskimo by Georg Gerster, Rapho Guillumette; Ethiopians by Ivan Polunin, Bruce Coleman Inc. 104–105

PART THREE   FROM SUBSISTENCE TO SURPLUS: ECONOMIC EVOLUTION Rubbing of a scene from "The Churning of the Sea of Milk," Angkor Wat, Cambodia. Courtesy of the Weyhe Gallery, New York 110

CHAPTER FIVE   MAN AS HUNTER   Detail of a rubbing from Angkor Wat, Cambodia. Courtesy of the Weyhe Gallery, New York 117   Courtesy of the American Museum of Natural History   120   Lennart Nilsson, Black Star   127   Georg Gerster, Rapho Guillumette   133   Courtesy of the American Museum of Natural History   138

CHAPTER SIX   PRIMITIVE TILLERS OF THE SOIL   Rubbing from Palenque, Chiapas, Mexico, by Robert S. Lindsley. Courtesy of the Seattle Art Museum   144   Picture from Napoleon Chagnon, *Yanomamö, The Fierce People*, Holt, Rinehart and Winston, Inc., New York, 1968, p. 2. Reprinted by permission 149   Picture from Robert Gardner and Karl Heider, *Gardens of War—Life and Death in the New Guinea Stone Age*. Random House, Inc., New York, 1968, p. 11. Reprinted by permission   153   Paolo Koch, Rapho Guillumette   159   Harrison Forman   163

CHAPTER SEVEN   MAN AND BEAST: THE PASTORALISTS   Rubbing from Angkor Wat, Cambodia. Courtesy of the Weyhe Gallery, New York   170   Jean-Dominique Lajoux, Rapho Guillumette   178   John Moss, Black Star   184   Culver Pictures, Inc.   189

CHAPTER EIGHT   PEASANTS AND FARMERS Rubbing of an early Scottish carving by Ann Parker and Avon Neal   196   Federico Borromeo   198   Georg Gerster, Rapho Guillumette   207   Thase Daniel, Bruce Coleman Inc.   213

CHAPTER NINE   WEALTH AND SOCIAL CLASS Carving after a rubbing of "Slave Panel Three" by Ann Parker and Avon Neal   220 Courtesy of the American Museum of Natural History   225   Joseph Martin   227 Courtesy of the American Museum of Natural History   238

PART FOUR   THE HUMAN BOND   Rubbing from Angkor Wat, Cambodia. Courtesy of the Weyhe Gallery, New York   244

CHAPTER TEN   MARRIAGE AND FAMILY Rubbing of a maternity figure, San Augustine, Columbia, by Robert S. Lindsley. Courtesy of the Seattle Art Museum   249   Tony Howarth, Woodfin Company and Associates 263   Courtesy of the American Museum of Natural History   266   Erich Hartmann, Magnum Photos   271

CHAPTER ELEVEN   KINSHIP AND LINEAGE Rubbing of a medieval Yugoslavian carving by Ann Parker and Avon Neal   273

CHAPTER TWELVE   FROM TRIBALISM TO STATE   A detail of a rubbing from Angkor Wat, Cambodia. Courtesy of the Fogg Art Museum, Harvard University, Cambridge, Massachusetts   291   Courtesy of the American Museum of Natural History   303 Hubertus Kanus, Rapho Guillumette   306 M. Biber, Rapho Guillumette   313

CHAPTER THIRTEEN   THE RULE OF LAW Rubbing from an Irish gravestone by Ann Parker and Avon Neal   314   Courtesy of the American Museum of Natural History 323, 326   Harrison Forman   332 Guiron Le Courtois, Turin National Library, Editorial Photocolor Archives, Inc.   334

PART FIVE   EVOLVING VIEWS OF THE WORLD   Rubbing of an Assyrian bas relief by Ann Parker and Avon Neal   338

CHAPTER FOURTEEN   THE AWESOME SPIRITS   Rubbing from Angkor Wat, Cambodia. Courtesy of the Fogg Art Museum, Harvard University, Cambridge, Massachusetts   343   Emil Schulthess, Black Star   353   Culver Pictures, Inc. 361   Courtesy of the American Museum of Natural History   364

CHAPTER FIFTEEN   THE GROWTH OF THE GODS   Rubbing of Stele Raimondi, Chavin de Huantar, Peru, by Ann Parker and Avon Neal   366   Courtesy of the American Museum of Natural History   371   Culver Pictures, Inc.   374   Drawing adapted from Robert Bellah, "Religious Evolution," *American Sociological Review*, vol. 29, pp. 358–374, 1964 381   Raghubir Singh, Woodfin Camp and Associates, Orion Press/Scala   384 Courtesy of the American Museum of Natural History   387

CHAPTER SIXTEEN   EXTENSIONS OF COMMUNICATION   Rubbing of "Musicians with Banners" from Angkor Wat, Cambodia.

EVOLVING
LIFE STYLES

1176

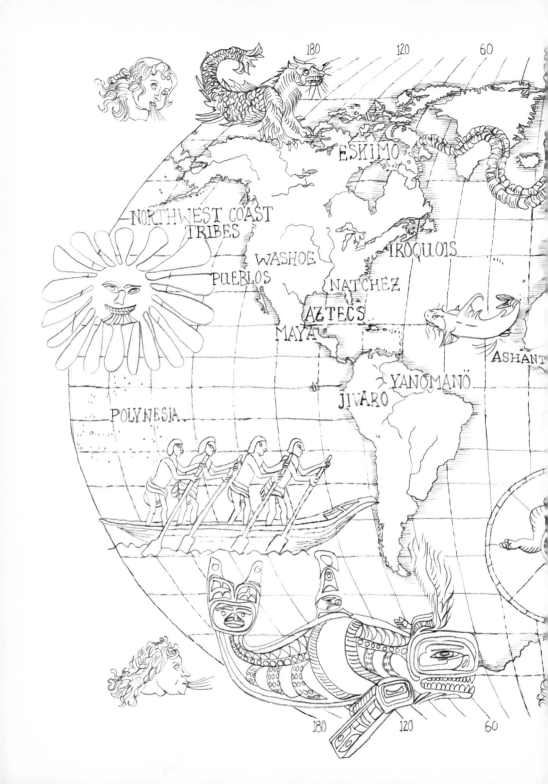

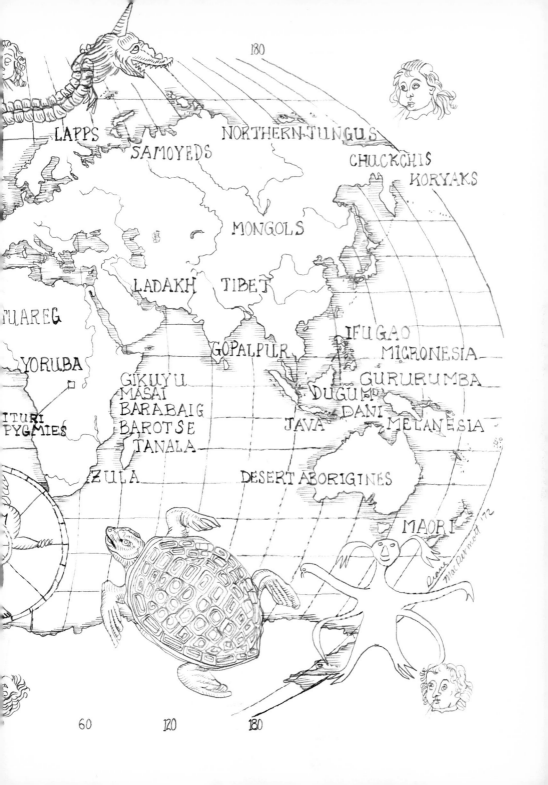

180

LAPPS

SAMOYEDS

NORTHERN TUNGUS

CHUCKCHIS

KORYAKS

MONGOLS

LADAKH   TIBET

TUAREG

YORUBA

GOPALPUR

IFUGAO

MICRONESIA

GIKUYU
MASAI
BARABAIG
BAROTSE
TANALA

GURURUMBA

DUGUM
DANI

JAVA

ITURI
PYGMIES

MELANESIA

ZULA

DESERT ABORIGINES

MAORI

60   120   180

McGRAW-HILL BOOK COMPANY

New York   San Francisco   St. Louis   Düsseldorf   Johannesburg   Kuala Lumpur   London
Mexico   Montreal   New Delhi   Panama   Rio de Janeiro   Singapore   Sydney   Toronto

ELBERT W. STEWART

Chairman, Department of
Sociology and Anthropology
Bakersfield College

EVOLVING
LIFE STYLES

An Introduction to Cultural Anthropology

This book was set in Elegante by Applied Typographic Systems. The editors were Ronald D. Kissack and Eva Marie Strock, the designer was Janet Durey Bollow, and the production supervisor was Michael A. Ungersma. The drawings were done by Diane MacDermott.

The printer was Halliday Lithograph Corporation; the binder, The Maple Press Company.

Cover: Mayan Tree of Life, Mexican National Monument, Movida, adapted by Janet Durey Bollow.

EVOLVING LIFE STYLES
An Introduction to Cultural Anthropology

Copyright © 1973 by McGraw-Hill, Inc. All rights reserved. No part of this publication may be reproduced, stored in a retrieval system, or transmitted, in any form or by any means, electronic, mechanical, photocopying, recording, or otherwise, without the prior written permission of the publisher.

Printed in the United States of America.

LIBRARY OF CONGRESS CATALOGING IN PUBLICATION DATA

Stewart, Elbert W.
    Evolving life styles.

    1. Ethnology.   I.   Title.
GN315.S72   301.2   72-12685
ISBN 0–07–061349–4
ISBN 0–07–061334–6 (pbk)

1234567890   HDMM   79876543

Preface   xv

PART ONE
THE SCIENCE OF HUMANITY   1

One   The Discovery of Culture   5

Two   The Modern Anthropological
           Enterprise   30

PART TWO
THE EMERGENCE OF MAN   55

Three   Evolution of
           the Cultural Capacity   59

Four   To the Ends of the Earth:
           Cultural and
           Physical Variation   87

PART THREE
FROM SUBSISTENCE TO SURPLUS:
ECONOMIC EVOLUTION   111

Five   Man as Hunter   117

Six   Primitive Tillers
           of the Soil   144

Seven   Man and Beast:
           The Pastoralists   170

Eight   Peasants and Farmers   196

Nine   Wealth and Social Class   220

Contents

PART FOUR
THE HUMAN BOND   245

Ten   Marriage and Family   249

Eleven   Kinship and Lineage   273

Twelve   From Tribalism to State   291

Thirteen   The Rule of Law   341

PART FIVE
EVOLVING VIEWS OF THE WORLD   339

Fourteen   The Awesome Spirits   343

Fifteen   The Growth of the Gods   366

Sixteen   Extensions
           of Communication   391

PART SIX
THE QUICKENING PACE OF CHANGE   419

Seventeen From Stone to Steel:
           Technological Evolution   423

Eighteen   Man As Evolutionist   444

Glossary   463

Index   477

To
Karen, Mike,
Mary, and Jean

Anthropology has a wider appeal today than ever before, partly because at a time when the world seems to be rushing toward systems of mechanistic uniformity it is heartening to look at other life styles, to find that great diversity has always characterized mankind and that it continues even today. It is important that we no longer look upon contrasting life styles with ethnocentric horror or with amused tolerance, but with genuine interest. It is a thesis of anthropology that only by studying man in all his cultural diversity do we learn to know him. For the anthropologist, to "know thyself" means to look outward, not merely inward.

Although the substance of a cultural anthropology book is to a great extent the study of custom, or of life style, it seems important to start with a general description of the full range of anthropology as a discipline. To know man as a cultural being it is necessary to know something of his remote origins, of his physical traits, of the artifacts left by his ancestors, and of the thoughts and cultural concerns reflected in his linguistic patterns. It is also of interest to review the origin of anthropology, the long process by which men began to overcome their

Preface

narrow mindedness enough to seek to understand their fellow men. For this reason the first chapters are devoted to a description of the origins of anthropology, its tremendous scope, and the many enterprises in which it is now engaged. Anthropology seeks greater knowledge of man partly through a mere compulsion to know, but, it is hoped, also with the thought that greater knowledge of man will enable us to avoid many of the mistakes—even disasters—of narrow vision and ignorance of possibilities.

In the major portions of this text, which concentrate on the cultures of many peoples of present or recent times, two approaches are used to give system and order to the presentation. In Part Three, a large number of societies are described, starting with hunting and gathering and moving through primitive horticulture, pastoralism, and finally peasantry and plow agriculture. The approach in this respect is somewhat empirical, with a presentation of evidence leading to conclusions about changes in productivity and in social organization and world views. This empirical approach not only presents many life styles but, consistent with the title of the book, shows those styles in a context of evolutionary change.

A cultural-evolution framework is used to bring a sense of unity and direction to the study and to make it meaningful to the student. Different cultural evolutionists give the concept of cultural evolution different shades of meaning. "General evolution" refers to the generalistic cultural drift of the entire human species, at present toward urban-industrial states. "Multilineal evolution" refers to the many different lines of development cultures can take, depending partly on the natural environments in which they are found, partly on their contacts with other cultural ideas, and partly on basic philosophies related to but not entirely determined by either natural environment or cultural contacts. In many of the descriptions of cultures in Part Three, multilineal types of development will be obvious, with peoples living in unproductive desert lands displaying certain similarities in development and those in lands of natural abundance showing other types of similarities. In the final chapters, though, where communication and technology are discussed, the perspective becomes increasingly that of general evolution—a general widening of cultural possibilities for all mankind because of the growth and diffusion of technologies and ideas.

The picture of evolving cultures is rather similar to that of a great river fanning out into a delta near its mouth, where it is hard to tell which of many alternate channels is the main one. To a degree, the water courses seem confused and contradictory; yet there is a common gravitational force that moves them eventually in a similar direction. In the case of mankind, too, there are multiple channels of movement, but there are also forces that prevent diversity from being infinite and unintelligible. Despite their very interesting and important diversity of culture, all human beings are of one species, with enough similarity of minds, emotions, desires, and potentialities to prevent total chaos and mutual unintelligibility.

After examining a variety of cultures at many levels of development, certain aspects of life styles will be looked at in more detail. The whole subject of the emotional, moral, legalistic, and even mystical ties that hold men together must be examined. Are there trends in the degree to which kinship welds people together into a common bond and in the way people solve their quarrels, dispose of troublesome cases, and maintain social control? Such questions lead to consideration of the modern state, nationalism, ideologies, and their problems.

Several other areas of human life are given special treatment in the perspective of evolving cultural systems. The first of these is the great area of interpretation of the world through magic, religion, and ideology. First the seemingly random differences in belief are discussed, then attention turns to the trends that lead from animism to the foundations of the world's great religions and to the impact of modern science and modern ideologies. Another line of development relating to man's perception of the world also is traced, and that is his capacity to communicate, first only through the spoken word and then through art, notations, pictographs, and eventually writing. The result of this intellectual achievement is shown to have a profound effect on the cumulative and inventive possibilities of culture.

Finally, before an anthropology course can have its full impact as something of major significance to the modern world, it is necessary to trace the growth of technology and its transformation of the world. Along with technology comes an increasing pace of events, greater precision, a greater ability to penetrate secrets and to probe the unknown, and the type of science that increasingly influences its own maker and may thoroughly remold him. Man in previous times could see life as the repetition of similar cycles of birth, maturity, and death, with each generation living much as other generations had and would on through the cycles of eternity. Now we no longer presume to say what forms the lives of the future will take and sometimes even fear "lest existence, closing your account and mine, should know our like no more." We alternate between utopian hopes for the future and Orwellian fears. Probably the future holds neither heaven nor hell for us, however. Students of anthropology cannot help but hope that, whatever happens, the great diversity and adaptability of mankind will continue into the future and new life styles will evolve into varied patterns so that the nightmare of the total homogenization of the human species will not be realized.

ACKNOWLEDGMENTS   In the production of a book an author is always in need of the help of a number of people, and in this case the help has been generous and of the highest quality. First, I wish to acknowledge the contribution of an extremely able editor, Ronald Kissack, for the many ideas that have helped make the subject matter clear, readable, and student oriented, as well as for the selection of photographic material for the text. Others who have made direct contributions to the production of this book include an extremely thorough and helpful production editor, Eva Marie Strock; an artistic and imaginative book designer, Janet Bollow; and the very talented illustrator, Diane MacDermott.

I am also grateful for the unusual care and effort expended by the following reviewers and for the quality of their suggestions: Michael D. Sullivan of De Anza College, Cupertino, California; Joseph R. Walsh of Bucks County Community College, Newton, Pennsylvania; Barry D. Kaas of Orange County Community College, Middleton, New York; and Willis E. Sibley, Chairman of the Department of Anthropology, Cleveland State University, Cleveland, Ohio. The book has been greatly strengthened by following many of their comments about organization, emphasis, style, illustrative material, and definition of terms. The production schedule and book length precluded incorporating all suggestions, but many were used, and all were well considered.

I wish to thank also a number of my colleagues for their wealth of information and ideas: Leonard Lieberman, John Dumitru, Caroline Davis, John Lyman, and Mita Dhariwal. My appreciation also to Michael Stewart for a number of helpful suggestions regarding the first chapters and for indexing this text. Finally, I wish to thank two outstanding professors: Daniel Crowly of the University of California at Davis and Robert Murphy, now of Columbia University, for presenting anthropology as a subject not only of science but of art, music, folklore, humor, philosophy, and all that helps mitigate the burden of being human.

ELBERT W. STEWART

EVOLVING
LIFE STYLES

PART ONE
THE SCIENCE
OF HUMANITY

"The science of man" is the usual designation for anthropology, but here "the science of humanity" is chosen, to stress not only the idea that anthropology deals with all humanity but also that it partakes of the nature of the humanities as well as that of the sciences. Scientific method calls for great care and precision and checking and rechecking of data. In this respect, anthropology is scientific. In much of its substance, however, anthropology enters the territory of the humanities, studying art, religion, philosophy, myth, and folktale and making a science of their interpretation. Like the humanities, anthropology often finds itself dealing with questions to which there are no final conclusions or agreed-upon evaluations. Of the hundreds of societies and life styles encountered it says only that each has the right to be understood empathically and to be interpreted to the world without bias.

Cultural anthropology has sometimes been described as "the science of custom," yet it will be found in the following pages that far more than customs and folkways are studied in this branch of anthropology. Moreover, the subject matter of the other branches has its bearing upon culture. Some of these will be discussed briefly in the second chapter. It is important also to know what attitudes have prevailed about people whose ways are strange and how these attitudes have been changed by anthropological concepts. We shall see that since ancient times a few real scholars have tried to make sense out of the diversity of human ways, but that it was not until the nineteenth century that some of the necessary points of view developed, and really not until the twentieth century that methods of study advanced to a point that could be designated as scientific. Before culture could be understood, many new approaches had to be found. Living cultures had to be studied systematically and compared. Strange new languages had to be learned and understood thoroughly before the secrets of cultural attitudes and beliefs could be penetrated. More had to be learned of how cultures develop, and the road led much further than the historian's customary road back to Greece and Rome or Egypt. The search led to all parts of the world, to the record of simple societies as well as advanced, and incredibly far into the past. Not only were cultural remains sought but also the record of the physical evolution of the human species and how man developed the capacity for culture.

The first step in understanding anthropology, then, will be to see how the concept of culture evolved and what conflicting attempts have been made to explain the characteristics of culture and its direction of change. What have anthropologists surmised about the human record and the human direction? What is the total scope of their field? How do their diverse activities all relate to the central theme of man's cultures or styles of life?

As is the case with many of the social sciences, anthropology is of surprisingly recent origin. It would seem that the social sciences, particularly anthropology, the science of man, should have developed long ago. In many respects human beings have always seemed thoroughly fascinated by themselves, compulsively making up myths and stories and philosophies to explain their origin and to give themselves a sense of cosmic importance. Why, then, did such storytelling and philosophizing not result in a much earlier development of a science of man? In earlier times were foreign people and foreign customs simply of no interest, or was it that things foreign were looked upon with misgiving and dread? How did the idea develop that all people and all cultures should be studied, not just Western civilization and the cultures that seem to be an immediate part of its line of development? What discoveries and insights broadened our horizons enough to make all mankind part of one scientific discipline, and why is such a study gaining enthusiastic response from the present college generation?

Chapter One
The Discovery
of Culture

To anthropologists, all the diverse cultures of man are equally worthy of study and understanding.

Long before the development of anthropology, peoples who had newly come into contact held great fascination for each other, but each generally considered the other peculiar and inferior. Sometimes strange new people have been approached openly for trade or stealthily for plunder. Occasionally they have been bargained with in an attempt to gain allies, and sometimes women have been traded to seal the bargain. During the expansion of the Western world, strange peoples were conquered in the course of empire building and their lands were exploited for the raw materials of industry. For years many of the new lands were also raided for slaves.

Not all Western expansionists were conquerors or slave raiders or even merchants; some had the pious ambition of converting others to their own religion, to the greater glory of the white man and his God. Rarely in the long story of new contact between peoples, however, was the stranger looked upon as an equal, with a way of life to be understood rather than scorned. He was not seen as the bearer of a culture as valid for the resolution of the riddles of mankind, as distinctively human, as full of potentialities, and as worthy of study as any other.

Anthropology looks upon all people in this manner. Consequently, anthropology is more than a science; it is a growing area of the humanities as well. Philosophically, it looks for many levels of meaning in the record of man and speculates about his future. Artistically, it tells the story of the peoples whose cultures have survived and of those whose cultures have been crushed under the weight of war, famine, plunder or under the equally ruthless jugger-naut of technological civilization. It attempts to tell the story with scholarly accuracy but also vividly and compassionately, entering into the thoughts and lives of the people through the medium of the cultural concept and the belief that all peoples possess a common humanity.

THE CULTURE CONCEPT   The culture concept is essentially the idea that the wide differences between groups of people are determined mainly by their cultures, not by their races or biological types. Cultures are the distinctive ways of life developed by different bands, tribes, and nations over long periods of history and passed along to each individual as he matures and becomes a member of his own social group. Culture encompasses language, means of making a living, arrangement of family life, locus of group loyalties, and ways of perceiving the world—both the physical world and the world of spirits, demons, and gods. Culture sets controls over human drives, influencing eating habits, hours of sleep, maturation, the display of emotion, and sexual relations. Culture pro-vides for reproduction and care of new members and patterns of child rearing that perpetuate its own values and points of view. Culture includes techniques and skills and is able slowly to change with the development of new techniques and ideas or as a result of borrowing ideas and skills from other cultures.

All peoples develop cultures, and there is a unity behind the diversity of culture. All cultures make arrangements for livelihood, for family structure, for social control, and for psychologically sustaining myths and systems of belief. Such similarities in cultural content, along with the ability of the infant of one group to learn the culture of another, convince us of a great similarity in the mental and emotional characteristics of all segments of the human species, a concept sometimes referred to as "the psychic unity of man."

THE CURRENT APPEAL OF ANTHROPOLOGY   The notion that differing cultural patterns are a valid explanation for most human behavioral contrasts is not new or revelatory for the present college generation, nor does the present generation find it hard to accept the idea that all people are of one species, both physically and mentally. The last few years have seen a great increase in the size of anthropology classes and a swelling of the ranks of trained anthropologists. Undoubtedly the growing acceptance of anthropological views and the growing interest in anthropology are rooted in an age of rapid communication and expanding world travel. Another reason for the interest, especially in America, is our increasing awareness of the multiracial and multicultural nature of our own society. There is probably yet a third reason, and that has to do with a critical attitude toward man's present condition.

We live in a world that has become disillusioned with many of its old explanations and attitudes, and especially with those which seem to divide people against one another. We are tired of nationalistic and racial bigotry and see the hope for our continued survival and happiness as depending on broader perspectives and greater mutual understanding. There is also a felt need for more time for reflection on the course over which we have traveled and the road ahead; too long have we dared not take a moment out from the pursuit of material satiation. The world's leading anthropologists have been a strange breed in this respect, interested in the far away, the unusual, the unknown, admiring the craftsmanship of the Pomo basket weaver and the harpoon of the Eskimo, treasuring ancient potsherds, and treating a two-million-year-old tooth as though it were a Kimberly diamond.

There is definitely a touch of romanticism about anthropology, and that is probably one of its attractions for the present age. Our age has some of the attitudes of the early romanticists of literature: wishing to look beyond the present and the mundane, to glorify the elemental, to take a new look at the primitive and peasant worlds and at nature. Romanticism can be overdrawn, of course, as it was in Rousseau's image of the "noble savage." Not all primitive life is noble; much of it is laden with hardship, disease, and even cruelty. No modern anthropologist will be romantic enough to picture the simpler life as an earthly paradise, but he may find important values that have been left behind. Whatever else he finds, simple honesty or chicanery, shrewdness or guilelessness, he will find societies that form a continuum with all the other human societies that exist.

Another appeal of anthropology for the student is that it lacks some of the narrowness and extreme specialization of many academic disciplines. In earlier days all leading American anthropologists were trained in both the physical and the cultural aspects of the discipline. The scope of anthropology has become too great to allow the same unity as before, but even now the lines

INCREASING AWARENESS OF SIMILARITIES AMONG RACES
EXPANDING KNOWLEDGE OF THE WORLD
INTEGRATION PROBLEMS OF MULTIETHNIC SOCIETIES
DISILLUSIONMENT WITH ETHOCENTRISM AND RACIAL BIGOTRY
MAN'S GROWING CAPACITY FOR SELF-CRITICISM
INTEREST IN THE UNUSUAL AND UKNOWN
NEED FOR A BROADLY BASED INTELLECTUAL DISCIPLINE
DESIRE TO FIND MEANING IN MAN'S EXISTENCE
UNCERTAINTY ABOUT MAN'S FUTURE AND SURVIVAL

of communication within the anthropological field are open and clear. Its central concern with culture gives it unity as a discipline. Within its universe lie much of the mystery and wonder of the world—ancient artifacts, human and protohuman remains of early Pleistocene times and before, the palaces and temples of early civilizations, music and the arts, myths and tales, social class systems, and the beliefs and skills and techniques of people at all levels of cultural development. Undoubtedly, the attempt to integrate and make sense of the total range of human experience helps to give anthropology its appeal. Margaret Mead, probably the anthropologist best known to the average layman, sums up the discipline as follows:

> Anthropology is a uniquely situated discipline, related in diverse ways to many other disciplines, each of which, in specializing, has inadvertently helped to fragment the mind of modern man. *Anthropology is a humanity*, represented in the American Council of Learned Societies, concerned with the arts of language and with the versions that human cultures have given of the definition of man and of man's relationship to the universe; *anthropology is a science*, concerned with discovering and ordering the behavior of man-in-culture; *anthropology is a biological science*, concerned with the physical nature of man, with man's place in evolution, with the way genetic and racial differences, ecological adaptations, growth and maturation, and constitutional differences are implicated in man's culture and achievements; *anthropology is a historical discipline*, concerned with reading the record of man's far past and establishing the links which unite the potsherd and the first inscriptions on stone, in tying together the threads between the preliterate and the literate world wherever the sequence occurs, in Egypt, in China, in Crete, or in a modern African state. *Anthropology is a social science*, although never only a social science, because in anthropology man, as part of the natural world, as a biological creature, is not separated from man as a consumer or producer, member of a group, or possessor of certain psychological faculties. *Anthropology is an art*. The research skills that go into good field work are as complex as the skills of a musician or a surgeon. [Italics added.][1]

THE APPEAL OF THE UNUSUAL   Anthropology, then, has many aspects and attractions for the student. It is well to add that anthropology is a narrative of many of the most absorbing details of various patterns of life. Anthropologists have long avoided making their study a mere collection of cultural curiosities, for their purpose is to find meaning, not simply to collect accounts. Never-

[1]Margaret Mead, "Anthropology—an Education for the Future," in David G. Mandelbaum et al., *The Teaching of Anthropology*, University of California Press, Berkeley, 1963, p. 596. Originally published by the University of California Press; reprinted by permission of the Regents of the University of California.

theless, there is no question that for the layman one of the fascinations of anthropology is simply the narrative of the strange and unusual. Even if we do not penetrate deeply into the origin or functions of family diversity, we are, nevertheless, amazed to learn that our Nigerian visitor, dressed as we are and communicating very well in our own language, is one of the ninety children of his father, the district chief, and that he calls all twenty of his father's wives "mother." We try to picture the family and the different way of life implied and are unable to do so. Our visitor tells us that the huge family in his culture is now on the decline but that it has been a great source of comfort and security to him.[2]

We are perhaps encouraged to study further and learn of brothers who must share one wife, of Eskimo wife-swapping arrangements, and of wife hospitality. In some places sexual relations are severely regulated; in others they are given but the minimum of regulation. Then we hear of whole new classes of cultural phenomena. We learn of people whose conditions of life are so hard that they find it necessary to kill part of their female babies to keep down the population and must leave the aged to die or even help them on their way with a blow on the head. We find that in yet other societies the aged are allowed to dominate and in some cases even tyrannize. Children are reared in widely differing manners, sometimes overwhelmed with love and sometimes reared sternly, with more emphasis on status than on pure affection. Sometimes the rites of puberty for young boys are so severe that a few die; yet the rites are felt to be so important that they must be continued. Eating habits differ greatly, both in the foods consumed and in table manners; but usually some foods are taboo. Always there are beliefs about the supernatural, and these ideas sometimes lead to a fearsome preoccupation with witches and sorcerers and with the means by which their evils can be thwarted.

Such comments on culture as the ones just given need to be ordered. Customs and beliefs must be explained as the people who practice and believe in them would explain them; they also need deeper explanation through cross-cultural analysis, to show why they are necessary or at least commonly found at certain levels of development. Before anthropology was born as a discipline, the knowledge of strange customs was in the nature of the unexplained account just presented and was sometimes discussed in books with such titles as *The Abominations of Heathenism*. It would be the task of anthropology to make order out of what appeared to be cultural chaos, but anthropology was a long time being born. Many scientific findings and new viewpoints had to develop

[2]From conversation with Anthony A. U. Idiong, Anang chief, Abak Igot, Southeastern State, Nigeria.

before the importance of culture was discovered. Fear of foreigners and intense belief in the superiority of their own ways prevented many people of the past from developing the inquiring attitudes required of anthropology.

<table>
<tr><td>ANTHROPOLOGY IN THE
PRESCIENTIFIC PAST</td><td>However, there were occasional writers from the ancient Mediterranean civilizations and elsewhere whose narratives displayed some of the interests of anthropology. Herodotus (464–425 B.C.) was the</td></tr>
</table>

most helpful writer of antiquity in this respect, commenting on some of the peoples around him and relating details of their cultures. He observed that all people prefer their own customs and think of them as best. Herodotus even concluded that particular customs may be more suitable in some places than in others, depending on how they fit in with the general way of life—a notion now referred to as "cultural relativism." His accounts were often quite detailed and informative, but sometimes he relied on hearsay, as when he reported that far western Libya was a land "of creatures without heads whom the Libyans declare to have eyes in their breasts, and also the land of wild men and the wild women."[3]

On the other hand, Herodotus based his accounts of the Egyptians, Persians, and Scythians on his own observations and omitted the fanciful. He told of the Scythian burial of the deceased king and of the killing of fifty youths so they could go with him as servants, a custom that would be found in many places and be described by many other historians and anthropologists in the centuries to come. He recounted many of the Egyptian customs and wondered at the sight of the great pyramids, already old and mysterious in his day.

Had others followed the lead of Herodotus, anthropology might truly have had its roots in antiquity, but there were few others. Megasthenes gave an early description of the caste system of India, and Caesar later wrote about Gaul and Britain—very disdainfully of Britain. Another Roman, Tacitus, wrote glowingly of the Germans and supplied considerable information about their customs. To some degree, though, his work was propagandistic. He attempted to glamorize the Germans in order to encourage his increasingly corrupt Roman compatriots to accept the simple but wholesome ways of the northern barbarians. The recognition of the importance of a scientific, objective view of culture awaited later times.

---

[3]Francis R. B. Godolphin (ed.), *The Greek Historians*, Random House, Inc., New York, 1942, vol. I, pp. 247–252.

NON-EUROPEAN WRITERS   Non-European people, too, have been interested in the study of foreign cultures. Early descriptions of the Mongols and other peoples of central Asia came from the Chinese. Several Arabic scholars have added to our knowledge of the customs of people foreign to them. Alberuni, an Arabic writer, has left a description of India in the eleventh century. One of our first accounts of the Scandinavian invaders of Russia comes from Ahmed ibn Fadlan, writing in the tenth century. His impression of the Northmen included their gigantic stature, florid complexions, uncouth manners ("they are the filthiest race that God has ever created"), their public sexual enjoyments, and their custom of cremation. Like the Scythians described by Herodotus, they did not allow a dead chief to go to the next world alone but killed a beautiful girl to go with him.[4]

The most famous of the Arabic scholars was Ibn-Khaldun of the fourteenth century, whose philosophical writings influenced the Renaissance in Europe. In the anthropological field, Ibn-Khaldun left descriptions of the Bedouin Arabs and contrasted their life styles with those of the urban civilization to which he belonged, speculating on reasons for the divergence of cultures.[5]

THE AGE OF EXPLORATION   What should have been the greatest possible age for the development of anthropology was the Age of Exploration. Surely, one would think, accounts made at the very time of discovery of the New World, of the first trips around Africa to India, and of the first circumnavigation of the earth would be of priceless anthropological value. Actually, much description survives from that age, but it is likely to be the story of discovery and conquest, not of the cultures of the Indians and the Africans. Both Indians and Africans are often dismissed as total savages, living as beasts.[6] Had Henry the Navigator (1394–1460) lived longer, he might have insisted on scholarly accounts of the peoples discovered, but his followers were interested in gold, not native peoples.

Spain discovered the New World in the late fifteenth and early sixteenth century, just as the last of the Moors were driven out of Granada and a few years after Their Most Christian Majesties Ferdinand and Isabella united their kingdoms and elevated the Court of the Inquisition to governmental rank. The

[4]Ahmed ibn Fadlan, "Scandinavians on the Volga in 922," in Alan Dundes (ed.), *Every Man His Way,* Prentice-Hall, Inc., Englewood Cliffs, N.J., 1968, pp. 14–22.
[5]Ibn-Khaldun, *An Introduction to History: The Muqaddimah,* trans. Franz Rosenthal, N. J. Dawood (ed.), Routledge & Kegan Paul, London, 1967.
[6]Katherine George, "The Civilized West Looks at Primitive Africa, 1400–1800: A Study in Ethnocentrism" *Isis,* vol, 49, pp. 62–72, March 1958.

Strange theories arose among the
Europeans to try to explain such New
World civilizations as the Aztecan
and the older Teotihuacan ruins
depicted here.

intellectual atmosphere did not seem conducive to the objective study of the religions of conquered peoples overseas. Yet some of the Spanish friars of the early 1500s recorded the Aztec story carefully, feeling a strong compulsion to learn Aztec beliefs in order better to convert them to Christianity. Bernardo de Sahagún, especially, wrote much about the lives and customs of the Aztecs, their arts and technology, their governmental system, and their great city of Tenochtitlán. Records of events in Peru were not so carefully kept, but several Spanish writers did keep records, especially Pedro de Ciesa and the half-Inca writer Garcilaso de la Vega. The records eventually were found by friends of the American historian William H. Prescott, who more than a century ago wrote accounts of the conquests of Mexico and Peru that are still classics in the field.

The Age of Exploration vastly increased knowledge of the world and of the cultural variety to be found, but the narrative was more frequently one of high adventure and the lure of gold and plunder. Even the interpretation of the cultural findings sounds strange to modern ears. Mexico had a host of gods, some of whom, especially Huitzilopchtli, had a thirst for human blood; and the success of the Aztecs depended upon keeping their gods satisfied. When the Spanish learned of the massive human sacrifices to Huitzilopochtli, they wondered if he was not actually one of the many manifestations of Satan. There were other strange discoveries. The Aztecs used a sign of the cross in some of the ceremonies, and they even had an initiation rite in which sprinkling was done, as in Christian baptism. One theory that emerged was that these people had once known Christianity but had been misled by the wiles of the Devil and had descended. (In the United States, Cotton Mather had a very similar idea about the origin of the Indians—they had been led far away from Christian influence by the crafty Devil.) The parallel seen in these religious symbols and customs was a case of complete misinterpretation, so easy for observers from a distant land, but from the Christian point of view the parallelism was helpful; it facilitated the conversion proces.[7] One pagan goddess of mercy remained confused in the Aztec mind with the Holy Virgin of Christianity. For more than a century the Virgin of Guadalupe was, in the minds of the Indian pilgrims, none other than their old earth and fertility goddess, Tonantizin.[8]

There were other interesting theories about the peoples of America, more common in other parts of Europe than in Spain. One of these—and a

[7]B. G. Hedrick, *Religious Syncretism in Spanish America*, Museum of Anthropology Miscellaneous Series 2, Southern Illinois University, Carbondale, Ill., December 1967.
[8]Eric R. Wolf, "The Virgin of Guadalupe: A Mexican National Symbol," *Journal of American Folklore*, vol. 71, pp. 34–38, January 1958.

theory that died hard—was that of degradation: the backward peoples of the world were backward because they had sinned and the Lord had punished them for their sins. This was one of the ideas that anthropologists eventually laid to rest.

THE BEGINNING OF CULTURAL DISCOVERY   In later centuries of American exploration, the scholarly Jesuits made careful studies of the Indians of the Mississippi Valley and of parts of Canada. Especially important was Father Lafitau, who made studies in cultural comparison that would do credit to an anthropologist of modern times. Lafitau in the seventeenth century and the Scottish historian William Robertson in the eighteenth century concluded that there was probably little innate difference between Indians and Europeans and that observable differences reflected mainly variations in culture and rearing. One of the major insights of anthropology was taking root; culture was being discovered.

The discovery of culture was aided by Thomas Jefferson.[9] Among his innumerable interests was American Indian languages. He found time for a study of these, and he was also the first to carefully excavate one of the large Indian mounds (barrows) of the Ohio Valley, doing so with all the precision and care of a modern archaeologist. Although he, like many Americans of his time, speculated on the possibility that Indians were a lost tribe of Israel, before the end of his long life (1743–1826), he reached the conclusion that they had migrated from Asia by way of the Bering Strait. In his day he was almost alone in this opinion. Long before Charles Darwin introduced his theory of evolution, Jefferson believed the human race had evolved from lower forms of life. Before the idea had become prominent in the thinking of social scientists, he concluded that accidents in historical development accounted for the difference between Indians and whites, not racial traits. He expressed well the modern point of view of cultural relativism:

> Men living in different countries, under different circumstances and regimens, may have different utilities; the same act may, therefore, be useful, and consequently virtuous in one country which is injurious and vicious in another differently circumstanced.[10]

The point of view that cultural differences are merely a matter of historical circumstance and that all races are capable of similar development presupposes that tremendous amounts of time have been necessary to develop the differences encountered in the world. Yet the prevailing point of view

[9]Lowell D. Holmes, "Jefferson's Avocation," *Natural History*, vol. 74, pp. 58–62, November 1965.
[10]Ibid., p. 61.

before the nineteenth century was that the earth was only about 6,000 years old. Much had to be learned about time.

THE KNOWLEDGE OF GEOLOGICAL TIME   Before further advances in anthropology could be made, certain other ideas in addition to that of cultural perspective had to be developed. Was it possible that the European ancestors had once lived in a manner similar to that of the American Indians? Was the study of the Indian capable of giving the European some insight into his own past?

Early in the nineteenth century a Frenchman named Jacques Boucher de Crevecoeur de Perthes (1788–1868) found hand axes and flint knives buried deep in the soils of France in the vicinity of Abbeville. Were the ancestors of the French once a Stone Age people, and was their age to be reckoned in tens of thousands of years? Boucher de Perthes's question was at first greeted with skepticism and even derision. He lived in a time when public opinion considered Bishop Usher's dating of the age of the earth to be just about right. The earth, said Bishop Usher, had come into existence in 4004 B.C. on a morning in late October. Historical records made it clear that France had had a Bronze Age culture by the time of the Romans. How could so much cultural evolution have taken place in so short a time?

In the 1830s the question was answered to a large degree by Sir Charles Lyell, the Father of Geology, who began the explanation of the long processes of geological time, of erosion and deposition, and Ice Ages. Even then, though, the findings of Lyell were not applied to human affairs, and man's antiquity remained in dispute for another 30 years. Lyell had no radioactive time clock such as can be used now, but he did make it clear that terrestrial time should be dated in millions of years, not mere thousands.

In 1831, just a year or two before Lyell's major work in geology went to press, a young man named Charles Darwin set sail from England on *H.M.S. Beagle*, paying his own costs so he could go along as a naturalist observer. Everywhere he went he observed the processes of change caused by adaptation to environment, whether in the cultures of the primitive Tierra del Fuegans or in the species of animal life in the Galápagos. Darwin concluded that species change in response to environment by a process of natural selection. For nearly 30 years he observed and experimented to prove his point. Finally, in 1859, his first book appeared, *On the Origin of Species by Means of Natural Selection, or the Preservation of Favored Races in the Struggle for Survival.* The intellectual world has never been the same since. The following year, Boucher de Perthes, then an old man, was finally given official recognition as the discoverer of a new science of prehistoric man.

The idea of biological evolution was not really original with Darwin. The Roman scholar Lucretius had believed in a type of evolution. Immanuel Kant and Johann Wolfgang von Goethe had speculated on evolution, as had Darwin's grandfather, Erasmus Darwin. The French scholar Jean Baptiste Lamarck had destroyed his own academic reputation with his lectures on evolution. However, although the other men predated Darwin, it was Darwin who gave a plausible explanation and presented the evidence, and he did so at a time when the intellectual world was ready to listen.

DARWIN AND THE SOCIAL DARWINISTS   One reason why the intellectual world was willing to listen to Darwin was that social scientists had been thinking along similar lines about societies. De Perthes had concluded that cultures are stratified just as are the layers of the earth. Thomas Malthus, David Ricardo, and other early economists had introduced the idea of struggle for survival into the study of human affairs. The sociologists William Sumner and Herbert Spencer took up the theme and have sometimes been referred to as "social Darwinists," although Spencer objected to the term, claiming his ideas preceded Darwin's.

The cultural anthropologists best remembered for an early interest in evolution were not exactly the same as either the biological Darwinists or the social Darwinists, as will become clear after a description of their views. There were two aspects of cultural evolutionism that linked it to Darwinism, however. First and most important, it introduced a long-range scheme for describing the course of human cultural development, just as physical evolution provided a pattern for understanding the entire process of differentiation and development of life forms. Second, the evolutionary perspective was introduced into cultural anthropology at about the time that Darwin's theories began to influence biology and physical anthropology and was generally regarded as an offshoot of Darwinism.

DARWINISM AND CULTURAL EVOLUTION COMPARED   Darwinian evolution contends that species change as a result of the need for adaptation to changing environments and that there are struggles among species for living space within their environments. Changes are gradual, not generally rapid and catastrophic, and are the cumulative result of tiny degrees of individual variation. Those individuals who cannot meet the requirements of living in the form of adaptation to environment die young without issue; the "fit" in a Darwinian sense are those who survive and leave offspring, who in turn reach maturity and reproduce their kind. These ideas were adopted by Sumner and Spencer and were

DARWINISM

EMPHASIS ON STRUGGLE FOR SURVIVAL AMONG INDIVIDUALS AND SPECIES - LEADING TO NATURAL SELECTION AND "SURVIVAL OF FITTEST."

BELIEF IN VESTIGIAL ORGANS AS REMNANTS OF EARLIER STAGES OF DEVELOPMENT.

SOCIAL DARWINISM

DARWINIAN IDEAS APPLIED TO INDIVIDUALS AND SOCIETIES, RATIONALIZING INDIVIDUALISTIC, HIGHLY COMPETITIVE SOCIAL SYSTEMS.

BACKWARD SOCIETIES SEEN AS REMNANTS OF EARLIER STAGES OF DEVELOPMENT.

NINETEENTH-CENTURY CULTURAL EVOLUTION

EMPHASIS ON SIMILARITY IN ALL HUMAN TYPES. SEARCH FOR UNIFORM STAGES OF DEVELOPMENT; IMPLIED BELIEF IN INEVITABILITY OF CULTURAL DEVELOPMENTS.

SAME VIEW OF PRIMITIVE SOCIETIES + SUPERSTITIONS AND OLD CUSTOMS AS VESTIGIAL REMAINS OF ANCIENT TIMES.

believed in by the early cultural evolutionists in anthropology. However, the anthropological cultural evolutionists gave evolution a different shade of meaning. The idea was not that cultures evolve through the destruction of the weak, but simply that they all evolve in a fairly uniform manner, although at varying rates.

EDWARD B. TYLOR   The general scheme of cultural evolution was laid down by Edward B. Tylor in *Primitive Culture* (1865) and more dogmatically by Lewis Henry Morgan in *Ancient Society* (1877). Tylor, the son of a wealthy English Quaker family, had health problems in his twenties and was advised to travel. He visited the Caribbean and then Mexico and was excited by being able to observe the Mexican pyramids, but even more by observing the scourging rites of religious penitents in Mexico, which seemed exactly the same as those in ancient Egypt he had read about. It occurred to him that the same patterns often repeat themselves in successive civilizations as they go through comparable stages of development. Or could it be that some customs survive beyond their time, like the vestigial organs described by biologists? Both ideas took root in Tylor's thinking. He later read the works of Lyell and became interested in the discoveries of Boucher de Perthes. He became convinced of the stratification of historical cultures, realizing that only the most primitive remains are found in the lower strata.

Although Tylor became aware of the great gap between primitive cultures and industrial societies, he did not subscribe to the old idea of degradation or to the idea of mental differences between peoples. He concluded that all human peoples have similar minds, capable of similar reasoning. In his later analysis of supernatural beliefs, he attempted to demonstrate the similarity of thought processes of all people, and he accepted the emerging belief in cultural relativism. In his words, "Never measure other people's corn by our own bushel."[11] We shall encounter the ingenious Tylor interpretation of supernatural belief in Chapter Fifteen. It is enough to say at this point that he hypothesized a progression from a simple belief in spirit beings in all things to belief in higher and more dominant spirits and gods or even a single god. He contended, though, that elements of the older ideas still persist in modern-day superstitions.

LEWIS HENRY MORGAN   Morgan was an even more thorough systematizer than Tylor and attempted to arrange all cultures in an ascending order, moving from lower, middle, and upper savagery to lower, middle, and upper barbarism and finally to civilization. Upper barbarism was, in his analysis, the period when man learned to write. Lower savagery was a remote time when man was little separated from the beasts. Middle and upper savagery were exemplified by the Australian aborigines and the Polynesians, respecitvely. The Iroquois represented lower barbarism, the agricultural Zuñi, middle barbarism, and the Homeric Greeks, upper, developing gradually toward modern civilization.

The scheme was overly ambitious, and Morgan was often careless with details, but there were certain merits to his thinking. Like Tylor, he believed in the "psychic unity of man" (his own phrase), the idea that all races have similar capacities. He also believed in cultural relativity—that all people should be judged in terms of their own cultural values. More so than Tylor, he believed in cultural evolution as a kind of inevitable force, occasionally slowed or even turned back but inevitably drifting toward greater possibilities. It is probably this almost mystic idea of inevitability that modern cultural evolutionists would object to most in Morgan's ideas.

In detailed studies the cultural evolutionists of the nineteenth century generally concentrated on evolution of a specific institution, such as the family,

[11]Abram Kardiner and Edward Prebble, *They Studied Man*, New American Library, Inc., New York, 1963, pp. 50–68.

religion, or government. Henry Maine, in *Ancient Law* (1861), traced the growth of legal principles from kinship ties to territorial ties and finally to contract. In 1841, J. K. Bachofen of Switzerland, in *Das Mutterecht,* suggested a dubious evolution from matrilineage (families tracing descent through the mother's line) to patrilineage (father's line) and the consequent emergence of male dominance in the family.

THE GOLDEN BOUGH   Bridging the nineteenth and twentieth centuries was the extremely gifted writer Sir James Frazer, whose *Golden Bough*,[12] published in thirteen volumes, from 1890 to 1911, became the most widely read anthropological work produced until that time. Frazer advanced a semievolutionary theory of religion, positing a progression beginning in animism and leading to the sacrificial god. Although not a great theorist, Frazer was a master of literature. A recluse, living his life among books and aided by his equally bookish wife, Frazer combed through most of the vast literature on mythology that was then available. He was particularly interested in the custom of human sacrifice, attributing it to beliefs in holophrastic and contagious magic. Holophrastic magic is based on the idea that the part can stand for the whole; thus one member of society can be sacrificed and symbolize the sacrifice of all. Contagious magic similarly holds that a spiritual unity—a kind of contagion— unites forever things that were once united, in this case the society and its sacrificial victim. Thus the sacrificial blood of one has a spiritual relationship to all. In these ideas Frazer perceived parallels between the thinking of primitive and modern man, and the gulf between Christian belief and the sacrificial being of earlier forms of religion narrowed. His theories challenged, as does much of anthropological research, Western civilization's certainty of its uniqueness and intellectual profundity.

Above all, however, Frazer was a romantic, fascinated by the world of the imagination. He wrote of himself:

> The dreamland world of fancy
>   There is my own true home,
> There are the purple mountains
>   And blue seas fringed with foam;
> . . . .
> And there the deathless garlands
>   That crown the chosen head,
> When youth's brief June is over
>   And youth's brief roses dead.[13]

[12]Sir James Frazer, *The Golden Bough,* with notes and foreword by Theodore H. Caster (ed.), Mentor Books, New American Library, Inc., New York, 1964.
[13]Sir James Frazer, "June in Cambridge," quoted in Kardiner and Prebble, op. cit., pp. 77–78.

Although Frazer has been criticized for depending on secondary sources of material and for consequent errors in detail, he actually did more than describe a "dreamland world of fancy." He was among the first to seek for meaning in that world, to show that it was more than idle fancy, that mythology is as much part of the modern world as of the primitive, and that "much that we are wont to regard as solid rests on the sands of superstition rather than the rock of nature."

By the time *The Golden Bough* was completed, "youth's brief June" was coming to a close for the school of anthropologists just described. They had awakened interest; they had added significantly to the discovery of culture and to cultural relativism. They had dealt heavy blows to the old ideas of cultural degradation and had discovered man's unity behind his diversity. They had the effect of encouraging others to go into the field to study primitive life, but they had done little firsthand research themselves and are referred to as "armchair anthropologists." The idea of cultural evolution as a way of seeing mankind was to be eclipsed, later to revive in new forms, with corrections and refinements, more attention to detail, and far more firsthand knowledge of the incredible variation of which human cultures are capable.

FROM THEORY TO FIELD: FRANZ BOAS AND HIS FOLLOWERS   A new direction was given to American anthropology by the German-born Franz Boas (1858–1942)[14] and to English anthropology by Bronislaw Malinowski and A. R. Radcliffe-Brown. Throughout his long life Boas was a man of great energy and strong convictions. Generations of American anthropology students were to refer to him as "Papa Franz" and were to be profoundly influenced by his personality, methods, and views. In 1896 he wrote a book in opposition to what he regarded as careless and premature theorizing about cultural evolution. His contention was that the first duty of anthropologists was to go out and study the primitive peoples and their ways before they disappear. For him, historical studies attempting to show the relationships between cultures were commendable, but history is not the study of cultural evolution; it focuses on particular events, not on grand theory.

The Boas methods resulted in careful research and documentation, the study of cultural diffusion (the spread of an idea or technique from one culture to another), and the idea developed by some of his students that cultures should be studied as a whole rather than compared in such areas as religion, family, art forms, or rites. His extremely influential book *The Mind of Primitive*

[14]Kardiner and Prebble, op. cit., "Franz Boas: Icy Enthusiasm," pp. 117–139.

CONTINUITY AND CHANGE IN CULTURAL ANTHROPOLOGY

NINETEENTH CENTURY	EARLY TWENTIETH CENTURY	LATER TWENTIETH CENTURY

IDEOLOGICAL PRINCIPLES

"PSYCHIC UNITY OF MAN." INTEREST IN ALL CULTURES. OPPOSED "DEGRADATION THEORIES."

GENERAL AGREEMENT ON SAME PRINCIPLES; STRONG OPPOSITION TO RACISM.

RESEARCH METHODS

LARGELY LIBRARY RESEARCH AND REPORTS OF TRAVELERS.

FIELD WORK, TRAINED OBSERVERS, CAREFUL METHODOLOGY.

FIELDWORK, TRAINED OBSERVERS, CAREFUL METHODOLOGY. MORE CROSS-CULTURAL COMPARISONS.

THEORETICAL INTEREST

CULTURAL EVOLUTION. SEARCH FOR UNIFORM STEPS IN DEVELOPMENT.

DECLINE OF CULTURAL-EVOLUTIONARY INTEREST. FUNCTIONALISM. CULTURE AND PERSONALITY.

FUNCTIONALISM. PROBLEMS OF SOCIAL CHANGE. NEW TYPES OF CULTURAL EVOLUTION: MULTILINEAL, GENERAL.

Man was an assault against racism, explaining the cultural, not biological, origins of differing thought patterns. Cultural relativity, already commented on by Tylor, was orthodoxy to Boas; and he realized that one problem with cultural evolution is that it violates cultural relativism to some degree, making the anthropologist judge of which of various cultural forms is "most advanced." Boas turned his attention to Indian languages and linguistics in general and later became especially interested in studies of culture and personality.

Among his students were such able anthropologists as A. L. Kroeber, Robert Lowie, Edward Sapir, Clark Wissler, Ruth Benedict, and Margaret Mead. His severest critic, Leslie White, said Boas so completely avoided theory as to make anthropology afraid to draw any conclusions. Field work was certainly improved under Boas, but sometimes it grew repetitive. In order to complete their field work, later students were studying the same Indian tribes over and over. An Oglala Sioux has recently written a rather clever song entitled "The Anthros Are Coming," the gist of which is "My God, we're about to be studied again!"

23

The life of Boas happens to have been almost coterminous with that of the great psychoanalyst Sigmund Freud, and the interest in psychology generated by Freud spilled over into anthropology, apparently approved but not led by Boas himself. Two brilliant women with a great gift for writing began to turn their attention to culture and personality studies. Ruth Benedict wrote *Patterns of Culture*,[15] a book with a strongly psychological orientation. She expounded on the idea that primitive cultures fit into patterns, have an internal consistency about them, and mold the character of the people into such patterns. The pattern can emphasize serenity and cooperation (exemplified by the Zuñi in her study), hostility, sorcery, and fear (as in Dobuan culture), or wild ecstatic rites and an emphasis on prestige and rivalry (as in the Northwest Coast Indian tribe, Kwakiutl). Her examples may be overdrawn to some extent, but in a style both descriptive and poetic she focused attention on the extreme variability of world views and demonstrated that it is just as valid to say cultures make men as to say men make cultures. It is also to her credit that she saw the personality type as the result of an entire pattern of life and belief, not just of infantile and childhood patterns.

Mead, whose career in anthropology started soon after Benedict's, has turned her inexhaustible energy in a similar direction, focusing especially on child-rearing patterns and personality and also on how cultures decide what are proper masculine and feminine personalities and mold the two sexes into conformity with the pattern. She has also been a pioneer in studies of social change and the impact of the Western world on primitive cultures.

Field research, greatly inspired by Boas, had vastly increased the scope of cultural anthropology, added to its stock, and cast more light on the mysteries of cultural variability. Much of the riddle of culture still awaited explanation, as it does today, but new insights were provided by students whose original inspiration seems to derive from the great French social scientist Émile Durkheim.

NEW SYSTEMS OF ANALYSIS ÉMILE DURKHEIM Durkheim belongs partly to the nineteenth century (1858–1917), but his thinking sounds very contemporary. Although he called himself a sociologist, he is claimed by the two related disciplines of sociology and anthropology and is highly honored in both. A French citizen, he was strongly loyal to France, supporting her cause vigorously in World War I. His son was killed in the war, and he himself died within a few weeks of his son's death. It may well be that his own na-

[15]Ruth Benedict, *Patterns of Culture*, Mentor Books, New American Library, Inc., New York, 1964.

tional sentiments influenced his thinking to some degree. At any rate, such a detail of his life helps one to remember that for Durkheim the individual can be understood only as part of a collective identity, a culture, that determines for him not only his customs and values but his ways of conceptualizing reality.

The Durkheim book that is more distinctively anthropological than sociological is his *Elementary Forms of the Religious Life*,[16] first published in 1912. Developed from secondary research on the Australian aborigines, it purports to arrive at the earliest known form of religion and possibly the prototype of all religions. His assumption that a knowledge of the Australian aborigines, the world's most primitive people, would necessarily cast light on the origin of all religions is a strongly cultural-evolutionist point of view of the nineteenth-century variety and would not be regarded as a certainty now, because too much diversity in belief has been found among the most primitive peoples. In the study of the aborigines, Durkheim concluded that religion arose out of the collective sentiments of the people and their need for solidarity. Dances, ceremonies, and rituals, and the emotions engendered by them, were the essence of the tie that binds, and so were the churinga and other sacred objects of the people. The sacred objects were collective symbols; the gods were simply the reflection of the social order, the ultimate collective representation.

COLLECTIVE REPRESENTATIONS   Two conclusions of *Elementary Forms of the Religious Life* were to bear further investigation in years to come. First, in looking at religion, Durkheim was interested not in the beautiful or dreadful myths that fascinated Frazer, but rather in what function religion served for society. This question he could answer rather succinctly: it gives people a collective identity and a membership and importance in the world, and it explains their social order to them. Especially for primitive cultures, religious conceptualizations are the cultural matrix which can be changed only at the cost of a thorough shaking of the social order and a melting of the glue that holds it together. Second, Durkheim demonstrated that symbols, or collective representations, are the means by which people relate to the natural world, the substance of their thought. Symbols, be they words, rituals, banners, images, designs, sacred numbers, or anything else, influence human thought processes. The latter idea was arrived at independently by a number of linguists, including Benjamin Lee Whorf. The leading European theoretical anthropologist of the present, Claude Lévi-Strauss, recognizes Durkheim as an intellectual

[16]Émile Durkheim, *Elementary Forms of the Religious Life,* George Allen & Unwin, Ltd., London, 1957.

forebear and carries the idea of collective representations and perceptions of reality into the fields of both linguistics and mythology. Lévi-Strauss will be discussed further in Part Five.

FUNCTIONALISM   Durkheim's interest in the study of social function had more immediate influence, which has appeared under two closely related labels, "functionalism" and "structuralism." Both systems were developed by British anthropologists.

Bronislaw Malinowski was born in the part of Poland then ruled by Austria. At the outbreak of World War I he was traveling in Australia and was arrested as an enemy alien, but he persuaded the British government to allow him to pursue his anthropological work in the Trobriand Islands, east of New Guinea.[17] Unlike many of the nineteenth-century anthropologists, Malinowski believed that research work should be done in the field, by living with peoples and learning their language. He is therefore important as a field researcher as well as a theoretician. Malinowski was impatient with grand theorizing of the Morgan type and had little interest in speculating about either general evolution or specific histories. What he was interested in was the analysis of cultures as entities and the demonstration of how each part (economics, trade, ceremony, kinship system, and the like) contributes to the maintenance of the whole. His rival for leadership in British anthropology was Radcliffe-Brown, whose very similar approach is called structuralism and centers in society rather than culture.

Culture, as we have seen, is a total pattern of life; "society" refers to the people who follow the culture; in actual usage it is a little more limited than "culture," and has often been used to refer specifically to social organization. Radcliffe-Brown focused his attention on society and its structures: social classes, kinship, government, and law. Both Radcliffe-Brown and Malinowski present viewpoints that emphasize the effects of technical change, such as the introduction of some of the products and technology of Europe, on such features as work habits, living arrangements, barter, bride price, relations between men and women, and urbanization. Their theories were practical for anthropology, since they focused attention on the problems of change. There are limitations to functionalism, however. It tends to look upon cultures as ends in themselves. Even such customs as ritual cannibalism can be analyzed in terms of contribution to the maintenance of the system. It must be granted that structural-functionalism tends to be value-free and in that sense conforms to

[17]Bronislaw Malinowski, *Argonauts of the Western Pacific*, E. P. Dutton & Co., Inc., New York, 1961. (Originally published in 1922.) Chapter I outlines his theory and method.

the ideal of the objectivity of science, but it is less given to conclusions about long-range social trends than is a cultural-evolution view. Finally, since each cultural system is seen as a meaningful entity, any change can be seen as at least temporarily disruptive, and structural-functionalism therefore can lead to a conservative bias, although such was not the intent of its early proponents.

THE NEW CULTURAL
EVOLUTIONISTS

Although there was a need for reexamining the overly simplified theories of cultural evolution of the nineteenth century, it was hard to blot out of the mind all speculations as to what the prevailing trends of human cultures have been. In the last three decades new interest has arisen in the idea of cultural evolution, and some of the new cultural evolution perspectives are the fundamental basis for the organization of this book. V. Gordon Childe and Leslie White have been the leaders of a new cultural evolutionism, and they have many followers and many colleagues who are at least partly in accord with their thinking. Julian Steward has developed cultural-evolution theories of a less generalizing type than White's, and so have Elman Service, Peter Farb, and Yehudi Cohen. In sociology, the eminent theorist Talcott Parsons has recently published a book with a strongly cultural-evolutionist perspective, and Gerhardt Lenski, in *Human Societies*, has written a text in macrosociology that applies a cultural-evolution scheme. Since sociology has generally covered the territory of industrial civilizations and anthropology that of primitive cultures, there is a difference in emphasis, in spite of common interests and concepts.

DIVERSITY IN CULTURAL EVOLUTION   Although there is an increasing interest in cultural evolution as an organizing principle for the study of anthropology, there are questions presented by this approach. For example, Japan and the industrial nations of the West stand at nearly identical technological levels, and their people display the same abilities, but the cultures are by no means identical. Certainly, local variations in the pattern of cultural evolution must be taken into consideration. Another rather obvious problem is that, even if people display capacities for similar development under similar conditions, the conditions are never, in fact, the same. One obvious reason for this is the matter of geography; the Eskimo culture could hardly have taken the same course as those of the irrigated river valleys to the south. Problems of this type are resolved by modern cultural evolutionists in various ways. One resolution of the problem is to think of evolution as multilineal, as in the theorizing of Steward.

Steward contends that parallel developments occur in certain geographical areas, such as arid regions, some types of river valleys, or boreal forests.[18] A few examples will suffice. One of the most obvious parallels is that among early civilizations in the valleys of the Tigris-Euphrates, the Nile, the Indus, and the Hwang Ho. Many of the similarities were commented on by Childe as well as by Steward. Another interesting perspective on the parallel developments of such areas is provided by Karl Wittfogel, who maintains that the need for control of rivers led to the first large-scale social organizations and the first all-powerful governments.[19] In his analysis, where this need existed, cities developed more as administrative centers of government than as independent trade centers, thus tending to make such civilizations less changeable than many others. Dynasties and conquests followed one another, but the systems remained very much the same.

Robert Suggs, in *Island Civilizations of Polynesia*, shows a constant repetition of a similar pattern of development as Pacific people moved from one island chain to another.[20] There are early stages of incipient agriculture, developmental stages characterized by large altars and stone platforms, expansionist periods, and classical periods of megalithic temples. The descriptive terminology is very similar to that used by both Childe and Steward, who speak of preagricultural periods, incipient agriculture, formative eras, florescent eras, and eras of cyclical conquest to describe the Mesopotamian civilizations.

The parallel development theory can also be carried to the land of the Maya and the Valley of Mexico in the New World. Recently, Farb has written a book on the American Indians, presenting with clarity and logic the many developmental levels of the North American peoples. Impoverished geographical environments and their results are shown, revealing the limitations geography can place upon possibilities and presenting parallels with developments in other geographically impoverished areas. The parallels between the Aztec total state and the states of ancient Egypt and Mesopotamia become clearer than ever before. His accounts give a sense of direction, not a mere recitation of strange times and places.

---

[18]Julian H. Steward, *Theory of Culture Change*, The University of Illinois Press, Urbana, 1955. See especially chap. 4, "Levels of Sociocultural Integration," pp. 43–63.
[19]Karl August Wittfogel, *Oriental Despotism: A Comparative Study of Total Power*, Yale University Press, New Haven, Conn., 1957.
[20]Robert Suggs, *Island Civilizations of Polynesia*, Mentor Books, New American Library, Inc., New York, 1957.

LESLIE WHITE AND GENERAL EVOLUTION   For years White has felt that only a cultural-evolution framework can make anthropology of real value to the modern world.[21] Once his was "the voice of one crying in the wilderness," but now he has company. White is the strongest advocate of a type of general cultural evolutionism, rather like a greatly refined, amended, and updated edition of Morgan. His view is that there is a prevailing direction toward greater technological and organizational complexity, in spite of the fact that a few isolated cultures have not followed the general trend. Whether cultures develop through invention or diffusion is irrelevant to him, since he is speaking of the human species as a whole. He sees the discovery of new sources of energy, the invention of new tools, and the environment as major factors in the development of civilizations. The early forms of energy were fire, for hollowing out tree trunks for boats, for ceramics and metallurgy and for slash-and-burn agriculture. Agriculture itself increased the caloric intake and the energy of the human being; and animal power was the first great breakthrough in human development of nonhuman energy. For White, there are regularities in the development of state power, of priest classes, and of wars of conquest after agriculture is well developed. Economic structures change. Theology reflects new interests. The old animalistic gods become anthropomorphic, then nationalistic gods, and in some cases universalistic. The cults of various savior gods develop as men long for the greater freedom of days before they were united into empires. White, of course, would not deny wide variations in the pattern, but he thinks it is the duty of anthropology to look for pattern behind the diversity.

It must not be concluded that the cultural evolutionists are the only anthropologists interested in theoretical understandings of man, physically, mentally, and culturally. A word has already been said of the linguists and the study of collective representations and of the study of culture and personality. In the next chapter we shall look at the total range of anthropology, seeing what is being done in physical anthropology, archaeology, and linguistics as well as in cultural anthropology and how all these fields relate to the basic study of culture.

[21]Leslie A. White, *The Evolution of Culture: The Development of Civilization to the Fall of Rome*, McGraw-Hill Book Company, New York, 1959. See especially chap. 2, "Energy and Tools."

Chapter Two
The Modern
Anthropological
Enterprise

Anthropologists are the practitioners of a science that extends its interests far and wide, often cooperating with other sciences in its attempt to learn more about man, his variability, his adaptability, his history, prehistory, origins, and his primate kinsmen. Anthropologists can be found at work in the bush country, meeting and conversing with the inhabitants, learning their beliefs and their rituals, often identifying strongly with the tribes among whom they live. They can be found also at all kinds of diggings, cleaning and piecing together potsherds with infinite care, whisking away the dust and debris from buried artifacts in tombs and collapsed dwellings, meticulously recording each detail found. They may be digging into the recent past of a century ago, the historical antiquities of a thousand years ago, or the prehistoric remains of many hundreds of thousands of years ago. They may be working in laboratories, studying blood types, proteins, or the genetic codes contained in the molecular structures of DNA chains. Or anthropologists may be at work studying monkeys or the great apes, not just in zoos, but in their natural habitats, knowing that other primates, like human beings, become neurotic if housed in prisons—the animal prisons we call zoos—and their natural behavior patterns are distorted. Increasingly in recent years anthropologists work in urban settings, in ghettos, in poverty areas, among unusual sects and cults—anywhere that promises new insights into cultures and subcultures.

What do all these pursuits have in common? How is the field of anthropology divided? Do the divisions represent a pulling apart of anthropology into specialties unacquainted with one another, or do anthropologists still have a sense of united purpose?

DIVISION AND UNITY   The subject matter of anthropology can be divided for the sake of analysis in more than one manner, but the accompanying chart focuses upon three major approaches to the study of man: his culture, his physical nature, and his historical and evolutionary development. Such a classification is convenient for conceptualizing the field, but it is more an analytical tool than a reality. A glance at the chart will show, for instance, that primatology has been placed under physical anthropology and primate evolution under evolutionary development—just one indication that fields overlap. It will be noted, too, that there are many other studies closely related to anthropology. No approach to the study of man can be isolated from all others.

Archaeology is the study of the remains of past peoples and their cultures and activities. Since archaeology is interested in both the relatively recent past and the events of hundreds of thousands of years ago, it is classed sometimes with cultural and sometimes with physical anthropology or as a separate branch of its own. Whatever the classification, archaeology is part and parcel of the general anthropological enterprise, drawing from other branches of the science and adding immeasurably to them in return. The following pages will comment briefly on several of the above-designated divisions of cultural anthropology and add a few comments on the present directions of physical anthropological research.

ETHNOGRAPHY   Not all texts make a distinction between ethnography and ethnology, but there is an important difference. Ethnographies are descriptive studies of societies at one moment in their history and form the basic data for ethnological studies. Ethnologies include comparative studies, developments over a period of time, and theoretical conclusions.

31

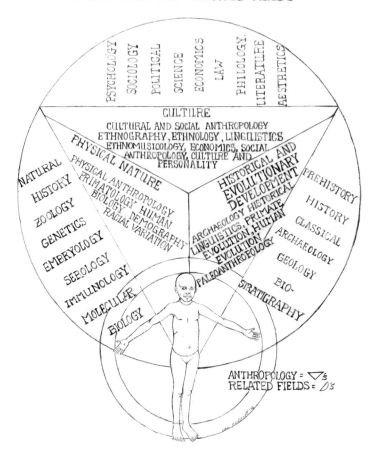

The essence of ethnography in the days of Boas was to describe a world that was about to disappear before our eyes. Now the frequent problem is to describe a particular stage in the development of a people as their traditional culture contacts and responds to the inroads of civilization. Rarely is a new and "uncontaminated" culture found anymore, although this ideal was closely approached by Robert Gardner and his associates when they contacted the Dugum Dani of New Guinea;[1] and an anthropological opportunity of the type has recently presented itself in the Philippine Islands with the discovery of the

[1]Robert Gardner, *Gardens of War: Life and Death in the New Guinea Stone Age*, Random House, Inc., New York, 1968.

Tasaday—a people who have hidden themselves away deep in the forest and avoided contact with the outside world until the last few years.[2]

In spite of the near exhaustion of the undiscovered primitives, the ethnographic field still holds a wealth of interest and has a sense of immediacy about it, because there are still societies that differ vastly from the great technological-urban homogenized mass that is conquering the world. In John Middleton's words, "This is the last time in history when there are still other societies, different from our own, to observe and to learn from; and it is the first time in history when we can no longer imagine the kind of life our granchildren will lead."[3]

Ethnography is still the foundation of cultural anthropology, and hundreds of graduate students are doing their studies in the waning world of cultural differences. They have developed rules for their discipline: Become familiar with the culture area; learn the language. Usually it is best to live in the midst of the people, where one must be willing to be observed as well as to observe. Beware of local taboos, such as moving into a house that has recently been contaminated by death. Take notes frequently, before memories become confused.[4] Situations will differ, but every effort must be made to learn what the people expect of a stranger and of a special stranger who has come from a faraway land. Finicky attitudes must be left behind, especially where food sharing is the rule and almost any "creeping thing that creepeth upon the earth" might go into the evening meal. The people must be accepted as equals, and their culture must be respected. Naturally, the anthropologist is not a man without values of his own, and he is not expected to discard them as he packs up his belongings and heads into the field; but at the very least he must regard himself as a guest, not a judge. What he wants to know is *why* people see witches and ghosts and how they behave in their presence, why a young man's death must be attributed to sorcery but not an old man's death, why one man's art is considered better than another's, how crop failures are explained, how the sick are cured, how evil spirits are removed.

Frequently an anthropologist must listen to strange ideas and even seem to concur in rather amusing judgments. Laura Bohannon's description of an attempt to tell a story (*Hamlet*) to the professional storytellers of Tiv is a classic. Her listeners interpreted the Hamlet story in a way strange to Western ears,

[2]"Tasaday Tribe," *New York Times Magazine*, July 11, 1971, p. 3
[3]From *Studies in Social and Cultural Anthropology*, edited by John Middleton, copyright 1968 by Thomas Y. Crowell Company, Inc. with permission of the publisher.
[4]Margaret Mead. *Male and Female*, William Morrow & Company, Inc., New York, 1955, chap. 2. See also Philip L. Newman, *Knowing the Gururumba*, Holt, Rinehart and Winston, Inc., New York, 1965, pp. 5–8.

thinking well of Hamlet's uncle because he had done precisely the right thing in marrying his deceased brother's wife—one of their cultural "rights." They knew Hamlet was insane because he saw a ghost, and they know that there aren't really any ghosts—just bad dreams caused by witches. After sternly correcting Bohannon in detail after detail of the plot, they finally admonished her to go home and listen more to the wise old men of her tribe so she could "learn wisdom."[5]

Interesting contrasts in thinking become clear immediately. One young woman anthropologist spent more than a year living with the Utkuhikhaling-miut Eskimo to study them at close range, learn their language and their skills, and make close friendships. It was decided that the best way for her to live with a family was to become the adopted daughter of her host; then all would be proper. The trouble was, though, that she did not act like a proper daughter; she expressed her own opinions rather than quietly obeying. She made suggestions; she even showed irritation and anger on occasion. She finally realized her errors but was already ostracized, looked upon as either incorrigible or feeble minded.[6]

Another anthropologist tells of the worry over his health that became obvious in the New Guinea village in which he lived. The men observed that he spent too much time with his wife and admonished him that such behavior makes one prone to illness and causes considerable spirit loss.[7]

In short, the ethnographer's life is full of surprises, not always pleasant. Sometimes, if he lives in isolation from the outside world, he finds himself taking on more and more of the attributes of the people around him, unconcerned about the passing of time, interested only in the small talk of the village, and even learning to acquiesce as he hears discussions of who has bewitched whom.[8]

Earlier ethnographies were nearly always of preliterate people. Recent studies have turned increasingly to peasants, to uprooted people living at the fringes of cities in newly developing lands, or to others who have had to develop a distinctive mode of existence—the rural Hutterites or Amish, southwestern Mexican villagers, or the people of urban ghettos and barrios.

---

[5]Laura Bohannon, "Shakespeare in the Bush," *Natural History*, vol. 75, pp. 28–33, August–September 1966.
[6]Jean L. Briggs, "Kapluna Daughter: Living with Eskimos," *Transaction*, vol. 7, pp. 12–22, June 1970.
[7]Newman, op. cit., p. 41.
[8]From author's notes on Robert F. Murphy's experiences among the Mundurucú of the Amazon Valley.

Ethnology is a study of cultures that attempts to draw conclusions or solve particular problems— the relationship between culture and basic human nature, the psychological problems of sudden change, the economic consequences of new agricultural techniques introduced into a traditional gardening society. All the theories discussed in the first chapter are examples of ethnology, but usually modern ethnologies are more limited in scope. Two studies, one by Malinowski and the other by Mead, are important early examples.

While Malinowski was studying in the Trobriand Islands, he became interested in Freud's theories, especially the Freudian idea of the psychosexual development of the individual.[9] In Freud's opinion there is an inborn tendency for boy infants secretly to hate their fathers as competitors for the mother's love. This tendency, in the Freudian analysis, is the beginning of psychosexual development in the male. Consequently, said Freud, psychoanalysis would uncover resentments against the father held by the male child, but resentments that he would try to hide even from his own consciousness.

Malinowski tested the theory on Trobriand Island boys and found that they had deeply ambivalent feelings toward their mother's brother but not toward their biological father—their *tama*. The difference was a matter of family structure. In the Trobriands, children were treated with great indulgence by their fathers; but their disciplinarian and the man responsible for their proper upbringing was their mother's brother. Malinowski, then, felt that he had demonstrated that the so-called Oedipus complex was a misnomer. European boys did not resent their fathers because of jealousy of the mother nearly as much as because of fear of the strong hand of discipline, usually wielded by the father. In this way, Malinowski had attempted to shed light upon a particular problem of human nature through the comparative method of anthropology.

Similarly, Mead attempted to solve a problem about human nature in her first important field study, a study of the Samoan Islanders.[10] Her question was whether the observations about the emotional storms of adolescence so frequently made in Europe and the United States were valid for all human beings or only for particular cultures. After completing her study, Mead concluded that the problem of difficult adolescent years is not a psychophysical necessity but is culturally conditioned. In the Western world, the youth is bothered by decisions about school and occupation and often has guilt feelings about

[9]Bronislaw Malinowski, *Sex and Repression in Savage Society*, Meridian Books, The World Publishing Company, Cleveland, 1965, pp. 124–137.
[10]Margaret Mead, *Coming of Age in Samoa*, New American Library, Inc., New York, 1963.

breaking with his parental home, about his premarital sexual experiences, and about normative differences between his generation and that of his parents. Among the Samoans of those days (the study was made in the 1920s), no such problems existed. All types of premarital sexual relations were accepted with equanimity. Children of unwed mothers were readily accepted into the large family group (including many aunts and uncles and grandparents), and there was no stigma about unwed motherhood. Amusingly, one of the few acts looked upon with scorn was the attempt to be sneaky about sexual affairs rather than win the girl's consent. A young man who was caught entering an attractive unmarried girl's hut at night, trying to slip into bed with her, was called a *moetetoto* and was the object of scathing derision and taunts and slurs from the entire village. However, if he succeeded in his attempt and avoided getting caught, he might boast about the matter later. Obviously, the norms were very different from those of the United States. Mead's contention was not that we should all become Samoans, but she was a pioneer in the idea that rigid puritanism takes a heavy psychic toll and is a rare phenomenon in the world.

In studies of the type just mentioned, anthropology thinks of the world as a great laboratory full of ready-made experiments. All cultures have produced normative regulations regarding sex, maturity, marriage, and family. All have ideas about the supernatural realm, ways of healing, art and means of expression, proper roles for their members. All are faced now with adjusting to social change. Anthropology cannot order cultures to experiment, but the existent variety of cultures is closely equivalent to laboratory experiments, ready to be recorded and classified.

One important direction of ethnology in recent years has been toward statistical comparisons. George Murdock has pioneered in the statistics field, developing the Human Relations Area Files. Many of the main attributes of a particular culture are entered on punch cards, succinctly, then fed into a computer to match particular variables with those of other cultures. For example, we might wish to know what correlations exist between economic systems and the dominance of males over females. A statistical comparison shows that pastoral societies, where men are almost solely in charge of the means of livelihood, are strongly male dominated and that plow-agriculture societies are almost equally so.[11] Primitive hunting-and-gathering societies are frequently male dominated too, but not so frequently and by no means so

[11]George P. Murdock, *Ethnographic Atlas*, The University of Pittsburgh Press, Pittsburgh, 1967. Tables of African tribes, pp. 62–76, show only one exception to rule of patrilineal organization of tribes whose living is derived 50 percent or more from herding.

totally. In such societies, the collecting done by women makes an important economic contribution. The old stereotype of the most primitive men as brutes, dragging their women off to a cave, is a pure figment of the imagination.

Interestingly, another study of Murdock's shows that in a random selection of forty societies, women are given almost equal rights with men in obtaining divorce.[12] In the same study, Murdock brings us to realize that marital instability is not merely a symptom of civilized, effete, or decadent societies. All societies have the problem, and they attempt to meet it in a variety of ways.

Much anthropological study is pure science, pursued for the sake of knowledge as an end in itself. The knowledge often has practical applicability, but the application is merely a by-product. Some anthropologists, as well as government officials and foreign-aid workers, have also tried to make a practical, applied science of anthropology, trying to put new findings to work immediately to help solve human problems.

APPLIED ANTHROPOLOGY   In the past 15 or 20 years, attempts to apply anthropological knowledge in practical ways have increased. Anthropological knowledge is used by government officials occasionally and by businessmen, missionaries, and casual travelers. There is no doubt in the minds of anthropologists that the image of the United States would be vastly improved if more of our people understood and took seriously some of the anthropologist's viewpoints. As Sol Tax[13] points out, the main practical service of anthropology is to teach the world what it has learned and thus promote the understanding of man by his fellow man. Usually, he goes on to say, when the need extends beyond teaching to the practical politics of applying anthropological learning, the anthropologist drops out. He is still needed, however. Public administrators are so often unaware of the fact that those persons with whom they interact in an "underdeveloped" country are too much like themselves to really represent the people, since they are part of the small educated elite. Often the anthropologist alone could tell them of the gulf that separates the educated elite from the rank and file. The peasants of Russia and China rebelled against the elite classes, and in both cases at a time when the Western world was blind to the seriousness of the problem. There was little understanding of the peasant. Eric Wolf[14]

[12]George P. Murdock, "Family Stability in Non-European Societies," *The Annals of the American Academy of Political and Social Science*, vol. 272, pp. 195–202, November 1950.
[13]Sol Tax, *Horizons in Anthropology*, Aldine Publishing Company, Chicago, 1964, pp. 248–257.
[14]Eric R. Wolf, *Peasants*, Prentice-Hall, Inc., Englewood Cliffs, N.J., 1966, pp. 106–109

explains the peasant as a human type living in a position of constant exploitation, with resentments against the urban society only lightly veiled and able to burst forth with brutal violence if his precarious balance with the urban system breaks down.

Only rarely is the anthropologist in a position to apply his knowledge to such a situation or to the aid of the underdeveloped world in general. One striking example of success, however, points the way to what could be done. Under the direction of Alan Holmberg and with the support of Cornell University, the little village of Vicos, Peru, became the center of an anthropological experiment. Vicos was an old manorial domain, badly kept up and owned by absentee landlords who were willing to sell their interests to Cornell. The description of the community sounds impossibly medieval for modern times. The peasants (or serfs) owed much of their labor directly to the lords of the manor; their land was the lords' property, for which they owed rent in kind. The peasants had to repair roads and bridges, maintain irrigation ditches and other public works, all for a few cents pay per day plus a few cocaine leaves— and even this pay had not been given for the last several years. The houses were ill repaired and the land was infertile and unproductive. Although there was a pretense of local self-government, the governing committee was appointed by the overlord and the church and was safely controlled by the old order.

In the experiment, the best sociological and anthropological knowledge was put to work, along with soil science and agricultural and marketing information generally. An important step was to put the village government in the hands of real representatives of the people. The experimenters were aware of the need to "make haste slowly," so the policy was to replace old leaders gradually with young men who had been away in the military service (a requirement in Peru, even in peacetime). The returned servicemen had a view of the world outside Vicos and were therefore more amenable to change than the older generation.

Over a period of a few years leadership changed, fields were restored to productivity, new crops were initiated, the people were thoroughly won over. Many other landlords, looking on, became nervous for fear their peasants might also agitate for more rights, but the government continued to permit the Vicos project.[15]

There are not many stories of such total reorganization, but anthropologists have been able to help with foreign-aid programs, with the training of

[15]Alan R. Holmberg, "The Changing Values and Institutions of Vicos in the Context of National Development," *American Behavioral Scientist*, vol. 8, pp. 3–8, March 1965.

Peace Corps members, and sometimes with the introduction of new foods and agricultural methods. Often they have been called upon to do governmental staff work in such places as Basutoland and the trusteeship territories of the Pacific.[16] To doctors and hospitals anthropologists have been able to explain some of the problems of introducing modern medical care—such problems as native food taboos for pregnant women, the horror of having a baby in a place where death sometimes takes place, the fear of separation from relatives at a time of physical crisis, the fear that witches might get hold of the afterbirth or blood and work evil spells upon both mother and child.[17]

More attention needs to be given to some of the unforeseen consequences of changes introduced by the Western world. Occasionally African and Asian societies have copied the prejudices of the West and have given up types of food that are rejected by our folkways but were a source of protein in otherwise poor diets. Examples of such food include dog meat and insects as well as whole-grained cereals rather than the refined flour preferred in the West.[18]

There are cases, as in East Africa, where new ideas have interfered with old customs that helped to keep population under control, such as lengthy taboos on sexual intercourse after the birth of a baby. Such taboos often lasted until weaning, which might be 2 or 3 years after the birth of the baby. When men had several wives, the taboos were kept; now that the practice of polygyny has been discouraged, the old taboos fall into disuse and birthrates climb.

Another area of application of anthropology is in urban projects. Oscar Lewis has hypothesized that despite all the cultural differences to be found from country to country, there is a culture of poverty that is widespread throughout the world and has great similarities in all countries. It is a culture not only of economic poverty but of spiritual poverty. In his analysis, such a culture does not exist among many of the rural poor of India, poor though they are, because each is bound by his traditional culture and has a place within it. It applies more particularly to the uprooted, who must flee from rural poverty to the cities, there to compete for insufficient and very poor jobs, to experience a decline in the father's status as he fails to find employment, to find tempers frayed and marital relationships brittle. Such insights have led to more attempts to study urban minorities in an anthropological manner and to increase societal awareness of the problems discovered.

[16]Lisa R. Peattie, "Interventionism and Applied Anthropology," *Human Organization*, vol. 17, pp. 4–8, November 1958.
[17]Margaret Mead, *Cultural Patterns and Technical Change*, Mentor Books, New American Library, Inc., New York, 1955, pp. 204–219.
[18]Frederick J. Simoons, *Eat Not This Flesh*, The University of Wisconsin Press, Madison, 1961.

Languages are studied in other disciplines besides anthropology, but anthropology has its special interests in the systematic study of languages, known as "linguistics." There are a number of questions that anthropological linguists would like to answer, including questions about the relationship between language and the perception of reality and about how the transition to written language has been made. These questions will be pursued in a later chapter. At present we shall turn our attention to some of the other work of the linguists.

STRUCTURE OF LANGUAGE   Anthropologists have often faced the problem of learning unknown and unwritten languages. This problem is declining in importance to some degree, since there are few if any undiscovered people left; but many of the languages anthropologists must study are very difficult to learn, partly because there are no texts or college courses in them and partly because their rules of structure and pronunciation are extremely different from those of the languages of Europe. The basic sound elements of a language, called "phonemes," must be learned correctly, or embarrassing mistakes in pronunciation can be made. Sometimes the sounds are not the simple vowel and consonant sounds we know but include clicking sounds, throaty, guttural sounds, extended tones, or high, low, and sliding pitch. Most people have heard that Chinese requires proper pitch but do not know that pitch is an essential of meaning in many languages of Africa and in some American Indian languages, including Navaho. A careful system of sound symbols (similar to the diacritical marks in dictionaries) has been devised by linguists for designating exact phonemes.

The way languages are pieced together syllable by syllable must also be studied. It seems natural to us to add suffixes and prefixes, but we do not add a syllable in the middle of a word to change tense or person, as some African languages do. Some Indian languages (Kwakiutl, for example) have reality tenses, indicating whether the action was witnessed, was simply heard about, or appeared in a dream. Intermediate tenses are sometimes included, as in Veracruz Aztec *nimayana*, "I'm hungry," *nimayana?*, "I was hungry" (the question mark denotes raised voice), and *nimayanaya*, "I was hungry and may still be hungry." The syntax, or order of words in a sentence, also differs from language to language. Sometimes statements are compressed into very few words, as in our case of "good-bye," short for "God be with you." We have very few such compressions, but the Eskimo language is full of them, so that five or six Eskimo words may convey the message of fifteen or twenty of ours.

Such differences must be studied and understood by the linguist and by the anthropologist working in a strange language area.

LANGUAGE AREAS   Anthropological linguists also study languages to trace the relationships between groups of people. Considerable work was done in linguistics by Boas in the Northwest Coast of North America, and Kroeber did much more work on the languages of the American Indians. From such research work, we find languages falling into families, just as Italian, French, Spanish, Portuguese, and Romanian all fall into the family of Latin languages. Much detective work can be done in tracing ancient relationships between people on the basis of language resemblances. It is interesting to note, for example, that the Aztecs are linguistically related to the Great Basin Shoshoni, whose culture in pre-Columbian days was extremely primitive compared to that of their advanced kinsmen in Mexico. The Navaho are related to the people of the Lake Athabasca region in Canada, and though the languages differ enough that communication presents considerable difficulty, the Navaho still find it much easier than communication with the Hopi and Zuñi who live right next to them. History can be reconstructed, often, by studies of linguistics. The closest resemblance to the ancient Egyptian language is now found in Ethiopia, indicating the early spread of Egyptian influence far up the Nile.

One of the most familiar examples of tracing language relationships is that of the Indo-European languages. We usually think of the languages of the Mediterranean region as belonging to one family and of those of northern Europe as belonging to another. Actually, they are related, as are the majority of the languages of Europe, the Hindi language of India, and the Iranian or Persian language, all belonging to one great family known as the Indo-European group. Greek is part of this family, and so are the Slavic languages of Russia and much of Eastern Europe and also the nearly extinct Celtic languages of the Scotch, Irish, and Welsh. Magyar (Hungarian) is not included, however, but belongs to a different language system that includes Finnish and certain languages of western Siberia. The Basque language is another that is not included, but it might have been spoken before the coming of the Indo-European peoples into western Europe.

The vocabularies of languages can provide a key to where the original speakers of a language first lived. If all the languages of the family have many words in common for farm animals but widely different words for ocean, fishing, and navigation, then it can be assumed that the place from which the language originally spread must have been an inland area, possibly of farmland. Such is believed to be the case with the Indo-European languages; the probable homeland, or *urheimat*, is in the steppes of southern Russia.[19] It can also be deduced that the linguistic ancestors worshiped a pantheon of gods, made human and animal sacrifices, and used horses.

Similarly, the mystery about the origins of the Gypsies was finally solved by linguists. The Gypsies had long been an enigma, wandering throughout Europe, speaking a language no one understood, and rumored to be of Egyptain origin (whence the word "Gypsy"). The truth first dawned when a Czech Sanskrit scholar recognized a few Gypsy words. Investigation proved the origin of the European Gypsies to have been India, but their language has picked up enough European words to cause significant differences.[20]

Languages constantly change, borrowing new words through contacts with other languages. Sometimes migration paths can be partly verified by words that have been added to a language over a period of time. Often names change slightly from culture to culture but remain identifiable, as when the Hebrew yvh came to be pronounced yahweh in Hebrew and Jehovah in English. An ancient Canaanite god, Baal, is found by slightly different names in other parts of the ancient world. Alexander the Great appears in Arabic tales as Iksander.

Sometimes old remnants of earlier languages are preserved in the form of incantations, oaths, and rhymes. Etruscan words were preserved long after Rome conquered Tuscany and the language changed to Latin. The words were used mainly for magic spells and curses. Sometimes foreign words persist as nonsense verse. For example, in 1949 children on the Danish island of Anholt were heard reciting the rhyme

> Jekk og Jill
> Went op de hill
> Og Jill kom tombling efter.

Investigation indicated that the "Jack and Jill" rhyme had been learned by their ancestors from English soldiers stationed on the island during the Napoleonic Wars and had persisted as a nonsense jingle.[21]

GLOTTOCHRONOLOGY   Fairly precise dating of certain American Indian languages has been done by the linguist Morris Swadesh, using a method called "glottochronology." Swadesh has observed that languages change their basic

---

[19]John Geipel, *The Europeans*, Western Publishing Company, Inc., Racine, Wis., 1970, pp. 63–65.
[20]Jean-Paul Clebert, *The Gypsies*, trans. by Charles Duff, Penguin Books, Ltd., Harmondsworth, 1963, pp. 18, 235–240.
[21]Geipel, op. cit., pp. 92–93.

vocabularies at a fairly constant rate of around 15 to 20 percent per thousand years. On this basis he would assume that two closely related Indian languages that differed by about 30 or 40 percent of their basic words must have been the same language about 1,000 years ago. Thus the historical problem of the separation of two groups would be solved with a fair degree of accuracy. The method has utility especially when language clues are the only means of dating such an event, but there is a margin of error. Some languages seem to have changed more rapidly than others, and a few (Icelandic, for example) very slowly. Nevertheless, it can be seen that glottochronology and other forms of language analysis are very helpful to the anthropologist in the study of the histories and relationships of cultures.

An interesting sidelight on the subject of linguistic changes over a period of time can be gained from reading Geoffrey Chaucer (1340?–1400), who wrote in the language of the common people of England of his time. The following passage, taken from his account of Troilus and Cressida (Criseide in Chaucerian spelling), is easier to understand than much of Chaucer, but even it requires considerable study.

> It is wel wist how that the Greekes stronge
> In armes with a thousand shippes wente
> To Troyewardes, and the citee longe
> Assegeden—neigh ten yeer er they stente—
> In divers wise and in oon entente:
> The ravishing to wreken of Elaine,
> By Paris doon, they wroughten al hir paine.

A liberal translation into modern English would read:

> It is well known how the Greeks, strong
> In arms, with a thousand ships went
> To Troy, and the city long
> Was besieged—nearly ten years before they stopped—
> In various ways and with one intent:
> To revenge the ravishing of Helen
> By Paris [which caused them to] undergo all their troubles.

ARCHAEOLOGY   Archaeology is the study of the artifacts of the past with the purpose of increasing our knowledge of the lives and cultures of the people who produced them. The role of archaeologist is more than that of a mere digger among remains. He is the expert at their interpretation and often aids and is aided by historians and prehistorians. To many people, archaeology has meant mainly classical archaeology, or the study of the ruins of the classical civilizations of the Old World. For most American students of archaeology, it is just as much, if not more, the study of the prehistory of the American Indians, Africans, and Asians.

Just as the cultural anthropologist is interested in a wide variety of cultures, the archaeologist is interested in many forms of archaeological excavation, covering a great range of time and space. Sometimes archaeological findings are for periods that are recorded in history, but the records can be greatly supplemented by archaeology. Historians and other narrators have often left records of elite upper classes or the dramatic events of struggle and conflict, but have said little of the lives of the common people or the artifacts made by them. Even when old sites are found and studied, much interpretation is needed, and a certain imagination for reconstructing the actual lives of the people. As James Deetz says:

> An Indian village on the Missouri River in 1750 must have been a lively place. Barking dogs running between large earth-covered houses; children playing on the roofs; women making pots and chatting by the doorways; a party of men returning from a hunting expedition laden with bison meat—all contribute to a picture of confusion, sound, and motion. The same village in 1965 is a silent cluster of dim green rings of grass on the brown prairie, the only sound that of the wind, the only motion and life that of a tumbleweed rolling across the low mounds and depressions, and of a hawk circling high in the sky. The people are gone, and the only things which attest to their former presence are fragments of the objects which they made and used, buried in the collapsed remains of their dwellings.[22]

Even such a site, however, can give types of information that narrators of the past did not relate—preferences in art forms and crafts, size and configuration of villages, size, shape, and arrangement of houses, ecological and climatic data, and possibly a few details of food preferences and preparation.

The site discussed by Deetz belongs to a culture of known date. Often the date is not known, and one of the tasks of archaeology is to estimate dates and sequences of findings.

DATING ARTIFACTS   At one time the only possible ways of dating objects of the past were by association with other objects or by guessing the length of time it would take them to become buried in the sediment in which they were found. In the Near East so many *tells* (mounds containing the remains of suc-

44   [22]James Deetz, *Invitation to Archaeology*, Natural History Press, Garden City, N.Y., 1967, p. 8.

cessive civilizations) were found that relative dating could be fairly certain and the results could even be correlated with historical events or legends. The legendary Troy was discovered by Heinrich Schliemann late in the nineteenth century, and he had been helped in his search by Homer's descriptions. It is noteworthy, though, that for all his persistence and scholarship, Schliemann made a mistake as to which of several strata in the tell was the historic Troy. Much experience is needed in the interpretation of data from the past, and much has been learned since the nineteenth century.

Where there is no way of guessing by stratification or history or legend, dates are sometimes established by tree-ring dating, especially in the American Southwest. A yet better method with wider applicability is that of radiocarbon dating, developed in the 1940s. Living plants and animals, in the process of breathing, absorb small amounts of the radioactive isotope carbon (C^{14}), and the percentage contained in living tissues is fairly constant. When death occurs, C^{14} no longer enters the organism, and that which is present deteriorates into common C^{12} at a half-life of 5,730 years. Half-life means the time required for half the radioactive material to change into the nonradioactive form. Since accretions of half, plus one-fourth, plus one-eighth, ad infinitum, do not add up to the total number 1, there would, theoretically, always be a residuum of C^{14} left in any matter that had once known life. Actually, though, the amount becomes too small for accurate measurements if the method is applied after all but about one two-hundred-fiftieth of the C^{14} has changed to C^{12}, so the method is accurate only for dates no earlier than about 50,000 years ago.[23]

In cases where archaeology goes so far back in time as to merge with human paleontology, another dating method can be used, potassium-argon. Argon is a heavy gas formed from the atomic decomposition of potassium at a half-life of 1.3 billion years. It is only rarely that potassium is found in the right strata to make it useful, but it was found in Olduvai Gorge at the site of one of Louis Leakey's most important discoveries, an ancient protohuman skull (to be discussed in Chapter Three), and a date of approximately 1,750,000 years ago was determined.

ARCHAEOLOGICAL RECORDING   In the opening pages of the present chapter, mention was made of the infinite care with which archaeologists work, and the point needs to be emphasized. The untrained amateur who goes out and digs up an Indian grave and proudly takes home a skull and two or three arrowheads is making no contribution to archaeology. What he is doing is destroying a record, making it impossible for a trained archaeologist to explore the site

[23]Deetz, ibid., pp. 33–42.

Careful methods are needed to glean all the information an archaeological site can yield and to avoid mere grave robbing.

systematically and obtain the types of information such exploration would produce. Archaeology depends as much upon proper methods as upon analysis. Sites are mapped out by a grid system, and every fragment found is described as to its location along the grid. In the United States the most commonly used system for recording the locations of the sites themselves is one that gives a number for the state in which found and the initials of the county. The relative date of the site as compared to others in the county and the initials of the archaeologist doing the digging are also included. The material and records should be preserved at universities or museums.

It is one of the tragedies of archaeology that so much of the excavation of the past can be described only as grave robbing. C. W. Ceram, in *Gods, Graves, and Scholars*, tells of one Egyptian village in which generations of people had made their living selling the plunder of Egyptian tombs.[24] The only consolation in this case is that at least a few poor Egyptian fellahin were making a living

[24]C. W. Ceram, *Gods, Graves, and Scholars: The Story of Archaeology*, rev. ed., Alfred A. Knopf, New York, 1967, pp. 165–175.

from the practice. Often the treasures of antiquity have been stolen with no benefit whatever to the people of the country in which they were found. Modern governments with treasured antiquities—Egypt, Iraq, Mexico, Peru, China—are making determined efforts to bring the robbery to an end. Nevertheless, lucrative channels for the looting of Mexican temples still exist; much is smuggled out illegally and, after changing hands, ends up in "respectable" collections.[25] Most Indian artifacts in the United States have nothing like the same monetary value as some of the antiquities of Mexico, but all anthropology students should realize that amateur collecting results in unrecognizable jumbles of artifacts that perhaps could have added colorful details and meaningful sequences to the tragic story of Indian America.

NEAR EASTERN ARCHAEOLOGY: UR   The artifacts of Egypt are more familiar to most people than those of Mesopotamia, partly because Egyptian building was so monumental and permanent and partly because Egypt has been studied longer and more thoroughly than Mesopotamia. Nevertheless, some of the most exciting finds of the twentieth century have been made in the ancient land of the Tigris-Euphrates. Although the discovery of Ur is by no means recent, it is very important and tells much about the dawn of what is probably the world's first urban civilization.

Ur was one of the great cities of antiquity, possibly having had a population of more than 100,000 during its times of greatness. It was abandoned shortly before the beginning of the Christian era and deteriorated into a series of great mounds, visited only by occasional shepherds and made featureless by the drifting sands of twenty-five centuries. Its excavation was directed by Sir Charles Leonard Woolley during the years 1924 to 1935 and is of particular archaeological importance because it revealed a succession of levels of civilization, starting with the founding of Ur in about 5000 B.C. and progressing through its growth to a great city by the time of the royal tombs, about 2800 B.C. The royal tombs (sixteen were discovered) reveal a Bronze Age culture, the use of domes and arches, wheeled transport, finery for its nobility, jewelry, and semiprecious stones. In the royal tombs is found evidence of the burial of many servants and valuable artifacts with the deceased—in one case seventy-five servants, as well as oxen and ox carts. Here was a prominent early occurrence of the custom Herodotus was to describe over 2,000 years later and that was also practiced in the First Dynasty of the Old Kingdom of ancient Egypt and in the early Shan Dynasty of northern China. Since only the royal tombs contained buried servants, indications are that social class had become widely

[25]"Smuggling of Artifacts Rampant in Mexico," *Los Angeles Times*, September 1971, part I, pp. 4–5.

differentiated by that time and that royalty had more than a touch of divinity. In a later chapter we shall refer again to Mesopotamia, as an illustration of certain uniformities in the growth of civilizations and the development of noble classes.

RECENT FINDS IN THE NEAR EAST   Less well known than the great Mesopotamian city of Ur are some of the remarkable discoveries of the last decade or so. Archaeologists have unearthed evidence of agriculture's beginnings in the Near East in the form of grain storage bins and sickles. In Turkey they have found a trade center, Çatal Hüyük, dating back to 6000 B.C., older than the earliest ruins of Ur or the first pyramids of Egypt. The city was Neolithic, with obsidian and bone tools, since metals were not yet in use. The houses were rectangular, of mud-brick construction, and closely packed together. There were large communal ovens and a shrine room dominated by two giant bull heads.[26] The cult of the sacred bull, later significant in Crete, apparently dates back at least as far as Çatal Hüyük.

Older yet is the earliest town at the location of the biblical city of Jericho, a walled town existing almost 10,000 years ago and the oldest yet discovered. It, too, had large ovens for the baking of bread, and there are evidences of grain storage, although it is uncertain whether wild grain was collected or agriculture was already practiced to some degree.

PALEONTOLOGY AND ARCHAEOLOGY   Since archaeology is primarily the study of artifacts, some very ancient findings without tools or other cultural remains belong more to human paleontology than to archaeology. However, there are cases where it is possible to make surmises about the way of life of our ancestors of a much more remote time than is usually studied by archaeologists. Such evidence obviously cannot come from villages or towns, since none existed, but sometimes ancient camp sites or hunting grounds can yield information.

In the Ambrona Valley of Spain, F. Clark Howell discovered an ancient hunting site of about 300,000 years ago. Men apparently drove animals into a marsh, where the heavier ones, such as the woolly elephants that lived in Europe in those days, would be mired in the quicksand. The bones of smaller elephants, horses, and other animals were found, along with hand axes, cleavers, and stone scrapers. It looked as though the meat had been cut from the large elephants and all the bones left; whole sections of the other animals had apparently been carried off to camp. The evidence indicates hunting

[26]James Mellaart, "A Neolithic City in Turkey," *Scientific American*, vol. 210, pp. 94–104, April 1964.

Anthropologists at Jericho have unearthed the oldest walled town yet discovered, nearly 10,000 years old.

parties of considerable size and the use of the marsh over a long period of years. The fauna indicates the great antiquity of the find, and stratigraphy and pollen dating are consistent with the estimate of 300,000 years ago. One other interesting feature is that there is much evidence of fire, widespread, as though torches had been lit to drive the animals into the marsh. Howell believes this is precisely what happened and that this site presents the first clear evidence of such a technique being used. There are no human bones in the site, but the date indicates that the people were of a type now called *Homo erectus*.[27]

The Ambrona site is clearly one for which all help from history, legend, and myth have long since disappeared. It takes archaeology far backward in time to a point where artifacts become few and their purposes indistinct. Increasingly the help of other sciences, such as pollen analysis and paleobiostratigraphy, is needed to help date the material. The attempt to connect such finds with a general developmental framework of the human race is a major task of physical anthropology, which we shall turn to briefly.

[27]F. Clark Howell, *Early Man*, Time-Life Books, New York, 1965, pp. 85–106.

Since the present text is addressed to the subject matter of cultural rather than physical anthropology, just a few remarks will be made about the latter at this time. The original interests of physical anthropology were to trace the origin of man from earlier forms of life and to describe the variations in human types that have developed. Much progress has been made along both lines. Not only have many more remains of different stages of human evolution been discovered, but more can be deduced about the probable ways of life and capabilities of earlier human beings and prehumans. For example, the initial impression of Neanderthal man was that he was a terribly lowly brute, far removed from mankind of today. As more knowledge of Neanderthal man and his culture (Mousterian) has developed, he has come to seem more an important pioneer of human culture and a creature very closely related to modern man.[28]

Progressive discoveries have also pushed back the boundaries of our knowledge of the probable ancestors of man to over 2 million years ago, with at least one jawbone and tooth dated at over 3 million years ago. New dating methods have been of inestimable value to physical anthropology; pollen dating, especially, has made records of climatic changes much clearer than before. In a recent finding at Nice in southern France, for example, pollen samples indicate that the trees of the time were of boreal-forest type, indicating a very cold, moist climate, comparable to that of northern Finland. The time of the site is around 110,000 years ago, during one of the advances of the final (Würm) Ice Age.

Much has been learned about the causes of variations in human types. In recent years, physical anthropologists have delved deeply into the fields of genetics, serology, and blood proteins. Rather than merely describing in detail all the physical variations of racial or subracial types, they are looking for genotypes, that is, the possibilities that are carried in the long chains of molecules (DNA) that transmit heredity. Immunology, mutation, and susceptibility to disease are increasingly important topics. These studies place anthropology squarely in alliance with biology in seeking deeper understanding of the operation of heredity. In the next chapter, quite a bit will be said about the evolutionary development of the human race as revealed by fossil remains and about the arguments over racial variation. At this point it might be interesting to mention a new type of approach to human origins and relationships.

[28]Francois Bordes, "Mousterian Cultures in France," *Science*, vol. 134, pp. 803–810, September 1961.

TRACING RELATIONSHIPS   For a number of years comparative studies have been made of blood proteins and chromosome patterns of man and the great apes. It was not surprising to find that man's closest relatives by this type of measurement were the great apes, especially the chimpanzees and gorillas. It was, however, rather surprising to find how close the resemblance is. In both blood proteins and chromosomes, man is as close to the chimpanzee as the chimpanzee is to the gorilla. The orangutan stands at a slightly greater distance, the gibbons and Old World monkeys are further removed, and the New World monkeys even further. Previous to the time of serology and blood protein and chromosome studies, there even had been some speculation as to whether man might be more closely related to some of the monkeys than to the great apes. It was thought that we might be making too much out of superficial resemblances to apes in size and morphology but overlooking some very different special adaptations. Now it is clear that the more apparent resemblance to apes was of real significance.[29]

Recently, two members of the anthropology staff at the University of California at Berkeley have developed an ingenious device for making another measurement of the difference between man and the other primates.[30] They (Vincent Sarich and Allan Wilson) have hypothesized that certain blood and chromosome characteristics change at a constant rate as species advance along the evolutionary scale. The easiest characteristic to work on first was blood albumins, with which they worked out an "immunological distance scale" including man, the great apes, the orangutans, the gibbons, and the Old World monkeys. Just as in the protein studies, the distances between man and chimpanzee and between chimpanzee and gorilla were equal, and greater differences separated man from the orangutans, gibbons, and monkeys. Calculating the separation of the Old World monkeys from the ancestors of the great apes as mid-Oligocene (about 30 million years ago), a fairly well-accepted date, and estimating the rate of change of serum albumin as being constant, they came up with a figure of from 5 to 8 million years ago as the time of separation of our ancestors from the great apes. Their scheme of phylogenetic development follows.

It should be pointed out that the studies of Sarich and Wilson have not yet gained wide acceptance and, like any calculations of such remote evolutionary changes, must not be taken as the final word. Their study, however,

[29]Morris Goodman and Sherwood L. Washburn, *Classification and Human Evolution*, Aldine Publishing Company, Chicago, 1963.
[30]Vincent Sarich and Allan Wilson, "Immunological Time Scale for Hominid Evolution," *Science*, vol. 158, pp. 1200–1203, December 1967.

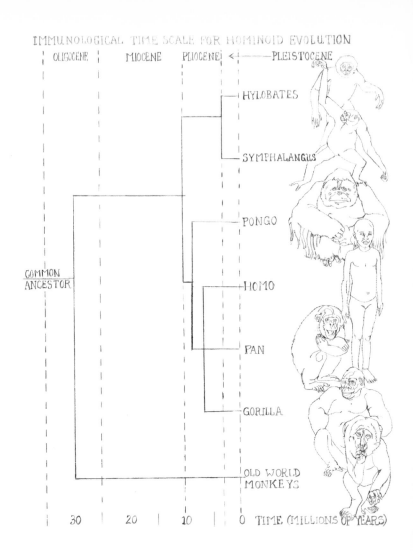

IMMUNOLOGICAL TIME SCALE FOR HOMINOID EVOLUTION

| OLIGOCENE | MIOCENE | PLIOCENE | < ———— PLEISTOCENE |

HYLOBATES

SYMPHALANGUS

PONGO

COMMON ANCESTOR

HOMO

PAN

GORILLA

OLD WORLD MONKEYS

30   20   10   0 TIME (MILLIONS OF YEARS)

provides an interesting illustration of one of the directions in which the search for man's ancestors can lead and of the cooperation between anthropology and biology in the enterprise.

SUMMARY   One chapter is obviously inadequate for describing all the activities and branches of anthropology. Several of those included in the chart near the beginning of the chapter have been omitted, particularly the more specialized fields. Nevertheless, this brief glance has demonstrated the great scope of anthropology. We have looked at ethnographic descriptions and ethnological theories and at the attempts to apply anthropological learning to the practical problems of emerging nations and people having difficulty adjusting to the requirements of the modern world.

Some of the anthropological disciplines with which we have dealt add greatly to our knowledge of historic and prehistoric developments. Historical linguistics tells much about the interrelationships between peoples and in many cases demonstrate common origins for people whose known history would indicate they had always been separate. Archaeology, too, has been a great source of enlightenment about past cultures and has supplied cultural interpretations based on artifacts whose meanings would be obscure to the casual observer. Recent developments in dating methods have aided archaeological research and made dates and sequences much more certain.

In the very distant past, archaeology merges with the study of fossil man, or paleoanthropology, and the study of the record of human evolution. These subjects and the study of living primates will be given attention in Chapter Three. The attempt at biological dating discussed in the present chapter was used to illustrate the connection between anthropology and molecular biology. Whether such studies prove fully accurate or not, they at least show the possibility for new types of cooperation between sciences.

PART TWO
THE EMERGENCE
OF MAN

In Part One we studied the development of anthropology as an academic discipline and the often conflicting points of view that arose along with that development. We also looked into the far-flung enterprise of anthropology and the many approaches it uses to study mankind and to discover the interconnection between man as a physical being and man as a cultural being. In the course of the discussion, the idea of Darwinian evolution was introduced. It seems a logical next step to go briefly into the record of the evolutionary development of the human species and the concomitant development of the capacity to create culture.

In treating the emergence of man, a full course in physical anthropology would give detailed coverage to the development of all the traits of the primates—the order of animals that includes all the monkeys, apes, and man, as well as several more primitive types, such as tarsiers and lemurs. In this brief discussion, comments will be limited almost entirely to types of beings called "hominids," a term including man, his immediate ancestors, and such closely related species as the type of ape-man whose remains were first found in South Africa and who has been given the general name of australopithecine. In contrast, the word "hominoid" describes man and his more distant relatives, the great apes. What are the traits that all hominoids have in common? What traits are confined only to hominids and which only to man?

Next it is important to look at a
particular trait of the hominids, and
especially man—the capacity to adapt
to so many parts of the world.
Monkeys have a fairly wide distribution,
although those of the New World differ
from those of the Old. Apes are limited
to the Old World only, and at least one
surviving species, the orangutan, is
limited to Borneo and Sumatra. Man,
on the other hand, was able to spread
to and flourish in all parts of the world
except Antarctica. At what time and by
what means was this highly adaptive
species able to spread so widely? Does
racial variation have any relevance to its
adaptability? What traits were eventually
to make man dominant over all other
species?

The overwhelming difference between man and the other animals lies in the capacity to build cultures. Only man can explain new ideas and techniques to his offspring and thus pass them along to future generations. Primatologists have become increasingly fascinated with certain species of monkeys and apes and have found them to have greater learning capacity than was once supposed and even the rudiments of invention; but the gap between them and man remains enormous. We are no longer so anthropocentric—so arrogant about our species—as to be horrified, as our nineteenth-century ancestors were, to be told that the apes are our close relatives; but we still wonder how so much difference came about. What do the records of the past tell us of the evolution of the cultural capacity? What can we learn from primate comparisons? What was the relationship to later evolution of upright posture, manipulative hands, and the ability to make tools? To what degree did early man become the architect of his own evolution? Finally, why did it take man so long to examine critically the record of his remote ancestors?

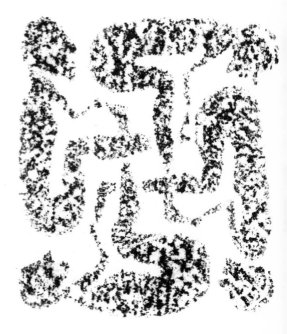

Chapter Three
Evolution
of the
Cultural Capacity

Since ancient times, fossilized bones of extinct species have been uncovered in the sediments of the earth. In eastern Asia the fossilized remains of giant animals were ground up and sold in apothecary shops as powdered dragon bones, alleged to have wonderful powers to cure illness and restore sexual vigor to the impotent. In the West a few of the ancients of Greco-Roman times had found remains of marine life and had correctly assumed the seas once covered parts of what is now land. They also found enormous bones that they interpreted more fancifully as the bones of Cyclopses, giants, griffins, and unicorns. Such ideas were by no means limited to the uneducated. Even Leonardo da Vinci, whose mentality dwarfs that of almost any person living today, made drawings of the dragons that might account for such bones. Giovanni Boccaccio, author of the famous *Decameron*, was convinced he had found the bones of a Cyclops. In the eighteenth century, Otto von Guericke, the mayor of Magdeburg, was able to find enough bones in the Harz Mountains to construct a skeleton of a unicorn—in his excited opinion possibly the very one mentioned in the Book of Job![1]

There were equally strange reports of remote races of men, including men with ears so long they could use them for blankets to cover themselves at night.[2] Corolus Linnaeus (1707–1778) was the first great classifier of living species and a scientist of high repute. Even he, however, gave some credence to reports of fantastic beings, especially fantastic human beings. He gave modern man his present name, *Homo sapiens* (thinking man), but added also the species *Homo monstrosus*, to include giants and strangely deformed races rumored to exist. There had been reports of large-headed, pin-headed, goat-headed, and dog-headed people and even of people with no heads at all. Linnaeus listed the goat-headed people as *Simia satyrus* (simian satyrs). The word "simian" refers to apes and "satyrs" to the mythical half-man, half-goat creatures of Greek mythology. Apparently Linnaeus thought of satyrs as apelike. He also listed pygmies as simians, *Simia sylvanus* (simians of the woods). Linnaeus's follower, C. E. Hoppius, added *Homo troglodytes* (human beings living underground) and *Homo luciferus* (human beings with tails—like the devil Lucifer).

Many sophisticated men of science were skeptical about the findings of mythological creatures. Following the lead of the great Arab scholar Avicenna (A.D. 980–1037), they explained fossilized bones as being the result of a mysterious stone-making natural force that sometimes shapes rocks in ways

[1]Herbert Wendt, *In Search of Adam*, Houghton Mifflin Company, Boston, 1956, pp. 3–10.
[2]Annemarie de Waal Malefijt, "Homo monstrosus," *Scientific American*, vol. 219, pp. 113–118, October 1968.

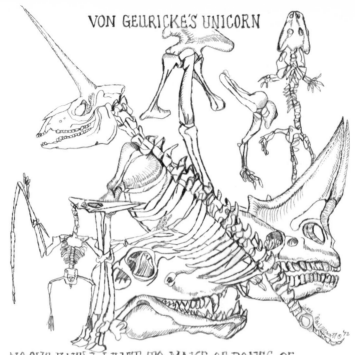

VON GEURICKE'S UNICORN

NO ONE KNEW WHAT TO MAKE OF BONES OF PREHISTORIC ANIMALS. DID THEY PROVE THE TRUTH OF MYTHOLOGICAL BEINGS, OR WERE THEY INDICATIONS THAT CHANGES IN SPECIES ACTUALLY DO TAKE PLACE?

that closely imitate actual life forms. Some clerics, on the other hand, contended that the bones were placed by the Devil to deceive the mind of man, and many more thought they were the remains of animals drowned in the Great Flood of Noah's time. A lively controversy grew between the "Floodists" and the "anti-Floodists." Voltaire jabbed at the Floodists with his devastating wit, but even he was unable to offer an adequate explanation for the mysterious bones. The first of the mammoth bones were explained away neatly as the remains of some of Hannibal's elephants; but what were they doing in so many different parts of Europe? How did they get into remote Siberia? Swedish soldiers of the unfortunate army of Charles XII, held prisoner in Siberia, reported the first of the mammoths in the early 1700s, frozen in the ice, their flesh still preserved. Later in the century, elephant tusks were purchased from Tungus tribesmen, who led explorers to the great animals they called *mamontokovast* (from which we derive the word "mammoth"). Finally, in the early

61

nineteenth century, the scientific world began to recognize the existence not only of mammoths but of many kinds of extinct animals.[3] Had some great cataclysm killed them, or is it simply in the nature of things for species to change?

The idea of a changing world and changing species, previously speculated upon by a few, was gaining acceptance as a result of the work of such scholars as Lyell and Boucher de Perthes but became a widely accepted view only after the publication of Darwin's *Origin of Species*. The sporadic and accidental discovery of bones was replaced by a frantic search for the past, and not just for lower animals but for man himself. Had men lived in a world of much larger animals than are now extant? Was it possible that the human species itself had changed and that men and animals are linked closely together in the same evolutionary process?

THE SEARCH
FOR PREHISTORIC MAN

Not even the evolutionalists could conceptualize easily what type of creature was ancestral to man. The first Neanderthal skull was actually unearthed in Spain long before the publication of *The Origin of Species*, but no one knew what to say about it or where to classify it. Even the Darwinists seem to have expected to find a being with a skull and brain very similar to that of modern man, but probably with massive jaws. As a matter of fact, Neanderthal man did have a large brain, but the shape of the skull was different from that of modern man, with a large, bun-shaped occiput (rear section) and smaller and less rounded forehead and with massive brow ridges. The puzzling nature of the large cranium of Neanderthal was such as to lend credence to the idea that man's brain had grown first and then he had achieved upright stature. A great hoax was perpetrated that tended to confirm the idea of brain evolution followed by evolution of other parts of the body. An Englishman pieced together a late Pleistocene skull and an ape jaw with modified canines and called it "Piltdown man." To their credit, a few anthropologists, including Franz von Weidenreich and Aleš Hrdlička, never did believe in Piltdown man, but most people did. Piltdown man provided an ancestor whose brain had grown first and whose manual dexterity, we could assume, had developed as a consequence. Eventually the idea of mental growth followed by bodily anatomical changes was to be proved completely wrong. Better dating methods later proved Piltdown man to be one of the greatest scientific hoaxes ever perpetrated.

[3]Wendt, op. cit., p. 41.

In popular literature the misrepresentation of prehistoric man was even more amazing. Even to this day, Stone Age men are often pictured as struggling in a world of dinosaurs, although dinosaurs had become extinct 80 million years before man appeared on earth.

THE FINDINGS IN EUROPE   Much early searching was done in Europe, partly because it was the convenient place to look and partly because Europeans seemed to take pride in finding ancient remains in their own soil. France developed an early interest in anthropology and proved to be a rich mine of prehistoric skulls and artifacts. Neanderthal craniums and skeletons were found in Belgium and Germany and in many sites in France. The Neanderthal culture was named "Mousterian," after the village of Le Moustier in southern France. Also found in France were some of the first skulls of modern types of man, the best known being named "Cro-Magnon man," after a village of that name in the Dordogne Valley.

A dichotomy of human types was hypothesized from the first. Neanderthal man seemed very primitive and brutal in appearance, with sloping brow, heavy brow ridges, clumsy posture, and bowed legs—a point exaggerated by the fact that one of the first specimens studied was that of an old man with arthritis. Neanderthalers were thought of as subhuman brutes, and every attempt was made to explain that they could not possibly have been our ancestors. Stories were invented of a conflict between Neanderthal man and Cro-Magnon man and the triumph of the latter—a dubious tale, as we shall see.

THE ASIAN SEARCH   The search for prehistoric man in Asia is nearly as old as the search in Europe. In the early 1890s, an army surgeon, Eugene Dubois, obsessed with the idea of finding the remains of prehistoric man, succeeded in getting a government appointment to the Dutch East Indies (now Indonesia). With a combination of insight, persistence, and incredible luck, he found what has since been called "Java man." He named his specimen *Pithecanthropus erectus* (apeman that walked erect), but it is now included in the species *Homo erectus* (upright man). A femur was found of a type to suggest upright posture. The skull was much more primitive than any ever found before, with a cranial capacity of about 900 to 1000 cc (modern men average around 1500 cc). The specimen had extremely heavy brow ridges and jaws. The brow ridge, which exists only in very rudimentary form among modern men, had the function of protecting the eyes in the days before the frontal lobe of the brain was large enough to call for a brain case that extended above the eyes.

The Dubois findings gave considerable aid to the Darwinists, although arguments arose as to whether the skull was protohuman or merely that of an ape and whether the femur found near it actually belonged with the skull. Other researchers, including Davidson Black, continued the digging, and more teeth and bones were unearthed, but not nearly enough for a complete skeleton. Dubois grew weary of the argument over the importance of his findings and locked them up in his house in Leiden, Holland, until 1921, when he finally published descriptions. He had more specimens that had been made known, but by that time Dubois had lost all interest in the subject.[4] In the mid-1930s, G. H. R. von Koenigswald made many more findings of Java types, some of approximately the date of Dubois's Java man and some of a later type.

PEKING   In another part of Asia an equally exciting find was made some years later. Black and Weng Chung Pei (and later von Weidenreich) took a great interest in some teeth found among the powdered dragon bones being sold at Chinese drug stores and decided to see if they could lead to bones of prehistoric man. Their search took them to Choukoutien Cave, near Peking, where they found many specimens of a *Homo erectus* type originally called "Peking man" or *Sinanthropus*. The skulls bore a resemblance to those found in Java but were more advanced, with cranial capacities of 1000 to 1200 cc, getting to the lower margin of modern man. The posture was undoubtedly upright. The skull was thick, the forehead sloping, and brow ridges continued to be massive. Along with the human bones were found large numbers of animal bones, often broken open, probably to get the marrow. Peking man was an able hunter, bringing back to his cave bones of antelope and deer, camels, horses, bison, and even rhinoceroses and elephants. The Peking people must have lived in bands and hunted together, or such catches would not have been possible. For the first time there was good evidence that man used fire, but there is no certainty that it had not also been used much earlier.

Along with the broken animal bones were human skulls, broken open at the base. Evidently Peking man practiced brain cannibalism. Often among recent cannibals, cannibalism has been accompanied by headhunting, but not always. New Guinea highlanders have practiced cannibalism as a sign of mourning and respect for the dead and, possibly, as a ritual unification of the world of the living and that of the dead.[5] There is no way of knowing the intent of the Peking men; maybe they were only after food, but the very fact that the brain was prized seems to indicate some idea of the head as a spirit center. Possibly a dim idea of the dualities of the secular and the sacred, of some

[4]Ibid., pp. 291–301.
[5]Carleton Gajdusek, "Physiological and Psychological Characteristics of Stone Age Man," *Engineering and Science*, vol. 33, pp. 27–28, April 1970.

haunting spirit or mana lurking in an unseen world, was already taking shape in the human mind. Perhaps man had entered the mysterious realm of magic and spirit that would be the preoccupation of his descendants for thousands of generations. Eventually this realm would include rites and myths, gods and devils, and imaginings of other worlds.

AFRICA   While the interest of the world was focused on Europe and Asia, miners were at work in South Africa, at the quarry at Taung about an hour's drive north of Kimberley. In 1924, a blast threw out a fragment of bone that attracted the attention of a quarryman, M. de Bruyn. The fragment was a small skull, the skull of a child, a gorilla or chimpanzee pup, or perhaps something of greater importance. The skull was sent to an anatomist, Raymond Dart, who immediately recognized its significance. The skull of the Taung child was not that of a chimpanzee or gorilla or of any known species; it was a species quite possibly on the main line of human evolution and much closer to the anthropoids (apes) than any hominid yet found.[6] The teeth (baby teeth) were remarkably human. Even the skull, in Dart's opinion, showed signs of hominization, although the size was no greater than that of a chimpanzee, 500 to 600 cc.

Other scientists were called upon to review the evidence, but they all agreed that Dart was wrong; he had only an interesting variation on a species of ape, nothing of any more significance. He received so little support in his theories that he was about ready to give up in disgust when the elderly Scottish paleontologist Robert Broom heard of the specimen and went to South Africa. Broom immediately agreed with Dart, wrote a description of the teeth and the general skull shape, and started a search for mature specimens. Twelve frustrating years passed, but from 1936 onward specimens began to "rise from the ground," first from a quarry at Sterkfontein. Then Broom was given a skull from Kromdraai, found by a schoolboy, Gert Terblanche, who also had a pocketful of teeth and a jawbone he had found. Terblanche led the way to the quarry where he had been looking, and a new type of South African man was discovered, "Kromdraai man," more rugged in appearance than the specimens from Sterkfontein. Then a whole series of adult skulls, along with other bones, was found at Swartkranz. Africa was being recognized at last as the possible place of origin of the human species. Broom and Dart, along with their early allies John T. Robinson and William J. Sollar, were no longer alone. The great Jesuit scholar Teilhard de Chardin had joined their team. After the discovery of the Swartkranz skulls the whole scientific world was convinced of the importance of the South African finds.[7]

[6]Robert Broom, "The Ape Men," *Scientific American*, vol. 181, pp. 20–24, November 1949.
[7]Ibid., p. 23.

Australopithecine skull. In South Africa
startling finds were made of a creature
far more primitive and remote in time
than any previously discovered hominid.

LOUIS S. B. LEAKEY Far to the north, in the country now called Tanzania, in a gorge that contains the sediment of at least three million years, a determined and indefatigable anthropologist, Louis S. B. Leakey—soon joined by his wife, Mary—started to dig in the late 1920s. They and their family returned to Olduvai Gorge every summer, sometimes interesting others in the diggings. The bones of many extinct species of animals were found and also pebble tools but for many years no clearly identifiable hominid bones. Then one day, when Leakey had retired early because of a headache, his wife made the find they had been looking for—a hominid skull, resembling the finds in South Africa, particularly the Kromdraai skull. Leakey named the specimen *Zinjanthropus bosei*, but it has since been considered one of the australopithecines.

Since the sediment in which *Zinjanthropus* was found was overlaid with volcanic rock and potassium was contained in this rock, it was possible to obtain a date by the potassium-argon method. Two tests were made, with a laboratory in Holland giving a date of 1,300,000 years ago, and one in Berkeley, California, giving a date of 1,750,000 years ago. In the years since, the Berkeley date has generally won acceptance. The antiquity of hominid remains now stretches backward in time incalculably, to a date earlier than had generally been considered the beginning of the Pleistocene.

Since the uncovering of *Zinjanthropus* there have been other discoveries by Leakey, one or two specimens of a smaller, less rugged sort, which he has named *Homo habilis* and believes to be more directly in the line of human development than the australopithecines. Others consider *Homo habilis* to be a variety of the same species as the australopithecines.[8] Whatever the case, the antiquity of man's ancestors has been moved backward far beyond expectation, and yet more is to be found. In the summer of 1969, a graduate student in anthropology, on an expedition first headed by Camile Arambourg and later by F. Clark Howell, found a hominid tooth in the Omo Valley of Ethiopia dated at 3,500,000 years ago.

THE STAGES
OF HUMAN EVOLUTION

Since the last few pages have been written primarily to narrate the finding of man's ancestors, they have described specimens in the order in which they were found, not in their order of development. It seems necessary at this point to use a short summary to clarify the chronological order of the types of fossil man found in Europe, Asia, and Africa. There are differences of opinion as to how each type should be classi-

[8]C. Loring Brace, *The Stages of Human Evolution*, chap. 9, "The Australopithecine Stage," Prentice-Hall, Inc., Englewood Cliffs, N.J., 1967.

fied, especially in the case of Neanderthal man, who will be given more consideration later. For the present, the simple classification used by Loring Brace in *The Stages of Human Evolution* seems most useful.[9] He speaks of four stages of human evolution: the australopithecine, the *Homo erectus*, the Neanderthal, and the modern stage. Dates are very difficult to estimate, but the following are fair approximations for at least a few specimens that have been dated. It will be noted that there are long time gaps, which may be filled or partially filled in the future. In the transition from the Neanderthal to the modern stage, there is undoubtedly a certain amount of overlap that does not show up in the dating scheme on page 69.

TIME AND MAN   It is virtually impossible to construct a time line that would show the existence of man in scale with the age of the earth. Denoyer-Geppert has produced a chart that represents the earth's entire history as one year.[10] On such a scale, the first life appears late in August; the first mammals appear around December 25. On the twenty-seventh day of the last month of the year, the first primates put in their appearance. About 6 hours before midnight the australopithecines are born. At 11:57, 3 minutes before the stroke of midnight, modern man appears.

The rate of human evolution has been extremely rapid in terms of the earth's history and compared with the rate for many other species. Evolution is not a rigid process set to a time clock but moves at uneven rates, both biologically and culturally. On the time scale just used, man and his hominid relatives have been on earth only a few hours. His more distant primate relatives have been here for several days. What traits were they developing that have a bearing on the evolution of man?

THE PRIMATE RELATIVES   So far the discussion has been about types of animals called hominids, beings that either are men or definitely developing in the direction of mankind and are more nearly human than any of the living apes. There are much older types of beings, generally regarded as "pongids" (apelike), that could possibly be ancestral to both man and ape. There are several species of a genus called *Dryopithecus* that could conceivably be ancestral to the hominids. Findings of the dryopithecines have been made over a long period of years in Europe, eastern Asia, and Africa, and the specimens range in age from about

[9]Ibid., pp. 59–107.
[10]John Sternig, "Picture History of the Earth" (chart), Denoyer-Geppert Science Series, Chicago, 1963.

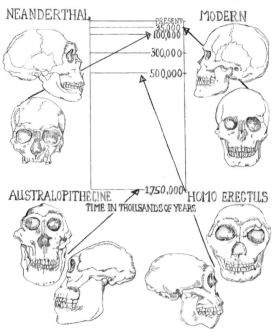

THE FOUR STAGES OF HUMAN EVOLUTION

NEANDERTHAL   MODERN

PRESENT
35,000
100,000
300,000
500,000

AUSTRALOPITHECINE   1,750,000 HOMO ERECTUS
TIME IN THOUSANDS OF YEARS

20 million to 10 million years ago. There is also *Ramapithecus*, first found in India, of about 10 million years ago, showing more advanced development than *Dryopithecus*, with a general reduction in tooth size, especially of the canines. A few anthropologists would call *Ramapithecus* a hominid; most would still include him with the pongids, but all would see him as a possible progenitor of the hominids.[11] We shall not dwell upon these and several other kinds of prehominids that have been found and studied, because it is even harder to make surmises about them than it is to guess the way of life of the australopithecines. Fossil remains show something of the gradual pattern of physical development of man's primate relatives, but for behavioral comparisons anthropology must turn to the studies of living primates, especially the apes and Old World monkeys.

As was mentioned in the previous chapter, certain of the great apes are our closest living relatives. The relationship between man and the other primates is shown in the figure below. Pongids include the present-day great apes

[11] C. Loring Brace, Harry Nelson, and Noel Korn, *Atlas of Fossil Man*, Holt, Rinehart and Winston, Inc., New York, 1971, pp. 11–18.

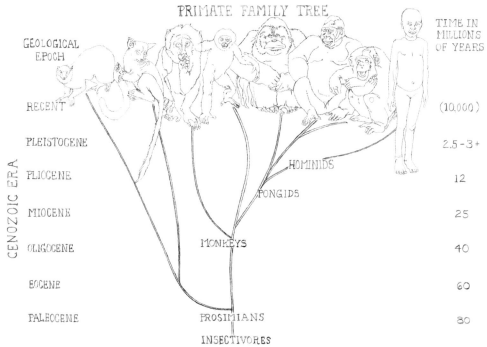

PRIMATE FAMILY TREE

GEOLOGICAL
EPOCH

TIME IN
MILLIONS
OF YEARS

RECENT (10,000)

PLEISTOCENE 2.5 - 3 +

PLIOCENE HOMINIDS 12

PONGIDS

MIOCENE 25

OLIGOCENE MONKEYS 40

EOCENE 60

PALEOCENE PROSIMIANS 80

INSECTIVORES

CENOZOIC ERA

A FAMILY TREE DIAGRAM SHOWS THE APPROXIMATE RELATIONSHIP BETWEEN THE OTHER PRIMATES AND MAN.

and also the earlier, extinct types of apes, such as the dryopithecines. The figure also shows that the stem of primate development probably stretches back 80 million years or more to types of insectivores similar to the modern long-snouted tree shrew. Next appear the ancestors of the present-day lemurs and lorises—small, furry, big-eyed arboreal animals with five-toed hands and feet. The New World monkeys branched off from the main stem of development back in Eocene times, possibly before the mid-Atlantic rift formed and the continents of Africa and South America drifted apart. Some of the New World monkeys have the distinction of being the only primates able to cling to and swing from branches by means of prehensile tails, but they drop out of the main line of human evolution.

The Old World monkeys include the baboons, a type that has partly abandoned tree life and lives much of the time on the ground. Baboons have been studied extensively in the wild, and so have macaques, monkeys that are distributed all the way from North Africa through southern and eastern Asia. The apes include gibbons, orangutans, gorillas, and chimpanzees. Gibbons are purely aboreal, with very long, strong arms for brachiating (swinging from branches). The orangutans, although very much larger and classified differently, are also particularly well built for brachiating. The other two types of great apes have been studied more in the wild than have orangutans, because the latter are very elusive, few in number, and found only on Borneo and Sumatra. They seem to live in small primary-family groups, are of gentle, non-aggressive disposition, and are purely vegetarian.[12] It is to the studies of the other great apes and baboons and macaques that we must look for clues to human behavioral traits.

THE JAPANESE MACAQUE   Japanese monkeys have been studied extensively, both in Japan and in the United States. They display certain social traits that point in the direction of culture: specifically, new learning is transmitted and becomes habit among certain groups.[13] When young monkeys were given candy, they soon took a liking to it, and the candy was adopted as a part of the eating pattern of their band, although not of other bands. The eating habit spread to the mothers but only very belatedly to the fathers, who were much slower to take up a new custom.

The same behavior was noted in teaching macaques to swim. A few of the infants were enticed into the water and soon learned it was fun to play and swim. Later the mothers also took to swimming for fun, but not the adult males. The conservative nature of adult males may once have had an adaptive value. At earlier times, the protector of the band probably needed to be of a disposition to look upon new ideas with caution. In the case of the macaques, as young males matured they continued the new cultural habits, to which we could almost apply the human word "subculture." New ideas, such as washing sand from potatoes, occurred to young members only.

BABOONS   Baboons have been studied extensively in their native habitat in Africa. In some respects the baboons are of particular interest for our guesses about early hominids, although they are genetically further from us than the chimpanzees and gorillas. They are ground-dwelling animals, as we imagine our early ancestors to have been, and therefore meet many of the problems of survival that early australopithecines may have met. Baboons travel in bands of forty to eighty individuals, and when they move, the adult males form a protective guard for the group, with the most powerful males staying near the mothers and infants. They are highly social, living always close to one another.

[12]Thomas W. McKern and Sharon McKern, *Human Origins*, Prentice-Hall, Inc., Englewood Cliffs, N.J., 1969, p. 136.
[13]"Monkeys, Apes, and Men," CBS television production, summer 1971.

Sherwood Washburn and Irven DeVore describe the troop as composed of emotionally involved, cohesive members united by a wide range of common interests, not just the mating instinct.[14]

Baboons eat mainly a vegetable diet but also eat some meat and are fond of birds' eggs. They have a symbiotic relationship, each depending on the other, with impallas and zebras that graze in the same area and share the same water holes. The baboons utter a very loud, human-sounding shout to warn of the approach of cheetahs or lions. The impallas, for their warning mechanism, have a keen sense of smell, which baboons lack.

Baboons spend much of their time grooming one another, a job performed mainly by the adult females. Starting with infancy, the baboon becomes accustomed to having another pick through his fur, removing dirt and parasites. The animal being groomed gives every indication of great pleasure in the act; the grooming is often mutual. Washburn and DeVore suggest that the act of grooming is a major part of the development of affective and social feelings. As with many animals, there is hierarchy of positions, with a certain amount of quarreling until a rank of dominance is achieved. The dominant males usually operate in groups, but occasionally a single male dominates, protecting against intruders from other bands and also preventing fighting within the group. As do their human relatives, baboons find social cohesiveness a necessity for survival.

CHIMPANZEES   The most thorough student of chimpanzees in the wild is Jane Goodall (now the Baroness Jane van Lawick), who studied in Tanzania in 1963 and returned again for further observations from 1965 till the present.[15] In social organization, chimpanzee behavior is more rudimentary than that of baboons, in spite of their higher intelligence. The reason appears to be that since they spend nearly all their time in trees, they are less in need of the protection that organization gives. In two important respects, chimpanzees resemble human beings more closely than do baboons: they actually make and use crude types of tools, and the mothers seem to recognize kinship over a long period of years. One reason for Goodall's return to Africa in 1965 was to observe a female chimpanzee with which she had made friends previously and which she was told was about to have a baby. By the time she arrived, the baby

[14]Sherwood L. Washburn and Irven DeVore, "The Social Life of Baboons," *Scientific American*, vol. 614, pp. 62–71, June 1961.
[15]Jane Goodall, "Chimpanzees of the Gombe Stream Reserve," in Irven DeVore (ed.), *Primate Behavior*, Holt, Rinehart and Winston, Inc., New York, 1965, pp. 425–473. See also Jane (Goodall) van Lawick, *National Geographic*, vol. 128, pp. 802–831, December 1965.

was already born and was held protectively and jealously by the mother. No other chimpanzee was permitted to hold the baby except one eight-year-old girl, which Goodall had previously believed to be the daughter of the older chimpanzee. The preferential treatment of the girl chimpanzee convinced Goodall that the two were, indeed, mother and daughter and still recognized the relationship.

Families are merely mother-child groupings. Males are promiscuous. At night chimpanzees build individual nests in the trees, breaking branches and using leaves to make the bed springy and comfortable. Their eating habits are largely vegetarian, but they also eat insects and small animals. Occasionally they go on a hunting expedition, kill a small monkey, and eat him at a common feast reminiscent of human parties. Two examples of their "tool" invention are the crumbling of leaves to make a sponge to soak up water from water holes for a drink and making a "lollipop." The lollipop consists of a twig broken to the right length and thrust down a termite hole to collect termites. The termites are licked off as one might lick a lollipop, and then the twig is inserted again into the termite nest. These are crude tools, of course, but they do show inventiveness. There is also a protocultural aspect to such inventions. One chimpanzee learns from imitation of another. Probably the greatest handicap for chimpanzees is the lack of speech. Although they make twenty-three or more distinct sounds, conveying warnings and emotions, they are incapable of true speech. However, one recent researcher has found that a chimpanzee can be taught to manipulate visual symbols and even fit them together into rudimentary sentences; one chimpanzee has mastered 130 such "words."[16]

In an age when much attention is focused on the quarrelsome nature of man, it is interesting to ask whether he shares this disposition with his primate kinsmen. Goodall's chimpanzees were generally unaggressive and cooperative, but they showed jealousy and quarrelsomeness when they were given too many bananas. Sudden wealth seemed to have the effect of legendary pirate's gold.

There is one other disturbing note about the chimpanzee disposition. In West Africa some chimpanzees live at the edge of the savanna, with less tree protection than the bands in Tanzania. They use sticks to threaten and to hit their enemies more than do the Tanzanians. In an experiment, a simulated panther was placed in their territory. They attacked it with sticks, always

[16]Ann J. Premack and David Premack, "Teaching Language to an Ape," *Scientific American*, vol. 227, pp. 92–99, October 1972.

gingerly and retreating to trees after striking a blow. Eventually they came close enough to determine it was "dead." They continued to club it, managed to sever its head, and took it away in a manner reminding one of the head trophies of certain recent primitive human tribes.

A certain amount of research work in art has indicated chimpanzees can become thoroughly absorbed in finger painting and even observe margins in doing the painting. One anthropologist reports having observed a chimpanzee sitting quietly for 15 minutes or more watching the sunset, absorbed in the changing light until the gathering of darkness.[17] Perhaps the anthropologist's conclusions were overdrawn, but quite possibly not. The gulf between men and chimpanzees is great, but it seems to be a matter of degree, not of kind.

GORILLAS   Gorillas are much heavier than chimpanzees and spend much of their time on the ground, although they nest in trees at night. Their diet is purely vegetarian and they eat enormous amounts of food. In social organization, gorillas range between baboons and chimpanzees, living in groups of from two to thirty individuals and showing the frequently encountered tendency toward dominance by the strongest males. As with female chimpanzees, there seems to be a monthly estrous cycle, similar to that of human females, and babies are carried almost the same length of time, 34 weeks. Babies are nursed for 2 or 3 years. There is less grooming behavior among adult males than in the case of baboons, but females and the young engage in considerable grooming behavior. Generally speaking, despite their appearance, gorillas live quiet lives, playing amicably together, and usually are not aggressive in their behavior toward neighboring bands.[18]

COMMON TRAITS   A short glimpse at a few of the most carefully studied primates shows a few clues to human development and also a considerable amount of confusion. If it could be demonstrated that there is a clear and unequivocal progression of a whole series of traits through monkeys to the apes and finally to man, the primate studies would be extremely illuminating. Obviously, such a direction is only approximated, and, as with any attempt to find the human direction, there seem to be divergences and even what look like regressions in the record. "Regression" is almost certainly a poor term for description of

[17]Sarel Eimerl and Irven DeVore, *The Primates*, Time-Life Books, New York, 1965, p. 70.
[18]McKern and McKern, op. cit., pp. 136–138.

primate direction, however; what looks like regression (as in the case of a simpler social organization for chimpanzees than for baboons) is merely an adaptation to different problems of life. Not all the conclusions that can be drawn from primate studies are of a nature that applies to primates alone. A dominance hierarchy is common in much of the animal world, as are affection and systems of warning. There are a few traits, though, that seem to progress in general terms through the primate order, and they make man the most successful representative of the order.

1   *Brain.* The primate brain is large in proportion to the total size of the animal, the difference is especially noticeable in man. Increasingly, mentality begins to supplement instinct as we move up the primate order to the gorillas and chimpanzees. Finally, with man, the whole concept of instinct becomes debatable, and survival depends overwhelmingly on learning and intelligence.

2   *Ontogenetic growth* (the natural history of the individual, beginning with the fertilized egg). The developmental rate of the individual lengthens in the higher species of the primates. Chimpanzees reach puberty at about the age of eight, human beings, at about twelve to fourteen. Childhood is long in both cases and is a time for play, curiosity, and learning. A Dutch anthropologist once suggested that man is simply an ape who took too long at growing up. The statement is not intended as fact but as an illustration of the great importance of the developmental years of childhood.

The period of pregnancy is long in the case of the great apes and man. Especially with man, the infant requires long periods of care, but the infant's care among apes is also much longer than in the case of other animals, as much as 3 or 4 years with chimpanzees.

The dependency of mothers and the young is provided for by social organization in the case of the baboons. For the gorillas and chimpanzees, tight defensive organization has not arisen, probably because gorillas have few natural enemies and chimpanzees can retreat into the trees.

3   *Sexual nature.* As Washburn points out from his study of baboons, it is easy to go too far in attributing the roots of social organization to continuous sexual interest, even though such interest is present on the part of baboons, chimpanzees, gorillas, and human beings. No doubt the need for many kinds of cooperation has contributed to the social nature of man as well as apes and baboons. The other species cannot tell us how important sexual nature is to the maintenance of relationships, but the majority of human beings would give it a strong vote of confidence.

4   *Hand and eye.* Man and ape, and also the monkeys, have a type of visual acuity that exceeds that of other animals, and they also have close coordination of hand and eye. Dogs, in contrast, depend very little on their eyes but strongly on the sense of smell. The higher primates have only a slightly useful sense of smell but have such good senses of sight and touch as to diminish its importance. The primate hand differs slightly from species to species but is always five-digited and dexterous.

5   *Posture.* The hand as a tool and as a maker of other tools is closely connected with upright posture, the trait of mankind alone. However, all the primates presented in the above examples can use their hands to some degree for throwing objects. Gorillas scramble across the ground almost upright but use their long forearms for support. Gorillas, chimpanzees, and even baboons can stand on their hind legs temporarily to free their hands for uses other than walking or running. For man, upright posture and the freeing of the hands preceded a spectacular growth of the brain as he progressed from the australopithecine level to the level of *Homo sapiens.*

The traits of the primates are not held in equal degree by all. It might be said that one of the outstanding traits of the primate order is a high degree of variability, with different types of social organization, different means of using their generally highly developed forelimbs and hands, different means of locomotion, and differences in dietary habits. With the lower primates, most of the adaptation is genetic, physical, and instinctive. For man, the adaptive ability is only minimally a matter of physical change but primarily a matter of culture and the making of tools.

THE TOOL MAKER   It was Washburn who first brought a new approach to the question of how evolution progressed in the human species,[19] and the idea has been further elaborated by other physical anthropologists, including Howell. Washburn's approach concerns the simultaneous development of upright posture, tool use, and greater mentality and the ways in which the three changes interacted and reinforced one another as evolutionary forces. Earlier surmises about man assumed that he had somehow progressed to a physical state that would be recognizably human and then, equipped with superior mentality, hit upon the idea of using sticks and stones for weapons. We have seen, however, that the rudiments of tool making are present in the chim-

[19]Sherwood L. Washburn, "Tools and Human Evolution," *Scientific American*, vol. 203, pp. 62–75, September 1960.

panzees and must assume that they were present among the progenitors of man, even those we would not class as belonging to the genus *Homo*—the australopithecines and, conceivably, types that predated them.

What probably happened is that in the remote past, in late Miocene times, there was a widespread distribution of apelike creatures such as *Ramapithecus*. These early apes, in their search for food, often came down from the trees at least temporarily. They may have walked on all fours, but with their weight placed mainly on the hind legs, enabling them to rise erect when necessary to look around for enemies—the type of knuckle-walking done by chimpanzees. Probably at the edges of the great forests there were more tempting food items on the ground than there were in interior forests. Possibly animals living near the forest edge had more survival potential if they were able to roam the ground for considerable periods. However, the ground was not safe. The time of the early australopithecines was a time of gigantism in some types of animals, with sheep 7 feet tall and pigs as large as a rhinoceros. Judging by findings in the close vicinity of Leakey's *Zinjanthropus* specimen, the australopithecines ate many plants and roots and also hunted small animals such as lizards and snakes or the infants of such larger species as antelopes. They were, like modern man, omnivorous, eating anything with food value.

EARLY HOMINIDS   It is obvious that in their environment the early ape-men would have been comfortable only near the trees and must have retreated into the trees a good part of the time. In the trees perhaps they used stone tools for cracking nuts or for helping to break the branches from which they made their nests. On the ground they used rocks for braining small animals and maybe even for cutting them up. A hand equipped with a heavy rock is a far better weapon than a bare fist, and if a sharp-pointed rock is found or fashioned, so much the better. It is easy to imagine that the use of tools began to have a survival value in some environments and that those ape-men best able to make and use tools were the ones most likely to survive and leave offspring. Hence, as Washburn contends, tools were both a product of evolution and a means to further evolutionary development.

The tool-making animal had an advantage in evolution with respect to selection and may have had advantages in other respects as well. In many species, the more capable males are able to mate with a large number of females and leave more descendants than the less capable. In some species, less dominant males are completely eliminated from the breeding stock. The effective use of stone tools could well have helped to establish dominance within the band. Washburn also suggests that other types of social selection

Crude stone tools. Some of the earliest tools are collections of chipped stones showing little workmanship but already giving man an advantage in the competitive struggle for survival.

might have gone on. The man-apes probably found great advantage in working together for protection, and the selective advantage went increasingly to the more cooperative males.

For some of our conclusions about tools we do not have to rely entirely on guesswork. In Olduvai Gorge, and at several sites in South Africa, there are pebble tools in association with the ancient, Lower Pleistocene hominids. Some of the tools are not worked at all, and others are worked only very crudely, but they are gathered in places where they do not occur naturally, such as caves and other places that gave shelter to the australopithecines. In some of the caves are antelope bones that are a subject of debate. Dart thinks they were used as weapons; C. R. Brain is convinced they and hominid skulls were both dropped into caves by leopards. Others surmise that the early hominids were scavengers, dragging to their caves portions of antelopes they had stolen from hyenas or other animals.[20]

[20]F. Clark Howell, *Early Man*, Time-Life Books, New York, 1965, pp. 63-69.

Leakey is convinced that some of the very early Pleistocene types, especially *Homo habilis*, used fire and probably frightened animals by use of it. A long gap separates the time of australopithecines from that of the next stage in human evolution, the *Homo erectus* types, and we can only imagine the intermediate stages of evolution. Tools remain crude and few in type, but gradually chipped hand axes along with scrapers begin to dominate, replacing the dawn Stone Age pebble tools.

Homo erectus became a great hunter, able to bring down giant mastodons, tigers, and woolly rhinoceroses, probably driving them over cliffs by the use of fire. As we have seen, the findings at Choukoutien give a hint that a spiritual life may also have been developing. Certainly the brain was growing by this time. Whereas the australopithecines had had cranial capacities of only about 600 cc, some of the *Homo erectus* types had capacities of around 1000 to 1200 cc. The findings in the Ambrona Valley of Spain, mentioned in Chapter Two, were probably the remains of a hunt, or a series of hunts, by *Homo erectus* types.

NEANDERTHAL MAN . Neanderthal man occupies the time span of approximately 100,000 years ago till about 35,000 years ago. It was the finding of Neanderthal skulls that began to give the Darwinists some of the evidence they were looking for, but the skulls also left serious problems. One of the difficulties was that much more human-looking skulls were found that seemed to belong to a date only slightly more recent than that of the Neanderthalers. Since many people of about the time of Darwin were deliberately looking for a kind of "missing link," they might have had a tendency to reconstruct the Neanderthalers as much more crude looking than they actually were. True, they had large faces, virtually no chin, very large teeth, poor posture by our standards, heavy brow ridges, and sloping foreheads. Nevertheless, as Francois Bordes, one of the world's greatest authorities on prehistoric tools, points out, the Neanderthalers were culture-bearing beings to a much greater extent than any previous types, and deserve their place in the category of *Homo sapiens*.[21] The Mousterian culture of Neanderthal man included not only the ability to hunt the great animals of the last Ice Age—reindeer, wild oxen, bison, mammoths, woolly rhinoceroses, cave bears, and many others—but hints of a further development of tools. There were more blades and scrapers and elongated points and the very beginnings of the use of bone tools. The dead were ceremonially buried, which indicates afterlife beliefs. Paints were used, especially red ochre. There also seems to have been a bear cult, as evidenced by bear skulls gathered

[21]Francois Bordes, "Mousterian Cultures in France," *Science*, vol. 134, pp. 803–810, September 22, 1961. Bordes's view is strongly championed by Brace in *The Stages of Human Evolution*, pp. 83–96.

into piles in caves. Neanderthal man, says Bordes, was far from an apelike being, but was a pioneer of human culture, and the gulf between him and the present types of man has been considerably exaggerated. His rugged frame and very considerable weight might have helped him to survive in Europe during the last Ice Age. Whatever the case, for the first time man did not have to retreat very far before the glaciers. Some anthropologists consider Neanderthal man a type that disappeared at the end of the Würm, to be replaced by more modern types of man that had evolved elsewhere, but such types are yet to be found in any considerable numbers. Bordes ends his comment with the statement that the ancestor of present-day man had to be Neanderthal man; there is simply no other choice. He uses the old quip about Shakespeare to illustrate the relation of Neanderthal to modern man. "If it was not William Shakespeare who wrote *Hamlet*, it was another man who lived at the same time and whose name was also William Shakespeare."[22]

To be fair to both sides of the argument, it must be admitted that certain cave findings in Palestine at Mt. Carmel indicate a type a little more advanced looking than Neanderthal man. He could have been the "modern type evolving elsewhere." Or he could have been, as Bordes would contend, simply a variation on Neanderthal man as he himself gradually changed into the less rugged-looking type of man found today. Whatever the problems of placement, Neanderthal man has won at least part of the argument in recent times. He is now called officially *Homo sapiens neanderthalensis*, implying that he is of the human genus and of the human species. The only distinction between him and modern man made in taxonomy is to call modern man *Homo sapiens sapiens* in contrast. *Sapiens* means "knowing" or "thinking." We now flatter ourselves by repeating the word in our own self-description.

The comments on evolution have pertained almost entirely to tools and to some evidence of the emergence of magico-religious beliefs. Some reference has also been made to the growth of the brain. The brain of Neanderthal man was as large as that of modern man, but it might have had some disadvantages in a weaker development of the frontal lobe. Washburn presents a diagram of the brain showing the areas associated with various functions. It is particularly the areas connected with speech, both vocalization and symbolization, that have probably progressed most since the time of Neanderthal. Nevertheless, Neanderthal man was a culture builder and possibly held spiritual beliefs.

Neanderthal man was extremely variable in type. Bordes has dug through the accumulated debris at Combe Grenal in the Dordogne Valley of southwestern France. There he has found sixty-five levels of occupation, ranging

[22]Bordes, ibid.

from around 110,000 years ago down to about 35,000 or 40,000 years ago. There is great fluctuation in tool techniques. In one case Bordes has found a posthole, indicating the building of shelters. The same type of evidence has been found at Lazaré Cave at Nice on the French Riviera. Whatever else can be said of Neanderthalers, they were able to survive through the end of the last interglacial period and through the first advance of the Würm, in the glacial period turning increasingly to cave dwelling and probably to the use of animal-skin clothing. Types similar to Neanderthal are widespread in eastern Europe and Africa, and one or two specimens have been found in eastern Asia. One of the mysteries is that some of the later Neanderthalers of Europe seemed "bulkier and more beetle-browed than their predecessors."[23] No doubt questions about Neanderthal man will remain for many years to come.

THE NEW TYPE   Several new types of man appear in Europe after about 35,000 years ago, the most frequently found variety being Cro-Magnon. Like his Neanderthal predecessors, Cro-Magnon man hunted the abundant large animals of the final stage of the last glacial period and did not retreat from the cold but adapted to it by clothing. Unlike Neanderthal man, he is generally pictured as tall and handsome, and modern men like to think of themselves as his descendants. We have no way of knowing whether he was dark or light and whether he had Mongoloid eye form. There is considerable evidence that he, like his predecessors, practiced ritual cannibalism, as many later people have done. He gave great care to the burial of the dead, undoubtedly had a rich ceremonial life, seems to have believed in the magico-religious properties of a variety of art forms, and eventually became an artist of great note.

During the time from 35,000 years ago up to about 10,000 years ago, the pace of cultural advance quickens. The long hundreds of thousands of years of hand axes and scrapers is replaced by a profusion of stone and bone tools—awls, needles, beautifully polished spear points of many cultural traditions, hooks, hafted axes, atlatls, long-bladed knives, harpoons, and a wide variety of objects of art. The art, in particular, seems to have been born almost without parents, developing over a 25,000- or 30,000-year span—slowly by our system of timing but incredibly rapidly compared with the slow advance of earlier times.

DISCOVERY OF THE ARTISTS   Some fox hunters on the estate of the Spanish nobleman Don Marcelino de Sautuola lost one of their dogs, as though the

[23]Howell, op. cit., p. 126.

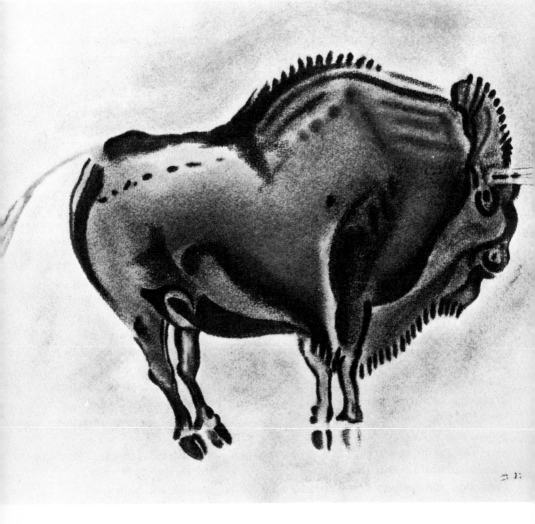

The paintings at Altamira Cave in Spain
were at first believed to be a
fraud—surely no Stone Age people
could produce art work "good enough
for the Louvre!"

earth had opened up and swallowed him. Soon they heard him whispering from down below and found that the earth actually *had* swallowed him. They found the opening to a cave, gouged it out enough to make their way down to rescue the dog, and reported the matter to De Sautuola.

De Sautuola looked into the cave superficially but found nothing of interest and had it closed up for fear children might fall in. Nine or ten years later, at the Paris Exhibition of 1878, he became interested in some of the artifacts being found in southern France and decided to look in his cave for possible stone knives or arrowheads. He succeeded in finding a stone ax and an arrowhead or two and went back to explore further. His little daughter went along and was able to crawl into passages too narrow for de Sautuola. There, in an inner recess, she saw by the dim candlelight a large number of red bulls painted on the walls. She called to her father, who finally managed to get in and confirm her finding of a veritable Stone Age Louvre.

De Sautuola became feverishly excited and wrote to Madrid to send a scholar to look at the findings in the cave. Eventually a professor came to look over the cave painting. He saw the red bulls and cows and calves, bison and wild boars, and large numbers of horses, beautifully painted, natural, and lifelike. Professor Vilanova was convinced that he had found not only a rare collection of Stone Age paintings but masterpieces. After establishing the association of the paintings with the tools found on the floor of the cave, he was ready to risk his reputation on pronouncing them genuine, and he had them copied for the world's authorities to see. A conference was held in Lisbon, attended by the best authorities from France and other parts of Europe, and both De Sautuola and Vilanova were pronounced frauds. No Stone Age people could have turned out such work, which the famous prehistorian Cartailhac described as nearly as good as any work of the French impressionists. De Sautuola had copies of the paintings published but could awaken no further interest for years, and he died 23 years later an embittered man. His daughter Maria waited for confirmation of the authenticity of the cave paintings.

In 1903 the confirmation came, interestingly, from one of the sharpest critics, Cartailhac. Cartailhac had been made aware of similar cave paintings in France by a young priest named Henri Breuil, who was to take up the cause of cave art and its Paleolithic origin, to convice skeptics, and to crawl through caverns and copy Stone Age paintings until his death in 1961 at the age of eighty-four.[24]

More caves were found in Spain in the next few years, along with several in France. It was in 1940 that the most famous of the Stone Age caves was

[24]Wendt, op. cit., pp. 327–333.

discovered by four French boys, and by that time the "age of skepticism" was past. Men had found ancestors whom they no longer regarded as brutes but were inclined to look upon almost in awe. The cave art, and much other art as well, has now been studied, cataloged, and arranged into periods. The paintings covered a time span from about 35,000 years ago till around 10,000 years ago. The styles of art change from crude drawings of the earliest period (Aurignacian) to the finished product of the most productive period, known as Magdalenian. The most beautiful of the paintings are supreme works of naturalistic art, brightly colored with pigments that soaked into the limestone and lasted undimmed through the thousands of years. A magnificent bison of the Altamira cave and one or two of the figures of Lascaux display shading effects that give a slight feeling of perspective—a difficult problem for artists of all ages. The Upper Paleolithic age also produced a large number of stone and ivory carvings, the first of which are called "Venuses"—the Venus of Willendorf (Austria), the Venus of Bassempouy (France), and the Venus of Vestonice (Czechoslavakia). They seem to be fertility symbols, the first in particular being gross and undoubtedly intended to emphasize pregnancy. Sometimes they are regarded as goddesses of fertility, and the interpretation seems highly plausible. Both human and animal fertility were of great importance for the continuation of humankind and the animals on which it lived. A large number of the female animals in the cave at Lascaux are pregnant.

It is a good guess, too, that much of the painting was associated with hunting magic. In the cave at Les Trois Frères is a part-animal, part-man figure, clad in skins, with the antlers of a stag and the beard of a man. The figure is most commonly supposed to be a shaman connected with ceremonial magic. Elsewhere are animals with spears through them, which might denote a belief in imitative magic—the idea that imitating an event will help it to come about.

The great flowering of naturalistic art came at the end of the Old Stone Age, or Paleolithic. The following period is generally referred to as the Mesolithic (Middle Stone Age), and its major characteristic is a change of habits from primary dependence on the animals that flourished during the last Ice Age to a more intensive use of grain. Sometimes Mesolithic tribes settled along seacoasts and depended to a great extent upon fishing. Fishhooks, nets, and great mounds of shells and bones attest to their success. Grain-gathering people made sickles with saw teeth by insetting tiny bits of sharpened stone into curved-wood or ivory blades. These tools, called microblades, were used for cutting grain. After years of dependence upon the harvesting of wild grains, the idea of planting evolved, probably first in the highlands of Turkey or Iran and later and more productively in the river valleys below. When agriculture developed, surpluses were possible to support craftsmen and soldiers, astrologers and priests, kings and aristocracies. Wheeled transport developed, along with far-flung trade routes and an Age of Metals. The pace of such development was widely different in different parts of the world, depending partly on natural geographical conditions and on the possiblities of contact with other societies; but the general course of man was in the direction of more efficient technology, more complex organization, and a wider range of cultural possiblities.

No longer were the hominids dim of mind, only a step or two above the animal world. So great had become the gap between the new species and its forebears that until the time of recent primate studies it was assumed that the difference in mentality was a matter of kind rather than merely of degree—an issue still in some dispute. The long process of evolutionary development had now led to the creative urge of the artist and to speculations into the mysteries of life and death and reproduction, of natural forces to be controlled by dexterity and wit, and of unknown forces to be approached only with awe, exorcised by the shaman, manipulated by ritual and spell, but forever beyond the range of understanding.

SUMMARY   Before the nineteenth century, the development of cultures was believed to have taken place in only a few thousand years. Fossil remains were interpreted in mythological terms or were ignored, but the discovery of their true meaning started man on a search for the ancestry of all species, especially his own. The search began in Europe and Asia and more recently in Africa, where the largest amount of the most ancient evidence is found.

The search for the fossil evidence of man as a physical being led to increasing speculation as to his cultural development throughout the Pleistocene and even before. Since there is little evidence of the way of life of a million or more years ago, we look to our primate relatives for suggestive evidence. Baboons, macaques, gorillas, and chimpanzees develop different social systems in response to different needs but show such rudiments of culture as baboon protective organization, macaque development of new cultural habits, chimpanzee tool making, some kinds of kinship recognition, and possibly an incipient capacity for symbolic communication.

The australopithecines also made crude tools, and the *Homo erectus* types used fire and effective cooperation on the hunt and may have had spirit beliefs. Neanderthal types advanced the art of tool making, probably built shelters, used animal-skin clothes, and practiced ceremonial burial of the dead. Their successors, the Cro-Magnons and other more modern types, built further upon the cultural foundations laid by the Neanderthal men. The most beautiful of Stone Age art appeared, with evidence of a belief in imitative magic. Shamanism appeared and probably social organization at least at the band level. A profusion of hunting tools were developed that ensured more food supply until the Ice Age animals declined in numbers and new cultures had to be worked out—cultures that would eventually lead to agriculture and Neolithic towns and then to an Age of Metals and the great historic cities of Egypt and Mesopotamia. The cultural capacity was making man adaptable to all climates and climatic changes and ultimately would make him the dominant species of the earth.

The human species and its hominid predecessors have spread widely over the earth. It is tempting to say that once man had achieved his present physical form and intelligence, he set forth in a high spirit of adventure to explore and conquer his world, but there are two errors in the assertion. In the first place, the earlier hominids had already spread over many parts of the world long before true human types evolved. Such types as *Ramapithecus* were by no means confined to India but have been found also in Europe and Africa. The australopithecines could quite logically be renamed, because they were not merely "southern ape-men" but were found in many parts of Africa, and what may be their cultural remains have been found recently in Asia and Europe. *Homo erectus* types have also been found in the three continents of Europe, Asia, and Africa, and the Neanderthalers were widespread in North Africa, western Asia, and Europe.

The second flaw in the assertion about the adventurous spirit of early man is that we have no way of knowing whether there was any such spirit. We do know that modern hunting people

Chapter Four
To the Ends
of the Earth:
Cultural and
Physical Variation

are inclined to roam over a considerable territory, but, nevertheless, a limited and well-known one. Hunting is easier and the world is safer in a known terrain. Why, then, did the early hominids and the later human beings spread so widely over the world? What caused the human species to experiment with a variety of cultural adaptations to different climes? Did human types also make physical adaptations, as many species of mammals have? What special traits made it possible for mankind to become the most widespread of living species? Was racial variation connected with long physical adjustment to differing climates, diets, terrain, and ways of life? If race does not explain physical adaptation, then what does?

HUMAN DISTRIBUTION   In modern terms we would say that people tend to move to places of economic opportunity. Our prehistoric ancestors were undoubtedly the same in their motivations, except that economic opportunity was almost exclusively a matter of food supply. There were times, too, when early tribes were driven out of a territory by natural disaster, such as the advance of a new Ice Age. It was only during the Würm that people were able to continue to occupy Europe; previously they had retreated in the face of the cold. One reason for the difference is that Neanderthal types seem to have been specially equipped for the cold, with short, bulky bodies and short limbs that limit the area of heat loss. A more important reason is that before the end of the Würm, men were learning cultural means of surviving the cold—the making of animal-skin robes, methods of making and using fire, the use of cave shelters, and probably the building of semisubterranean houses. There was an abundance of Arctic-type game in Europe in those days, and man was able to live as a hunter as long as he was equipped to withstand the cold. His settlement of Europe had become permanent.

In many parts of the world permanent settlement had come about much earlier. Human habitation is very ancient in India and in the lands between India and the Pacific Coast of Asia, and it is also very ancient in North Africa and in China. The lands of late settlement were the Americas and Australia and much later yet the islands of the Pacific. There are also scattered areas of mountain, desert, and tundra and certain regions of dense rain forest whose habitation is recent compared with much of the world. The story of the peopling of the earth is a story of trial and error and of triumph and tragedy before man invented the incredible variety of cultures that planted him securely in all continents except Antartica.

There are many dates of early American artifacts
that are fairly certain, and there are many that
are in considerable doubt. In the United States,
widely distributed projectile points (called "Clovis
points") are found, dating from 15,000 to 11,000 years ago. Recently in South
America, at Cerro Chivateros on the southern coast of Peru, artifacts have been
found dating back to about 14,000 years ago.[1] Such an ancient date in South
America is particularly significant because a long period must have elapsed
between the time of the first crossing of the Bering Strait region, where a land
bridge existed during the last glacial advance, and the time of arrival in South
America. There are also findings on the coast of Venezuela at El Jobo dated at
about 16,500 years ago.[2] More ancient evidence becomes increasingly tentative.
In northwestern Texas charcoal samples from what are thought to be hearths
have been carbon-dated at 38,000 years ago.[3]

There are numerous other sites that could possibly date back to 30,000
years ago or more. They are referred to as pre-projectile-point sites, since the
artifacts consist only of crudely worked stone, not spear points. An element of
doubt exists about some of the chipped stones, because it is not always easy to
tell whether chipping has been done by man or has occurred naturally. Another
problem with the pre-projectile-point sites is the great difficulty of dating.
Nevertheless, there are enough sites to give plausibility to the very early arrival
of man in the Americas, and the existence of a land bridge over the Bering
Strait area as far back as 40,000 years ago would make it possible.[4]

The most exciting research on early man in the Americas has been under
way since 1964, near Barstow, California, in a desert area where a large lake
(Lake Manix) existed during glacial advances.[5] Much of the work has been
supervised by Ruth DeEtte Simpson, although until his death in 1972 it was
sponsored by Dr. Leakey, a man with strong faith in the extreme antiquity of
human life in America. For several years Simpson had been finding large,
crude hand axes and chopperlike implements with a tentative date of about
19,500 years ago in the area of former Lake Manix. Such findings led to the

[1]Edward P. Lanning and Thomas C. Patterson, "Early Man in South America," *Scientific American*,
vol. 217, pp. 44–50, November 1967.
[2]Louis A. Brennan, *American Dawn*, The Macmillan Company, New York, 1970, pp. 141–143.
[3]Peter Farb, *Man's Rise to Civilization as Shown by the Indians of North America from Primeval Times to
the Coming of the Industrial State*, Avon Book Division, The Hearst Corporation, New York,
1968, p. 241.
[4]Betty J. Meggers, *Prehistoric America*, Aldine-Atherton, Inc., Chicago, 1972, pp. 7–15.
[5]Louis S. B. Leakey, Ruth DeEtte Simpson, and Thomas Clements, "Archaeological Excavations
in the Calico Mountains, California: A Preliminary Report," *Science*, vol. 160, pp. 1022–1023,
May 1, 1968.

SITES INDICATING POSSIBILITY OF TWO SEPARATE WAVES OF ANCIENT IMMIGRATION TO AMERICA

LAND BRIDGE FROM 50,000 to 40,000 YEARS AGO AND 28,000 to 10,000 YEARS AGO

△ PRE PROJECTILE POINT SITES, 30,000-20,000 YEARS AGO

⊕ PALEO-INDIAN SITES, EARLY PROJECTILE POINTS APPROXIMATELY 15,000-10,000 YEARS AGO

recent diggings into the alluvial material deposited by streams flowing into the ancient lake. Chopper tools have been found at levels throughout the alluvium, whose age is estimated by geologists at about 50,000 to 80,000 years. Dating is extremely difficult, and there is still debate as to whether the chipped stones actually show human workmanship. The argument in favor of human occupation is that the stones are not only chipped in a manner suggesting human workmanship but are of better quality chalcedony than the unworked stone in the area, suggesting human selection. Furthermore, another test hole at some distance away from the main site produced no stones the researchers believed to show human workmanship, again suggesting that they had found a place frequented by prehistoric men. Leakey and Simpson were convinced of the validity of the finds, and the previously mentioned French expert on stone tools, Bordes, the Hungarian expert Lasslo Vertes, and the American J. Desmond Clark have all supported the claim of human chipping of the stones.[6]

A different type of evidence for the considerable antiquity of the American Indians in the New World is based on physical type. The late-Mongoloid type, with short limbs, flat face, Mongoloid eye form, and broad and fat-padded cheeks is most prominent in northeastern Asia. This description also applies fairly well to the Eskimo type, but it does not describe the earliest American skeletal remains. The late-Mongoloid type seems to have developed since the earliest American Indians crossed from Siberia.[7]

Whatever the argument over the antiquity of man in America, there is no doubt in the minds of leading anthropologists that he came from eastern Asia, across a land bridge, and he came in pursuit of the great animals of Pleistocene times (the time of the Ice Ages)—mammoths, long-horned bison, giant sloths, camels, and horses. Turning from the uncertain earlier dates to the well-accepted dates of around 15,000 to 12,000 years ago, one can describe the way of life of the early Americans with a degree of certainty. Their favorite game seems to have been the mammoth, which may have been driven with fire into traps in the earliest times in America. What is more certain is that the Pleistocene animals were hunted by men using spears with 3- or 4-inch stone points, the previously mentioned Clovis points—named after the town in New Mexico where they were first found. The Clovis people often separated young mammoths from the herd, finding them easier prey than the adults.

A later hunting culture's main diet seems to have been the long-horned bison, as the woolly mammoths began to disappear. Soon the long-horned bison also disappeared, as did the giant sloths and tapirs and the horses and camels. (American wild horses of historic times are the descendants of horses that escaped from the Spaniards.) The primitive American hunters apparently were becoming too efficient. The American Indian was already working out new cultural patterns, however. An area of intensive foraging of grain, nuts, and herbs was developing on the deserts of the United States and southward into Mexico. In southern Mexico, in the vicinity of Tehuacan, a grain was found that was being domesticated and improved upon as much as 6,000 years ago and developed into the staple crop of the continent, maize.[8] The corn culture was eventually distributed all the way from Chile to southern Canada.

[6]Brennan, op. cit., pp. 147–151.
[7]William W. Howells, "The Distribution of Man," *Scientific American*, vol. 203, pp. 112–120, September 1960.
[8]Richard S. McNeish, "The Origin of New World Civilization," *Scientific American*, vol. 211, pp. 29–37, November 1964.

The Indians of the New World developed 240 varieties of potatoes, many types of beans, and peanuts, artichokes, peppers, squash, sunflower seeds, avocados, cacao, manioc—a majority of the food products of the world. They also cultivated cotton, sisal, rubber, and tobacco, such poisons as curare, and several drugs, including psychedelic mushrooms, parica, cocaine, and peyote. They domesticated llamas and alpacas, guinea pigs, and turkeys.[9] Obviously, the men who peopled America could adapt to new situations. In the far north they hunted and fished; in temperate areas they supplemented their diets with gardening; in some places they became fully agricultural and even began the development of urban civilizations.

The Americas are vast, and their climate and terrain include all the types found on the earth. Partly as a result of this natural variety, the American Indians covered the entire cultural range from Old Stone Age to the early civilizations of Mexico, Guatemala, and Peru. The next continent to be discussed was much more limited in its Stone Age possibilities.

SETTLING AUSTRALIA   Australia forms a sharp contrast with the Americas—smaller, more largely desert, longer separated from the rest of the world. Its trees are of distinctive types not found elsewhere, as are its animals, such as the platypus, kangaroo, koala, bandicoot, vulpine oppossum, and Tasmanian wolf. Most Australian species are marsupials, giving birth to immature young that must be carried in pouches. The more advanced mammals found on other continents are met in Australia only in the form of rats, bats, and dingoes (wild dogs). Not a single cultivable food plant is native to Australia—no wheat, no rice, no corn, potatoes, or beans. The continent remained out of the roads even of navigators and explorers, and its colonization by Europeans started almost three centuries after the beginning of colonization of the Americas.[10]

The northern coast of Australia stretches into a fairly rainy tropical climate, and the eastern highlands are also moderately well watered; the vast interior, however, is a dry, baked land, with thornbush and scrub trees and in some places only tufts of dune grass or saltbush, growing around the holes where seasonal streams have died in the desert, for in this whole continent only one river makes its way to the sea. Nevertheless, *Homo sapiens* found his way even to this uninviting land and has lived there for many thousands of years.

[9]Erland Nordenskiöld, "Primitive Man as Inventor," in Walter Goldschmidt (ed.), *Exploring the Ways of Mankind*, Holt, Rinehart and Winston, Inc., New York, 1960, pp. 130–137.
[10]Kaj Birket-Smith, *Primitive Man and His Ways*, trans. Roy Duffell, Mentor Books, New American Library, New York, 1963, pp. 15–51.

Social and physical scientists of many types have taken an interest in the Australian aborigines. Their culture was the first step on Morgan's cultural-evolution scale and the basis for Durkheim's theory of religion and Freud's theory of totemism and taboo; but there have not been enough archaeological studies. A radiocarbon date of about 13,500 years ago has been obtained for findings near Melbourne, but the general impression is that the aborigines came along before that.

Recently, near the headwaters of the Murray River, artifacts have been found and dated at about 16,000 years ago and charcoal below the artifacts, at about 18,000 years ago.[11] The artifacts date to late Pleistocene times and to a cultural period in Australia when stone tools were extremely crude and none were hafted (fitted with handles).

A comparison of the elements in Australian culture makes it seem likely that the ancestors of the people of the central and western deserts came earlier than those of the people in the north. Most of the stone tools of these desert people are crudely chipped, and the bow and arrow is not used; in fact, it is used only around Cape York in the north. The people closer to New Guinea have similar initiation ceremonies, the bull-roarer (a narrow stick on a string, swung around the head to produce a loud whirring sound), a multipronged fish spear, and canoes.

Further south the culture is more impoverished, but it contains most of the basics of the Old Stone Age—a throwing stick (atlatl), drills for making fire, stone axes, dome-shaped huts to break the wind, boomerangs, wood or bark vessels, and digging sticks carried by the women.

Even further south, on the island of Tasmania, the culture of the now extinct Tasmanians was yet more rudimentary. The Tasmanians were the only people in the world never to have developed any type of hafted tools. They used only hand axes and scrapers little advanced over those of the Middle Pleistocene.[12]

Crude though the aborigine culture is, it has allowed the survival of a small population, rugged in appearance and undoubtedly thinned out by natural selection pressures. The aborigine reminds us that much of what is written about man's fragility compared with the physical strength of many other species is greatly exaggerated. The human being has great endurance—can track game in the most intense heat, can keep going even after his prey begins to wear out, and can subsist on almost anything. Grubs, ants, and lizards

[11]D. J. Mulvaney, "The Prehistory of the Australian Aboriginies," *Scientific American*, vol. 214, pp. 84-93, March 1966.
[12]Ibid.

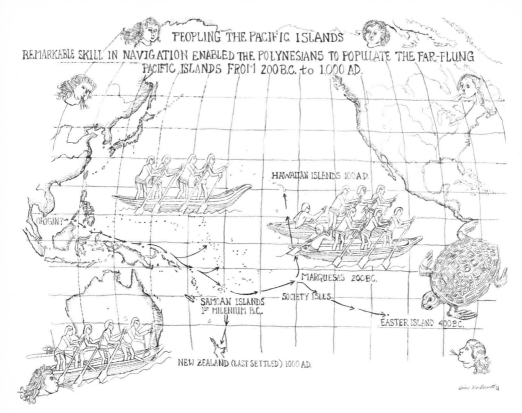

PEOPLING THE PACIFIC ISLANDS

REMARKABLE SKILL IN NAVIGATION ENABLED THE POLYNESIANS TO POPULATE THE FAR-FLUNG PACIFIC ISLANDS FROM 200 B.C. to 1,000 A.D.

ORIGIN?

HAWAIIAN ISLANDS 100 A.D.

MARQUESAS 200 B.C.

SOCIETY ISLES

SAMOAN ISLANDS 1ST MILENIUM B.C.

EASTER ISLAND 400 B.C.

NEW ZEALAND (LAST SETTLED) 1000 A.D.

make up a steady part of the desert aborigine diet, and so do grass seeds and roots and berries. With good luck, the diet is supplemented with kangaroo, bandicoot, or wild rat.

SETTLING THE PACIFIC   The peopling of the islands of Polynesia is much more recent than the original settling of America or Australia.[13] The islands of the Pacific are generally grouped into three major categories: Melanesia, Micronesia, and Polynesia. Melanesia includes the islands to the east of New Guinea—the Solomons, the Bismarck Archipelago, the New Hebrides, and New Caledonia. The people of the smaller Melanesian Islands are very dark and resemble the black people of New Guinea, a population of very great antiquity. The Micronesian people are located east of the Philippines in the Mariana (of which Guam is the largest), Marshall, and Gilbert Islands. The word "Micronesia" (small) comes

[13]The following description based on Robert C. Suggs, *The Island Civilizations of Polynesia*, Mentor Books, New American Library, New York, 1960.

from the size of the islands. The Micronesians show a blending of Malayan and Melanesian stock.

The Polynesian Islands are the remaining islands of the Pacific, forming a triangle from New Zealand to Hawaii to Easter Island. The Polynesians are believed to be a blend of peoples, partly Malayan, perhaps partly of an ancient Caucasoid race from India, and partly Melanesian. Whatever their origin, they are generally of a yellow-brown color, have black, wavy hair, and are tall and muscular but given to corpulence with increasing years. It is believed that the ancestors of the Polynesian people spread from Malaya down into parts of Melanesia and from there eastward into the Pacific, reaching the Samoan Islands during the first millennium b.c. By 200 b.c. they had reached the Marquesas and the Society Islands, including Tahiti and Bora Bora. They discovered the Hawaiian Islands and started settling them around a.d. 100 and reached Easter Island about a.d. 400. The last of the great island groups to be settled was New Zealand, around a.d. 1000, where Polynesian inhabitants are now known as the Maori.

It seems likely that the need for new lands for growing populations caused the Polynesians to explore more islands, but explorations could have resulted from schisms that developed. The different island groups tended to go through a long settlement period, a developmental stage of many centuries, and then an expansion period. The expansion period came about only when populations became fairly crowded.

There has been much discussion about how the Polynesian people happen to have traveled such distances over the open ocean; no other primitive peoples have even approached their feats. Even ancient Greek and Roman boats tried insofar as possible to stay within sight of land because their knowledge of navigation was poor. The Polynesians undoubtedly discovered new islands by accident many times, but there is evidence that they eventually made journeys back and forth for the sake of settlement. When they settled new islands, they evidently took plants with them. As early as 1769 the botanist on Capt. James Cook's ship *Endeavor* commented that breadfruit, pandanus, yams, sugar cane, and taro must have been imported from the west. They built boats of three basic designs: small dugout outriggers, large planked outriggers, and double-hulled canoes. Marquesan war canoes were as much as 50 feet long. The largest canoe ever built by the Marquesans, according to their legend, was 100 feet long and 6 feet wide. It took a great cargo of grapefruit to the east, from Hava Oa to a land called Te Fiti (Peru?) and returned to its home port. The Marquesans also used rafts, but rafts were much less important to them than Thor Heyerdahl, author of of Kon-Tiki, suggests.

Not only had the island people learned to build boats, but they obviously had to have learned the arts of navigation. It is fairly simple to make use of the North Star when traveling at night, but on most of their voyages they were too far south for that, sometimes even south of the equator. Although there is a constellation called the Southern Cross, it is not at true south and lacks the utility of the North Star. It is believed that other stars were used for navigation, but such navigation is very complicated, since the stars seem to move across the sky in the night and also to change positions in the course of the year, as the earth makes its journey around the sun. Corrections would have to be made on an hourly and seasonal basis to judge even approximate locations or to estimate directions.

The habits of seabirds were learned, and wind and cloud patterns and ocean currents. A type of knotted rope was used that had the function of recording estimated distances, and bamboo charts of the island groups were made. Thus a new cultural development helped the spread of the human species to far-scattered parts of the globe.

THE HARD LANDS   There are many cases in which people have settled in barren lands because they have been driven out of their homes by enemy people or by changes in climate, and, again, survival has depended upon developing new cultural ways. The Bushmen of the Kalahari Desert were once a large people, stretching southward from their present homeland into the South African veld and into the Drakensberg Mountains. The white migrants into South Africa and the large African people from further north have outcompeted them for the land, and they have retreated farther and farther into the desert. They have learned new means of survival—the use of poisoned arrows for hunting large game animals, an uncanny ability to track game, cooperative customs of food sharing, and hospitality with the use of the rare water holes of the desert.

In the north of Africa is a much larger desert, the Sahara, and even this desert is populated, although thinly, by *Homo sapiens.* It is even less hospitable than the Kalahari, and there are stretches that are without inhabitants, though most of it is at least traversed. In the worst of this desert, men have found a new means of cultural adaptation, a dependence on a particular animal, the camel. The camel is specially made for the desert, with inner eyelids to protect against the wind and flaps that close over his nose to keep out the driving sand. The camel is ill tempered and considered proud and arrogant. Legend has it that the reason for his arrogance is that Muhammad once whispered into the camel's ear the secret name of God, now known only to the camel. Whatever

Muhammad did for the camel, he did not make him easy to live with, but somehow he was domesticated, and much of the desert can be traversed because of him.

The Sahara once had more rainfall than now, but that was long ago, even before Greek and Roman times. Over a period of thousands of years, the adaptive capacity of the only culture-bearing animal has been put to the test.

There are many other peoples who have had to adapt to hard climates or terrains or who are interesting exceptions to the usual adjustments of man. The Eskimo and Aleuts are good examples; so are the reindeer-herding Lapps and Samoyeds, the Yahgan of Tierra del Fuego, the Incas of the extremely high Andes, the Tibetans, and many others. Some of these people will be met in the following chapters. All throw some light on how mankind has been able to reach the *ultima Thule*—the "end of the earth"—and survive. The secret is a matter of "adaptability."

Adaptability refers to the ability to meet successfully the circumstances posed by the environment. In the case of a very cold environment, for example, some animals are adapted because of heavy fur coats. Man adapts, instead, by cultural traits such as fire, housing, and warm clothing. There is no question that the overwhelming amount of human adaptation has been of the cultural type. However, there remains some conjecture as to whether different varieties of man also show a certain amount of physical adaptation to different environments and whether the physical adaptations have had something to do with the development of "races."

Race is a word used by anthropologists to refer strictly to physical varieties—a breeding population that shares genetically transferable characteristics such as skin color, eye color and form, hair color and texture, bodily build, and such nonapparent traits as blood-type distribution. As such, race has no connection whatever with culture, because all races of mankind have equal ability to create culture. Race becomes a culturally involved concept only in that groundless prejudice and discrimination often make success in a society more or less difficult, depending on one's race. In our discussion in the next pages we shall be interested only in physical traits. We shall note that some types of physical differences are important in adaptability but whether they should be tied into the concept of race is doubtful.

PHYSICAL ADAPTATION   Anthropologists would agree that the predominant trait making hominids adaptable to all parts of the earth has been the cultural capacity, whether it be that of the first crude tool makers or that of the most sophisticated modern

97

industrial-scientific societies. However, at the time when cultures were very crude and there was little protective clothing and shelter, could the processes of natural selection have fostered the development of types specially adapted for different parts of the world? To at least a limited degree, anthropologists would concede this possibility, but there is much argument as to the degree to which actual geographical adaptation has taken place and whether it is possible to relate these adaptations to race. Superficially, it seems that darker people are better adapted to the tropics than lighter people. Black coloration has developed only among Africans and Melanesians. Does this mean that they constitute some kind of special variation on *Homo sapiens* called a race? It is generally believed that Mongoloid eye form is protective against strong winds and bitter cold, but it does not appear among northern European people regardless of the climate. Does this mean that it is characteristic of a long-established human variety properly called the Mongoloid race? To the superficial observer, the answer is very doubtful.

Leonard Lieberman has used a very apt description for two schools of anthropology in attitudes toward race. He calls the two schools the "splitters" and the "lumpers," the one wishing to make minute studies of mankind that tend to divide the human species into large numbers of races and the other tending to lump all kinds of people together into one common human species whose variations are not of a type that are meaningfully explained by the racial concept.[14] Let us look first at the more traditional school, the splitters.

TRADITIONAL RACIAL CONCEPTS   The term "traditional racial concept" needs a little qualifying, because the racial tradition is not very long. The ancient Greeks and Romans were aware of different types of people but did not think of them as races in the sense of being important subdivisions of mankind. The racial concept in this sense did not become important until the seventeenth, eighteenth, and nineteenth centuries, when it became useful for justifying slavery and imperialism. The human race was conveniently divided into three major branches and probably several minor branches. The names of Joseph Arthur De Gobineau of France, John Stuart Chamberlain of England, and John Lothrop Stoddard and Madison Grant of the United States are associated with an extreme type of racist thinking which contended that great mental differences exist among races and warned of the dangers of mixing races. It just

---

[14]Leonard Lieberman, "The Debate over Race: A Study in the Sociology of Knowledge," in Herman K. Bleibtreu and James F. Downs (eds.), Glencoe Press, Beverly Hills, Calif., 1971, pp. 213–236.

happened that the Caucasoid race, to which they all belonged, was perceived as superior to the others, and especially the Nordic branch of the Caucasoid race.

Fortunately for the name of anthropology, its early leaders were not racist in the sense of trying to assign labels of inferiority and superiority. Morgan and Boas, despite their great differences, were both of the opinion that men the world over had similar potentials. Differences among types of people were to be explained purely in cultural terms, they said, not in racial terms. Boas even demonstrated that certain traits widely accepted as racial were not purely hereditary but could be influenced by diet and environment—size and head shape were his major examples. He also made studies of the children of mixed Hottentot and white parentage and found them to be physically superior to their parents in terms of number of healthy offspring produced. Rather than fearing the terrible results of racial mixture, he seems to have believed hybrid vigor was just as possible for the human race as for other types of life.

However, neither Morgan nor Boas denied there was such a thing as race, nor did they try to stop their followers from classifying people. For years much of the energy of physical anthropologists was devoted to classifying and describing races and trying to determine the origins of such mystery people as the Ainu, an apparently Caucasoid people of Hokkaido in northern Japan. The popular idea of three basic races—Caucasoid, Negroid, and Monogoloid—was widely accepted. A diagram by Kroeber frequently reproduced in textbooks showed the three major races as equispaced circles with others in between them, verging toward one or two of the major races. It should be added that Kroeber was no racist in the inferiority-superiority implications of the term. Like his old friend Boas, he was a cultural determinist.

THE ANTIQUITY OF RACES   Even many of the splitters, who divide mankind into a number of races, have thought of races as a recent development. They have commonly pictured an intermediate type of human beings migrating from the Near East northward into Europe, eastward into Asia, and southward into Africa and gradually developing the characteristics of the people of those continents, all in the span of time since *Homo erectus* turned into *Homo sapiens*, a matter of perhaps 100,000 years. The Asian people also migrated later to America, and somehow black people migrated into Melanesia and Australia.

A fundamental difference in the perception of races is developed by those who suppose races are of extremely ancient origin, dating back to the mid-Pleistocene, possibly 500,000 years. Von Weidenreich, who followed Black and W. C. Pei in the discovery of Peking man and is better known than either, assumed Peking man was ancestral to the present Mongoloid race. He also assumed Java man was ancestral to the present Australians and that some early *Homo erectus* type in Europe was ancestral to the Caucasoid race. Although ancestors of the African people had not yet been discovered, he assumed that they would be and that they would be found to be distinct since mid-Pleistocene times.

Just as the ideas of Weidenreich were beginning to seem passé, Carleton Coon revived them in a book entitled *The Origin of Races*.[15] Using recent evidence and relying heavily on slight differences in dentition, Coon distinguished five different races of great antiquity—European, Asiatic, Australian, and two races from Africa, the Congoid (Negroid) and Capoid (Bushmen and Hottentots). Coon's book has been criticized on several grounds. For one thing, it presupposes a type of parallelism in evolution that does not exist among other species. It also pays insufficient attention to migration and intermixing, which seem to have taken place even before the hominids became clearly human. Finally, it is accused of showing a racist bias in favor of the Caucasoids. Europeans are demonstrated to have "crossed the threshold" to human at an earlier date than the other races. "Crossing the threshold" refers to developing a brain of a particular size. Although the statement is never made quite so bluntly, it is implied that those who crossed the threshold first remain somewhat ahead of the others, even though it is reasonable to argue that order of arrival is irrelevant as long as definitely modern human brain-size is achieved; but Coon does not reassure us on this point.

Sarich, who also believes in the antiquity of races and is attempting to prove it by DNA studies, is among Coon's critics on his racial implications. In his opinion, the major races have attained equal capacities, but a further knowledge of them could be helpful in the study of hereditary diseases, blood types, and immunology—not for rating purposes.[16]

GEOGRAPHICAL RACES   Many modern anthropologists and biologists, including Coon, Stanley Garn, and Theodosius Dobzhansky, wish to redefine race in yet another way. Rather than assign all races to three or four basic types, with intermediate races between, they wish to describe races from a point of view of gene pool and geographical location. By "gene pool" is meant the total number of genes in a breeding population, transmitted to offspring unmixed with those of other populations. Gene pools exist in geographical areas where the popula-

[15]Carleton Coon, *The Origin of Races*, Alfred A. Knopf, Inc., New York, 1962.
[16]Vincent Sarich, "Human Variation in an Evolutionary Perspective," printed lecture, Department of Anthropology, University of California, Berkeley, 1971.

tion must have bred for long periods of time with little mixture from outsiders. On this basis, such races as European, East Asian, Hindic, North African, Central African, American Indian, Melanesian, Polynesian, and the like, can be differentiated. Although the idea seems rather sensible, it has the objection of carrying splitting to the ultimate conclusion, with some "splitters" finding several hundreds of races. The differences in number of races depend upon how fine the perceived points of differentiation are. The majority of anthropologists who do a great amount of splitting are interested in examining races, subraces, and even "microraces" from the points of view of mutation, genetic drift, natural selection, and new mixing—all of which help account for racial variation. Such microraces as the Greenland Eskimo and the Pitcairn Islanders are biologically as well as culturally interesting, and the extreme splitting approach may produce valuable studies in blood types and immunology. The question that others raise, though, is whether the word race is correct for describing these human variations.

THE NONRACE CONCEPT   Ashley Montagu, Jean Hiernaux, Frank B. Livingston, C. Loring Brace, and others think it would be well to eliminate race as an anthropological concept.[17] Of course, some people are dark and some light, some tall and some short, but there are always people in between. Some of the lumpers would simply call race a matter of "clines," or gradations from one type to another, much like gradations on a relief map or isobars on a weather map. Brace says that race almost *has* to be talked about as a sociological concept because even myths are of sociological importance as long as they are believed; but he doubts whether racial categories are correct descriptions of human variation for anthropological purposes. It is important to point out that very competent anthropologists line up on opposite sides of some of the questions about race—how many races, how ancient, how they have come about, and how physically adaptive they are. Extremely few are racists in the sense of regarding race as important for discussing human abilities and potentials. An interesting analysis of the nonracial explanation is presented clearly and succinctly by Brace, whose major point is that such so-called racial traits as color, dentition, body size and build are perfectly explainable in nonracial terms. Some of his explanations follow.[18]

Color   Dark color, says Brace, is definitely adaptive to hot, tropical conditions. Natural selection weeds out the light and preserves those with heavy melanin

[17]See Ashley Montagu (ed.), *The Concept of Race*, The Macmillan Company, New York, 1969.
[18]C. Loring Brace, "Non-Racial Approach Toward the Understanding of Human Diversity," in ibid., pp. 103–152.

CONFLICTING VIEWS REGARDING RACE

	RACIAL EXPLANATION	NONRACIAL EXPLANATION
REALITY OF RACES?	REAL., MAJOR DIVISIONS OF MANKIND.	MERE VARIATION, BEST REPRESENT. AS "CLINES."
ANTIQUITY?	VERY OLD, PROBABLY AT LEAST MID-PLEISTOCENE.	RECENT AND CONSTANTLY CHANG VARIATIONS.
HOW MANY?	THREE TO FIVE MAJOR, NUMEROUS MINOR OR SUBRACIAL CLASSIFICATIONS.	EITHER NONE OR AS MANY AS ONE OF TWO HUNDRED WITH SLIGHTLY OVERLAPPING TRAITS.
IMPORTANCE	SOCIOLOGICALLY IMPORTANT BECAUSE OF RACIAL ATTITUDES.	
	POSSIBLE DIFFERENCES IN TEMPERAMENT AND CAPACITIES.	ONLY REAL IMPORTANCE IS POSSIBLY IN IMMUNOLOGY MEDICAL PROBLEMS.

in Africa, northern Australia, and Melanesia, although evidence from blood typing, culture types, linguistics, and archaeology indicates no connection between Africa and Melanesia. In Australia, the northern people, being more tropical, are darker than the desert people to the south. In the desert, deep tan is needed, but not black pigmentation. Over a period of thousands of years a number of lighter people have been preserved. None of them are really fair complexioned, although some of the children have light hair and relatively light skin at birth. It can be objected that many relatively light people do live in the tropics, especially the Javanese and the Brazilian Indians. Brace contends that this is simply because they are fairly recent arrivals. Also, the natural process selecting for dark color is far less intense now that most people are protected by clothing and shelter. The lightest skins occur among the very people whose ancestors were first to wear clothes and whose climate has remained cloudy—northern Europeans.

Hair   Very briefly, kinky hair, according to Brace, seems to have at least a minor selective advantage of better insulation in some of the hot regions of the world. It exists in Africa and in slightly different form in Melanesia. There are also "traces of it in southern Arabia," and it becomes more pronounced among some of the hill tribes of southern India, some of the Malay jungle people, the Andamanese, and the Philippine pygmies. Some would try to explain these resemblances on the basis of racial migration; Brace contends that similar natural selection processes have produced similar results.

Teeth   After examining the subject of color, Brace presents an analysis of certain characteristics of teeth. Very large teeth are said to be a primitive trait, and certain tooth characteristics are supposed to be racial. Actually the largest teeth among living human beings are found among the Australians and the next largest among the Eskimo. It might sound plausible to some people to find a relationship between black color in Africa and black color in Melanesia, but hardly anyone would imagine a relationship between the Eskimo and the Australians. Instead of looking for racial relationship, let us look instead to natural selection factors. In most parts of the world the function of teeth is simply to grind up food that is already cooked and is fairly soft. In Australia, teeth are used to grind up tough roots, often covered with sand grains, and teeth are also used for tools. Wooden objects being worked on are often held in the teeth. Strong teeth are necessary for survival, and it is easy to imagine people with small, weak teeth being eliminated and leaving no heirs, so that large teeth are retained generation after generation. For the Eskimo, although the technology is more advanced and the Eskimo are highly inventive, the

Despite exceptions to the rule, cold
climates are associated with short,
stocky build and hot climates with tall,
slender build, as shown in contrast
between Eskimo and Ethiopians of Lake
Tave region.

teeth still perform an important function, and large, strong teeth are called for. The Eskimo fisherman kills his fish by breaking their backs with his teeth; he holds ivory and bone objects in the best vice he has—his teeth—as he works on them. His wife chews animal hides by the hour to soften them for sewing with bone needles (bone needles are passé now, but we are speaking of the traditional culture). Hence, for both these peoples, strong teeth are part of the equipment of survival. If we turn to look for the smallest teeth in the world, Brace informs us that they are found among the very people who have subsisted mainly on cooked cereal grains for the longest historical period—a band of people running from the ancient Near East through the river valleys of India and on into southern China. The people are not of the same race, but there has been no natural selection pressure for large teeth, so they are similar in dentition.

Size and shape   There is a very general rule about body size and shape that many anthropologists agree on (again, not quite all), and that is the tendency for bodies of animals (including human beings) to be adjusted either to maximize or to minimize heat loss, depending on the climate. Cold lands should produce physiques that are fairly broad in proportion to height, are able to store a certain amount of subcutaneous fat, and have relatively short arms and legs. Long arms and legs tend to dissipate heat rapidly; think only of how rapidly the extremities of the body grow cold on a cold day. Long, slender types should be found in hot climates. In checking the hypothesis against the facts, one can note the stocky people of the Arctic tundras and the very tall, long-legged people of the highlands of eastern Africa. Pygmies, Brace suggests, may also fit the type, since small size is a solution to the heat problem as well as long arms and legs. There are certainly exceptions to such a rule, but there are more positive than negative cases as Brace sees the matter. It might be noted here, too, that one of Brace's intellectual opponents, Coon, also believes in this body-build type of adaptation, known as Bergam's rule. William Howells comments on such a rule, too, saying that the "average body weight of man goes up as the temperature goes down,"[19] but this is pertinent only in cases where types have lived in cold areas for long periods of time.

Defective traits   Considerable work has been done on the occurrence of genetically connected unfavorable conditions in different human populations. Brace uses only one example, but it is rather intriguing. Keen eyesight, he reasons, including color vision, is necessary for survival among hunting people; those with defective eyes would tend to be weeded out by natural

[19]Howells, op. cit., p. 116.

selection, including those with color blindness. Then, he asks, where is the highest incidence of color blindness found? Precisely among those people who have abandoned a hunting way of life for the longest period of time—European people, Near Eastern people, and the Chinese. In these areas color blindness has proved only a slight handicap to survival, so it has not been weeded out by natural selection.

Such are a few of the examples brought up by Brace of selective factors that really are not racial or can be thought of as racial only by an odd stretching of the entire concept of race. No one would claim at this point of development of anthropology that anyone is certain of the answers about all selective factors. For a number of years many studies of blood types have been made, since they are discrete factors, easier to trace genetically than such multiple factors as size and weight. Another area of investigation is in the field of immunology, and the effects that ravaging diseases have had on populations.

Dobzhansky is especially interested in the disease aspect of evolution.[20] He gives considerable information about the effects of tuberculosis on populations, contending that it wiped out many of the most susceptible people of the British population in the eighteenth century and began to decline long before penicillin or any other cure was known. Similarly, in the case of American Indians, those who survived the tuberculosis ravages of the nineteenth century were those with the greatest genetic immunity. Dobzhansky also speculates that one reason bubonic plague no longer spreads in devastating epidemics is that the present human population is descended from those people with a considerable degree of resistance. We really have no idea what effect germs have had on the present distribution and varieties of the human race. Whatever their effect, however, mankind has survived and finally flourished, until our very multitude threatens to be our undoing.

SUMMARY   Well before our ancestors had achieved the *Homo sapiens* stage of development, they had started to spread over many parts of the Old World, but the journey to the ends of the habitable earth was completed only by *Homo sapiens*. Glacial advances locked up enough water in the form of ice to lower the sea level and leave a land bridge across the Bering Strait area, over which hunters traveled to the Americas in search of game. Somewhat later, men from the region of New Guinea spread southward into Australia and Tasmania, whether in pursuit of better lands or by accident we do not know; but we do know that

[20]Theodosius Dobzhansky, *Mankind Evolving*, Yale University Press, New Haven, Conn., 1962, pp. 302–306.

they lived in an unusually isolated state, developing unique cultural forms and changing their ways slowly, if at all, because of the lack of diffusion of new ideas.

In more recent times human cultures have made the adaptations necessary for permanent settlement of Arctic tundras, high mountain terrains, and barren deserts. The remarkably skillful Melanesian and Polynesian people discovered and inhabited nearly all the islands of the Pacific, completing the task with the occupation of New Zealand about A.D. 1000.

In their journeys to the ends of the earth, men have also evolved certain physical differences, some of which seem clearly adaptive to climatic variations and to differences in means of livelihood. Besides the commonly accepted idea that amounts and types of pigmentation are selective factors, it seems very likely that other traits, such as body build, dentition, and immunity to disease have been highly selective. Populations showing certain combinations of physical differences have been classified into races, but the racial classifications are inexact and not agreed upon by all anthropologists. A careful study of specific selective factors may prove more useful in learning about the human species than the study of classifications based on the concept of race.

PART THREE
FROM
SUBSISTENCE
TO SURPLUS:
ECONOMIC
EVOLUTION

After discussing the emergence of man and his capacity for cultural adaptation to nearly all parts of the world, the next logical step is to describe some of those cultural adaptations. What have the styles of life been like in societies making their living in such diverse ways as hunting and gathering, fishing, planting a few crops, herding animals, or turning to fully developed agriculture with the use of farm animals or machinery? Do other cultural traits seem to correlate with means of making a living and the amount of goods that can be produced?

The following chapters will present pictures of many ways of life, showing ecological adjustment of man to different terrains and climates and at different cultural levels. The first societies to be studied are those subsisting by hunting and gathering. Considered along with them is one society in which fishing becomes even more important than hunting and in which natural abundance makes possible considerable advances over the usual hunting-and-gathering way of life.

The hunters are obviously the people with whom to start. They still pursue the way of life of mankind through the vast majority of his existence, with men working on spears and arrows and women digging roots with sharpened sticks (dibble sticks) and searching for berries, nuts, grains, and herbs. It is a way of life with a measure of freedom but also with great uncertainty. What are the other traits that accompany the hunting-and-gathering way of life—what types of food ceremonials, social interaction, and world views—and what are the possibilities for achieving a more secure existence?

The next stage of development beyond the hunting-and-gathering level is that in which men and women supplement their food supply by simple methods of cultivation. A certain amount of hunting remains, since hunting is a hard way of life to abandon, not only because it brings good protein food but because it is a relatively free-ranging style of life, unencumbered by the hard work of gardening and the constant need for developing new land as old land wears out. The transition was undoubtedly made by slow degrees, possibly first in Anatolia or Iran or perhaps in Southeast Asia. Two of the cases to be studied here, particularly that of the Yanomamö, are still transitional between hunting and gardening. In the New Guinea tribes described, hunting plays a smaller role, and in the case of the much more advanced Yoruba of Africa and Pueblos of the Southwestern United States, the contribution of hunting to the economy declines even further. All the peoples described use relatively simple tools— dibble sticks, hoes, and shovels; but their productivity is greater and more dependable than that of the hunting-and-gathering people. As productivity increases, what happens to social systems? Is there more rivalry and divisiveness? In what ways do views of the world change? Does man-to-man equalitarianism continue, or do the first signs of social class begin to develop?

It is difficult to decide what style of life should be studied after simple horticulture. An orderly development would suggest turning next to more highly developed agriculture, with the use of farm animals. There are good reasons, though, for studying herders, or pastoralists, next, because their way of life does not place them in a position immediately preceding modern industrial society. Like simple horticulture,

pastoralism is more limited than is highly developed agriculture in its possibilities for laying the foundations of viable states and urban civilizations; but placing it before plow agriculture does not imply that it necessarily developed first as a way of life. More likely, the pastoralists learned the use of domestic animals from farming peoples and adapted them to their own seminomadic existence.

The last groups of people to be studied in this part of the book are peasants. Peasants differ from farmers in that they are more tradition bound, more likely to produce many goods for their own use rather than for the market economy, and generally more exploited by the upper classes in the urban civilizations to which they are attached. The last of the peasant studies—that of the Greek villagers—shows a transition toward the situation of the modern farmer.

Conclusions are drawn about the connection between the possibility of accumulating wealth and building cities and the evolution of social class systems. Factors other than wealth are of importance, but it will be seen that surplus wealth is one of the basic determinants of social stratification.

Each of the discussions of life styles is divided into at least three sections: technology and production, social organization, and world view. In anthropology, the word "technology" does not necessarily imply advanced mechanical equipment; it refers to all types of tools and weapons—spears, spear throwers, bows and arrows, sleds pulled by dog teams or reindeer, fishing boats, hooks and nets, needles, dibble sticks, hoes, plows, and storage facilities. "Social organization" refers to the ways in which people relate to one another as family members, kinsmen, members of social classes, clubs and associations, and in more formal types of institution. Social organization also implies rules and regulations that hold people together in social systems. "World view" includes magic and religion, moral philosophies, and much more. It includes all that people believe regarding the nature of existence, the role of man and the other animals in the scheme, man's relation to the natural species and the phenomena about him, and what man is and should be.

In connection with kinship as a major part of social organization, a few words are used that are not fully discussed until Chapters Ten and Eleven, so enough definition must be inserted at this point to make them intelligible. The words "matrilineal" and patrilineal" are used. Matrilineal refers to the practice of tracing descent through the mother's line rather than through the father's or equally on both sides. Patrilineal refers to the more common practice of tracing descent through the father's line. The word "lineage" obviously refers to the line of descent and hardly needs definition, but it should be noted that line of descent is far more important for many of the people to be studied in the next few chapters than it is for the majority of the people of the modern industrial world. Often one's lineage defines one's identity, importance, loyalties, inheritance, allies, and enemies.

Technology, social organization, and world view are all so important that they will be given special treatment in later parts of this book, but the cultures described in Chapters Five through Eight could not be introduced without some reference to the subjects at this point. These cultures will also constitute good, concrete examples to clarify the discussions presented in the remainder of the book.

Man has been a hunter, gradually improving his hunting skills and weapons, during at least 99 percent of his time on earth. The rate of invention in early times was incredibly slow, however, so slow that unless one makes a real study of early Stone Age tools they all seem to be alike and far from promising. The earliest sediments yield mainly pebble tools. After that come hand axes and scrapers. Hafted tools and weapons and the bow and arrow are inventions of the latest moment of time compared with hand axes, but they were very important in the advancement of hunting skills and probably made possible extensive population growth before the discovery of agriculture. Many of the weapons of the expert hunter diffused all over the world in prehistoric times and probably help to account for why the human population no longer seemed to display the pattern of advances and retreats that it did in early phases of the Pleistocene.

Adaptations to a hunting life are different in different places and times, but, as has been mentioned before, they generally call for cooperation on the part of a hunting band, especially when the animals hunted are much larger than the hunters themselves. Some of the Congolese Pygmies of today still hunt elephants; the Kalahari Bushmen hunt wildebeests and giraffes, and the Eskimo and Aleuts hunt

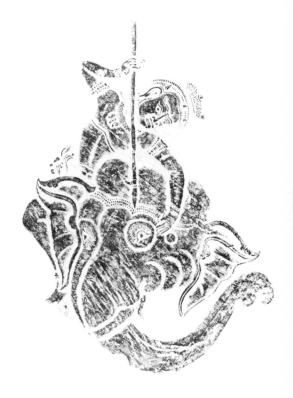

Chapter Five
Man as Hunter

whales and walrus. All these enterprises call for group cooperation, for the right equipment and knowledge, and often for ceremonial magic as well. The remaining hunting peoples of the world are widely scattered over the globe, so that many kinds of terrain and climate and social adaptation are represented. Behind the variety is there a basic way of life? Can generalizations be made beyond merely the means of livelihood and its limitations? Are there common traits in family structure and other elements of social organization? Are there common traits in systems of magic and religion and in ways of interpreting the world?

THE SURVIVING HUNTERS Some of the best-known hunters and gatherers in the world are the Eskimo of northern Canada, Alaska, and Greenland.[1] Many may be found today living near towns, looking for scarce jobs, and sending their children to American or Canadian schools. Their way of life is rapidly disappearing, and much of their pride and independence along with it, but many of them still hunt for a living. The following description is based mainly on conditions of years ago, when the tools and weapons were of native craftsmanship and the way of life was integrated.

The Indians of the Northwest Coast of North America—the Haida, Kwakiutl, Tlingit, Bella Coola, and many others—were exclusively hunters and gatherers until recent years and, as we shall see, among the more prosperous of the world's hunters. To the east of them in inland Canada are the remnants of hunting tribes. Further south, in the United States, a certain amount of hunting and gathering is done by the Shoshoni of the Great Basin and by a few surviving California Indians in the northeastern part of the state. Most of the people of the Great Plains and from there eastward had done considerable hunting but were also gardeners.

The surviving hunters of South America are the Siriono of eastern Bolivia, a few tribes of southern Argentina, and the scattered remains of the people of Tierra del Fuego.

Contrary to much popular belief, the overwhelming majority of the peoples of Africa have long been gardeners or pastoralists, doing considerable hunting in favorable locations but past the stage of a purely hunting existence. The Pygmies of the Congo basin, however, are still hunters and gatherers, as are the Bushmen of the Kalahari. Both groups are of considerable interest and have been studied in recent years.

[1] For a more thorough description of the hunting-and-gathering way of life, see Elman R. Service, *The Hunters*, Prentice-Hall, Inc., Englewood Cliffs, N.J., 1966.

In Southeast Asia are the Semang—a pygmy people of the Malay Peninsula—and the Andaman Islanders. In the Philippines are a few Negrito peoples, somewhat similar to the Semang, still living in a hunting existence. The peoples of New Guinea, near the Semang, are more advanced in their means of subsistence, generally growing yams and raising pigs for the major part of their living.

Finally, there are the Australian aborigines, mentioned at some length in the previous chapter. Many of them now work on cattle ranches or live at the fringes of the white cities, but in days past they all lived in hunting bands and a handful still do. Since their technology was the most primitive discovered in historic times, we will start with a description of their way of life and then take up a few examples of other hunting-and-gathering societies.

THE ABORIGINES OF AUSTRALIA   Much of Australia is poorly endowed by nature, and the western desert is a particularly harsh, unproductive land.[2] For thousands of years, however, people have survived in this land, with men hunting the larger game and women digging roots and gathering grass seed and other foodstuffs. Since food is scarce, no edible thing is passed over, and lizards, snakes, and frogs; grubs and ants; seeds, nuts, and berries of all available kinds are collected. Coastal aborigines eat shellfish and do not scorn dead whales or any other dead sea life washed ashore. The animals are not fierce, so the division of labor between men and women is not decided on the basis of danger but more on the basis of the great distances covered in tracking and the use of the spear. Food supply is precarious, especially for the desert tribes, and all the tribes have elaborate rituals for assuring an abundance of game. Settlements on the desert are impermanent, and the bands must range over a wide territory to find a living.

TECHNOLOGY AND PRODUCTION   Australian tools are extremely limited in number, for like all hunting-and-gathering peoples, the aborigines must be mobile and cannot carry too much equipment; but for the aborigines especially, tools and weapons are minimal. The women carry an all-purpose wooden bowl, called a *biti*, for collecting everything from ant larvae and lizards to grass seeds for flour. The *biti* is the winnowing basket and the mixing bowl; it is the pitcher for carrying water from the sparse water holes, and it can double as a

[2]The following description, except for the section on world view, is based on Kaj Birket-Smith, *Primitive Man and His Ways*, trans. Roy Duffell, Mentor Books, New American Library, New York, 1963, pp. 15–51.

Ngatatjara man trimming a spear with hafted stone adze. Tools and possessions are severely limited among wandering hunting-and-gathering people, especially Australian aborigines.

shovel for digging lizards and reptile eggs out of the soft soil. The main digging implement, though, is a dibble, the kind of sharpened stick that is the possession of women gatherers in all arid lands. Women usually also carry a flat stone for grinding grass seed, from which they knead a dough that is baked in the coals and ashes to make their bread.

Men's tools also are few in number and serve a variety of purposes. Before steel axes were available, axes were made of stone, usually quartzite or a low-grade chalcedony, and tied to handles with cordage—hardly adequate for striking heavy blows. Now there is usually a steel axe in each band. The men carry spears and a spear thrower and in some places a curved club called a boomerang. Australian boomerangs are not as exclusive to Australia as is sometimes believed, nor are they used by all aborigines. The more useful type is a weapon that gives the advantage of a whirling force but does not return. The kind used for sport does return, and its use is among the more widely acclaimed arts of the Australians. Only in northern Arnhem Land are bows and arrows used; the majority of Australians are among the very few hunters never to have learned of them.

For many of the desert tribes, the only clothing is a belt of human hair, worn around the waist. There are no blankets at night but only fires for warmth, even when night temperatures drop below freezing. The most common shelter on the desert is a mere windscreen, made of broken branches. At times a more adequate shelter is made with grass and leaves thick enough to keep off the rain.

SOCIAL ORGANIZATION   For people whose means of livelihood is extremely limited, large aggregations are impossible except at certain times of the year. Most of the time the people wander in very small bands of a few families, but tribes come together for initiation rites, funerals, and totem festivals. The social organization, which at first glance seems incredibly simple, turns out to be quite complex. There are prescriptive rules of kinship and marriage, sometimes calling for marriage to a first cousin but often for a more distant cousin, such as father's mother's sister's daughter's daughter. In some tribes marriages have to be to people outside the immediate group, a custom called exogamy, and the tribes are divided into subsections for marriage and ceremonial purposes. For example, in the Nyul-Nyul tribe of western Australia, there are four sections: Panaka, Burong, Karimba, and Paldjeri. The Aranda complicate the rules even further, with eight sections, so that Panaka men marry Purula women and beget Bangata children. The Bangata boys will eventually marry Mbitjana women and beget Panaka children; the Bangata girls will marry Mbitjana men, but their children will be Ngala, who marry Knuraia and beget Mbitjana children. This arrangement, which at first looks like utter confusion, is actually patterned for long-range circularity. It has the function, as marriage so often has, of keeping people tied together in cooperative alliances, it is hoped avoiding quarrels. Frictions may also be avoided by the prescriptive nature of the rules, whereby each man knows what women are available to him and that he will be assured a mating partner.

The rules of kinship do more than provide a means of getting a mate. They determine the rules of food sharing. They also determine friend and foe, and in some tribes a man to whom no relationship can be traced is automatically regarded as an enemy. In some tribes kinship organization was extended into clans, an unusual development among hunting-and-gathering people.

A few tribes, especially the Murngin, often raided one another, but warfare was desultory among most Australians. Sometimes war was a ritualized combat between opposing sides, in which men threw their spears at one another from a considerable distance. As soon as one of the participants was badly wounded, the fight was over. As with other small hunting populations, lives were too few to be spent in large numbers and there was no wealth to invite aggression.

The absence of wealth also means an absence of any well-marked class system. The men of prestige were the old men, who were able to set the rules and maintain what authority there was. The older men were accorded defer- ence and often had extra wives. Their knowledge of the old days, the traditions, and myths was valuable. The area in which they were most notably supreme, however, was in the religious and ceremonial life, which rested on a view of the world unfamiliar to people of Western culture.

THE WORLD VIEW   The world view of the Australians differs from place to place but always contains three essential elements: an unusually close associa- tion between myth and ritual, strong totemic beliefs, and magic rites for the production of animals and plants. Usually the earth is believed to have been here always, but the original ancestors, or the sky god, or, in some versions of the creation tale, a number of giant semihuman beings, arose. The earth was given its present shape, and hills and streams were created. The heroes of the Dreamtime, as the Australians call the indefinite past, made all the tools and weapons used today, but, more important, they made all the animal and plant species of the land. They also made sacred objects called "churinga," and placed them in the hands of the men to guard. The old men have cared for them ever since. The word churinga usually refers to a bull-roarer, a stick attached to a string and whirled about the head; it makes a roaring noise as it is whirled. In Central Australia churinga also refers to larger objects of wood or stone on which designs denoting the spirit type and location are carved. Both human and animals spirits are associated with these spirit centers, and it is from them that a totemic relationship between man and animal arises. People are born affiliated with one totem or another and are of the same spirit as their totem animal. Often the exogamous rules are related to totem animals. A kangaroo man cannot marry a kangaroo woman, for example, but must instead marry one of the others, possibly an opossum woman.

Several mythologies tell of how the men came to be in charge of sacred ritual. Sometimes the myths say that religious rituals first belonged to women but later passed into the hands of men.[3] Boys are initiated into manhood with

[3]A. M. Panoff, "Oceania: Society and Tradition," in *Larousse World Mythology*, Librairie Larousse, Paris, 1963. American edition, G. P. Putnam's Sons, New York, 1965, pp. 511–517.

bloody rites, including circumcision and subincision, sometimes the knocking out of a tooth, and the letting of blood to flow over the churinga or other ceremonial objects. The sacred secrets of the tribe are conveyed and all the detailed descriptions of the creation of the territory of the particular tribe. The secrets belong only to males; women are threatened with death for seeing or touching a churinga.

Man and nature are closely connected in Australian myth, and life is a cyclical matter of birth, death, and rebirth. Such a cycle of birth and rebirth of the spirit is one of the common ways of resolving the agony of man's certain knowledge of eventual death. Above all, the Australian view gives life meaning and provides authority and rules in a society whose means of living force its division into very small units with little secular cohesion. It was his study of the Australians that led Durkheim to his famous conclusions about religion: that it arises out of ceremony and group feeling and that the gods are themselves manifestations of group identity and cohesion. We must look at many more world views and theories before returning to the Durkheim explanation. The Australian world view also emphasizes the male-female dichotomy often encountered in myth, along with other cycles and dualities. In kinship and ceremonial life the Australians display great complexity and intricacy in contradistinction to their very simple technology.

THE ITURI PYGMIES   The Pygmies of Africa inhabit much of the Congo Basin and are believed to have lived formerly in a more extensive territory. The anthropologist Colin M. Turnbull has spent several years with the Pygmies of the Ituri Forest, to the north and east of Stanleyville in central Africa, and regards them highly for their kindness, their skills, and their almost total freedom from fear in what others regard as their dark and forbidding forest.[4] Like the Australian aborigines, they wear little or no clothing, do no farming or gardening, and make only temporary shelters. There are also resemblances in social organization, since they, like other hunting people, must travel constantly in small bands for hunting efficiency. In appearance, however, they are very different, being the world's smallest people, averaging only 4'5" to 4'8", whereas the Australians are of average stature. Many other differences are dependent upon contrasts in habitat and technology.

[4]Colin M. Turnbull, *The Forest People: A Study of the Pygmies of the Congo,* Simon & Schuster, Inc., New York, 1962. See also Colin M. Turnbull, "The Lesson of the Pygmies," *Scientific American,* vol. 208, pp. 28–37, January 1963.

The Ituri Forest is not the type of jungle that is hard to slash one's way through (tropical rain forests seldom are), but to many people it is oppressive and overpowering. Little direct sunlight breaks through the heavy overhang of trees and vines, and everything is constantly damp and warm. Eerie noises make other nearby peoples superstitious about the forest, but not the Pygmies. To them it is home and shelter, and they know its secrets, its benevolent plants and its poisons, how to track its game, where to find honey and roots and mushrooms, and when the delicious termites will swarm. The sounds of the forest are no menace to them; all are understood. "They know the secret language that is denied all outsiders and without which life in the forest is an impossibility."[5]

The game available to the Pygmies is more plentiful and much of it larger and more dangerous than that of the Australians. Pygmies hunt antelopes, monkeys, birds, buffalo, and even elephants. For the larger animals poisoned arrows, spears, traps and rope nets are used; the smaller ones are killed by arrows which are usually poisoned. The bows are not particularly large or powerful, and even with the poison it takes some of the animals a considerable length of time to die. The Pygmies are skilled at tracking them, as hunters must be to survive. Pygmies also make baskets for gathering and sometimes a little pottery.

One reason the Pygmy technology is more advanced than that of the Australians is that they live close to horticultural peoples and are described as living in symbiotic relationship with them. The Bantu tribes and the Sudanese near them trade metal and agricultural products for meat. Earlier investigators considered the Pygmies to be so dependent on the larger Africans around them as to exist in a state of near servitude. Turnbull does not agree with this appraisal. They are a very independent people, having as much bargaining power in their hands as their trading partners. The Pygmies with whom Turnbull lived did, however, send their children to initiation rites of the Bantu neighbors. Pygmies speak the language of their neighbors, with only a few words of their original language remaining. It is believed likely that their belief in a sky god is also borrowed.

Hunting magic is supplied partly by a wind instrument called the *molimo*, used only by the adult males. Women and children are supposed to believe some type of animal makes the strange noise that issues from the forest. The *molimo* ceremony cleanses away bad luck. A more positive hunting magic is a paste made from various parts of an antelope, especially the heart and eyes, and smeared on the men going on the hunt. When the hunt is completed, all

[5]Turnbull, *The Forest People*, p. 4.

the game is brought home to camp and divided fairly, after considerable argument. Among most hunting people there is no storage and all game must be eaten at once. One man's luck must be shared with others if all are to survive.

SOCIAL ORGANIZATION   Pygmy social organization is of a band type. Marriages must be with members of another band, and, at least for the Ituri bands known to Turnbull, cousin marriages are strictly forbidden. One incident he tells of illustrates this point and also the importance of group-opinion control in a small band. Two members of the band were caught committing incest, cousin mating with cousin. The situation was horrifying to the band, and the guilty man was sent out into the forest, unable to face the people. However, the Pygmies are essentially kindly and could not leave him alone where he might easily die. It soon developed that several members were smuggling a little food to him. Soon the stern discipline collapsed completely, and he was allowed to come back, provided he show proper humility.

To the Australians, initiation rites make the young man a member of the exclusive male group and able eventually to become part of the ruling elders. For the Pygmies, the initiation is an almost foreign ceremony, carried on by the Bantu, but including their own puberty-aged boys. The boys are circumcised and take their place henceforth with the adult males, but less is made of the event than is the case with many tribes. The Pygmies' real test of manhood is the very practical one of whether the boy has become an able hunter. The general rule seems to be that when the young men become part of a male group that has great solidarity, the puberty rites are severe and very important. Pygmy men must form solidarity for the hunt, but socially they are less aloof from the women and children than are many primitives. Puberty rites for girls at the time of first menstruation are held by the Pygmies themselves. The rites consist of a few days' seclusion of the girl followed by a feast and singing and dancing.

Usually the oldest man in a hunting band is headman, but not chief. The distinction is that the headman has an advisory role during the hunt but not at other times. His advice is taken because of his age and wisdom, not because of office. With a few exceptions, status rises with age among hunting bands because the memories of the old are the archives of history and legend, as well as repositories of knowledge about hunting and other survival skills.

THE WORLD VIEW   The Pygmies have a god, Khonvum, probably adopted from the Bantu people near them. He is at times identified as the sky god or as the Great Huntsman, whose bow is made of two serpents. He contacts men through the chameleon or sometimes in dreams through real or imaginary animals.[6] At times there is a long, unidentifiable cry in the forest, which the Pygmies say is the song of the chameleon.[7] However, the thing Ituri Pygmies regard as most sacred is the forest, and their god is conceptualized as the god of the forest. In the evenings they collect food from all people, which is to be eaten as they sing the songs of the forest to the tones of the *molimo*. There is little insistence on inequality of the two sexes, but when the *molimo* is played and the fire built, the ceremony belongs to the men. As in Australia, there are legends that say that once the *molimo* belonged to the women and that it was a woman who first brought fire, but now these things belong to the men.

In outward appearance, at least, the religion is one of ceremonial unity through ritual and worship of the god of the forest. One of the Pygmies is quoted as saying:

> The forest is a father and mother to us, and like a father or mother it gives us everything we need—food, clothing, shelter, warmth, and affection. Normally everything goes well because the forest is good to its children, but when things go wrong there must be a reason.[8]

The informant continued that when things go wrong, it must be that the forest has gone to sleep and is no longer watching them, so they must sing to waken it and make it happy.

The Pygmies have remarkably little belief in witchcraft or sorcery. When a death occurs, the Bantu people start divination to find out the cause; the Pygmies merely mourn the dead.[9]

As with the Australian aborigines, ritual and religion are inseparable, social unity through rites is strong, and man is closely related to nature. However, there is no totemism and no notion of cycles of rebirth.

THE WASHO The Australian aborigines and the Congo Pygmies are well-known peoples inhabiting very large territories. For comparison it seems important to study one of the small and little-known groups of hunting-and-gathering people. The Washo have been chosen for this purpose, as they are described by James F. Downs.[10] In certain characteristics they are similar to the Great

---

[6]R. Bastide, in *Larousse World Mythology*, G. P. Putnam's Sons, New York, 1965, p. 520.
[7]Turnbull, *The Forest People*, p. 2.
[8]Ibid., p. 89.
[9]Ibid., p. 41–45.
[10]James F. Downs, *The Two Worlds of the Washo: An Indian Tribe of California and Nevada*, Holt, Rinehart, and Winston, Inc., New York, 1966.

The Ituri Pygmies live in intimate relationship with the forest, where "normally everything goes well because the forest is good to its children."

Basin Shoshoni, being a nonaggressive people with a simple technology and dependent purely on hunting and gathering. However, they inhabited a more fruitful territory in the past, and they also differed linguistically. Their language bears a distant resemblance to the language of the Achomawi or Pit River people of northern California and also to that of the Chumash of the coast of central California, but it is not related to the Uto-Aztecan dialects of the Shoshonean peoples near them. The Washo were never a numerous people, having numbered at most not more than 3,000.

They centered around Lake Tahoe and the steep Sierra slopes to the east and extended out into the arid Carson Sink of Nevada, so that their territory had great variety in altitude and climate and in its abundant flora and fauna. Such varied conditions led to a way of life that maintained a seasonal cycle, taking the Washo down into the desert in the cold winter months and up into the Sierra in the spring. Even the floor of the desert is from 3,000 to 4,000 feet above sea level, receives occasional winter snow, and is by no means utterly dry and lifeless. The mountains to the west rise to 12,000 or 14,000 feet, and Lake Tahoe itself is at an elevation of 6,000 feet. The best way of describing the livelihood of the people and their technology is to follow them through a typical year, as season followed season, bringing excitements and trials in the old days before the mountains of the Washo became ski country for winter sports and before their desert valleys were paved with highways and dotted with farms, towns, and junkyards.

PRODUCTION: THE RESOURCES OF THE LAND   Even down in the desert the winter was long and cold, and after a time the stores of piñon nuts and other foods ran short. Before the snow melted off the mountain slopes, the first of the Washo were climbing the eastern slopes to tap the fishing resources at Lake Tahoe, and by June the entire population was on the shores of the lake. As the fish began spawning runs into the smaller streams, they became easier to catch in large numbers, so some were dried on racks in the sun and kept for later days. Later in the year fishing became more difficult, requiring more skill, and was often abandoned in favor of hunting.

Hunting started almost as soon as fishing in the spring but reached its height in early autumn. Whereas fishing was done by men, women, and children, hunting was a man's activity. Old men, unable to follow game long distances, sometimes trapped squirrels, gophers, and chipmunks and were joined in these activities by young boys, not yet ready to be hunters of big game. Hunting was done with well-made bows strung with tough sinew, and arrows of obsidian or flint; but the greatest hunting skill was not in the making of weapons but in the stalking of animals. As with all hunters, survival depended to a great extent on knowing the habits of the animals, finding their traces, following them for miles if necessary, and getting so close it would be nearly impossible to miss the mark. The hunting apprenticeship called also for learning the magic and rituals for each class of game, and ritual magic grew in importance as it was directed at increasingly difficult types of prey. Deer and antelope were greatly prized, particularly in the fall, when they were well fattened. There were two species of mountain sheep, even harder to stalk than deer and antelope, calling for more magic, and therefore a fine prize for proving the manhood of the hunter.

The animal possessed of the greatest supernatural power and regarded with awe was the bear, always hunted cooperatively by several men. Bear meat was reserved only for the men of the hunting party, and it alone was not shared, breaking the usual food-sharing rule for all family members of hunting bands. The Washo were not alone in giving a sacred significance to the bear;

our Paleolithic ancestors seem to have done the same, and there is still a sacred bear rite among the Ainu of Hokkaido in northern Japan.

Rabbit hunts were very common and less of a manly accomplishment, but they show the cooperative nature of the hunters. Rabbits were rounded up and driven into nets made of sage fibers and sometimes were killed in large numbers.

The women, with their dibble sticks, were indispensable to the life of the band, knowing all the edible roots and bulbs that grew in the desert and on the mountain slopes. So much knowledge was needed of the innumerable plants and the soils in which they might be found that Downs comments, "It might be said that fishing and hunting were arts, but gathering approached a primitive applied science."[11]

The most important gathering came late in the season and is still carried on by the remaining Washo people who live near Garberville in the Carson Sink. The piñon harvest drew all the bands together, and men, women, and children participated in knocking the pine cones from the trees and breaking the nuts loose from them. Tons of piñon nuts were gathered, for they would be the major food supply for the hard winter, when snow covered the ground and fishing and gathering were impossible.

TECHNOLOGY   Among the Washo, baskets were made for utility and also as an art. It is a general rule that hunting-and-gathering peoples make some kind of basket, but, as we have seen, the Australians did not. Washo women made large, loosely woven baskets for collecting piñons, very tightly woven baskets for holding water. Cooking was done by a method called "stone boiling." Hot stones were dropped into baskets of water until they brought the water temperature to a boil. This technique was common to many California Indian tribes and to others of the Great Basin region. Fish traps were made of woven fibers, as were the rabbit traps previously mentioned. Hunting called for bows and arrows, but fishing called for a more advanced type of Washo technology, including dams and weirs, fishing platforms, fishhooks, and nets.

The houses, called *galesdangls*, were very crude, conical-shaped structures, made of limbs leaning together. Sometimes they were covered with thatch, tules, or mud and used through the winter. The word *galesdangl* referred both to the house and to the family inhabiting it.

SOCIAL ORGANIZATION   As in the case of the Australians and the Pygmies, the Washo traveled in very small bands of only one, two, or three families. The

[11]Ibid., p. 21.

inhabitants of a *galesdangl* were considered a family, although occasionally unrelated people might join such a group. Marriages were usually monogamous, but occasionally a man might have more than one wife, especially if his first wife bore no children. It was also possible for polygyny to come about on the request of parents. If their elder daughter married a man who was a good hunter and provider, they might suggest that one of the younger daughters also marry him. In a few rare cases, polyandry (the sharing of one wife by two or more men) was practiced. This generally happened when a younger, unmarried brother expected to share a man's wife. Polyandry occurs fairly often among people who practice junior levirate, which is the custom of having a younger brother marry a man's widow. Sometimes in such a society the younger brother, knowing that he could conceivably inherit his brother's wife, feels that he has an interest in her, and "anticipatory levirate" is practiced. Such was the case occasionally among the Washo.

Kinship was traced through both the mother and the father and all cousins were called "brother" and "sister"—a system of kinship terminology called "classificatory" or "lumping." No two people with a common grandparent could marry, which excluded all close-cousin marriages. However, no kinship was traced back as far as great-grandparent, so descendants of the same great-grandparents could marry. The kinship rules were immediate and practical. One could be expected to come to the aid of anyone classed as brother or sister, as brother or sister to parents, or as grandparent. Since it was highly improbable that any great-grandparents would still be alive, the network of obligations ended at that point, and it is not illogical that the feeling of kinship also ended.

There were no permanent chiefs, but there were temporary political leaders. Sometimes the Washo held well-organized antelope hunts in which one man became the leader, the "antelope shaman," with temporary power to make decisions. As with many other Indian hunting tribes, only on special occasions was any one man elevated above others in authority.

The Washo were divided into regional groups, east, north, and south, depending on the location of winter quarters. These groups met at times for celebrations and games and for religious rituals but otherwise had mainly the function of identity. There was no requirement that each group perform rituals for the others or marry members of the other groups, as is sometimes the case with such tribal divisions.

THE WORLD VIEW   The world was believed to have gone through a series of stages, and its present inhabitants are the creatures of the fifth stage. In one version of the creation myth, the Washo and neighboring tribes were made by Creation Women and in another version, by Creation Men. As in the beliefs of the aborigines, the gap between men and animals was not very wide; all animals had spirits and differing degrees of power, the bear, as previously mentioned, being particularly strong in spiritual force. As with the neighboring Shoshoni, the coyote was woven into many myths and legends, sometimes as trickster or villain, sometimes as a likable rogue. There were, of course, mythological creatures and sorcerers and ghosts. Ghost fear was particularly strong, and the dead were seen as always malevolent unless they lay at rest as they were supposed to. Inconsistently, ghosts both haunted the world and also wandered off to a distant and happy land of the dead.

Lake Tahoe had a particular significance to the Washo, as did the Truckee River and other bodies of water in the vicinity. Deep in these waters lived water babies—supernatural beings with long black hair and great power to do ill or good. Some said that the very sight of a water baby brought death. There were shamans, however, specialists in supernaturalism, who could appeal to them for help in curing, and sometimes precious baskets were submerged in the lake as offerings. Shamans were possessed by spirits called *wegaleyos*, and for the most powerful the *wegaleyo* might be a water baby. Shamans so possessed could walk under Lake Tahoe to the far southern end and there eat poisonous plants that increased their power. Some could even follow spirits of the dead to the very borders of the land of the dead and, if they caught them in time, bring them back. The free wanderings of shaman spirits were by no means unique to the Washo, but are encountered among the next hunters we will consider, the Eskimo.

As with the other hunting-and-gathering peoples discussed, the spirits were mainly those of nature. Man, nature, and animals were linked closely together. The way of life supported little status differentiation among people and no hierarchy of gods.

THE ESKIMO No other hunting people of the world have attracted as much attention as have the Eskimo, not only for their ability to survive in some of the least hospitable parts of our planet but also for their highly developed technology and social customs that have made such survival possible. The number of Eskimo is variously estimated at from 20,000 to 40,000 and may once have been as high as 100,000. Since they inhabit a territory stretching from Alaska to Greenland, theirs is one of the most thinly populated areas of the world, averaging less than 1 person per 200 square miles. All the way from Alaska to

Greenland, the Eskimo are recognizably the same people, with a language that changes only slightly from place to place. The culture and technology is similar throughout the vast territory, except in the case of the Polar Eskimo of western Greenland, who had become so isolated from the rest of the world that they were unaware of the existence of any other people. The Polar Eskimo had lost the skill of kayak making, but it was brought to them again by Baffin Island Eskimo in the middle of the nineteenth century.[12]

The Arctic land of the Eskimo differs to some degree in climatic severity, with the ocean moderating the climate in coastal areas. In all the land, though, there are long months of darkness or semidarkness in the winter, with temperatures of -50° F or less, howling winds, and cutting snow and sleet. There are only 3 months of summer, when the surface of the ground thaws to a depth of a few inches and moss and sedges grow and flowers bloom. In the short but intense summer, salmon and birds are abundant, along with Arctic hare, caribou, and walrus. In the winter months, seal meat becomes the major resource and the Eskimo hunter must wait hour after hour at the breathing holes of seals to harpoon them instantaneously when they appear. The process demands tense alertness. Knud Rasmussen tells of one Eskimo watching sleeplessly beside a seal hole for 2½ days before he was finally able to make his kill.[13]

TECHNOLOGY   Most people learn a little bit about the life of the Eskimo during childhood and know of some of the inventions for which they are famous. Often, though, there is little awareness of how remarkable much of the technology is. Snow houses, built by most of the Eskimo, involve the principle of the arch—a construction principle beyond the ability of a number of advanced civilizations, such as Aztec, Mayan, Inca, and ancient Egyptian. The Eskimo and Aleuts alone made light, skin-covered boats, called respectively kayaks and bidarkas. The Eskimo harpoon is a remarkable weapon, with a detachable barbed point that holds the seal or walrus with great tenacity. Only the Eskimo designed sleds and trained dogs to pull them. Only a few people, including the Eskimo, Aleuts, and Nootka, dared hunt whales in small boats, and only they made clothing fitted to the body, with animal fur turned inward for warmth, and able to protect against the bitterness of the climate. The Eskimo were almost unique, too, in the three-pronged weapon with which they speared fish, the hide thongs they used, the sharpness of their walrus-tusk knives, and the efficiency of the bone needles and sewing techniques of the women. A few of

[12]George Peter Murdock, *Our Primitive Contemporaries*, The Macmillan Company, New York, 1936, Chapter 5, "The Polar Eskimos."
[13]Elman R. Service, *Profiles in Ethnology*, Harper & Row, Publishers, Incorporated, New York, 1971, p. 68.

In a modern walrus hunt in the
Bering Sea a new type of boat is used,
but clothing and harpoon remain
essentially those of the ingenious Eskimo
of earlier times.

the Eskimo even learned to make tools of raw copper, and they were among the extremely few primitive hunters ever to have learned to obtain and use metal in the absence of contact with more modern peoples.

SOCIAL ORGANIZATION   The Eskimo were given different names by their discoverers, such as Polar Eskimo, Copper Eskimo, and Alaskan Eskimo, but these were not their own names for themselves. The Eskimo affix *miut* refers to a territory, and the people called themselves Itivimiut, Takamiut, and Sirqinirmiut, indicating the territories in which they lived. Such peoples, though, were not tribes in the sense of having tribal organizations and chiefs. Like the other hunters and gatherers we have discussed, they lived mainly at the band level. In the winter, when long hunts became fruitless or impossible, they lived in clusters of as many as 50 to 100 people, close to good sealing grounds. In the spring and summer, one or two families often composed the social unit, especially when traveling far in search of game.

There were no prescriptive rules about marriage or complicated processes for tracing kinship. First-cousin marriages were permitted but not preferred. The marriage system could be thought of best as a very practical arrangement for making sure almost everyone found a mate. Although a few people existed without mates, it was a hard life for a woman without a husband to do the hunting and provide food, and it was difficult for a man to exist without a wife to do the long hours of chewing needed to soften hides for sewing, make clothes, do the cooking, and provide sex. Life was often so hard that not all children could be reared; those born defective were destroyed. Occasionally infanticide was practiced when a mother died and there was no one to nurse the infant or when there were more children than a mother could possibly support. Girls were killed more frequently than boys, since males were so extremely necessary for hunting. A sex balance was maintained, however, because more men than women were killed while hunting, by drowning at sea, or in a violent quarrel. If the numbers of men and women were not exactly even, it didn't matter too much because it was possible for one man to have two wives and occasionally for two men to be married to one wife. Monogamy was much more efficient in most cases, however, and was the most usual form of marriage.[14]

The Eskimo are famous for their wife-lending custom. A guest was often extended wife hospitality. Sometimes men of the same *miut* living some

[14]E. Adamson Hoebel, "The Eskimo: Rudimentary Law in a Primitive Anarchy," in John Middleton (ed.), *Studies in Social and Cultural Anthropology*, Thomas Y. Crowell Company, New York, 1968, pp. 93–127.

distance apart worked out arrangements for mutual wife lending whenever one happened to be passing through the territory of the other. Such borrowings were by consent of the husband, however. Wife stealing often brought about a deadly fight. The Eskimo have been praised for their hospitality, their generosity, and their good nature. There was a limit to the latter, however, and quite a few murders occurred over rivalry for women.

Warfare of any sustained type is impossible among most band-type societies, and what killings have taken place among the Eskimo have been matters of private quarrel. In the early days, though, the Eskimo showed a more militant spirit than did any of the previous three hunting peoples we have discussed. A number of early traders and Hudson's Bay Company workers and officials were killed by the Eskimo in the eighteenth century.[15]

Food sharing was highly developed among the Eskimo, as could easily be expected for a people who had to share. To the foreign observer, the custom looks like generosity; to the Eskimo himself, it is merely a matter of following the rules of reciprocity so that all may survive. Large animals were divided many ways, with specific portions for the hunter who made the kill, for the hunter's household, for men, for women, for everyone in the settlement, and for dogs.[16] Under the hardest of conditions food-sharing rules sometimes broke down. Old people often asked to be killed if famine threatened, for it would be impossible to keep them alive and they would be happier in the next life if they were killed than if they simply died a natural death. There are even known cases of eating the dead, so desperate was hunger during some of the worst times of famine.[17]

THE WORLD VIEW   As with many other peoples, there was a contradiction about afterlife belief, with simultaneous fear of the ghosts of the dead and belief that they went to some happy land of the dead.

The magical practitioner was the angakok—a shaman, who attempted to cure the sick but had the more important function of curing collective ills of bad luck. If hunting or fishing became inexplicably bad, the reason was very likely that someone had broken a taboo. The cure for such a problem was a type of public confessional meeting, in which the person who had broken the taboo admitted guilt. The guilty party was more pitied than hated by the group and was instructed to make amends. Confession alone seemed to be very important and could sometimes relieve the trouble. If bad luck continued,

[15]Nelson H. H. Graburn, *Eskimos without Igloos*, Little, Brown and Company, Boston, 1969, pp. 86–95.
[16]Ibid., p. 69.
[17]Ibid., p. 74.

the angakok might have to go into a trance in which his spirit could travel down under the ocean to consult with Sedna, the goddess of the sea, and bargain with her. His threats and promises might ultimately have their effect, and the goddess (an extremely unpleasant character) might be induced to favor the people again.

Naturally, there was hunting magic, particularly elaborate in the whale hunt. The hunted animals had spirits, and some type of libation or apology was made for having to kill them. The spirits of men and those of animals were similar, although there was no actual totemic belief. As with other hunting peoples, the world view included a close relationship between man and nature, and there was no elaborate theology, no hierarchy of gods, but simple rituals and taboos for keeping the species going, for ensuring food supply and good fortune.

THE INDIANS OF THE NORTHWEST COAST   The Indians of the Northwest Coast of North America are included in this chapter on hunters because they, like peoples already discussed, did no gardening. But their style of life was quite different from that of the four peoples just described. The difference resulted from the fact that fishing was even more important than hunting and permitted settlement in permanent fishing villages.

The Indian tribes of the Northwest Coast inhabit an area stretching from the northern extremity of California almost to the Alaskan Peninsula. They are best known for their colorful totem poles, which became increasingly them are the Bella Coola, Kwakiutl, and Nootka, and yet farther south, the product of great skill and an interest in artistic expression; the figures on them are connected with many myths and tales, family histories, and traditions. But above all, the poles were created to be impressive signs of family rank and could properly have been called "status poles."

There were many Northwest Coast societies with cultural similarities, the northernmost being the Tlingit, Haida, and Tsimshian; to the south of them are the Bella Coola, Kwakiutl, and Nootka, and yet farther south, the Tillamook, Coos, and Yurok. There were many more linguistic groups, but the ones named were among the more prominent.

Even the northernmost of the Northwest Coast tribes lived south of the Arctic Circle. Although the region is cool and extremely wet, it is modified by its proximity to the ocean, by the prevailing northwesterlies, and by the

[18]The following description is based on Philip Drucker, *Cultures of the North Pacific Coast*, Chandler Publishing Company, San Francisco, 1965.

Japanese Current. Geographers refer to the climatic type as "west coast marine," and it is a highly productive climate, supporting dense coniferous forests, with broad-leaved trees becoming more prominent toward the southern end of the climatic range. Life of all types was abundant in the old days and is to quite an extent even yet—deer and elk, black and grizzly bears, squirrels, weasels, pine martens, mink, beavers, land otters, ducks, geese, swans, ravens, and grouse.

The abundance of the waters was even greater than that of the land, with five species of salmon and several varieties of trout in the streams. In the coastal waters were herring, pike, halibut, smelt, and candlefish and many kinds of crustaceans and shellfish, including those that produced precious dentalium shells in the territorial waters of the Nootka. There were also seals and walrus, sea lions and sea otters, porpoises, and many kinds of whales. Amid the great abundance, the Indians needed only a well-developed hunting and fishing technology to become wealthy by primitive standards, and the needed technology was developed by these ingenious people.
them are the Bella Coola, Kwakiutl, and Nootka, and yet farther south, the

TECHNOLOGY AND PRODUCTION The majority of the Northwest Coast tribes built sturdy houses of cedar, or, in California, redwood, often of logs, split and planed. Cutting blades for chisels, drills, knives, and adzes were made of jadite, horn, or the incisors of beavers. Long before the area was opened up to Western exploration, unsmelted iron had made its way to the Indians of the region, possibly by trade with Siberians or from the wreckage of Japanese boats. The origin of the metal is still a matter of dispute, but iron tools were in use in considerable quantity by the time the region was explored by Captain Cook in 1778.

The same technology that permitted impressive houses and lodges and totem poles also made possible the building of seaworthy canoes, constructed with beauty and symmetry and in a variety of sizes and designs. Sea hunting was even more important than land hunting, and most tribes took large quantities of seal, sea lion, walrus, salmon, and other fish and sea mammals. The Northwest Coast was also one of the few areas of the world where primitive people matched their skill against whales, and whaling expeditions were a highlight in the lives of the Nootka. To ensure success, they hung skulls in whalers' shrines, brought along strings of human teeth, and had their wives lie quietly all day long so as to calm the whale. They embarked in two or three large canoes, manned by six or eight men each and equipped with enormous harpoons and floats and long coils of rope. It was necessary to approach a point almost directly above the whale to thrust in the harpoon, which was too heavy

Northwest Coast Indians were an affluent people compared with most preliterates, accumulating possessions, building sturdy houses and boats, and erecting totem poles for prestigious families.

to hurl except downward. The harpoon of the hunting chief was equipped with two elk-horn barbs that flared out as the whale struggled, holding it secure while other men got into position to thrust more harpoons into the stricken animal. Skill and daring were great, and long periods of training and expertise in magical protective techniques were required.

All the usual equipment and techniques were used for hunting land animals—bows and arrows, group drives of smaller animals, hunting dogs, spring poles, and snares.

The Northwest Coast produced many artistic and decorative objects in addition to the famous totem poles—elegant corner posts for houses, cedar boxes, carved bowls, decorative plaques made of copper, masks, and statues. There were occasional feasts and celebrations, featuring a lavish display of wealth, for these peoples lived in much greater economic plenty than any of the peoples previously described. Material abundance had its effect on the social system.

SOCIAL ORGANIZATION   Making their living from the sea as they did, the North-west Coast peoples were able to settle in permanent villages and had no necessity for limiting their possessions to the few items they could carry with them. In this respect they resembled horticultural peoples and actually had a better living than many of the latter. Like many farming peoples, they were able to store food, especially great quantities of smoked salmon.

Despite settled villages, however, the Indians were organized on a group level, linked together mainly by the kinship principle. The northerly tribes were matrilineal and the southerly tribes patrilineal, but in all cases, kinship was a major mechanism for managing obligations. Marriage systems differed, but there were usually preferences for marriage to relatives far enough removed to avoid incest violations but, nevertheless, kinsmen to some degree. Nearly all families received bride price for their daughters, and usually large-scale reciprocal gift giving was carried on by the two families involved—practices not to be found among the poorer peoples described earlier. Again, social control was based mainly on kinship, and so was justice.

In other ways, the Northwest Coast peoples differed greatly from the less affluent hunters and gatherers. For one thing, they had hierarchical systems of social class, and they had chieftains, who acted as ceremonial figures and as agencies of collection and redistribution.

The Kwakiutl, Haida, Nootka, and nearly all the other groups were divided into nobles and commoners in spite of the fact that nobles and commoners were kinsmen. Kinship prevented extremes of class division and helped maintain group solidarity. In another respect the system could be more accurately described as one of rank rather than social class, since no two individuals were exactly equivalent in rank and competition for position was strong. The situation was not too different from that of modern industrial societies in which large percentages of people consider themselves "middle class" but are nevertheless very different in actual rank and prestige. Below the nobles and commoners were a small number of slaves, usually war captives. The slaves, especially women and children captives, were rescued whenever possible by their own kinsmen, who paid ransom for their return. Men who were captured were often killed or, among the Kwakiutl, used for sacrifices.

Each local group had a chief, with ceremonial and religious functions and very much the embodiment of the group insofar as prestige was concerned. It was important that the chief be wealthy, and much of the wealth of the group was turned over to him; although the land and sea resources and great houses were actually collectively owned, they were spoken of as the property of the chief. This wealth made it possible for the chiefs to give the great celebrations called "potlatches" on the most important occasions—noble weddings, funerals, and, above all, the ascension of a new chief to office. Potlatches were grand affairs, in which much of the accumulated property of the chiefs was given as gifts, always in proportion to the rank of the members attending the feast. The guests' acceptance of gifts was their implied validation of the chief's right to his title; his ability to give generously was the mark of his greatness and the prestige of his entire group. Eventually, he, too, would be guest at a potlatch, and some of the gifts would be recovered.

RIVALRY, JUSTICE, AND WAR   The majority of the potlatches were such ecstatic and extravagant celebrations that the word has come into our vocabulary as the designation for an almost orgiastic party. Another word coming to our vocabulary from the Northwest coast—from the Haida and Tlingit—is "hootch," a contraction for their *hootchenoe*, a powerful rum they learned to make. Most potlatches were occasions for dancing and fun, although there were elaborate rules of protocol that pointed out official function. Benedict describes some of the potlatches of the Kwakiutl as so filled with rivalry for status that they seemed venomous, featuring attempts to humiliate and taunt any rival who could not afford such a lavish party. She tells of the pouring of precious oil on the fire to make it flame high in front of prestigious guests, who would try vainly to keep from noticing the heat for fear of losing face.[19] Philip Drucker says that apparently the extremes of rivalry developed in the nineteenth century, when diseases often wiped out the proper heirs to chieftaincies and bitter jealousies developed between men with approximately equal claim. Benedict makes the Kwakiutl appear to be a people who had developed a psychological compulsion for social climbing. This is no doubt partly true, but the function of the chief as a redistributive agency and a symbol of the group must not be overlooked.

As in the case of other hunting-and-gathering peoples, intergroup quarrels sometimes developed. In such cases a fight or feud could arise for the sake of doing justice and evening the score with another group. This type of fight, whether called "primitive justice" or "vengeful reciprocity," is not unusual among hunting bands. War waged for economic gain, however, *is* unusual among such people, but it occurred in the Northwest coast. Wars were waged for booty and slaves and even for taking over land and resources. It is ironic, but the intensity of warfare increases with the advance toward civili-

---

[19]Ruth Benedict, *Patterns of Culture*, Mentor Books, New American Library, Inc., New York, 1947, pp. 160–205.

zation. It may be that the Northwest Coast held all the population it could support and population pressure had something to do with the conquest of tribal lands.[20]

THE WORLD VIEW The world view was much more in conformity with what we have observed among hunting-and-gathering people than was the social system. Many young men went on spirit quests, and seeing the right spirits would enable them to become great hunters, warriors, or medicine men. Among the Yurok the women became the shamans. The other religious practices were mainly concerned with the ritual magic for hunting, fishing, and acquiring the great skills in woodworking for which the Northwest Coast was so outstanding. Animals had spirits, as was noted with the whale, and in the beginning a race of supernatural people had placed the animals here for man's later use, along with the kinds of spirits that could be appealed to by proper ritual and magic.

Celebrations were ecstatic, emphasizing what Benedict called the Dionysian spirit and making great issue over important events in the life cycle—puberty, marriage, investiture of chiefs, and funerals. The frantic celebration of such events is by no means unique to the Northwest Coast, but Benedict considered the Kwakiutl culture an extreme example of the type.[21]

In world view there is possibly one notable departure from other hunting-and-gathering peoples considered in this chapter. In all cases religious belief is a unifying influence among the people, and there is always a shaman of some type who specializes in religion and magic. Among the Northwest Coast Indians, however, a certain amount of religious charisma devolved upon the chief himself. Among the Nootka, only the chief had the mystic powers necessary to make a whale hunt successful. With other tribes there were chiefly functions of a magico-religious nature. Since the chiefs had no actual political power to make law, they cannot be compared with the god-kings of certain civilizations, but they might represent a step in that direction.

SUMMARY Hunting and gathering as a means of livelihood is the starting point for human societies. The majority of societies at that point have probably been of a type approximate to the first four described here, having to move frequently to find food and unable to accumulate more than the bare necessities of existence. The Northwest Coast represents a more advanced development, still

[20]Drucker, op. cit., p. 75.
[21]Benedict, op. cit., pp. 200–205.

MAN AS HUNTER

BASIC PATTERN   POSSIBLE DEVELOPMENTS

TECHNOLOGY AND POSSESSIONS

MINIMUM: SPEAR AND DIBBLE - SPECIALIZED   ADVANCED HUNTING, FISHING TECHNOLOGIES-
FOR TERRAIN-FEW POSSESSIONS -   SETTLED VILLAGES-WEALTH IN GOOD
NOMADIC LIFE.   FISHING AREAS.

SOCIAL ORGANIZATION

FAMILY AND BAND-EQUALITARIAN -   EXTENDED FAMILIES AND CLANS -GREAT
  HEADMAN WITH LITTLE AUTHORITY.   ATTENTION TO RANK-CHIEFTAINCIES.

WORLD VIEW

NATURE AND ANIMAL SPIRITS -HUNTING   SPECIAL RITES AND SPIRITS FOR
AND REPRODUCTION MAGIC-SHAMANISM.   IMPORTANT FAMILIES- TREND TOWARD
                                              ANCESTOR WORSHIP.

Diane McDermott '72

based on hunting and gathering, but in a rich territory where permanent dwellings were possible. In all cases, the essential social group is bound together by kinship or fictive kinship. In all cases the world view is intimately associated with the task of providing food. There is no priestly class, but animal spirits and shamanism are important and supernaturalism occupies a far wider area of life than in modern socieities. The economically poorer societies have no distinguishable social classes, no slaves, and no institutionalized warfare. High status goes to men, not to women, and is generally based on either hunting skill or shamanism. Food sharing is important in all cases, although in the Northwest Coast the sharing is indirect, with the chief acting as an agent of redistribution. Marriage systems vary, frequently permitting cross-cousin marriage and nearly always permitting at least a few cases of polygyny. The marriage systems always allow for the getting of wives by all men, whether through monogamy or polygyny or by a rare case or two of polyandry.

In the one case of a cultural area with social class (Northwest Coast), the system is modified by kinship of all members of a group except the war captives. The greater social differentiation seems to result from the availability of surplus goods and residence in settled villages where goods can accumulate, along with unequal distribution of control over goods and services.

Since the conclusions here are based on only five examples, one of which is in some ways atypical, the question arises whether other hunting-and-gathering peoples conform to a considerable degree to the same pattern. Elman Service's book *The Hunters* summarizes several additional societies and comes to similar conclusions.[22] Although there are variations in the societies, they can be thought of as having certain core characteristics, as in the accompanying illustration. The variations can be accounted for largely as the result of different environments, the diffusion of ideas from elsewhere, the techniques invented by the cultures, and the potentials for surplus goods.

[22]Service, *The Hunters*, pp. 81–111.

The most primitive level of gardening is the cultivation of fruits and vegetables by a simple digging stick—the type of gardening to be found in the Upper Orinoco region of Venezuela and in New Guinea. In West Africa horticulture is more advanced, the fields being more carefully tended with the use of iron hoes. Many horticultural peoples continue to depend partly on hunting and fishing to supplement their food supply. When hunting is a very important source of food, the men do the hunting while the women plant and weed the gardens; and sometimes if warfare is a primary occupation, the gardening is largely women's work. In other cases work is shared, especially if the gardens are the only source of food and tilling them therefore befits the dignified status of manhood.

In this chapter we shall also include certain tillers of the soil who use methods other than simple planting and waiting for the rain. The New Guinea people dig drainage ditches to prevent their crops from rotting from the effects of too much water, and the Pueblo Indians of the Southwestern United States practice irrigation and other methods of assuring water supply. None of these peoples, however,

Chapter Six
Primitive Tillers
of the Soil

employ animal power, and all are being used as examples of fairly simple farming techniques. The Indians of the Southwest and the Yoruba of Africa grow important cereal grains—millet and maize—and in this respect approach the advanced farming techniques that developed in the Near East and the Orient.

Obviously, a wide range of cultural developments and possibilities are brought together under the single theme of farming without plows and beasts of burden. Do farming techniques correlate in any way with other phases of cultural development within so wide a cultural grouping? What kinds of social organization do these gardening peoples have? What belief systems are encountered? Does violence tend to be more prevalent or less so as people move from a hunting to a horticultural way of life? Why did some of the peoples mentioned in this chapter reach the stage of kingly states while others remained at more primitive political levels? Finally, what are some of the details of the lives of a few representative groups of tillers of the soil?

TROPICAL SOUTH AMERICA The great Amazon Valley was once inhabited by Indians of many linguistic groups, scattered thinly along the vast expanse of the Amazon and its tributaries and extending along the eastern slopes of the towering Andes, and in the north, to the Venezuelan highlands. Many of the cultures have been described at length—the Caduveo, Bororo, and Nambikwara by Claude Lévi-Strauss,[1] the Camayurá by Edward Weyer, Jr.,[2] the Mundurucú by Robert Murphy,[3] the Tapirapé by Charles Wagley,[4] the Jívaro by a series of anthropologists, one of the most recent being Michael Harner,[5] the self-destructive Kaingang by Jules Henry,[6] and recently the Yanomamö by Napoleon Chagnon.[7]

[1]Claude Lévi-Strauss, *Tristes Tropiques: An Anthropological Study of Primitive Societies in Brazil,* Atheneum Publishers, New York, 1965.

[2]Edward Weyer, Jr., *Primitive Peoples Today,* Dolphin Books, Doubleday & Company, Inc., Garden City, N.Y., 1961, pp. 127–142.

[3]Robert F. Murphy, "Matrilocality and Patrilineality in Mundurucú Society," *American Anthropologist,* vol. 58, pp. 414–434, June 1956.

[4]Charles Wagley, *Tapirapé Shamanism,* Boletim do Museu National do Brazil (Antropologia), no. 3, 1943, pp. 61–92. Reprinted in Morton H. Fried, *Readings in Anthropology,* 2d ed., Thomas Y. Crowell Company, New York, 1968, pp. 617–635.

[5]Michael J. Harner, "Jívaro Souls," *American Anthropologist,* vol. 64, pp. 258–272, April 1962.

[6]Jules Henry, *Jungle People: A Kaingang Tribe of the Highlands of Brazil,* Vintage Books, Inc., New York, 1964.

[7]Napoleon A. Chagnon, *Yanomamö: The Fierce People,* Holt, Rinehart and Winston, Inc., New York, 1968.

Nearly all the tribes do considerable hunting but depend upon horticulture for the steady part of their diet, usually growing manioc, sweet potatoes, and plantains (a type of banana that is better for cooking than for eating fresh). In many cases these crops are supplemented by others, although the common Indian staple, maize, is peripheral to the area. The crops are mainly types that grow from shoots or tubers—a kind of agriculture that would be easy to discover. The preferred plants also show little seasonal change, matching the climate and making it possible to produce mature crops at all times of the year. Most of the people fish considerably, sometimes poisoning stagnant pools that are left after the water level declines, sometimes with fish traps or weirs. Much of the hunting is done with arrows with hard bamboo tips, good for shooting birds and monkeys but necessarily supplemented with poison for hunting larger prey.

Many of the Amazon peoples are diminishing rapidly in numbers, being killed off by the diseases of civilized man and also deliberately being driven from places where they are too much trouble or where they hold land that modern developers may be able to use. Those that remain in the rain forest find life more precarious as modern intruders burn off trees and destroy the game that has been a major part of the diet of Amazonian Indians.[8] Some of the groups, although diminished in numbers compared with centuries ago, continue in a little-changed way of life. Such is the case with the Yanomamö. Although they are at the outer fringes of the area, they constitute but a variation on cultural themes commonly encountered in the western Amazon Valley. They are a people among whom war is endemic, but in this trait, they only slightly exaggerate the picture of the area. South of them are the head-shrinking Jívaro and the Bororo, also intermittently at war and practicing ritual cannibalism.

THE YANOMAMÖ   The Yanomamö cultivate gardens and hunt in a territory partly in Brazil but mainly in Venezuela, near the headwaters of the Orinoco. They hunt wild pigs and anteaters, tapir, deer, monkeys, wild turkeys, and small birds. They also gather edible seeds, several kinds of palm fruits, tubers, Brazil nuts, and wild bananas. Some of the palms of their area are of value for dates, palm oil, and palm wine, and the heart meat of the tree is plentiful, tender, and tasty. After its pith decays for a month or two, the palm harbors large white grubs, and these, too, are a delicacy. A tree produces 4 or 5 pounds of grubs, some

[8]Christopher Weathersby, "Spoiling the Jungle Yields Few Riches," *Science News*, vol. 95, pp. 312–315, Mar. 29, 1969.

as large as a mouse. When wrapped in leaves and toasted in the hot coals, they are said to taste like bacon.

TECHNOLOGY AND PRODUCTION   As with most of the Amazon peoples, the Yanomamö use certain types of hard palm wood for bows and make arrows of the hardest species of bamboo, adding to the deadliness of their arrows by the use of curare poison. They make knives of the sharp incisors of a huge rodent, the agouti, or the canines of wild pigs. As is usual with horticulturists, but not with hunters and gatherers, they make pottery for cooking, but theirs is very crude and brittle. Contrary to the usual custom, men make the pots and are in charge of cooking in them during important feasts, the reason being that they regard women as to clumsy to handle pots without breaking them. Considerable effort is put into the building of houses (shabonos), of a circular type, covered with palm-frond thatching, neatly woven, and steeply pitched to shed the heavy rains. Better housing is encouraged by the relative permanence of the settlements of gardeners as opposed to the temporary camps of hunters. As in many parts of the tropics, the thatch becomes moldy and a home for armies of crawling roaches, scorpions, spiders, and other vermin. "Kaobawa's house was so badly infested at one point that the noise of thousands of scurrying roaches produced a constant, noticeable din in the village," says Chagnon of the house of his best informant and the man's two wives.[9] The people sleep in hammocks, fairly free of the insects, as do most of the people of that part of the world.

Cultivated crops constitute the majority of the Yanomamö food supply, so the gardens are highly valued and are an object of enemy raids. The preferred sites are in rather scarce supply, since reasonably flat land with less than average amounts of heavy forest growth is sought. Before a few steel tools were available through trade, all the big trees had to be girdled, left to dry, and then burned, or possibly just left standing. This type of gardening is referred to as "slash-and-burn" or "swidden" horticulture. New gardens are cleared of nearly all trees and underbrush and planted to several varieties of plantains, manioc (a root plant from which our tapioca is made), taro, and sweet potatoes. A little maize is planted, but is regarded as an emergency crop, not a staple as in so many of the Indian lands of America. The people also grow a little cotton, used for the sashes women wear around their waists and for the men's loin cloths. The gardens are not quite permanent because weeds and undergrowth intrude and fertility declines. Consequently, new land is cleared at one end of the garden as the poorest end is abandoned—abandoning the "rectum" and extending the "nose," as the Yanomamö phrase it.

[9]Chagnon, op. cit., p. 25.

The Yanomamö problem of rapid depletion of soil is a common one for slash-and-burn gardeners, especially in the tropics. Not only do cultivated plants take their toll of the humus and mineral contents of the soil, but heavy tropical rains cause severe leaching, draining soil nutrients downward to a depth below that of plant roots.

It might seem that a gardening people would be more peaceful than the hunters discussed in the previous chapter, but such is not the usual case. The Yanomamö carry warfare as a cultural value to greater lengths than do most primitives, and their lives are made up of constant raids and counterraids. The most frequent immediate cause of war is the escalation of suspicion and hatred between villages, culminating in charges of witchcraft against the shaman of the other village if someone dies or falls ill. Another war motive is the theft of women and food. Woman capture is important because of a numerical imbalance in the sexes. Yanomamö men greatly prefer sons to daughters, since sons will become fighters and since they also attest to the father's manhood. Especially if the firstborn is a girl, the mother may kill it to please the husband, and thus a woman shortage is created. Another problem is that the society has a taboo against sexual relations while women are nursing babies, and the women nurse their babies for 2 or 3 years—a common practice among primitives. A man's sex life is seriously frustrated unless he has extra wives or can capture a woman from another village.

The seizure of gardens or of their produce is also part of Yanomamö warfare. Sometimes a large village or a combination of allied villages will drive out the occupants of an enemy village and appropriate their bananas, plantains, and sweet potatoes. The territorial objective is more common among horticulturists than among hunting-and-gathering peoples. Constantly among the Yanomamö, alliances between villages for mutual protection must be made, with special feasts being held to get potential allies together to negotiate.

THE WORLD VIEW   The primitives discussed in the previous chapter were all fairly pleasant people whom most anthropologists have enjoyed knowing; but not all primitives are pleasant, least of all the Yanomamö, who pride themselves on their ferocity. According to Yanomamö belief, one of the mythical characters, Periboriwä ("spirit of the moon"), had come to earth repeatedly and devoured the souls of children. Finally some hunters became so incensed that they shot arrows at him as he was returning to the world above the clouds. One of the arrows wounded Periboriwä in the abdomen, and he bled profusely. Wherever drops of blood fell, they created Yanomamö men, who were fierce because of the fierceness of the blood. Where the blood was thickest, the men were too fierce, and they exterminated one another long ago, but in other parts the ferocity was just great enough to create superior men, the Yanomamö, whose name for themselves means "true men."[10]

Not all the fighting carried on is actual warfare. The Yanomamö have chest-pounding duels, in which antagonists exchange fisted blows to the chest, delivered with all the force possible. A "true man" cannot wither from the exchange of blows or his entire group of supporters will lose face, and they are determined not to. They will force their champion back into the contest, even though he may cough blood for days afterward. Sometimes chest pounding escalates into clubbing, with the object being to strike the antagonist on the head. Men are proud of the patchwork of scars on their heads from the clubbing contests they have endured. The next escalation is a contest with spears, but such contests are rare and are likely to lead to war between villages. In warfare, raids are usually sneak affairs in which few are killed. Cultural norms

[10]Ibid., pp. 47–48.

Chest-pounding duel among the Yanomamö. To prove their fierceness, participants take turns slugging each other on the chest or they may escalate the contest to a game of clubbing each other over the head.

thus provide the means for proving fierceness and "true manhood" without massive extermination as in the larger-scale wars of the world that calls itself civilized.

Yanomamö beliefs are much more complex than those so far encountered. The universe has four layers (a magic number among many Indian tribes), and there are many original beings who brought valuable plants and animals to the earth from one of the higher layers. There is also a kind of underworld in which dwell the evil Amahiri-teri, who come to earth to capture the souls of children and eat them, thus causing the children to sicken and die. Evil shamans are believed to do the same thing, and the illness or death of a child is usually interpreted as a sign that some shaman in an enemy village has been eating souls.

The Yanomamö imagination creates dramatic dualities. For every man born there is an animal of the same spirit, his spirit twin in a sense, that sleeps when he does, wakes when he does, eats when he does, and will die at the same moment he dies. Men also have another spirit, a guardian spirit, identified as a small demon (*hekura*) that dwells under rocks or in the mountains. This spirit can be contacted for psychic reinforcement, but only through taking a psychedelic drug made from the powdered bark of the *ebene* tree. With long tubes, Yanomamö men blow the psychedelic powder into one another's nostrils, causing coughs, pain, and dizziness but producing the sought-for dreams. The ritual is performed nearly every evening after gardening is finished. Chagnon had the misfortune of first meeting the Yanomamö when they were wild with anger because of a raid they had suffered the previous day, and they had enhanced their ferocity with the use of their favorite drug. His first contact produced an extreme state of culture shock, enough to strain an observer's scientific neutrality:

> I looked up and gasped when I saw a dozen burly, naked, filthy, hideous men staring at us down the shafts of their drawn arrows. Immense wads of green tobacco were stuck between their lower teeth and lips making them look even more hideous, and strands of dark green slime dripped or hung from their noses. My next discovery was that there were a dozen or so vicious, underfed dogs snapping at my legs, circling me as if I were going to be their next meal. I just stood there holding my notebook, helpless and pathetic. Then the stench of the decaying vegetation and filth struck me and I almost got sick.[11]

Chagnon eventually learned to get along with the Yanomamö, but only by assuming a fierce attitude that came close to matching their own.

[11]Ibid., p. 5.

SOCIAL ORGANIZATION   The Yanomamö live in slightly larger groups than most hunting-and-gathering peoples, with village populations numbering from 60 or 80 to 200 or 300. There is a village headman, without power to rule, but important in negotiations with other villages for gaining war allies and planning raiding parties. His power is informal, depending on his personal qualities, not on the legitimate power inherent in office.

The kinship and marriage systems are complicated by many exceptions to rules but are basically similar to those of many hunting-and-gathering peoples. There is, however, more emphasis on lineage. The naming of relatives is of a "bifurcate merging" type, meaning that father and father's brother are both called by the same kinship term, as are mother and mother's sister. In the younger generation, all children of the same patrilineage are called brothers and sisters, and those of lineages into which they are likely to marry are called brother-in-law and sister-in-law.

Marriage preferably takes place on a sister exchange basis. A man who marries a woman from an allied family feels compelled to provide a woman for his wife's kinship group, usually someone he calls "sister." Such a custom is common among people who think of marriage as a means of gaining and holding allies. Women are often beaten severely by these fierce people, but the woman whose brother lives near her and who has married on a proper exchange basis has an advantage over one captured and living far away. Her brother may come to her defense if she is too badly beaten. Although men are severe with their women, they pride themselves in providing well for them, especially by showing their prowess at hunting. A man's pride forces him to give meat first to his wife and children and sometimes even to his wife's relatives before thinking of himself. Obligations of this type, combined with strong feelings of lineage loyalty, marriage alliances, and negotiated alliances with other villages promoted by headmen, give a measure of cohesion to the people. They quarrel and fight, but, unlike the men who sprang from the thickest of Periboriwä's blood, they stop short of tribal extermination.

NEW GUINEA: THE DANI   New Guinea is one of the last parts of the world
AND THE GURURUMBA   with territories that have not been studied by
                     Western man and one of the few in which canni-
                     balism and headhunting have been practiced into
the last decade or two. Some of the eastern highland populations do not practice cannibalism in connection with headhunting but eat their own dead as a sign of ritual respect. The practice has resulted in a strange degenerative disease, *kuru*, which has killed 30,000 highland cannibal people in recent

years.[12] Others have until very recently practiced brain cannibalism, by breaking open the skull at the foramen magnum, just as seems to have been done by *Homo erectus* 300,000 years ago.

New Guinea is the world's second largest island, with a population of 2.5 million and containing over 400 separate cultures. Some of the people are rapidly making the transition into the modern world; others are still Stone Age people. In 1961 Robert Gardner and Jan Broekhuijse were the first outsiders to enter the territory of the warlike Dugum Dani of the Baliem River Valley in the western highlands.[13] A year or two earlier, Philip L. Newman made a study of the less isolated and less dangerous Gururumba of the Asaro Valley in the eastern highlands.[14] The two peoples are very similar in their horticultural way of life but differ in other respects. The Dani are, for instance, much more warlike and even more ghost haunted; they are also described by Gardner as more grasping and avaricious.

THE DANI   Most of our attention will be devoted to the Gururumba, because they are accessible enough and friendly enough to have been described more thoroughly insofar as kinship and supernatural beliefs are concerned. It took considerable courage to study the Dani at all.

The Dani inhabit a verdant valley in the region now held by Indonesia and referred to as East Irian. The territory can be recognized from a great distance by the high watchtowers that rise from all the villages to warn them of approaching enemies. Gardens are planted at a distance from the main streams because the streams are dangerous places where one can be ambushed and killed. An ageless feud goes on between the people of one side of the valley and those of the other, in which each death must be avenged. Just as the Yanomamö reinforce their fierce image of themselves by mythology, so do the Dani. According to Gardner:

> There is a fable told by a mountain people in the ancient highlands of New Guinea about a race between a snake and a bird. It tells of a contest which decided whether men would be like birds and die, or be like snakes which shed their skin and have eternal life. The bird won, and from that time all men, like birds, must die.[15]

[12]Carleton Gajdusek, "Physiological and Psychological Characteristics of Stone Age Man," *Engineering and Science*, vol. 33, pp. 26–33, 56, April 1970.
[13]Robert Gardner and Karl Heider, *Gardens of War: Life and Death in the New Guinea Stone Age*, Random House, Inc., New York, 1968.
[14]Philip L. Newman, *Knowing the Gururumba*, Holt, Rinehart and Winston, Inc., New York, 1965.
[15]Gardner and Heider, op. cit., p. 3.

The Dugum Dani stand guard at tall watch towers to defend villagers in the gardens against possible enemy attack or ambush. Raids, death, and revenge are central to the Dani life style.

Thus, according to Gardner, the Dani have rationalized death and also a behavior pattern that invites violent death. The bird spirit is the spirit of flight and daring, and the Dani identify themselves with birds in myth, in decoration, and in action. The bird imagery is carried further, and the soul is identified with "the seeds of singing," the loss of which brings death.

The Dani live in very small villages of thirty or forty people, but with what seem to be permanent alliances with other villages. Social organization is in this sense more stable than the shifting alliances of the Yanomamö.

The Dani are unusually haunted by the ghosts of the dead, so they avoid being out at night and take such ritual protections as sweeping ghosts out of the village with brooms. Special little huts are built for the ghosts to inhabit, in the hope that ghosts who are well treated will not be too harmful.

The gardening technology of the people is very simple. Their one tool is a digging stick. The harder work of ground breaking is done by men, and most of the planting and tending of crops is done by women. Since rainfall is extremely heavy in highland New Guinea, the fields must be planted in places of gentle slope so that drainage ditches can be maintained. The digging of drainage ditches is a technique usually encountered only among more technically advanced people. Part of the living of the people is derived from hunting, and they depend heavily on pigs for protein. Pigs are important as signs of wealth, for ceremonial feasts, and as pets particularly adored by children and old women. The gardening methods, the pig festivals, and the combination hunting and horticultural livelihood are common to much of New Guinea, including the now-pacified Gururumba far to the east of the Dani.

THE LAND OF THE GURURUMBA   As described by Newman, the Gururumba were at one time very similar to the Dani, avoiding flat lands at the bottom of their valley for fear of being ambushed, planting gardens of sweet potatoes, taro, and bananas, raising pigs, holding pig feasts, and hunting animals in the higher slopes of their mountains. The major difference is that they are now at peace, but there are other differences as well. Villages are larger, and there are elaborate men's houses, as in much of New Guinea. The Gururumba number over 1,100 people, all living in six villages. Although there are many more villages of similar people in the Asaro Valley, the six make up the largest meaningful organization of the Gururumba themselves. In the past they were a unit in warfare, and they continue to constitute a unit in ritual activities, especially the pig festival.

The land is cultivated at three levels. Near the river grow tall grasses used as roofing materials, for simple weaving, and for arrow shafts. Gardens are planted closer to the river than in the past, since planting there is no longer dangerous. The most intensive cultivation is at elevations of up to 7,500 feet (the valley floor is nearly 6,000 feet high), where the crops include taro and yams, bamboo, and bananas, and always there are the drainage ditches. At 7,500 to 8,200 feet are pandanus trees and more sweet potatoes, as well as cultivable wild plants, and it is here that the pigs do most of their rooting for food. The gardening techniques include not only drainage but a type of crop rotation, with one-third of the land lying fallow each year.

SOCIAL ORGANIZATION OF THE GURURUMBA   The people of the six villages that make up the Gururumba are divided into three patrilineal descent groups, each tracing its way back to a common ancestor of the distant past whose identity is not clearly known.[16] Most males of a village belong to the same descent group, but since married women nearly always move to the man's village (there are a few cases of the opposite type), the women are generally of different descent groups. The members of a descent group take one another's side in a quarrel, arrange certain ceremonies, and grieve together at funerals. They address one another by kinship terms, often calling all elders "mother" and "father" and age mates "brother" and "sister." Such terms are not applied to members of other descent groups.

Married women live in their own huts in the village, but men spend most of their time in the large men's houses, not spending too much time with their wives. The men expressed concern over the health and well-being of anthropologist Newman when they realized that he lived all the time with his wife. The separation of the sexes is insisted upon, and many taboos are imposed. Boys at the age of puberty move into men's houses, and girls move into a common house from the time of puberty until marriage. A type of men's fraternity is frequent in fighting tribes, and these people were hard fighters until recent years and still admire the trait of aggressiveness.

The greatest unifying ceremony is the pig festival, held every 4 or 5 years and put on by first one lineage and then another. The host group invites not only the six villages but people from even greater distances. Gift exchange is carried on to strengthen relationships, and hundreds of pigs are slaughtered, many having been brought in by other groups. The host group tries to show its strength and wealth by putting on a tremendous feast—a trait in ways similar to the potlatches of the Northwest Coast. Wealth in the form of feathers and shells is displayed and exchanged. Rituals are carried on to increase the future production of pigs and yams, since the host group virtually depletes its

[16]The material in this section is based on Newman, op. cit., pp. 27–38.

stock in the course of the festival. Flutes are played and *gerua* boards are displayed. *Geruas* are flat boards, sometimes shaped like a person, honoring the ghosts and ancestors and possessed of power to increase the future yield of pigs. The pig festivals are the types of celebrations that must be held by all such kinship-organized societies to bring kinsmen back together and prevent erosion of the ties that bind them together as one people.

GURURUMBA WORLD VIEW   Gururumba cosmology is very limited and explains only those things in the immediate area. Long ago a great male being passed through the Asaro Valley, teaching men how to grow yams and taro. When he died, his body sprouted many other plants that are valuable to the Gururumba. There are many rituals and spells to make plants grow and to give them longevity and fruitfulness. Spells are blown into the grass to do harm to anyone who steals from the gardens. There is also a ritual for inducing the ghosts of the dead to get inside the pandanus trees and make them grow and produce nuts—this in spite of the fact that ghosts are generally regarded as extremely dangerous. There are many nature spirits, often half man, half animal in form. Always males, they attack women and are believed to be the cause of the birth of twins.[17]

Newman's conclusion after living with the Gururumba was that their most important magico-religious beliefs are not concerned with the ghosts or spirits of the external world but with their own vital essence, *gwondefoje*. It is vital essence that gives the man power to accomplish, protects him from ghosts and bad luck, and causes his crops to grow and his children and pigs to remain healthy. The vital essence is largely sexual and can be destroyed with semen loss caused by witches or ghosts or by breaking any taboos regarding male-female relations. Many people impose severe taboos on menstruating women, but the Gururumba carry the taboo further than most, making sure that they do not contaminate men, gardens, or pigs during the menstrual period.

There are also strong ghost beliefs of a contradictory nature. Ghosts of the recently dead are *foroso* and are extremely harmful, causing accidents, illness, and even madness and death. After a funeral, the ghost of the deceased must be driven away with frightening noise and clamor. There are other ghosts, though, of a different type. The ghosts of remote ancestors, *abwaho*, are quite different. They do not enter personally into the affairs of men, but as a group they are important sources of vital energy for growing crops and raising children.[18]

[17]Ibid., p. 63.
[18]Ibid., pp. 84–90.

Many New Guineans have an interesting way of fitting the white European people into their cosmology. When Englishmen were first seen they were believed to be ghosts, and, since ghosts are known to be red, they were called the "red men." With the passing of time more was learned of the red men. They are an interesting people, who never are seen working or gardening but who have large numbers of goods at their command—goods brought over the oceans in ships and always with no observable effort. Obviously, the red men are a great source of goods and must have great magic. There have been attempts in New Guinea to develop the magic that will bring such cargoes—leading to a number of cargo cults. In Newman's account, although the Gururumba had no specific cargo magic, they did feel that all kinds of good things would flow their way as a result of having a red man in their midst.

In summary, the belief system emphasizes productivity, as is to be expected. Also, as is usual with people with no extensive political organization, superior gods are dim and unimportant in their thinking. What is important is the type of ritual magic that will ensure crops, animals, and perpetuation of their kind, and the more recent magic that might produce cargoes. The vital essence, *gwondefoje*, which Newman found so important to these people, has its counterpart elsewhere and will be encountered again as one of the varieties of the concept of mana. Obviously, many differences in world view are found among the world's gardening peoples. We will look next at a group among whom religion is more fully developed, with priests, many gods and spirits, and calendrical observances.[19]

THE SOUTHWESTERN PUEBLOS   The Pueblo villages of the Southwestern United States, mainly in Arizona and New Mexico, were first discovered by Francisco Vásquez de Coronado on his search for the fabled Seven Cities of Cíbola. The villages are the shrunken remnant of a culture that built the great cliff dwellings at Mesa Verde and elsewhere in the Southwest. The people were probably diminished in number by the great droughts of the thirteenth century that caused the abandonment of many village sites and relocation at the edges of the high mesas where they now live. They also suffered from the raids of Apaches and Utes and may have abandoned some of their sites for safer locations. Whatever their deprivations, however, many of the Pueblo peoples have maintained their old cultures with far less change than is the case with any other Indians of the United States. The same clans and tribes are still present, the same underground ceremonial chambers (kivas), the same types of hous-

[19]Ibid., pp. 81–82.

ing, the same cultivating techniques, and the same elaborate seasonal ceremonies for the production of rain for their dry lands, health for their people, and continuance of their kind. The many happy kachina spirits visit them each year, and they still have the cults of the sun, the rainmaker, the war gods, and the beast gods.[20]

TECHNOLOGY AND PRODUCTION   The Pueblo Indians—the Hopi, Tewa, Zuñi, Taos, and several other tribes—live mainly on high mesas and plant their gardens in the lands below their villages. The land appears so arid that agriculture would seem impossible, but underlying their lands are supplies of groundwater, seeping downward from the higher mountains to the north. The soft sandstone that makes up the top geological stratum of the mesas is underlain by a barrier of impermeable shale that makes for natural entrapment of groundwater to nourish the roots of corn and trees and in places causes springs and cienegas.

The Hopi, Tewa, and Zuñi have a good knowledge of their land. Their corn plantings are much deeper than those of modern commercial cultivation and are far apart, and twenty or more seeds are planted in a single mound. By the time the corn matures, the wisdom of the techniques becomes apparent. At times the winds dry out the surface of the land, and the only dampness is a foot or more below; the winds blow away top soil, and seed is also blown away if shallow planting is done. Before the corn matures, most of the great bundle of stalks that have sprouted will have been thrashed and destroyed by the winds and seared by the hot sun, but the inner stalks will survive and mature an abundance of small ears of maize.[21]

Peach trees are usually planted down slope from the springs so that they will benefit from deep groundwater. Near the springs a few crops are irrigated—squash, beans, melons, gourds, and some types of corn. Farther from the springs, where underground seepage and rain runoff must be depended upon, there is still a minimal amount of water management. Where gullies and arroyos begin to form, brush and soil are thrown in, stopping the erosion and destruction of the good fields. Fields are not abandoned. Nearly all are planted where a certain amount of mud is brought in during the rains, helping to restore the soil. The gardening tools, until recent times, consisted of the well-known dibble stick, a broad-bladed wooden spade, and a three-pronged

[20]Peter Farb, *Man's Rise to Civilization as Shown by the Indians of North America from Primeval Times to the Coming of the Industrial State*, Avon Book Division, The Hearst Corporation, New York, 1968, pp. 106–116.

[21]Discussion of Pueblo cultivation is based on C. Daryll Forde, *Habitat, Economy, and Society*, Dutton Paperbacks, E. P. Dutton & Co., Inc., New York, 1963, pp. 22–243.

Pueblo village scene. Among the Pueblo
Indians of the Southwest, both gardening
and building techniques are highly
advanced for preliterate horticultural
people.

wooden rake. The men do most of the gardening, but the division of labor is not absolute. Sometimes the women help with the planting, and they always help with the drying of peaches and corn and the storing of dried food for the winter.

House building, like the gardening techniques, is more advanced than that of other Indians of the United States. The houses are apartmentlike buildings of sun-dried brick supported by wooden beams. Sometimes, when a man marries into a crowded household, a new room is built for him and his wife, so the large houses grow in a haphazard pattern. Men always move into the households of their wives (matrilocal residence); the Pueblos trace descent through the female line.

The Brazilian and New Guinean horticulturists lived in areas of little seasonal variety, but seasons are important to the people of the dry plateau, which is covered by light snow in the winter and baked by the sun in the summer. The Hopi are one of many peoples greatly interested in the sun and its seasons. One of the important priests of the society is the Sun Watcher, who carefully observes the exact points of sunrise at all periods of the year so that plantings can be made at precisely the right time and the accompanying ceremonies and their magical protection will not fail. The Sun Watcher is only one of many important officials in Pueblo society.

SOCIAL ORGANIZATION   The Pueblo, especially the Zuñi, are organized into theocracies, highest authority being priestly. The level of organization is tribal. Tribes are divided into clans (for a description of clans see Chapter Eleven), in the Zuñi case thirteen in number, each one named for a different totemic plant or animal. Totemism has a variety of significances, but in Zuñi society the main function of totemic identification is to keep kinship clear in people's minds in order to avoid incestuous marriage, which to the Zuñi means marriage to anyone having any degree of relationship.[22] The clans stress kinship, hold land, defend their members, and make sure that their members stay in line. Each of the clans is made up of a number of smaller lineages, tracing descent through the mother's line.

The women are in charge of the households and of the cooperative grain-storage bins; they are also the owners of the fields. A man is an important member of his mother's household but a mere sojourner in his wife's. In his mother's house, he supervises his sister's children and defends his sister in case of disputes with her husband. In his own wife's house, he finds his brother-in-law to be a rival for the affection of his own children and a major

[22]Farb, op. cit., pp. 107–109.

authority of the household. Marriages break up frequently, without too much worry, for the children always have their mother and her brothers to care for them.

In many respects, the society seems to be structured to the detriment of the men, and yet men have highest prestige in precisely the area of Zuñi life that is most important—religion.

THE WORLD VIEW   The world view of the Zuñi was discussed years ago by Benedict.[23] Her description was of a much more serene, harmonious society than actually exists, but the Zuñi are a people of a strong discipline, so serenity appears strong on the surface. In the old days the war societies seem to have been very important and prestigious, and there were internecine fights within these societies.[24]

In other respects, the Benedict description of the Zuñi appears to be quite accurate. They are among the most religious of peoples. Religious ceremonies do not depend upon a solitary vision quest, as with many of the Great Plains Indians, but unite the tribe. Ceremonies are long and elaborate and occupy a good part of the time of the people.

The unseen world consists of a number of major gods in charge of the major natural forces, but there is no supreme god. Similarly, in the Zuñi social structure, there are several priesthoods of great importance, often inherent in particular lineages, but there is no supreme priest or priest-king. The kachinas, who represent lesser natural spirits of many kinds, come to visit the villages at times. As seen by the Pueblos, living in harmony with nature and the gods and spirits of nature is the supreme good. The older men usually belong to one or another of several sacred lodges that conduct initiation ceremonies for the young. The men dress in kachina masks for the ceremonies and believe themselves to be possessed by the kachinas at the time of the dance. The kachina masks are of great religious value, for it is the masks that make possession by the spirits possible and add sacred mystery to the secret rites.

The way of life of the Pueblos probably creates psychic tensions of an unusual type because of close crowding in villages and because of a family system that makes the role of husband an ambiguous one.[25] Throughout

[23]Ruth Benedict, *Patterns of Culture*, Houghton Mifflin Company, Boston, 1934.
[24]Farb, op. cit., pp. 119-120.
[25]Ibid. For a more thorough discussion of psychic tensions in certain Pueblo societies, see also Bernard J. Siegel, "Defensive Cultural Adaptation," in Hugh Davis Graham and Ted Robert Gurr, (eds.), *The History of Violence in America: A Report to the National Commission on the Causes and Prevention of Violence*, Bantam Books, Inc., New York, 1969, pp. 764-786.

history the tribes have divided and founded new colonies when internal tensions became too strong. The way of life is maintained against the pressures of the outside world only at heavy psychic costs and with very severe discipline. The inner tensions are fairly well hidden from the outside world, but they appear in the form of internal bickering and accusations of witchcraft. Nevertheless, despite its strains, the way of the Pueblos has shown an unusual tenacity in the face of long contact with Spanish, Mexican, and United States rule. The Pueblos still have an orientation that makes life meaningful, places them in the center of the concerns of a spiritual world, and fortifies them against the cultural disintegration that has been the fate of most of their kinsmen.

AFRICAN
HOE CULTIVATORS:
THE YORUBA

The African peoples, at the time of their discovery by Europeans, were assumed to be simple hunters and gatherers with only a very slight reliance on horticulture.[26] The Western world was surprised to learn of extensive African kingdoms, with strong interests in political elaboration and law and with hoe cultivation as the predominant way of life. Only a tiny minority of African peoples, such as the Ituri Pygmies and the Kalahari Bushmen, continued to live a hunting-and-gathering existence. The eastern highlands of Africa proved to be predominantly pastoral country, usually combined with horticulture. Central and West Africans show less interest in cattle, but live mainly from their gardens. Many of the people live in less elaborate states than the one about to be described, but the Yoruba are by no means unique. Equally large kingdoms arose among the Ashanti of Ghana and in Dahomey, and a few evolved farther south in the Congo Basin.

THE LANDS OF THE YORUBA   The Yoruba live in central and western Nigeria, their territory extending from the coast to the northern boundaries of the present state. The coastal region is low and swampy, with muddy barrier islands, except in the vicinity of the seaport of Lagos. This is a land of dense tropical forest and mangrove swamps, with tall palms rising above the roof of the forest. Inland from the coast the terrain rises steeply to a plateau whose elevation is 1,200 feet, where the forest is less dense and easier to clear. It is here and in the valleys farther northward that most of the people live. The climate is prevailingly warm and damp, but less so to the north. Summer rains are heavy, brought in by monsoonal winds blowing toward the partial pressure

[26]Discussion of the Yoruba, except for portion on mythology, follows Forde, op. cit., pp. 148–172.

Yoruba village of Nigeria. Yoruba horticulture is productive enough to support a wide division of labor and sizable villages, towns, and even cities.

vacuum of the Sahara; but in the winter, high pressure develops over the Sahara, driving winds southward to the lands of the Yoruba and keeping the temperatures down to 65° F or less.

TECHNOLOGY AND PRODUCTION   Although the majority of the Yoruba live in small farming villages, many live in towns and cities, and their way of life supports a division of labor not encountered in any of our previous studies. Village ironworkers specialize in extracting iron from the ferrous clays that occur in parts of the region, and their kilns produce 50 or 60 pounds of ore at a smelting. The pig iron is sent to the larger towns, where craftsmen repuddle it and cast and hammer it into hoes and knives, generally of better quality than can be purchased abroad. Copper and bronze are also worked, usually into statues and other decorative objects. Cotton is grown in the Yoruba country, and the women weave on hand looms. Many of the men are expert at wood

163

carving, and the Yoruba are among the African peoples whose art has appealed to recent schools of European and American artists.

The clearing of land and most of the farming is done by the men. The brief dry spell that occurs during what is mid-winter in more northerly climates is the best time for clearing. The relatively dry northern parts of the country are savanna, and all that is needed is to burn the grass. In the forests, more effort is involved, with larger trees sometimes girdled first, then left to dry before burning. Not all trees are necessarily cleared. Many kinds of palms are too valuable to destroy and are left standing in the gardens. The only fertilizing is the scattering over the land of ashes, and this is insufficient. Consequently, plots must be abandoned after 4 or 5 years and allowed as much as 20 years to recover. Land close to the larger villages and towns is exhausted, and farmland at considerable distances must be worked. This sometimes means that people must leave the main settlement for weeks at a time during important planting and harvesting seasons.

The steady sources of food are yams, millet, maize and cassava (introduced from America), bananas, peanuts, and several varieties of beans. Long, warm growing seasons generally permit two harvests, but also encourage weeds, so that constant hoeing must be done. Chickens and goats are also important to the Yoruba, but these people have few cattle and almost no pigs. Chickens are as important for divination as for meat and eggs, for it is believed that chicken entrails can foretell the future and find guilt in a trial. Wild palms are of such great importance that ownership can remain in the hands of the original claimants even though others work the land on which the trees stand. From palms come valuable dates, palm oil, and palm wine. Nigeria is densely populated compared with other parts of tropical Africa, and game is largely depleted except in the southeast, where hartebeests, waterbuck, elands, and antelope are hunted. Hunting is a specialty carried on by certain villages, which form almost a separate caste, marry always among themselves, and have only trade contact with others.

SOCIAL ORGANIZATION   The houses of the people are rectangular, with clay walls and thatched roofs that overhang the walls sufficiently to prevent their dissolution in the heavy rains. The houses of the more prominent families are built in large compounds entered through a single gate; many of the compounds accommodate polygynous families. Inheritance is through the father's line, but in many respects the society seems almost matrilineal. Mothers and senior wives are treated with great respect and have considerable influence, and a man considers himself emotionally closer to his mother's kinsmen than to his father's. In all likelihood, inheritance of property in the male line has only recently replaced inheritance through the mother's line,[27] possibly because of the importance of men in the heavy work of preparing new lands.

At the head of the largest group of Yoruba is the Alafin of Oyo, a priest-king with minor political power and very important religious and ceremonial duties. Below him in rank are several other sacred rulers, and each of the larger towns and its dependent villages has a district chief. Sometimes the chief's duties at the royal court keep him away, and subchiefs must be selected. Although the alafin appears to be an absolute monarch, even in the eighteenth and nineteenth centuries his power was controlled to some extent by the council of chiefs that selected the alafin from a sacred lineage and could, in rare circumstances, force his resignation or exile. There is also a secret society, the Ogboni (The Elders), that holds court and attempts to bring the chiefs under its control. Like many secret societies, it can become terrorist; at best it acts as a brake on tyrannical power.

The Yoruba, then, have traits of political absolutism, but with certain modifications. They also display a class consciousness of a type not encountered in any of the other cultures so far described. Large and powerful families sometimes allot lands to retainers who must turn over part of the product of their labor. Land, however, is not so scarce as to be a monopoly of the rich. Most villagers have their own gardens, and a man has title to any land that he himself has cleared. Slaves formerly constituted a large part of the population, but the slaves were not a badly oppressed caste and often had only the duties of turning over agricultural produce to their lords and serving them in time of war. There were, however, no legal rights for the slaves, and they could be sold to foreign traders, as many of them were in the days of the slave trade.

THE WORLD VIEW   Just as Yoruba society is presided over by lesser chiefs, great chiefs, and a supreme ruler, so are the gods arranged into a hierarchy. The head of the pantheon, Olorun, originally lived alone above a world that consisted only of water. He sent a son to earth with soil and a great chicken that scratched to make hills and mud flats and to leave areas of water. Olorun also created beings who have become the great gods of nature, sixteen in number,[28] and it is these gods that insist upon being observed in ritual and sacrifice, just as the chiefs are the usual recipients of labor and goods from the people.

There are other sacred attitudes reflecting an underlayer of belief probably older than belief in the great god. There are spirits dwelling in the land,

[27]Ibid., p. 150.
[28]R. Bastide, in *Larousse World Mythology*, G. P. Putnam's Sons, New York, 1965, pp. 531–535.

who help prevent illegal land seizure, for no one wants to risk hostile spirits. There are also religious societies—the Oro and the Egungun—each with its own deity and mythology. Members of the Oro and Egungun unite with their ancestral spirits when they die, and ancestors merge with some of the gods in the mythologies of the people. One of the deities brought the gift of divination; another, the goddess Shango, taught the arts of war. These two deities then, would seem to explain and justify warfare and trial by divination.

The Yoruba also illustrate a frequently encountered element of world view that became almost a preoccupation for Frazer in his *Golden Bough*. The great Alafin of Oyo has a degree of sacredness that identifies his being with the lives of the people and the welfare of the land. He presides over the magical ceremonies and rituals devoted to the major gods, the gods of particular towns, and the bringers of crafts and cultural skills. His performance of ritual and the animal sacrifices (also slave sacrifices in the old days) maintains the prosperity and well-being of the land. However, if the alafin grows too old and his health fails, he may be a threat to the vigor of the people and their land. He then is presented with a parrot's egg by the council of chiefs, who thus convey the message that he must kill himself so that a vigorous spiritual leader can be chosen and the welfare of the people can be preserved.

Strange as the custom seems to the modern Western world, it is a means toward political unity. Furthermore, the spiritual identity between leader and follower has its parallels in the magnetic attraction of some of the well-known leaders of recent history in more advanced social systems—Nikolai Lenin, Adolf Hitler, Kemal Ataturk, Fidel Castro, and, in a very different way, the great Mahatma Gandhi. The Yoruba have developed a type of mystic unity fraught with dangers but that seems to be a step on the road from small tribe to nation.

SUMMARY   In Chapter Five it was possible to present a large central core of common traits, surrounded by a rather narrow band of variables. In the case of horticulture, the variability is much greater and the common core possibly smaller, but a common core still exists. There are large numbers of horticultural societies, ranging from users of the digging stick to users of the hoe and including most of the rural people of tropical Africa and Melanesia and many of those of tropical South America. Not long ago the list also would have included such American Indian tribes as the Iroquois, Creek, Chickasaw, and Cherokee and innumerable others of the Eastern United States, along with most of the peoples of the Caribbean, Mexico, and Central America.

In the Valley of Mexico and in Peru the staple crops were maize, beans, and potatoes, and more irrigation and water management was required than is usual among simple horticulturists; but the tools were still digging sticks and crude, nonmetal spades and hoes. There were no plows or draft animals. Remarkable civilizations arose in spite of these shortcomings, and it is impossible to know precisely what their ultimate limits might have been had they been left free to develop. It seems likely, though, that the amount of agricultural surplus, upon which all urban civilizations depend, was more limited in areas without plows and animal power, and that circumstance placed an upper limit on cultural possibilities.

At the beginning of this chapter, several questions for investigation were posed. It is now time to attempt answers. In reply to the question of how the gardening techniques exemplified here correlate with other cultural traits, we can say first that they bring village life and fairly permanent settlement. Among hunters, only the Northwest Coast tribes had achieved permanent village life, and their livelihood, it will be recalled, was derived more from fishing than from hunting. There are more possessions in villages, since goods need not be carried around in constant migrations.

In social organization, the level of integration is usually higher, with lineages and clans replacing small bands. Social classes become a possibility, although not always a reality. Often the men still do considerable hunting, which adds to their status, but women continue to make important economic contributions just as the women of hunting-and-gathering peoples do. In Yanomamö society, the women are as subordinated as in any hunting culture, but among the Zuñi and the Yoruba they are not. Woman's status is generally lower than man's, but less so among some horticulturists than among the pastoralists or plow agriculturalists to be discussed in the next chapters.

Belief systems differ greatly in the cultures just described, but there is more possibility of important priestly roles than in hunting cultures. These roles become possible because there is extra product and labor to allocate. Crops and the land as well as animals enter into supernaturalism, and often the supernatural world is far more complex than among hunting peoples.

In reply to the question about violence and warfare, it is plain that a change comes about. Hunters are not necessarily mild—many of them beat their women and get into deadly fights with other men; but warfare is less frequent—often nonexistent—and its motives different. Hunters often fight for revenge or for manly prestige but seldom for plunder or for the seizure of land—only to retain their own territory. The latter motives become possible for horticulturists because there are goods to be seized and occasionally competition for good land. Since these societies are larger, warfare can be carried on more incessantly without total extermination. In two of the foregoing examples, the people are no longer carrying on warfare, but that is because Western civilization, with its very different violence patterns, has changed their way of life. The Zuñi are the most peace loving of the peoples discussed, but there is evidence that even they have done considerable fighting in the past.

To the question "Why have some of the societies advanced to the level of kingly states and others not?" it will have to be admitted that there are few certainties. Diffusion from Arabic-influenced cultures to the north is one likely explanation for the Yoruba. In all cases, terrain, climate, and the resources of the land must not be overlooked. The time element is also important. How long has horticulture been practiced as a way of life? It goes back thousands of years in central and southern Mexico, which helps to account for both the variety of Mexican cultures and their high levels of attainment. A final factor to consider is the elusive concept called "cultural ethos"—the tendency for a culture to find an internal and persistent value system, sometimes centering around one or two basic ideas. In the case of the Yanomamö, the importance of a man's conception of himself as a fierce "true man," following out a mythological definition of masculinity, can explain much about the culture, including its likely resistance to new ideas that might redefine social relationships. The very different philosophy of the Zuñi, giving man his place through a system of harmonies with kin, clan, religious societies, and the spirit world is another instance of how a central ethos can serve as a resister of change. Explanations of the origins of contrasting value systems are difficult. Perhaps societies faced with constant warfare develop myths for the justification of fighting and death (as among the Dani and the Yanomamö), but certainly the myths and resultant self-concepts become a cultural force in themselves. In sum, then, we should list cultural ethos along with such factors as diffusion, climate, environmental resources, and the length of time since the beginning of horticultural ways to account for the wide variations in cultural patterns among the primitive tillers of the soil.

The accompanying illustration summarizes graphically the types of variations that occur among horticulturists as well as show the central core of cultural traits found among these peoples. The variables are more prominent than in the hunting-and-gathering cultures and indicate how many more possibilities there are for the further evolution of culture once the threshold of settled village life has been crossed.

PRIMITIVE HORTICULTURE

BASIC PATTERN

POSSIBLE DEVELOPMENTS

ECHNOLOGY AND POSSESSIONS

HOE, DIBBLE STICK - SOME HUNTING CONTINUES - SEMI PERMANENT VILLAGES - INCREASED POSSESSIONS.

PERMANENT VILLAGES, LARGE TOWNS - DIVISION OF LABOR WITH MANY CRAFT SPECIALTIES - IMPROVED AGRICULTURE.

OCIAL ORGANIZATION

VILLAGE OR VILLAGE ALLIANCES - OFTEN LINEAGES AND CLANS - STATUS DIFFERENCES.

TRIBAL, WITH CLAN CHIEFS - CENTRAL COUNCIL, DEVELOPING TOWARD STATE POWER.

WORLD VIEW

NATURE SPIRITS, BOTH PLANT AND ANIMAL - SHAMANISM CONTINUES; OCCASIONALLY HIGH PRIEST.

POSSIBLE HIERARCHY OF GODS WITH HIGH PRIEST OR DIVINE CHIEFTAIN.

Diane MacDermott
'72

Chapter Seven
Man and Beast:
The Pastoralists

The introduction of domestic animals to pull plows and carts would seem a logical next step beyond the horticultural means of livelihood just described. In the river valleys of eastern Asia, India, Egypt, and Iraq such development occurred over a long period of time, but for several reasons it took many centuries for the use of domestic animals in agriculture to become widespread in other areas. In the case of the indigenous peoples of America the reason was obviously a lack of suitable animals for domestication. The horses of the Great Plains were descended from Spanish horses that escaped from the early explorers, and the sheep of the Navaho and the Pueblos were also introduced from Europe. In other parts of the world, the old life of hunting or of simple horticulture remained successful enough not to call for the great investment of effort required to change styles of life. In yet other places, domesticated animals became central to the lives of the people but not for agricultural purposes. We shall describe some of these people next, not because pastoralism preceded agriculture historically, but because pastoralism does not share agriculture's association with the development of permanent states and empires and urban civilizations.

Pastoralists have developed their ways of life in areas that permit contact with agricultural civilizations. Those of Mongolia and central Asia, especially, have looked hungrily upon the more luxurious civilizations near them. They have always traded with their neighbors, and sometimes they have raided them or even conquered them. Pastoralism, as one possible adjustment between man and beast, has had its impact upon history and has created its own particular values and colorful styles of life. Can pastoralism, then, be thought of as a highroad on the way to the more technically advanced civilizations, or is it only an interesting sidetrack? Are there any characteristic values and customs that apply to all pastoral peoples or any similarities in kinship organization or in ceremonialism? Does pastoralism usually lead to agriculture, or is it a very persistent system not necessarily followed by farming? Why have the great empires founded by pastoral peoples eventually crumbed to dust?

There are many pastoral peoples to consider, but the following will show a variety of adaptations to different climates and terrains and to different cultural areas. The Asiatic nomads are well known to history. Less well known are the East African pastoralists and the Saharan Tuareg, and still less so, such reindeer herders as the Tungus and the Samoyeds. We shall examine these peoples as the bearers of four alternative ways of life and shall look for both common traits and variations. American pastoralists are not included, because pastoralism was a very late development in America and has not had the same impact on history as that in East Africa, North Africa, and central Asia. The reindeer people are considered first because they live under the most primitive conditions and most closely approximate the life of hunters and gatherers.

THE REINDEER PEOPLE   Reindeer herders occupy a vast expanse of territory, ranging from the land of the Lapps in the Arctic regions of Norway, Sweden, and Finland and the Russian side of the Kola Peninsula.[1] In this great territory there are considerable differences in the degree of reindeer domestication and its importance relative to fishing and hunting. Besides the Lapps, who have carried reindeer culture to its greatest extent, important reindeer people include the Samoyeds, the northern Tungus, and the Chuckchi. The Samoyeds occupy the region around the estuary of the Ob River and the shores of the Kara Sea and eastward to the

[1]C. Daryll Forde, *Habitat, Economy and Society*, Dutton Paperbacks, E. P. Dutton & Co., New York, 1963, pp. 352–353.

Taymyr Peninsula.[2] The Tungus are a people whose southern relatives raise horses in the Trans-Baikal region of Siberia, but the more northerly range of the Tungus is much too cold for horses. In the extreme western parts of the reindeer country, in northern Scandinavia, the temperatures are modified by the North Atlantic Drift, an extension of the Gulf Stream, so that seaports remain ice free and the cold seldom reaches more than $-30°$ F. Farther to the east the climate becomes progressively colder, dropping to $-40°$ or $-50°$ in the north of Russia—much lower in Siberia. Some of the Tungus live in the region of the Verkhoyansk Mountains, the coldest occupied part of the world, where the annual temperature averages only $1°$ F and winter temperatures of $-97°$ F have been recorded. The Tungus territory stretches even farther to the east into the Kamchatka Peninsula, where the reindeer-herding Chuckchi also live. The bitter temperatures of their land explain not only why the northern Tungus have had to turn to reindeer rather than horses but also why they have not been able to change over to sheep, goats, and cattle as have some of the Lapps.

More has been written about the Lapps than about the other reindeer herders, but there is no agreement as to the origin of the Lapps. They are mentioned for the first time in the writings of Tacitus in A.D. 98. Nearly five hundred years later, the Byzantine scholar Procopius mentioned "stride Finns," deriving his term from the Norse description of the Lapps as "skiing Finns." The term is a misnomer; the Lapps use skis and are probably the original inventors of them, but they are not the same people as the Finns, either in appearance or in language. Unlike the other people of Scandinavia, they are of very short stature. Although they are sometimes believed to be of Asiatic origin, to the casual observer they look much more European than Asiatic, and they certainly have not moved in from the East recently. One evidence of their very great antiquity in their present home is the finding of skis dating back to 2000 B.C.[3] The Lapps were once regarded by other Europeans with a certain amount of superstitious dread. In 922 a Germanic prince sent his daughter to live with the Lapps in order to learn witchcraft. In the sixteenth century, Ivan the Terrible sent for Lapp magicians to explain a comet that had appeared in the sky.[4]

[2]Robert F. Spencer and Elden Johnson, *Atlas for Anthropology*, Wm. C. Brown Company Publishers, Dubuque, Iowa, 1960, pp. 36–37.

[3]Kaj Birket-Smith, *Primitive Man and His Ways*, trans. Roy Duffell, Mentor Books, New American Library, New York, 1963, p. 98.

[4]Edward Weyer, Jr., *Primitive Peoples Today*, Dolphin Books, Doubleday & Company, Inc., Garden City, N.Y., 1961, p. 152.

The Tungus were also noted in history for many centuries, as early as the ninth century by the Chinese, and were already using reindeer.

TECHNOLOGY AND PRODUCTION   Reindeer are put to a variety of uses by the peoples of Lapland and Siberia. To the extreme east, the Chuckchi and Koryak follow and keep some controls on very large herds of reindeer, killing them for food supply and for hides, but using them for no other purposes. Their sleds are pulled by dog teams, just as in the case of the Eskimo on the other side of the straits. The northern Tungus are the only people who ride their reindeer, sitting well forward on the shoulders, since the deer will not carry a man's weight as well as a horse. They also use deer for pack animals, loading them with as much as 150 pounds and finding that they can make much better progress through the snowy country than can horses.[5] Although Tungus deer pull sleds, Tungus use them less for that purpose than do the Lapps. More than anything else, they breed reindeer for milk, although the doe gives only about 1 pint of milk per day. They kill reindeer for feasts only on special occasions. The Samoyeds, to the west of the Tungus, also have their reindeer herds, using them occasionally for pulling sleds but mainly for meat. A female deer is used as a decoy to attract wild bucks for capture or slaughter or sometimes even to attract bears. There are long deer drives, herding the animals between rows of posts and eventually into a trap. The Samoyeds do not use their deer for milking or riding. At the western extreme, the Lapps use deer for pulling sleds, for meat supply, hides, and milk, and as pack animals, but not for riding.

In all cases the harness used for sleds seems to have been derived from dog sleds rather than from the harness used by horse-riding peoples further south. The sleds are of a rather similar boat-shaped appearance. The herds consist mostly of females, since males are more frequently slaughtered for food. The leaders of the herds are castrated males. In the old days, the herders castrated the male by biting its spermatic cords and crushing its sexual glands; now a knife is generally used.

For most of the reindeer people, the way of life is largely nomadic, and, as in the cases of hunters and gatherers, their possessions must be limited, but not as strictly as with the latter. Some of the Lapp people are now settled quite permanently, but a few of the mountain Lapps still make an annual trek of over 150 miles, moving from the lowlands where they winter to intermediate slopes in the spring, when the fauns are born, and then to the higher mountains for the summer. Such an annual trek is called "transhumance" and is

[5]Forde, op. cit., p. 354.

LAPPS

CHUCKCHIS

KORYAKS

TUNGUS

SAMOYEDS

DIFFERING USE OF REINDEER

LAPPS	SAMOYEDS	TUNGUS	CHUCKCHIS AND KORYAKS
PASTORAL	PASTORAL	PASTORAL	HUNTING
REINDEER SLEDS	REINDEER SLEDS	REINDEER SLEDS	DOG SLEDS
REINDEER AS PACK ANIMALS	REINDEER AS PACK ANIMALS	REINDEER AS PACK ANIMALS	
REINDEER FOR MILKING		REINDEER FOR MILKING	
		REINDEER FOR RIDING	

PASTORALISM INCREASES USE OF NATURAL FAUNA ABOVE THE HUNTING AND GATHERING LEVEL.

characteristic of pastoral peoples. Among the Tungus, considerably more moving is necessary, especially in the winter, when moss is the only food for reindeer. During the summer the people often move from the taiga (the great northern forest) up to the tundra along the Arctic coast, where there is an abundance of grass for the reindeer. Although summer is the time of abundance, during which the deer fatten up for the ordeal of winter, the mosquitoes are so thick that sometimes the reindeer herds stampede, and smokey fires must be built much of the time to save both the people and their animals. Sometimes even wild reindeer will come and join the domestic pack to escape the mosquitoes; and at other times they will do so to escape the wolves, against which they have little defense. Other attractions for the capture of reindeer are salt licks and even human urine, because the deer are starved for salt.[6]

In the hard winter months, the deer must uncover moss by kicking away the snow or breaking through it with their antlers. After 3 or 4 days the herd packs the snow so hard they can no longer dig through it, so the herders must pack their deerskin tents and move. Tremendous amounts of territory are needed for the pasturage of reindeer, estimated at from 1 to 4 square miles per animal.

SOCIAL ORGANIZATION   The social structure in some ways resembles that of the hunting-and-gathering peoples mentioned in Chapter Five. The groups must break up into small bands of five or six families during the time of constant travel, although they gather in larger numbers during the summer months. Lineage and clan are more important among these herders than is usual among hunters because there is important wealth in the form of animals to be inherited and because raids and skirmishes occasionally call for large-scale cooperative groups of fighters. The Tungus are divided into a number of clans, which trace their descent through the male line and usually have tutelary spirits. Members of clans marry into other clans, but always of the same tribe, which can be thought of as a people ranging the same territory and speaking the same dialect. Marriage of a man to his mother's brother's daughter is the preferred pattern. She is close enough to help preserve kinship loyalties but belongs to the clan of her mother, not to that of the young man she will marry. In the case of Lapps, Tungus, and Samoyeds, women have a fair measure of equality. The man's family pays a bride price (*turi*) of deer for a wife, but the woman's family also contributes a number of deer and some utensils, which constitute her dowry and continue to be considered her property. Marriages

---

[6]Ibid., p. 355.

are arranged by the two families in Tungus society, but in Lapp society Scandinavian ideas of free marriage are now more common. Polygyny is not practiced by the Lapps and is rare among the Tungus.

Some of the same types of mutual giving that were noted among the Eskimo are also in evidence among the Tungus—a necessity for people whose way of life is precarious. Although reindeer are thought of as the property of particular families, there are times when epidemics, cold, or wolves wipe out large numbers of animals. In such cases the bands get together in the summertime and redistribute herds so that none will have to go hungry. There are also winter storehouses, elevated log huts, containing stores of food, tent hides, clothing, and utensils, and anyone in need can use the supplies of his own tribe, but he is expected to leave a piece of wood with signs on it indicating his debt to the group.[7]

THE WORLD VIEW   The very word "shaman" is of Tungusic origin and refers to the magico-religious practictioner who cures the sick, communicates with the spirits, and divines the future, usually by being himself possessed of a spirit. Most shamanistic peoples also believe in animal spirits, and such is the case with the Tungus. One of their reindeer is set aside as sacred and is not ridden or worked. It carries the soul to the land of the dead and is intermediary between man and the spirits.[8] Deer are sacrificed at marriage ceremonies and on other important occasions. The ceremonial importance of the reindeer finds its parallel in the thinking of many other pastoral peoples about the animal of greatest importance to them.

The Lapps have been Christianized for many years, but their old ways also lent great ceremonial importance to the reindeer. Some of their mythology was undoubtedly influenced by Nordic myth, especially Tirms, the god of thunder, who seems to be the Lapp version of the Nordic Thor. In other respects, their view of the spirit world conformed fairly well to the shamanism of Siberia. Each household had a drum that the father could beat for the purpose of learning truth from the spirits. A brass object was placed on the drum skin, and its path across the drum was read by the father to find the auspicious time for moving herds. If his talent should prove insufficient, he could turn to the shaman (*noaidde*), who could drum until he fell into a frenzied trance and his soul went to the *saivo* country to gain knowledge from the spirits. There were also strange-shaped stones that had sacred power, called *seides*, in the mountains, and sacrifices were made before them for the increase of reindeer.

[7]Ibid., pp. 358–359.
[8]Ibid., p. 366.

As was noted among the Washo, the bear contained unusual spiritual force. The bear ceremony was at one time almost as important as the famous bear ceremony among the Ainu of Japan, and it has been noted in all the circumpolar cultures. The bear spirit was so powerful that the Lapps did not mention it in their own tongue but always used Norse words to describe it. When men killed a bear, they had to be sprinkled with blood-red juice from alder bark to neutralize the dangerous power; even the reindeer that pulled the sled that brought the slain bear back to camp was rendered sacred, and for a whole year no woman could ride on the sled.[9] The Lapps also had an underworld, conceived of as a happy land of the dead, but, paradoxically, they were afraid of ghosts and monsters called *stalo*. They shared with many circumpolar people the idea of a great pole running through the world, linking it with the heavens and with the underworld. In their animal-spirit beliefs they differed little from many of the hunting-and-gathering peoples we have studied but like all pastoralists found a special ceremonial significance in their own chosen animal.

TUAREG: BLUE MEN OF THE SAHARA

The French, who long administered Algeria and Morocco, refer to the Tuareg as "les hommes bleus," from the blue robes and blue veils the men wear and because the indigo dye of the clothing rubs off, giving even the men themselves a blue color. Lower classes may wear white, but noblemen are certain to be dressed in blue and to wear the veil high over the bridge of the nose, with turban pulled down low over the forehead, so that the eyes peer out through only a narrow slit in the blue. The nobles also wear a long two-edged sword with cruciform hilt, a spear, an antelope-skin shield, and a dagger hidden under the robes, attached to the left forearm by a leather strap. "The overall impression given by one of the fully armed warriors is almost awesome," says Robert Murphy, who spent a year with them in 1959-1960.[10]

The Tuareg are essentially camel herders and in the old days were warriors and raiders, living in many parts of the Sahara Desert. A majority of them now live in the greener regions of the Sudan, but they are a numerous people, approximately 250,000, so that even the minority still living in the desert constitute 15,000 or 20,000 people. The desert is largely what geographers call "reg" (rock and pebble) or mountain and "balsan" (barren plateaus inter-

[9]Birket-Smith, op. cit., pp. 101–102.
[10]Robert F. Murphy, "Social Distance and the Veil," *American Anthropologist*, vol. 66, pt. 1, pp. 1257–1273, December 1964.

Mounted Tuareg noblemen, in blue veils
and blue robes. Once raiders but now
leaders of caravans, the haughty Tuareg
dominate their part of the Sahara.

spersed with eroded hills). In southeastern Algeria is the Grand Erg Oriental (the Great Eastern Sand Desert), with the shifting dunes that exist in the popular stereotype of the Sahara but constitute only 5 or 6 percent of the total desert area. At the south of Algeria, where the present boundary line wedges down into Mali, are the Ahaggar Mountains—low mountains that gather enough of the sparse rain of the Sahara to have their periods of greenery and a few constant sources of water. Far to the east, at the southern extreme of Libya, is the Tibesti Massif, which has peaks rising to 11,000 feet and is the only place of extensive greenery in that part of the desert. There is more concentration of the blue men around these areas than elsewhere, especially in the Ahaggar region, for further out in the desert it is sometimes over 100 miles from one tree to the next. Nevertheless, the Tuareg cross these deserts and have been doing so for hundreds of years.

LIVELIHOOD AND TECHNOLOGY   The Tuareg are thought of first of all as the leaders of caravans, taking goods from south to north across the Sahara. Since ancient times they have brought goods from the Sudan—gold dust, ivory, peacock feathers, and slaves—to the Mediterranean coast, exchanging them for silk, sugar, and European sword blades.[11] From the Ahaggars they obtain salt that is taken down to Nigeria or even as far northward as Marrakesh near the Atlantic coast of Morocco. In the old days they robbed rival caravans or charged them for protection. The nobility of the Tuareg in particular thought it lowly and demeaning to engage in any kind of work except that of the sword.

As was mentioned in Chapter Three, camels are extremely well adapted to the desert but are ill-tempered animals, groaning and balking as they are being loaded for a journey. The camel mares are much more productive than the reindeer of the Tungus, giving 5 to 9 pints of milk per day, but they will not allow themselves to be milked unless their foals are nearby. If a foal dies, its hide must be stuffed and set up beside the mother before she can be milked.[12] Some Asiatic pastoralists do the same with cows, although it is not as much of a necessity. Tending the camel herds is exclusively men's work, but the milking is done by the women.

The camels are the animals with status, and Tuareg poetry is mainly about either war, love, or camels. Nevertheless, goats, and to a lesser degree sheep, are more important for the majority of the people. Women tend the goats and sheep and make butter and occasionally cheese from their milk. Since a Tuareg hesitates to kill a camel (a few of the tribes even make

[11]Birket-Smith, op. cit., p. 148.
[12]Ibid., p. 145.

camel meat taboo), goats are more important for meat. A certain amount of hunting is done in the Ahaggar region, where wild desert sheep are found. Sometimes there are great swarms of locusts, which are eaten by the Tuareg. Other kinds of food are looked upon with disdain, and only the slaves eat fish, birds or bird eggs, or the snakes and lizards that are quite abundant.

Although the Tuareg are mainly pastoralists, a little hoe cultivation is practiced in oases; such work is done by lower classes or slaves, however, not by the Tuareg themselves. There is also a low caste of smiths, greatly despised, but doing the leather work, working iron obtained in trade, making saddles and harness, carving wood, and sometimes working as barbers.

SOCIAL ORGANIZATION   The Tuareg do not make up a nation in any sense of the word, and they have often fought with one another; nevertheless, there is a bond of unity between them, with similar language, dress, and appearance throughout their extensive domains. Their highest effective level of organization is a confederation or alliance of tribes in some areas. Next in descending order is the tribe, with a chief of very limited power, then the subtribe, and finally the *irriwan*, consisting of as many as fifty households that have rights to a particular water well.[13] All groups are supposedly based on a kinship principle, although no actual tracing is possible beyond the level of subtribe.

As has already become apparent from the discussion of the work that is done, the society is highly class structured. The nobles are the *imjaren*, who demand fealty and various taxes and services from their vassals, the *imrad*. Far below the *imrad* in rank are the *iklan* (slaves), who act as servants to both the other classes. Koranic ideas regarding the treatment of servants do apply, however, and it is possible for a mistreated slave to insist on being sold to another master who will treat him better. In recent years the institution of slavery has declined greatly and so has the position of the nobles. The noble class in the old days was maintained to a great extent by warring and raiding. Extended periods of peace are often damaging to nonworking noble classes, and such is the case among the Tuareg, even though the social distinctions remain as strong as ever.

The Tuareg are unique among Muslims not only in having the men rather than the women wear the veil but in the generally high status given women. The majority of the tribes also defy what is the general rule among pastoralists by tracing descent through the mother's line rather than the

[13]Murphy, op. cit., p. 1261.

father's and being just as likely to settle near the wife's parental household as near the husband's. They were originally a Mediterranean people who followed the practice of tracing descent through the mother's line (mother right), and some of their customs must be survivals of a system that disappeared long ago in the Mediterranean region.[14] Women have considerable choice in whom they may marry, have equality in divorce, and may even visit on friendly terms with other men, provided they do not commit adultery. "Man-friends and woman-friends are for the eye and the heart, not for the couch," according to their proverb.[15] Even such a degree of familiarity between the sexes is horrifying to more conventional Muslims from Arabia, as are the unveiled women and veiled men.

Although the marriage system is said to be more-or-less free, there is a great preference for marrying cousins. As with the Bedouin Arabs, it is permissible to marry the father's brother's daughter (a parallel cousin), rather than marrying mother's brother's daughter, the more usual custom. The Tuareg custom may intensify kinship loyalty and keep herds and water rights in the family, but it fails to cement alliances with other families—a usual function of marriage. The close marriages combine curiously with the practice of considerable avoidance of parents-in-law. The parents-in-law can be approached, but always with great respect and restraint and with the veil worn high; such familiarity as having a meal with them must be avoided. Often, however, the parents-in-law are also aunts and uncles or cousins once removed, who otherwise would not call for so much social restraint.

The Tuareg nobles are a haughty and arrogant people. Murphy attributes the wearing of the veil partly to this characteristic, for it helps greatly to obscure one's feelings and to maintain social distance. The face is veiled most completely around important people or around those very relatives who must be partially avoided. Slaves do not wear veils and neither do boys before the age of puberty, indicating that they are a mark of status. Murphy also contends that the veil, in some respects, belongs to the realm of the sacred. The only adult men of noble birth who may discard the veil entirely are the hajjis—those who have made their pilgrimage to Mecca—but important chiefs with only secular status would never discard it unless they were also hajjis.

THE WORLD VIEW   The Tuareg are Muslims and as such believe in Allah and his prophet, in religious prayers, pilgrimages, and a heaven to come,

[14]Birket-Smith, op. cit., p. 150.
[15]Ibid., p. 152.

and ostensibly in only one God. They are, however, as baffling in their religion as in many aspects of their social system and their dress. Murphy says of them:

> The Tuareg, like their neighbors on all sides, are Moslems. They are noted, however, as infamous and unregenerate backsliders who observe neither proper law nor custom, who misperform the ritual postures in prayer, fail to make ablutions, eat and drink during the fasting days of Ramadan, and who have few of the wise and holy in their ranks. Despite the best Tuareg efforts to simulate orthodoxy in the presence of their censorious neighbors, these charges are substantially true.[16]

A word must be said in their defense, however. Fight as they will, they will not poison water wells or destroy date palms of their enemy, and they are not abusive toward women or slaves. They have an arrogance about them that is unnerving to most observers, but along with it goes a certain code of chivalry.

There are underlying beliefs that are not purely Muslim and that might predate their conversion to Islam. The desert is filled with hostile spirits that must be avoided, and there are spirits in certain trees; many kinds of amulets are used to ward off evil. Such ideas, though, could be found almost anywhere, even among Arabic Muslims, so they reveal little about the original beliefs of the Tuareg people. The Arabs claim the word "Tuareg" derived from *terek*, meaning deserter, but the evidence is that the Tuareg have not deserted Islam to the extent of adopting other religious views or even of allowing older ones to survive in any vigorous form.

PASTORALISTS
OF EAST AFRICA

The East African plateau is one of the world's major regions of pastoralism. The Jie, Dodoth, Turkana, Bunyoro, Barabaig, and the better-known Masai are among the pastoral groups. In a few cases, as among the Baganda and Banyankole of Uganda, pastoralists have achieved a master to vassal relationship with some of the horticultural peoples of the area, thus establishing organized kingdoms with more steady food supply and greater cultural stability than exists among most of the pastoralists. Most of the cattle-herding peoples live in the relatively cool highlands, where forests are thin and do not harbor the deadly tsetse fly. The lands of the Masai cover the central part of southern Kenya and

[16]Murphy, op. cit. Reproduced by permission of the American Anthropological Association from *American Anthropologist*, 66:1262.

northern Uganda, rising from the plateau to the slopes of Mount Kenya and Kilimanjaro and intersected by Africa's Great Rift Valley. Just below them, on the southern shores of Lake Eyasi are the Barabaig, a similar pastoral people, with whom the Masai fought frequently in the late nineteenth century in an attempt to expand their territory and pasturage. Since there are periods of drought and men desire very large herds, much grazing land is needed.

CATTLE AS A WAY OF LIFE: PRODUCTION   The pastoral tribes of East Africa belong to what is called the "cattle complex," characterized by extensive ceremonial use of cattle and deep emotional attachment to them.[17] Cattle are the basis of economic and emotional security; their number and quality are a measure of a man's prestige; they are the medium of payment of bride wealth and dowry and hence are indispensable to marriage; their butter has ritual value for anointing the triumphant warrior and the new bride; the infant is born on a cowhide bed, and when he dies, he will be borne away on a cowhide bier. Among the Barabaig at least, the infant's first food will be cow's milk, for they believe that the first few days' supply of mother's milk is contaminated. Throughout life, the cattle herder will think of milk, and next to milk, cattle blood, as the best food, the staff of life. Bulls are stabbed in the jugular vein from time to time to obtain the blood, which is drunk straight or mixed with milk or butter. Cattle have other uses as well. Cow dung is mixed with mud for the plaster of the walls of huts, and cow urine is used for cleaning bowls and as a disinfectant for wounds.

Different tribes build their houses in different patterns, but always close to the cattle. In the case of the Barabaig, the houses are figure-eight shaped, with one part of the house for the people and the other part for young animals. A small hut is built in the middle of the cattle kraal for the young bride, where she spends the first 3 days of marriage learning to recognize the cattle of her husband's family. The cattle are generally humpbacked zebu, mainly of mixed color, but those of solid color are the most highly prized and of the greatest ritual value.

The cattle complex takes its toll of the human population. Many of the cattle are carriers of tuberculosis, which is spread to the people, and cattle hides contain the spores of anthrax, a nearly always fatal disease. At night ticks spread from the cattle to the people, often giving them relapsing fever, which can be fatal to children or to any individual in weakened

[17]George J. Klima, *The Barabaig, East African Cattle Herders*, Holt, Rinehart and Winston, Inc., New York, 1970, pp. 4–6.

Masai at a cattle market at Naberera
Wells, Tanzania. Cattle are the main
focus of economic and ceremonial life
for the Masai and many other East
African pastoralists.

condition.[18] Other health problems not connected with cattle also exist. Malaria and veneral disease are common, and the latter often makes women sterile. When a woman is pregnant, she is spoken of as "one with enemy," implying that the fetus within her can cause her death, and, indeed, the incidence of death at childbirth is very high. When the child is born, the preference for a diet of cow's milk the first few days helps to raise the incidence of infant mortality. Nevertheless, there seems to be "a survival of the fit." Both the Masai and the Barabaig are described as strong, muscular people of tall stature and of Nilotic type, with straight, high-bridged noses and commanding appearance.

Besides cattle, most of the East African pastoralists raise sheep and goats, but neither of the latter are of the same importance as the cattle. A man would be ridiculed and considered of very low character if he were to kill one of his cattle to eat, but the other animals are slaughtered. Cattle are eaten only on the most important ceremonial occasions or if they get sick and die.

SOCIAL ORGANIZATION   The Masai and other pastoral peoples have very little by way of tribal organization. The people are patrilineal, identifying themselves as members of particular lineages and recognizing a number of other lineages as part of the clan. A few of the Masai clans have special duties. From one of them the *laibond* is chosen, a supreme priest with religious and ceremonial duties toward all the people. The *laibond* is always consulted before a major raid because he is believed able to divine the future and also to intercede on behalf of the people with the Masai god, En-Gai.[19]

The Barabaig, likewise, have nothing that can be called an organized state. The prestigious members of lineages and the elders can call interclan moots with the power to sit in judgment on individual cases. The most common disputes of a civil nature are over cattle rights; the most common criminal cases are accusations of sorcery.[20] Other members gain special prestige by killing "enemies of the people"—a lion, elephant, or rhino, or, until recent years, a member of one of the horticultural tribes near the Barabaig territory. For his service the killer (*ghadyirochand*) is given special insignia and can wear a leather cap with a strip of brass shaped like a lion's tail. Killing an enemy is the ceremonial equivalent for a man to a woman's

[18]Ibid., pp. 45–47.
[19]Forde, op. cit., p. 301.
[20]Klima, op. cit., pp. 79–85.

giving birth, so men have to observe the same taboos, taking a period for rest and convalescence and sometimes adorning themselves with women's ornaments.[21]

Although a degree of organization is recognized at the clan level and clans can on occasion unite for action, there are many respects in which organization goes little beyond the household level. Because room for cattle is needed, neighborhoods are widely dispersed. The household is surrounded by a thornbush fence 8 to 10 feet high; one can enter only after shouting for permission to do so. If permission is withheld, one must retreat quickly for fear of being accused of attempted sorcery or some other ill intent. In Jie households, the entrance to the house is a low gateway through which a person must crawl, exposing himself to danger if he is unwanted. The households are frequently polygynous, often with a separate hut for the senior wife and in some tribes for each wife. Sometimes the wives live in harmony, and sometimes severe rivalries break out among them, most frequently over whose son will receive the larger inheritance or how many cattle are available to daughters for dowry. The dowry provided by the bride is often considered hers to pass along eventually to her own children, so that, especially among the Barabaig, daughters become a drain on the household cattle wealth. In many other tribes the bride price is higher than dowry and daughters are an economic asset.

In most of the pastoral tribes the women are considerably subordinated. Not only is descent traced through the male line, but the newly married couple is expected to be virilocal, that is, to live in the close vicinity of the man's father. The Barabaig provide a partial exception to the rule of male dominance in that their women can hold a moot to protest treatment of any women of the clan, and the judgment of the women's moot is generally respected.

AGE SETS   A special feature of social organization among some of the East African pastoral tribes is that of the age set. Age sets are found among many other peoples, but there are a few cases in East Africa where they are more important than elsewhere. Among the Masai and the Barabaig, young men are not expected to marry at an early age because their age group has its military duties to perform and these duties will interfere with marriage. Consequently, women are about thirteen to fifteen years of age at marriage, and men marry at least ten years later, with many years of premarital affairs before settling down to a permanent mate or mates.

[21]Ibid., p. 59.

Circumcision of boys and clitoridectomy of girls are both considered necessary for maturity. In Barabaig society, the girls' ceremonies are private and secret, but the boys' circumcision ceremony is an occasion for general rejoicing and drinking of honey beer. In neither case, however, do children constitute a unified age set as they do among the Masai. For the Masai the ceremonial for boys is much more important and determines which ones will enter military service at the same time, become eligible for marriage at the same time, and eventually be recognized as elders at the same time. The age sets cut across lineage lines and give a sense of solidarity that would otherwise be lacking in the society.

THE WORLD VIEW   The cattle herders tend to see themselves as superiors relative to the gardening people around them. In many East African societies, herders also practice horticulture, but this has been true only in recent years among the Barabaig and is still looked upon with contempt by the Masai. In parts of Uganda, pastoralists have made of themselves an upper caste, living in economic symbiosis with horticultural people, but always looking down upon them and observing rules of social avoidance. Even among the Masai and Barabaig, there is a slight tendency toward caste exclusiveness. The workers in leather and iron form separate castes within the societies and must marry within their own clans, since no one else would lower himself sufficiently to marry one. It seems likely that these haughty attitudes toward craftsmanship have slowed down the development of ironmongery among many of the peoples of East Africa.

It is very common for people who place great emphasis on lineage also to reverence ancestors and give them ritual respect. Such is particularly the case for important ancestors, whose cattle, wives, and children were many and who lived long years on the earth and achieved honors as hunters and warriors. Such men are ceremonially honored at death, even with the sacrifice of an ox. In Barabaig society a large funeral mound is built, covered with grass sod, and the people gather round it and sing songs to their ancestral spirits and their god. With many of the pastoral peoples, there is an important tribal god, regarded as superior to all others. For people who die young or who are otherwise unimportant, the funeral is quite different. A ritual is performed, but only a goat is sacrificed, and the body is taken out into the wilderness to be eaten by hyenas rather than buried. The spirit will not be remembered as a significant ancestor.

Since much of the East African highlands is an area of intermittent monsoon and drought, there is ritual magic for bringing rain, and certain clans are regarded as especially good at rainmaking. Magic for protection of the herds is very important, and there is magic for ensuring success on raids and, as with all such people, magic for keeping people well and for safe delivery of babies. In these forms of control over the unseen forces, the high priest of the Masai is the ultimate power, and his services resemble those of the Yoruba Alafin of Oyo and those performed in many more highly organized societies. Several, but not all, pastoral tribes have a spiritual leader of this type.

SONS OF THE GREAT KHAN

As we have seen, many of the pastoralists of East Africa and even those of the Sahara have been raiders and sometimes conquerors, reaching outward for new lands for their cattle and sometimes for the products of horticultural peoples. Their ready mobility undoubtedly has a bearing on their predatory nature, as has the fact that the products of pastoralism are barely sufficient, requiring either trading or raiding for supplementation. Many pastoral peoples also have an aggressive cult of manhood, with fully armed warriors equipped to protect cattle herds and also ready for the offensive. Not all pastoralists have been successful at territorial expansion, though, and Marshall D. Sahlins suggests this variable: the degree to which the segmentary lineages, into which most pastoral nomads are divided, can be brought together to be mutually supporting in an emergency.[22] Sahlins compares the African Dinka and the Nuer, both pastoralists, but with different organizational possibilities, so that the Nuer have been able to expand their territories at the expense of the Dinka. (See Chapter Eleven for further discussion of lineages.)

Certainly, for the most famous pastoralists of history, the Mongols, a number of factors must have combined to create the greatest conquering armies of history, and one of these factors was the ability sometimes to form cohesive alliances. Other factors are the consequence of certain types of pastoral nomadism combined with a proper historical and geographical setting and an ingenious leader who saw the possibilities for empire building.

The land of the Mongols is an intemperate land, with intense summer heat and bitter cold, only thinly populated to this day; but it was here that Temujin, best known to history by the name Genghis Khan or the epithet the Scourge of God, was born in 1162. Although he was the first son of the

[22]Marshall D. Sahlins, "The Segmentary Lineage: An Organization of Predatory Expansion," *American Anthropologist,* vol. 63, pp. 322–343, April 1961.

The Great Khan in regal splendor discussing a truce with Christian crusaders. No other pastoralists became such great empire builders as the Mongols.

leader of one of the Mongol tribes, he had a struggle for survival in his early days because of jealousies between the tribes. Eventually he triumphed over his enemies, and, rather than seek divisive vengeance, he worked to unite and train the Mongol hordes into effective military forces.[23] Eventually they were to spread their power through all of central Asia and beyond— down into Persia and Turkey, where they menaced Islam, and throughout Russia and into the borders of Poland and Hungary, menacing Christendom and leaving much of Russia vassal to the khans until the victories of Ivan the Terrible. To the east, they descended into China, conquering the entire land and setting up a dynasty whose principle monarch, Kublai Khan,

[23]Harold Lamb, *Genghis Khan: Emperor of All Men*, Garden City Publishing Company, Inc., New York, 1927.

grandson of Genghis Khan, would be characterized by Marco Polo as the greatest emperor ever to have ruled or ever likely to rule. Two centuries later, a descendant of Genghis Khan, Tamerlane, united much of the empire again, and in the 1500s one of his descendants, Baber, established the Mogul Dynasty of India.

MILITARY TECHNOLOGY   At the height of their conquests, the armies of Genghis Khan killed and destroyed as few armies in history have, laying waste whole cities if any resistance was shown and putting their entire populations to the sword. Thus terrorism was used effectively along with extreme mobility, training, and weaponry to turn the Mongol hordes into a force dreaded by all of Europe and Asia. At their height, their fighting forces probably numbered no more than 130,000, and all of Mongolia could hardly have had more than 1,500,000 people. Besides being a conqueror, Genghis Khan was a giver of laws, the fifth of which states, "It is forbidden to ever make peace with a monarch, a prince, or a people who have not submitted." In the seventeenth law it is stated, "Men should occupy themselves only with hunting and war."[24]

In the centuries since the days of the Great Khan, many have attempted to duplicate his deeds, and legends have grown about him and his allies. In what was formerly called Russian Turkestan, members of the Great Horde, the Kazakhs, claim that their ancestors were among his first followers and preferred people. Throughout much of central Asia other nomadic peoples claim to be his descendants, and their way of life in some respects resembles that of the Mongols before the coming of the Great Khan. One of the tribes that has been studied is that of the Ordos Mongols of Inner Mongolia, north of the Great Wall of China.

PRODUCTION   The Ordos Mongols are similar to large numbers of semi-nomadic peoples of central Asia.[25] Those who are close to agricultural lands often practice a certain amount of agriculture now, but those in lands too arid for farming still depend largely or entirely on their animals. In the case of the Ordos Mongols, the ones close to the Yellow River are partly agrarian or depend heavily on sheep and goats rather than on horses and cattle. At greater distances beyond the Great Wall, the proportion of cattle

[24]Lamb, op. cit., pp. 201–203.
[25]Lawrence Krader, *Social Organization of the Mongol-Turkic Pastoral Nomads,* Indiana University Publications, Uralic and Altaic Series, vol. 20, published by Mouton and Co., The Hague, 1963, pp. 13–56.

and horses increases, although sheep and goats are always important. In the days of conquest, horses had the greatest importance of all animals; in later years cattle have become more of a medium of exchange and of payment for bride price and for debts and fines.

According to their own tradition, the Ordos Mongols moved southward into their present domains under the leadership of one of the later chieftains, Dayan Khan, who temporarily reunited the Mongols. He is said to have called the Ordos the guardians of the Master (Genghis Khan), and they consider themselves to have played that role. There is a legend among the Ordos Mongols that the tomb of Genghis Khan is in their territory.

TRANSFORMATION OF SOCIAL ORGANIZATION   Hsiao Ta-heng, a Chinese traveler of the sixteenth century, described the Mongol social system as it existed at that time. The Mongols were linked together into a confederacy composed of a large number of clans, each headed by a noble bearing the title of *taiji*. The *taijis* had the function of settling disputes within their realms, and a council of all the *taijis* could be held to settle disputes between *taijis* or clans, thus giving the system more unity than is found among many pastoralists. The numbers of herds and tents differed greatly, so that some people had more wealth and rank than others, even within the same clan. There is a similarity to the Northwest Coast Indians in the fact that all members of a clan were considered kinsmen and yet the leaders were nobles and the others commoners. At a lower organizational level, the family itself had great importance as a legal entity, and member could not testify against member.

With the rise to power of the Manchu Dynasty in the seventeenth century, certain of the Ordos submitted to Manchu rule and persuaded others to do likewise. They were given a fairly independent position in outward respects but became subject to Manchu manipulation. The old clans were united into seven banners, which were organized into a left wing and a right wing. The two wings became territorial districts, and the division into territories restricted the amount of nomadism that had previously been carried on. It should be mentioned that nomadism among pastoralists is never a matter of unrestricted wandering but often follows a yearly route (the transhumance mentioned previously). In the older days, the nomadic circuits were more extended, though, than after the Manchu period. The other change that helped the Manchus to establish more control over their northern territories was that they were able to influence the choice of the head of the Ordos confederacy.

At present the Ordos occupy the same territories as they did centuries ago. More of them have taken to agriculture than previously, but the majority still tend their herds. In the long years of Manchu rule, the position of the clans gradually declined. In the old days, the marriage system demanded alliances between clans by insisting on marriage outside the clan. Even in those days, though, cousin marriages were possible, since a man's mother was of a different clan from his own. Today the only rule against an incestuous marriage bars marriage to a person of the same last name, which, in effect, makes marriage to any cousin except the father's brother's children legal and possibly preferred.

The residence system is patrilocal, the wife moving into her husband's father's household. Descent is traced through the male line. As seems logical in such a case, a high payment of bride wealth is made by the husband's family in the recognition that the woman and her children will belong to their group. There is apparently no corresponding dowry payment. The result is that, although the woman is fairly paid for, she is placed in a position of little power and prestige compared to the Barabaig woman who brought a considerable dowry with her. Since not all men can pay the price of a bride, it is possible to earn a bride by working for her family, a custom encountered frequently and referred to as "suitor service." In the 1930s bride wealth consisted of ten horses and eight head of cattle, besides a few sheep and goats and a bridal headdress with silver and pearls.

Marriages are arranged at a tender age and are actually to be carried out much later, but the custom assures the families that selection will be theirs and not simply the choice of young people anxious to be wed. If an unwed girl becomes pregnant, it is possible to conduct a wedding ceremony in which she marries a prayer rug and thus provides the family name of its owner for the otherwise illegitimate child.[26]

THE WORLD VIEW   Although Genghis Khan and his immediate followers contacted many Christians and Muslims and took an interest in their ideas, the Ordos Mongols have been more strongly influenced by Buddhism and have been practicing Buddhists since the seventeenth century. One of the consequences is the existence of lamaseries in their country and a large number of Buddhist monks pledged to a life of celibacy. Although a shortage of males is by no means the only reason for the existence of polygyny, the prevalence of monasticism may have made polygyny a little more common than in the past.

[26]Ibid., p. 41.

Religions seldom exist in pure form, and Buddhism among the Ordos is mixed with other religious forms. The new bride must do obeisance to the domestic spirits of her husband's household, for example. There are also a few of the Ordos, living in the vicinity of Irkutsk, who are believed to have been influenced by Christians. They are ruled entirely by their priests and have a type of confession reminiscent of Christianity. Otherwise there is little outward evidence of their having been influenced by Christianity, unless, as is sometimes claimed, the name "Irkut" comes from the Greek word *arkhon* ("priest").[27]

Although the Ordos and many other Mongol people were converted to Buddhism, it is doubtful whether religion was the main reason why they eventually changed into a peaceful people. The Kazakhs, for example, who were converted to Islam, have also become pacified over the centuries. As military organization improved in other armies, the organization and mobility of the pastoralists began to count for less.[28] Probably even more important is the fact that the Inner Mongols were eventually to be absorbed by Chinese control, the Outer Mongols to become a state dominated by Russia, and the Kazakhs a Russianized people, forced to abandon their old independence and nearly all their nomadism.

SUMMARY In summary, it is clear that many of the pastoralists have been among the world's most colorful people. They have at times conquered and destroyed and later built empires of their own, but usually empires of short duration. Pastoralism, mainly because of the nomadism or seminomadism that it requires, does not accumulate the buildings, tools, inventions, and centers of government and exchange that are required for urban civilization. In this respect pastoralism can be thought of as a side branch on the way to the development of technological civilizations. Only under heavy economic pressures have pastoral nomads changed their ways into those of agriculturalists. They tend to be proud, independent people, placing great value in their animals and their general way of life and changing only with great difficulty.

Pastoralists have traded with settled agriculturalists throughout history, and often they have been a menace as raiders. There are a number of instances in which pastoral peoples have subdued gardening peoples and

[27]Ibid., pp. 42–44.
[28]Ralph Linton, *The Tree of Culture*, Vintage Books, Random House, Inc., New York, 1955, pp. 82–83.

set up castelike states, very durable and efficient means of exploitation. In the most dramatic instances, pastoral nomads have conquered the settled peoples around them, as in the case of Genghis Khan, who built the largest empire ever to have existed. Such empires, however, tend to wither away rather quickly. Part of the reason may be that the clan organizations of the conquering people are hard to expand to the extent necessary to sustain polyglot empires. As Ralph Linton has pointed out, the majority of the conquering peoples of Asia have eventually been absorbed by the very cultural systems they have conquered. The Mongols who went to rule China became Chinese, the invaders of Persia and Turkey became Persians and Turks, and the descendants of the Moguls became part of India. Their numbers were never sufficient to administer without the help of conquered vassals, and their military advantage was of little help in the long task of ruling a foreign people.

The pastoral peoples have certain cultural traits in common. Not only do they attend their animals with great care for economic reasons, but their favored animals have great ritual and social value for such purposes as bride price, dowry, and even for sacrifice. With rare exception pastoral peoples are grouped into lineages or clans, tracing their descent through the male line. Although the majority of pastoral men are rather overbearing toward women, this is not true of the reindeer herders or of the Tungus or Barabaig. With the exception of the reindeer people, the pastoralists have marked social class with haughty aristocracies. Pastoral peoples have continued mainly in parts of the world that are submarginal for farming, requiring vast amounts of land for support of cattle or other animals. This fact compels the nomadism that has made pastoralists extremely mobile as fighters but has generally left them even slightly less able than certain horticultural peoples to build urban civilizations.

PASTORALISM

BASIC PATTERN   POSSIBLE DEVELOPMENTS

TECHNOLOGY AND POSSESSIONS

WEALTH CALCULATED IN ANIMALS-
MORE POSSESSIONS THAN HUNTERS-
LIMITED BY NOMADISM OR
TRANSHUMANCE.

GAIN GOODS BY TRADE OR PLUNDER
PERMANENT CENTERS-AGRICULTURE TO
SUPPLEMENT FOOD SUPPLY

SOCIAL ORGANIZATION

NONEQUALITARIAN LINEAGES- SOME TIMES
ALLIANCES-SOMETIMES CEREMONIAL HIGH
PRIEST-LINEAGE CHIEFS.

POSSIBLE MILITARY POWER AND CONQUEST;
PERMANENT CASTELIKE STATES -
TEMPORARY EMPIRES.

WORLD VIEW

RITUAL VALUE OF ANIMALS - SHAMANISM-
MAGIC FOR CARE OF ANIMALS.

OFTEN CONTACT FOREIGN BELIEFS —
ISLAM, BUDDHISM, CHRISTIANITY-
MAJOR RELIGIONS MODIFIED BY OLD MYTHS
AND RITES.

1-72 Diane MacDermott

The peasant is like the horticulturist of Chapter Six in that he draws his livelihood from the soil. In most cases, he resembles the pastoralists of Chapter Seven in that he depends heavily on domesticated animals. In some ways, however, he is like neither of the others, because he belongs more clearly to a way of life that leads to modern, urban societies. For this reason he is being considered last in these discussions of preindustrial styles of life.

In anthropology a distinction is made between the primitive horticulture described in Chapter Six and the more advanced techniques of agriculture. In spite of its all-inclusive dictionary meaning, we will limit the word "agriculture" to include only well-irrigated fields or fields worked by animal-drawn plows. The ancient Incas, with their system of irrigation canals, had advanced beyond the level of primitive horticulture, and so had the Aztecs, the Egyptians, and the peoples of the Tigris-Euphrates, the Indus, and the Hwang Ho river valleys. The tomb art of Egypt and similar art work of Mesopotamia shows plows dating back to about 3000 B.C., in some cases pulled by cattle yoked by the horns.[1] At least that far back into history animal power was beginning to supplement human power and to increase the productivity of land.

Chapter Eight
Peasants
and Farmers

As plows improved, land no longer had to be abandoned when overrun by dense grasses that simple dibble sticks could not manage. In the fertile river valleys, better plowing methods were combined with water management, so that the muddy flow of the rivers could inundate the fields, adding fertility to the soil. Later, where plows became associated with rainfall agriculture rather than irrigation, as in the circum-Mediterranean civilizations and in medieval Europe, land had to be rested by some kind of fallow system; but even then there was no land abandonment, and usually the maximum period of fallowing was only a year or two. In Southeast Asia and in southern China rice culture was developed, intensifying animal use and irrigation and the constant working and reworking of the same soil. In all the irrigated lands it became possible for population to grow as never before and for cities and trade to flourish. In the rice lands of the East even more than in the wheat lands of the West, the land could now support incredible numbers of people; whole families could be sustained meagerly on a mere 2 to 4 acres of land. Everywhere the division of labor and specialization of occupations increased, especially in the cities that were fed by the agricultural surplus of the farms.

The way of life of the peasant and the farmer, obviously, would have to display great variability from West to East and over a period of time. Have there been any traits common among peasants throughout most of history? Ever since the dawn of recorded history, peasants have had to support the urban centers that have arisen. What is the relationship between the peasant culture and the urban culture? Are they separate, or do the two cultures blend together in a common meeting ground? Are there special beliefs, attitudes, and personality traits of peasants the world over? What are the variations in means of livelihood and in attitudes and beliefs that can be encountered in peasant societies? What are the steps from peasantry to the businesslike farm and the agricultural "factories in the field" of modern capitalistic and communistic countries? Have all peasant societies supported wide divisions of labor, status differences, and aristocracies and other social classes?

PEASANTRY
AS A WAY OF LIFE

Historically, peasants have been an object of both romance and derision.[2] A cult of the simple life, of the wholesome goodness of the land and its tillers, was part of the age of romanticism in English and western European literature, and the glorification of the peasant

Henry Hodges, *Technology in the Ancient World*, Alfred A. Knopf, Inc., New York, 1970, pp 87–88.
Most of the following discussion is based on Eric R. Wolf, *Peasants*, Prentice-Hall, Inc., Englewood Cliffs, N.J., 1966.

Upon the economic foundations of peasantry rose all the great civilizations of antiquity: Europe, Asia, Africa, and the New World.

continued in the writings of Leo Tolstoy of Russia. Others, from the age of aristocracies down to the times of modern capitalists, have looked with a certain contempt upon the peasant as tradition bound, unchanging, and so dull as to be unable to avoid easy exploitation—in the pitying phrase of the American poet Edwin Markham, "distorted and soul-quenched." Actually neither view has too much validity. Compared with the ways of life of hunters and gatherers, pastoralists, or primitive horticulturists, the peasant's way of life is much more stable and routine. The freedom to roam was sacrificed for a more steady food supply, but the inconstancies of nature and the good earth prevented that supply from being completely dependable. Moreover, it was necessary to support other classes from the product of the soil—craftsmen and merchants, officials and administrators, aristocrats and warriors and money lenders—who often took more than their share and left a threadbare life for the peasant. One guarantee remained, however: the peasant could not be exterminated, because he was the host on which all the others fed. Even early Russian communism, with its preference for the industrial workers over the peasant, was to learn that hard lesson. Although he may have been regarded as a beast of burden or a mere clod of the earth he tilled he became the basic producer of food from the time hunting and simple horticulture were abandoned until the recent development of massive, scientific, market-oriented agriculture. Upon the economic foundations of peasantry rose all the great civilizations of antiquity, East and West, Old World and New. Even to this day, peasants constitute the majority of mankind, and industrial society is still but a recent innovation, made possible only by long centuries of peasantry. Although their way of life may seem antiquated, peasants remain important. In the words of Eric Wolf:

> They are important contemporaneously, because they inhabit that ''underdeveloped'' part of the world whose continued presence constitutes both a threat and a responsibility for those countries which have thrown off the shackles of backwardness. While the industrial revolution has advanced with giant strides across the globe, the events of every day suggest that its ultimate success is not yet secure.[3]

The examples of peasantry to follow will demonstrate that their way of life is by no means uniform, and any attempt to treat it as such can lead to the failures of understanding that have characterized the foreign policies of the great powers in their dealings with the less industrialized parts of the world. Nevertheless, the peasants of the world are generally faced with many similar types of problems. Wolf sums up the production problems of the peasant as being fourfold: producing enough for a caloric minimum of food for himself and his family, enough for a replacement fund, for a ceremonial fund, and enough to somehow meet the demands imposed by the outsider.[4]

The need to produce a caloric minimum is so obvious as to require no elaboration. A replacement fund is a little more complex. Obviously, enough must be produced so that some can be left for seed for the following year. Cattle, sheep, goats, and chickens must also be replaced, and so must harness, plow, and other tools, as well as houses and storage huts. Some of the latter must be purchased on a competitive market. Even when all these needs are met, there are usually social requirements of peasant life, the "ceremonial fund." A certain extra amount must be produced to provide dowry for daughters of marriageable age or for bride price in some types of society. Calendrical celebrations must be observed, calling often for festivals put on by the village, sometimes accompanied by sacrifices. The observations of ceremony solidify social relations, give variety to the otherwise routine life, and help to unite the community with the sacred world in whatever way is deemed necessary, for peasants often see the fertility and

[3]Ibid., p. vii.
[4]Ibid., pp. 1–17.

productivity of the soil as a function of their own moral rectitude and ceremonial observance.

The problem of meeting the demands imposed by the outsider is the most difficult of the peasant's tasks. If he is unable to meet his ordinary replacement fund, he may have to borrow at usurious rates of interest. Usually the land is not his alone but is part of an estate to which he must pay rent either in money or in kind. Peasants, much more characteristically than the other types of food producers we have discussed, belong also to state systems. There are always governments to be coped with, demanding their taxes for the support of roads and public buildings, law enforcement, administrative officials, and armies and other demands of warfare. When the pressures of the outside become too great, the peasant must somehow cope with the problem either by increasing production or by limiting consumption. His position becomes precarious, and he dares try nothing new, because his present practices can barely support him. New products are risky. In more revolutionary modern times, there are instances of peasants abandoning old ways, reducing the ceremonial fund, or attempting new crops; but generally speaking, the peasant has been slow to innovate.

Peasant life is also characterized by points of view that are out of tune with the modern world's rush into rational production systems aimed at profit. Whereas the industrial worker becomes increasingly attuned to figuring his time in terms of money, such calculations are impossible for the peasant. The amount of time spent in plowing can no more be calculated in economic terms than can the amount of time spent by the mother nursing a baby or sitting up with a sick child. They are tasks that must be done for their own sake. Usually, too, the products of the peasant are in the form of perishable commodities that must be sold quickly. All goods reach the market simultaneously, so that prices are severely depressed just as the peasant is ready to sell, but he must buy his tools on a more controlled market. Although peasantry differs greatly the world over, there is a unity in problems and also a latent unity in resentments, resulting in occasional peasant uprisings of a shockingly bloody type.

Finally, in social organization, there are certain problems that must be met. Since peasantry lives generally outside the realm of hired labor, the occasional demands for more labor than the family can produce must be met in some other manner. Usually there is a kind of institutionalized village cooperation for such needs, in which one peasant is helped by others in the building of a barn or shed and will eventually be expected to reciprocate. Sometimes the problem is met by extending the family into a large cooperative group, as has been traditional in China. Such families, however, are probably characteristic only of systems in which it is possible for a family to expand onto new lands or where there are some means of utilizing large numbers of family members at different tasks.[5] In Java, where the crowding of agricultural land has reached heights attained nowhere else in the world, the family is a small, nuclear unit; no additional relatives can be employed efficiently, nor is there any possibility of acquiring new lands for such relatives. In such a case, new cooperative or hiring methods have to be worked out for getting additional amounts of work done.

In the following pages, we shall consider peasantry in southern India, in Java, and in Greece and see that common problems are met by different types of social organization and methods of production, but always there must be replacement funds, ceremonial funds, and rental funds. Always there is a closeness to the earth and to the small community, and always strong feelings exist as to the distinctions between peasantry and the outsiders.

A SOUTHERN INDIAN VILLAGE

India is one of the world's most heavily populated lands, with nearly 500 million people occupying a territory about one-third the size of the United States. The country is highly variable, with some of the wettest monsoonal terrain on earth, but with regions of severe water shortage in the northwest and in the southern plateau. There are the low, well-watered plains of the Ganges-Brahmaputra, close to the northern highlands that rise toward the towering Himalayas. To the south are two smaller mountain ranges, the Eastern and Western Ghats, rising to the central Deccan Plateau. Culturally the land is as variable as it is topographically and climatically. Although the great majority of the people of India are Hindus of one sect or another, its local gods, feast days, and sacred shrines differ widely, and so do its languages and dialects, its customs, levels of industrial development, its family and kinship systems, and its marriage systems. Yet the majority of Indians are peasants, living in thousands of villages, some of them quite shut off from the main currents of change that have been sweeping the country in the last decades. Such a village is Gopalpur, as described by Alan R. Beals in the 1960s.[6] The village lies close to Hyderabad in the central part of the Indian Peninsula.

[5]Ibid., pp. 65-72.
[6]Alan R. Beals, *Gopalpur: A South Indian Village*, Holt, Rinehart and Winston, Inc., New York, 1962.

The farmers of Gopalpur usually own 4 or 5 acres of good land, about the same amount of sandy land for planting millet, and part of an acre of rice land. They are plow agriculturalists, using a plow that now has a steel tip but otherwise has changed little if any for 3,000 years. Early in the spring the fields are fertilized with steer manure. The preparation of the land starts soon after *Ugadi*, the New Year's festival, in March or April. Leafy vegetables and chili, onion, and eggplant are planted in June, and sometimes peanuts, tobacco, or cotton. The farmers depend upon rainfall for most of their irrigation, but during the summer rains they try to collect enough water in their reservoirs to plant a small patch of rice. In the early fall they plant their major crop, sorghum millet, which will mature in the fall and winter months. Seasons in Gopalpur are a matter of wet and dry cycles, depending on the indraft of moist sea air toward central Asia during the months when temperatures rise in the interior and the outdraft of dry air from the interior during the time of Northern Hemisphere winter. Planting during the summer season, when rainfall is almost adequate, and harvesting during the dry period of winter keep both men and women busy, although at other times the farm work is mainly the work of the men.

The women prepare the meals, and if harvests are good, the meals are good. The women of the household grind the millet with a stone handmill. The meal usually includes beans and vegetables, as well as bread, and everything is well seasoned with chili. If the water buffalo is giving milk, clarified butter called *ghi* is made and poured generously over everything. The spices for which India was noted in medieval times are used today, and the food of even the poor peasants is far from bland.

Although the village is dependent mainly on agriculture, the agricultural techniques are poor and the productivity meager compared to the farmlands of China, Java, and Japan. Very little irrigation is used, although the underground water table is within 15 or 20 feet of the surface. A few trees are grown, but the potential for more fruit production is very great and poorly exploited. New types of millet and other grains could be introduced, as they have been in many parts of India, but the peasants have a well-founded dread of doing anything risky. By traditional methods they can hold on to life and food supply; if an attempt at something new should fail, as it sometimes has through insufficient knowledge of new techniques, it could spell disaster. Moreover, there are never funds left for experimentation with anything new. The men of Gopalpur must get their seed for planting from the wealthier men of the village, and at harvest time they generally return two sacks of grain for every one sack borrowed. The lenders are not happy to lend money for anything new and promising, since higher peasant productivity might lead to independence in financing.[7] The peasant must borrow at high prices to plant, but he sells his grain at much less than its true value, since he and all his neighbors harvest at the same time, when the market is glutted, and none have storage facilities to keep the grain from the rats or from spoilage. Even the government works against the peasant, controlling the price of grain in order to keep bread cheap enough so that the poor workers of the cities can have enough to eat. If the price of grain were to rise, there would be starvation among city workers; as long as the price is kept low, the already impoverished peasants must stand the cost, making the extremely low wages of industry compatible with urban survival. A few of the wealthier men of Gopalpur have been able to make changes because they have had the money to buy new fertilizers and better strains of seed. Perhaps the new techniques will eventually filter down to the poorest of the peasants, but such changes are slow in coming in as isolated a village as Gopalpur.

SOCIAL ORGANIZATION   In its political organization, Gopalpur has a type of village democracy, but in reality it is controlled by the *gauda*, the headman of the village, a man of greater wealth and higher status than the majority and the owner of extensive lands. In its subsistence patterns, the village has an extensive division of labor, with blacksmiths to make the tools, carpenters, stone workers, barbers, arrangers of ceremonies, basket weavers, and leather workers. Goldsmiths wander through the village from time to time, as do beggars, performers, repairmen, and washermen, whose duty it is to cleanse clothing ritually and to provide clean ceremonial cloth. Altogether about fifty *jatis* exist within Gopalpur or are represented by persons who visit the village sufficiently to be known to the peasants. A *jati* is an occupational group fitted into the hierarchical system of that part of India, with a position closely connected with the concept of caste but not quite the same.

Castes are major divisions of Indian society, most easily explained and remembered by foreigners as of four basic types—the priestly caste, the warrior caste, the merchant and artisan caste, and the servant caste. But within a particular village the real awareness of social position relates to the various occupational *jatis* that fill the tasks mentioned above and many more. Each *jati* has its position in society and its own customs regarding

Ibid., p. 79.

eating and ritual observance. Since the highest gods are vegetarian gods, those *jatis* that are of highest ritual purity eat no meat. Besides the one Brahman family—that of the *gauda*—there are several families of Lingayat priests, farmers, and carpenters who are vegetarians and of high rank. The Lingayats are a sect devoting particular attention of the worship of Siva. Below the Brahmans and the Lingayats are the majority of the *jatis* of Gopalpur, who may eat clean or pure meat—sheep, goats, chicken, or fish, but not beef or pork. Most of the peasants are of the pure-meat *jatis*. The Muslims who live in the village are generally ranked below the *jatis* of the Hindu peasants, especially those who are butchers and weavers. Even below them are the stone workers and basket weavers, who consume pork and are definitely polluting, and lowest of all are the leather workers, who eat pork and beef. There are a few converts to Christianity, but they are generally low-ranking people who make sandals, and they are hardly taken seriously as Christians by the villagers. "Real" Christians should be of high status, it is believed.

The marriage system obviously has to reflect *jatis*, since most *jatis* marry only within their own group. The *jati* is thought of as a related group and is similar to a large clan whose common ancestors are not really known. Since marriage to a person related through the father's line is forbidden, it is necessary for each *jati* to be divided into two different descent groups. To marry a person of one's mother's descent group is quite acceptable, since relationship to the mother's line is believed to be of little biological importance. It is believed that the male plants the seed in the womb of the female and she serves as the soil in which the seed of life grows, but not as a carrier of heredity. Hence it is quite acceptable and common for a man to marry his mother's sister's daughter or mother's brother's daughter but not his father's brother's daughter, who is of the same seed as the man seeking marriage. Another very common marriage is to one's own sister's daughter, since a wife should be many years younger than her husband.

Marriages are arranged and are considered the business of the entire village, especially those to people of other villages. The better the marriage arrangements made by the villagers, the better the reputation the village acquires for future marriage arrangements. Since the bride is typically nine or ten years of age and the groom is between fifteen and twenty-five, considerable strain is placed on the marriage from the first. Many young men grow impatient waiting for their wives to reach the age of puberty, when wifely duties and connubial relations can be expected. Sometimes they form alliances with other women, and their marriages, so carefully arranged turn out to be failures.[8] Attempts are made to prevent marriage failure by the usual community and kinship pressures and also by making marriages elaborate and expensive and remarriages almost prohibitive in expense. The cost of a first wife may be an entire year's work; if the first marriage fails and a second wife is sought, she will cost three times as much.

Kinship is important, since cooperation is required in special tasks and also in marriage arrangements and calendrical celebrations. Although women marry into other families, they are not really lost to the kindred, because marriage of a man's sisters brings brothers-in-law into his kindred group. A person's importance within his *jati* can be reckoned fairly well in terms of the number of his relatives, which helps to account for the extensive use of kinship terms. Father and father's brother are both called "father," and so are all male relatives of approximately the father's generation and belonging to his line. "Mother's brother" is a kinship term and also an honorary term. Since mother's brother had to consent to her marriage to one's father, he is a person of importance and is treated with deference. Other relatives of mother's family are sometimes addressed as mother's brother as a sign of special respect. Even strangers may be called by kinship terms, depending upon the relationship one wishes to establish with them, for in the kinship-dominated village it is best to conceptualize all people of any social importance in kinship terms.

THE WORLD VIEW   Although in Hindu belief all things are of Brahma, Brahma is manifested in many forms, including high gods and lesser gods and gods of special regions and occasions. In Gopalpur, only the Brahman *gauda* and the few Lingayat families worship such high gods as Vishnu, Siva, and Rama. The special gods of the village are Hanumantha and Bhimarayya, both warrior gods and both of a status that makes them more approachable than the high gods. Even they, however, are so high that only a Brahman dares touch their statues. Below the male gods are a number of female goddesses, to some degree playing the role of Earth Mother. They save the village from floods and epidemics, but only if the people are deserving, having lived right and made appropriate sacrifices. The goddesses, being of lower rank than the higher gods, are nonvegetarian and must be given offerings of meat and beer. Otherwise Mariamma could bring cholera and Pollamma could bring smallpox.

The way to goodness and to a happy reincarnation is believed to lie in renunciation of the things of the world and living the life of the holy

[8]Ibid., p. 30.

man. However, there are ambiguities about such a moral requirement, for they are not possible for all people. Only old men are likely to be free of obligations to children and kinsmen, so that they can live such a life. Most people are born at a level that requires many types of impurity, often inevitable in carrying out the tasks of their *jatis* and in eating the foods permitted for their *jatis*. However, say the people of Gopalpur, it is only those who have spent a life doing injury to others who must suffer tortures in the underworld and eventually be reborn as dogs, donkeys, or worms. People who live good lives are reborn as men, sometimes of very high rank, or even as manifestations of one of the lesser gods.[9] The quarrelsome or thieving man interferes with the harmony of social life and of the universe; the virtuous man contributes to such harmony, and he is the one whose future reincarnation is bright. This philosophy conforms to the needs of a stable agrarian life, in which the devout make no attempt to interfere with destiny by striving for positions to which they are not entitled by birth.

THE RICE LANDS OF JAVA   Java is an island of only 50,000 square miles, but it is the center of Indonesia politically and commercially and contains nearly 70 million inhabitants, more than half the Indonesian total, although it comprises less than one-fifteenth of the total land area. It lies only a few degrees south of the equator and has a good climate for cultivation of crops throughout the year, abundant rainfall, and rich volcanic soils. The two highest volcanic peaks rise to 11,000 and 12,000 feet. The higher lands produce rubber, kapok, tea, and coffee. The lower lands produce a wealth of agricultural products, by far the most important of which is rice. Rice is not only an important source of food but has a ritual significance, is the "staff of life." Although Western dietitians would not agree, to many of the rice people of the world, only rice is filling and adequate; other types of food are mere condiments. Rice is the main support of hundreds of millions of people of Asia, and it is able to support population densities impossible for any other crops. Nowhere else in the world does rice cultivation support so many people per square mile as on the tropical island of Java. Wolf estimates that the early Neolithic cultivators of the Near Eastern hills supported 25 people per square mile, ancient Mesopotamia perhaps 50.[10] The United States has a population density of about 55 persons per square mile. In constrast, the most densely populated parts of southern

[9]Ibid., p. 48.
[10]Wolf, op. cit., pp. 28–29.

Terraced rice fields demand more in
human labor than any other type of
farming land, but they also sustain the
maximum number of people per square
mile.

China support 2,000 people per square mile, but each square mile of some parts of rural Java supports 5,000.

RICE AND THE MINOR CROPS: TECHNOLOGY AND PRODUCTION   In many parts of Southeast Asia rice is cultivated in paddies, and much of the labor is done by water buffalo, but in the most crowded parts the farms are too small for animal power and reliance for power must return to man alone. The result is maximum productivity per unit of land but minimum per unit of human labor. Whereas plow agriculture in many parts of the world involves from 18 to 24 days of human labor per acre per year, in the most crowded rice lands of Asia, the figure is 178.2 man-days per acre.[11] Rice is a unique crop not only in the amount of work devoted to it and its total per acre productivity but also in the fact that its cultivation by a terrace system does not wear out the soil. In some instances the same rice paddies have been worked for thousands of years. Cattle manure, if available, is used, and so are human wastes, but primarily the restoration of the soil depends upon the muddy waters used for irrigation, which bring nutrients to the soil from higher elevations. Blue-green algae form in the water that stands in the rice terraces, fixing nitrogen in the soil; and other organic material is decomposed and transformed in the warm water, adding further nutritive value. Eventually the soils of rice paddies take on characteristics of their own, and even thin soils are enriched.[12]

A few characteristics of rice cultivation explain the tremendous amounts of work involved. Fields must be terraced for the application of uniform depths of water, and the water must flow from nutrient-bearing sources. Furthermore, flooding is as bad as too little water, so the level must be carefully controlled, increased from mere dampness at the time of planting to depths of from 6 to 12 inches as the plant matures and flowers and then gradually reduced till the field is dry at the time of harvest. Drainage systems are as important as irrigation systems in the cultivation of rice, and it is also important that the water not remain stagnant but be kept gently flowing. Occasionally, too, the water must be drained for the sake of weeding and fertilizing. The more carefully all these tasks are performed, the more mouths the rice paddies can feed, so that rice responds as no other crop to increasing inputs of labor. When swidden methods of horticulture are used, increased populations begin a deterioration of the soil and a

[11]Ibid., p. 28.

[12]Clifford Geertz, "Sawah," in Yehudi A. Cohen, *Man in Adaptation: The Cultural Present*, Aldine Publishing Company, Chicago, 1968, pp. 333–334.

dwindling level of productivity, and the same can be true of dry farming in the United States or Russia and of the overpasturage of animals in any part of the world; but in those very limited lands where rice cultivation conditions meet all requirements, wet rice is limited only by the law of diminishing returns. The time eventually comes when increased human labor can no longer significantly increase productivity; then the Asian peasants must resort to what Clifford Geertz calls "shared poverty," subsisting on less food than before.[13]

Although rice is being emphasized here, the peasants of Java do not rely upon rice alone, even in areas of well-developed rice paddies. The one or two acres of land are divided into *sawah* (terraced land) and *pekarangan* (mixed garden land). The latter will be planted to maize, cassava, peanuts, vegetables, and sweet potatoes, and the *sawah* will be replanted to wrest two rice harvests per year. The men plow and hoe, and the women plant and harvest. Although the population has exploded in recent years, placing heavy pressure on the land, most of the land is owned in small plots by the peasants who work it. The Javanese are also accustomed to markets and cash crops and watch closely their opportunities for buying and selling.

SOCIAL ORGANIZATION   At the local, village level there is little awareness of social class, since the peasants are fairly equal in status. The main exception to this rule arises from the extra land rights of village leaders and from the presence of some people without land. Most of the wet rice land is owned as transferable property, with land tenure being passed to the children of the household upon the death of the parents. In case there should be no heirs, the villagers who belong to the most important households redistribute the land to waiting candidates—people who have houses in the village but no land. Otherwise, the landless are the bottom of the social scale; the majority of peasants comprise the middle strata, and the village leaders, with extra land, constitute the closest approach to an upper class.[14]

The extended family of rural China is not typical of Java. Although Java has been influenced by India, there are no important castes or corporate kin groups. The social structure centers in the small nuclear family, as it tends to do in urban societies. Marriage is usually monogamous and is seldom with relatives of any degree. The young couple spends the first year living first with the husband's family and then with the wife's, but they eventually settle in a

[13]Ibid., pp. 334–335.
[14]Ben J. Wallace, *Village Life in Insular Southeast Asia*, Little, Brown and Company, Boston, 1971, pp. 109–115.

home of their own, not necessarily next to either parental family—a residence pattern called "neolocal."

The other important links in the social lives of the people are to the agencies of government and to the marketing towns. At the local level there is village democracy. Village leaders and subdistrict leaders are elected by the villagers; higher officials are appointed by the government. The position of village leader is very important, because it carries with it an allotment of communal land. Another elected official, the *lurah*, or secretary, is the chief intermediary between the village and the higher levels of government, forwarding requests for marriage or divorce papers, loans, registrations and permits, and bringing directives from the government.[15] Since the local officials must be residents of the village, their status is close to that of the peasant and there is probably little "insolence of office." On the other hand, they are likely to have had little experience of the outside world.

The Javanese towns display much more heterogeneity in statuses and walks of life than do the villages. There are the *prijaji*, or local gentry; the *wong dagang*, or traders; the poor, peasantlike *wong tjilik*; and the foreigners, the *wong tjina*, or Chinese. The gentry hold most of the white-collar jobs and make up the cultural elite. Although most Javanese are at least nominally Muslims, the traders make the greatest claim to Muslim piety. The *wong tjilik* do the common day labor. As in many parts of Southeast Asia, the Chinese dominate the large-scale trade. The Javanese Muslim traders are secure at their own small-town level, but the Chinese have formed the larger business associations, travel more, and know the ways of commerce better. Their extended families and associations give them access to pooled capital and pooled knowledge. The business advantages of the Chinese have led to resentments and sometimes even to persecution, not only in Indonesia but in other parts of Southeast Asia.

THE WORLD VIEW   Indonesia presents a confusion of religious orientations, but behind them all are certain viewpoints that provide a semblance of unity in perception of the world. The coastal people and small merchants are the ones most thoroughly Islamic in viewpoint and practice. At earlier periods in the long history of Java, much influence came from Hindus and Buddhists, and some of this influence still persists among the small-town gentry and among the rice growers of the central areas. In the more remote, mountain regions, the people remain pagans, having adopted neither Islam nor Hinduism, but remaining faithful to the animistic beliefs of the past. In actual practice, the

[15]Ibid., p. 126.

animistic spirits still remain even among the people who consider themselves Muslims.[16]

Among the typical peasants of the villages, the most important ritual is the *slametan*, a ceremonial feast having to do with appeasement of nature spirits and with magic and curing. *Slametans* are held to celebrate the major points in the life cycle—birth, circumcision, marriage, and death. There are other *slametans* for celebrating Muslim sacred days and, inconsistently, a third class of *slametans* for cleansing the village of evil spirits. Finally, *slametans* are sometimes held on irregular occasions, in cases of severe illness, before taking a long trip, or if sorcery has been suspected. The more devout Muslims ignore such celebrations, tending to think of them as pagan and idolatrous.

Although the Muslims are dominant politically and in outward religious expression, much of Javanese culture actually derives from India, and its carriers are the Hinduized gentry of some of the towns. Music, entertainment, and especially the incessant dramas taken from the great epic tale the *Mahabharata* are of Indian origin. There is also a philosophical emphasis upon harmony, found in many parts of the world, but quite compatible with much of Hinduism or even with the Taoism of China. More than in most parts of the world, morality is associated with aesthetics and harmony.

> Individuals who ignore the moral-aesthetic norms . . . who follow a discordant style of life, are regarded not so much as evil as stupid, insensitive, unlearned, or in the case of extreme dereliction, mad. In Java, where I have done field work, small children, simpletons, boors, the insane, and the flagrantly immoral are all said to be "not yet Javanese," and not yet Javanese, not yet human.[17]

The idea that all the elements of life and of nature must be in harmony is called *tjottjog*. In some respects this concept is met as far away as China, among Taoists, and in the Southwestern United States among the Pueblo Indians and the Navaho. As in India, evil is looked upon as unregulated passion and can be resisted only by self-control and passivity; but contrary to a common Indian point of view, tranquillity must not be gained through a retreat from the world but by living within it. Thus it seems that philosophically, with some modifications, India may have won out in the struggle for the mind of Java, but this may be true only because Java, too, is a land of millions of peasants, living peacefully off the land and seeking the harmony that is needed by the peasant in order that his fields may prosper and his line continue.

[16]Ibid., pp. 128–130.

[17]Clifford Geertz, "Ethos, World View, and the Analysis of Sacred Symbols," *Antioch Review*, vol. 4, pp. 421–437, 1957. Copyright © 1957 by The Antioch Review, Inc. First published in *The Antioch Review*, vol. 17, no. 4; reprinted by permission of the editors.

Greece, with an area of about 51,000 squares miles and a population of nearly 9 million, has a population density of approximately 176 persons per square mile. Since only one-quarter of the land is arable and the country is basically agricultural, intensive cultivation is necessary to support the people even very simply. Much of Greece is mountainous, the soil is rocky, and the climate is typically Mediterranean. Rainfall occurs mainly in the winter and in most places is inadequate for farming without irrigation. Although Athens is a large city of close to 2 million people, the majority of Greeks live in small towns and villages, many along the coast, engaged in fishing and shipping, some in the northern mountains, depending heavily on sheep and goats for a living, but the majority in farming villages. Vasilika, described by Ernestine Friedl,[18] is such a village, lying in the Boeotian Plain in the shadow of Mount Parnassus, to the northwest of the smaller Athenian plain of Attica. The Boeotian plain is blessed with a small river flowing from the mountains to the north and is better watered than most parts of Greece. Groundwater is close to the surface, and a number of wells equipped with diesel pumps are used for irrigation of cotton in the summer months. Vasilika, like many rural villages of Greece, has an older name given it back in the days of Turkish occupation. In 1955 the government changed its offical designation from Kravasaras to Vasilika, meaning "royal," actually the name of a nearby hill where the Greeks won a battle against the Turks in one of the interminable wars in the Greek struggle for independence.

TECHNOLOGY AND PRODUCTION   The farming in Vasilika is small-scale. Most of the plowing is done by horses, and vegetable crops, wheat for bread, and grapes for wine are grown mainly for home consumption. In these respects, the Greek peasant is typical of peasantry as discussed earlier. However, there are important differences between the Greek peasant and many of the more backward peasants of the world, the most important being that he thinks of himself as a businessman. In this respect, he could more correctly be called a modern farmer, although in his conception of the farm as a family enterprise and a place for growing much of his own subsistence he is still typical of peasantry. Friedl gives a good account of the increasing divergence from peasant thinking in her discussion of arguments between the purchasers of cotton and the Vasilika farmers. The farmers contended that the price was much too low and that once they calculated all costs, including wages for work-

[18]Ernestine Friedl, *Vasilika: A Village in Modern Greece*, Holt, Rinehart and Winston, Inc., New York, 1962.

Although tractors and other farm
equipment are sometimes rented, much
of the life of the Greek peasant depends
on animal and family labor, as with
peasantry everywhere.

ing members of their families, they showed no profit at all. The merchants purchasing the crops wanted to argue from the more typically peasant point of view: "But you can't count wages for women and children. After all, what else would they do?"[19]

In another respect also, Greece displays a transition from rural-peasant to more modern attitudes. The most profitable cash crop for the peasants is tobacco, but the government has to control tobacco production to prevent flooding of the market, so that each peasant is alloted only a small part of his acreage. One of the serious problems of peasantry is thus partly controlled— the problem of unlimited competition and the dumping of products on the market in sufficient quantity to break the price.

The first part of the yearly round of agricultural work begins with pruning the grape vines and hoeing the vineyards. Later in the spring cotton is planted, to be harvested in the fall, and late in the fall the wheat fields are sown. If at any time the pressure of work becomes too great for plowing by horses, it is possible to hire a tractor for part of the plowing. Since horses must be kept, and often there is a family cow as well, 4 or 5 *stremata* of land (4 *stremata* = 1 acre) are used for oats, barley, and clover. Some of the families own land at some distance from the village and depend to quite an extent on sheep and wool for their living.

Houses are built of stone, are rectangular in shape, and sometimes are two stories high. Houses are owned individually. Near the center of the village are the two coffeehouses, one of which is also the village store, that are the centers for gatherings, discussion, and argument for the village men, and between them is the marketplace, the *aghora*. The bus stops at the *aghora*, and peddlers shout their wares there, and dances and festivals are held at the *aghora* on important days. The other important village centers are the two churches, the larger one to Saint Athanasius, where regular liturgy, baptisms, and weddings are held. At the other end of the village is the small church of Saint Cosmas and Saint Damian, the village patron saints, where the *paniyiri* festival, which honors them, is held in July.

The houses of the villages are kept neat and orderly, with separate storerooms for tools and equipment, even such equipment as coffee grinders and pots and pans. The home-produced wine, cheese, olives, eggs, and bread are stored away. Orderliness is more than convenience; it is a social value. Meals, especially the evening meal, are of ritual as well as nutritional importance, and Greeks pride themselves on hospitality. There is always an abundance of nutritious, home-baked brown bread, which is the staff of life to Greeks, so

[19]Ibid., pp. 25–26.

much so that a meal without bread is almost a source of guilt feelings.[20] Along with the brown bread is another dish, often beans flavored with a variety of vegetables, nutritious, but simple. The wine, prepared by the Greek villagers, has a bit of resin added, giving it a strange taste to the novice, but one that is eventually appreciated. A few of the poorest of the peasants live in grinding poverty, but, generally speaking, recent improvements in irrigation, fertilization, and markets have brought the Greek peasant to the level of a frugal but adequate living. Like most peasants, he considers his life better than the lives of the city people in moral wholesomeness if not in level of prosperity.

SOCIAL ORGANIZATION   In spite of the governmental turbulence in Greece in recent years, there is usually tranquillity at the village level. A local village council is democratically elected and has certain functions in preparing village budgets. The more informal organization is that of the men in the coffeehouses, where conversation is incessant and often loud and vehement. To the average Greek villager social concerns are primarily the concerns of the family, an emotionally close family, cooperating for its survival and economic future and sometimes even attempting to survive in a joint household. Usually, however, if two or more brothers and their wives attempt to live together in the parental home, tensions and jealousies develop, so that if it is economically feasible, nuclear families live in separate houses.

One of the major concerns of the family is assuring the future of all children. Greek law provides for an equal division of property among the children, but the property of the daughters is given in the form of dowry at the time of marriage; the sons usually receive their share as an inheritance upon the death of the father. Sometimes, though, one son will be given the advantages of an education in the city so that he may become an official or a professional man, in which case it will be felt that his portion has already been granted, and the brothers remaining in the village will inherit the land. Parents are particularly concerned that good marriages be arranged for their daughters, and such marriages are impossible without at least a token dowry; much haggling and negotiation goes on over the matter.[21] Naturally, there is a desire that the marriage be harmonious as well as an economic success.

In the early days of Greek immigration to the United States, many of the young men came only to work a few years to earn enough money for dowry for their sisters, because they considered it beneath their honor to marry before

---

[20]Margaret Mead, *Cultural Patterns and Technical Change*, Mentor Books, New American Library, Inc., New York, 1955, pp. 87–88.
[21]Friedl, op. cit., pp. 48–60.

their sisters were adequately provided for.[22] Some remained indefinitely, eventually having brides sent to them from Greece. The old patterns of Greek rural life were extremely provincial as well as family oriented, and these patterns were maintained in America. Mutual assistance organizations were formed, but it was hard to get Greeks from Thessaly to cooperate with those from Boeotia, Rhodes, the Dodecanese, the Peloponnesus, or Epirus. This provincialism is now breaking down in modern Greece because of an increasing number of younger people migrating to Athens and other urban centers.

THE WORLD VIEW   The Greek people think of themselves as the first followers of Christianity, and rural Greece, especially, is steeped in Orthodox Christianity. A ritual of *agiasmos* ("making holy") opens every day at school, every public dedication, the building of every house, the undertaking of a journey. Saints' days are celebrated; children do not celebrate their own birthdays but rather the day of the saint for whom they are named. Priests are called in if a family has had misfortunes or illness to make things holy again. The Epiphany is celebrated, and Good Friday is observed. At Easter time, the people, including children, stay up all night, waiting for sunrise and crying in unison, "He has risen."

American sociologists have commented that the Greeks are an achievement-oriented people.[23] Their old enemies, the Turks, have characterized them as shrewd and cunning; and there is an expression in the eastern Mediterranean, "There is no such thing as a dumb Greek." The Greeks have a strong sense of pride and self-worth, called *philotimo*,[24] and consider a certain amount of boasting perfectly proper. One must maintain one's sense of worth at all costs. Orderliness, already mentioned, is a high value, and so are physical stamina, endurance and strength. Although women are expected to wait on men, it is not because they are regarded as weak or inferior. Even a woman is likely to be complimented by references to firmness and strength rather than to softness. If Lord Byron's line to a Greek maiden, "Kiss thy soft cheek's blooming tinge," had been addressed to a village girl, it probably would have fallen on deaf ears. Babies are swaddled in rural Greece, although that custom is now being abandoned. The reason given is "so that they will grow straight and firm." Physical fitness is carried so far as a value that a person with a deformity is more acutely aware of it in Greece than in many countries. Parents are ad-

[22]Robert James Theodoratus, "The Influence of the Homeland on the Social Organization of a Greek Community in America," doctoral thesis, University of Washington, Seattle, 1961.
[23]Bernard Rosen, "Race, Ethnicity, and the Achievement Syndrome," *American Sociological Review*, vol. 24, pp. 47–60, February 1959.
[24]Mead, op. cit., p. 63.

vised to think of eugenics when they select husbands for their daughters, just as the ancient Greeks did.[25] The emphasis on hardiness is generally attributed by the peasants themselves to their historic roots; their ancestors were of that type. Such values are found among many peasant people but in Greece are probably exaggerated as a consequence of historic tradition.

Certain other ancient traditions die slowly if at all. Many Greek children are still named after the philosophers and heroes of antiquity. Even some of the ancient beliefs survive in one form or another. A spirit called Hecate is responsible for sorcery; she is a survival of the ancient goddess of the underworld. Among some Greek peasants, the angel of death is called Charon—the ancient boatman of Greek mythology who rowed spirits across the River Styx.[26] Life is glorified, regardless of belief in a better world to come; this life is lived with zest. It is said that when the world was created, God placed soil and mud to make the lands of the world, but when he got to Greece he had only a pile of rocks left over, which he threw out to make that mountainous land, with its rugged contours, coastal indentations, and islands. Then, to compensate, he sent a rainbow, which entered into the people, making them colorful, excitable, and vivid, in contrast to the rocky land that became their home.[27]

In their self-image as businessmen, their achievement motivation, their admiration of education and hope of sending their sons to advanced schools, the Greek peasants are part of the modern world. In some of their personality traits and viewpoints, they are a unique people, having retained something of their traditions through 2,500 years of history and through long centuries of Turkish rule. In other respects, they are part of the world's peasantry, living from the soil, pulled between their own needs and the demands of the outer world, working long hours, producing goods that sell cheaply on the market, drawing a line of distinction between themselves and the supposedly less virile people of the city, and firmly committed to the interests of their own families above all else.

SUMMARY   The agricultural techniques of irrigation and plowing are necessary to the development of urban civilizations, and they create a way of life known as peasantry. Peasants work in various climates, with various crops, and at

[25]Ibid., p. 77.
[26]Martin P. Nilsson, *Greek Folk Religion*, Harper Torchbooks, Harper & Row, Publishers, Incorporated, New York, 1961.
[27]Irwin T. Sanders, *Rainbow in the Rock: The People of Rural Greece*, Harvard University Press, Cambridge, Mass., 1962, pp. 1–2. See also Eric Wolf, *Peasant Wars of the Twentieth Century*, Harper & Row, Publishers, Incorporated, New York, 1969.

various levels of technological development, but they have certain traits in common—a reverence for the earth, strong family orientation, village cooperation. Since their economic position is usually precarious, it is only under unusual circumstances that they dare experiment with new techniques; they tend to hold fast to the ways that have supported them, regardless of how meagerly.

Urban and state systems rest upon the peasant culture, providing organization and defense, markets, and ideas that diffuse slowly to the peasantry. The urban society also exacts its toll, buying at low prices from the peasantry but selling them goods at high prices, taxing the peasant, and often exploiting him by usurious interest rates. In all three examples used, it is clear that the urban culture is advanced beyond the simpler culture of the peasant in techniques, philosophies, and levels of organization and education.

In the Indian village, the Javanese village, and the Greek village there is much emphasis on ceremonialism and greater religiousness than in the city. There is a much-needed shrewdness, stoicism, admiration for hardihood, and an ability to live with a frugality that affluent parts of the modern world can hardly comprehend.

In the diverse examples of peasantry, it is clear that some have an orientation closer to that of the modern business world than others, and a further study of peasants would show even greater diversity along these lines. The progress toward modernity is connected with the level of advancement of the urban culture, the readiness of transportation and communication between the urban and the peasant culture, and many subtle traits of the peasant culture that help to determine its willingness to accept new ideas. The level of organization of the state is also of great importance in explaining the degree of advancement toward modern industrialism; and geographical factors, such as proximity to centers of diffusion of new ideas, climate and terrain, and types of soil and possibilities for irrigation all have their effect.

In all cases the peasant societies are associated with considerable degrees of class diversity. The peasants themselves may be quite equalitarian, but the urban centers with which they are connected are places of occupational diversity, accumulated wealth, power, prestige, and privilege—all the major criteria for social class differentiation, which must be described more fully in the next chapter.

BASIC PATTERN   POSSIBLE DEVELOPMENTS

TECHNOLOGY AND POSSESSIONS

PERMANENT VILLAGES, HOUSES, STORAGE-   MODERN FARMING WITH MECHANIZED
USUALLY FARM ANIMALS, PLOWS -   EQUIPMENT - FULLY DEVELOPED MARKET
PARTLY SUBSISTENCE ECONOMY.   ECONOMY.

SOCIAL ORGANIZATION

STRONG FAMILY AND VILLAGE TIES-   AGRARIAN REVOLTS - VOTING RIGHTS
SUBJECTS OF DEVELOPED STATE -   AND CITIZENSHIP - POLITICAL PARTIES.
SUPPORT ELITE CLASSES.

WORLD VIEW

PRAYER FOR HARVESTS - CALENDRICAL   MODERN SECULARIZATION - INCREASING
CEREMONIES - TRADITIONAL, REVERENT-   RELIANCE ON SCIENCE.
STATE RELIGION MODIFIED BY LOCAL BELIEFS,
SAINTS.

'72 Anne MacDermott

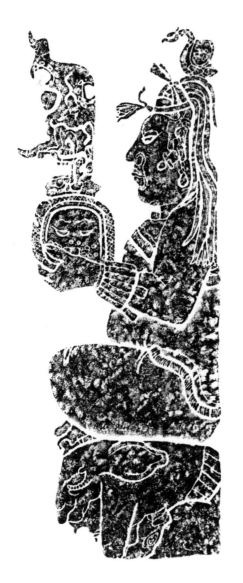

Chapter Nine
Wealth and
Social Class

Each of the last four chapters has included brief comments on social organization among the peoples studied, covering such diverse topics as family, social classes, and government. In some cases classes were a definite part of social organization, and in other cases they were not. The general evolutionary perspective assumes that class structures function differently as levels of subsistence become increasingly complex. Social class is nonexistent, or nearly so, at the hunting-and-gathering level, and it is always present in agricultural societies. In the stages between these two extremes, social class is usually present to some degree in horticultural societies and nearly always in pastoral societies. Slavery was found in one of the hunting-and-gathering societies (Northwest Coast) but was more prominent among some of the pastoralists. It existed in nearly all the early civilizations that were based on well-developed agriculture.

Obviously social status, rank, and class are somehow connected with ways of life and levels of development, but not so simply that all horticultural, pastoral, or agricultural societies have exactly the same class systems. Accumulated wealth is one important variable connected with class systems, but there are other complications to status and class. Northwest Coast chieftains had to give away wealth in order to maintain status, as has been true with many hunting peoples. Then, too, magico-religious powers and recognized skills are connected with class differentiation, depending partly on the values of the society. What determines high and low rank? How does a defined class system differ from mere differentiation of statuses or the ranking of individuals? What accounts for the extreme and rigid status differences that occur in caste systems? What types of social systems have made greatest use of the institution of slavery? Finally, what seems to be the trend of class systems in the modern world of increasingly educated, urban-industrial societies calling for intricate divisions of labor and new kinds of abilities?

STATUS WITHOUT CLASS   There are ways of classifying people in all societies, some of which are only slightly connected with the idea of social ranking. The many positions held in society are spoken of as "statuses," and the normative behavior expected of people occupying those positions is called "role." Some statuses are the accident of birth or the passing of time, and some are earned statuses; the former are called "ascribed" and the latter, "achieved." Thus we all have the ascribed status of male or female, and we also have ascribed age statuses that change gradually from childhood to adulthood and old age. Ralph Linton points out that in some societies status can even increase after death, as one becomes an ancestral spirit and receives great honors from the living.[1] Often in such societies the status of old age is a high one, partly because old people are few in preliterate societies and their memories are important and partly because the old person is right on the verge of joining the ancestors.

To return to male and female status, male status is nearly always given the higher respect, but the differences, as we have seen, vary from group to group. The fierce Yanomamö, for example, place women in an extremely subordinate position; among the peaceful Pygmies women are much less subordinate. It would seem that the statuses of women and the aged would have some connection with the values of the society, and this connection is often demonstrable. In Arapesh society, where values and personality structure emphasize a gentle disposition, the differences in tasks performed by each sex are not great, and the personality expectation for both sexes is compatible with what we would consider to be feminine traits.[2] In Eskimo society,

[1]Ralph Linton, *The Study of Man*, D. Appleton-Century Company, Inc., New York, 1936, pp. 121–122.
[2]Margaret Mead, *Sex and Temperament in Three Primitive Societies*, William Morrow & Company, Inc., New York, 1928.

where the division of labor is complete, the men must perform the daring tasks of hunting, and they are expected to be clearly dominant. In many historical societies, legends in praise of daring masculine roles, and an awareness of the dominance that goes with them, have been helpful in making the role of adult attractive to the growing boy. Where societal values are less adventurous, the masculine role need not be given such commanding status, as in the case of the Zuñi, where the only really superior masculine role is in religion and ceremony. Similarly, in societies with strong emphasis on family continuity, and often in cases where agricultural and other knowledge possessed by the aged is valuable to the group, the status of the aged can be very high. In a few cases, where the band could conceivably perish if it tried to support too many elderly members, the aged might be abandoned and left to die (often at their own request), as was once the practice among some of the Eskimo.

The types of status just discussed, based on age, sex, and skills, exist in all societies, but they are quite different from social class. Class is more than a mere matter of role differentiation; it involves groups with common status awareness, and it usually has at least a minimal connection with kinship and heredity. Even when status consciousness becomes very strong in particular families, however, the social system might yet fail to develop full-scale social classes, but might be based instead on ranking.

RANKING SYSTEMS   Many achieved statuses tend to rank people in a society on an individual rather than a social-class basis. Sometimes in American Indian societies, warriors or hunters of prominence could join military lodges or fraternities and thus enhance their rank. Members of the best fraternities formed superior social sets, but their status was not hereditary or familial. Tropical Africa has many secret societies that give a measure of rank, but they have other functions as well and are only secondarily sources of social prominence.

The more definitive cases of social ranking have occurred among hunting and fishing societies or primitive horticultural societies living in areas of natural abundance and producing surplus goods. Among several of the Indian tribes of the Southeastern United States were found chieftains with exalted rank, borne on litters to make sure they were undefiled by having their feet touch the ground. We have already commented on the splendor of the highest-ranking Northwest Coast chieftains and their close relatives. Among some of the Polynesians, high-ranking men could not feed themselves but had to be fed by people of lowly rank.[3] In Maori society, those chiefs who could trace their

[3]Raymond Firth, *Human Types*, Thomas Nelson & Sons, New York, 1957, pp. 202–203.

descent through the longest lines outranked all others and were often so sacred that they had difficulty finding women suitable to bear their offspring.[4] Reviewing cases of the pompousness of rank in many societies, Robert Lowie attempts to refute any economic interpretation, implicitly falling back on a definition of human nature to explain the extreme ranking systems: "Thus the utilitarian doctrine completely breaks down in the interpretation of aboriginal consciousness. Primitive man is not a miser nor a sage nor a beast of prey but, in Tarde's happy phrase, a peacock."[5]

There remains a question, however: if primitive man is by nature a peacock, why is there not such pompous display of rank among the lower hunters and gatherers? Why do such exaggerations of rank begin to appear only among peoples who have a degree of affluence by primitive standards and whose social organization has achieved or is tending toward a type of monarchy—conditions that probably existed among the Maori and other Polynesians, and were to be found among the Northwest Coast Indians? Leslie White answers this question with the assertion that such social systems were intricately connected with other aspects of the way of life: "Social organization here as elsewhere is a function of the mode of subsistence and of defense."[6] Implied in his statement is the idea that the level of subsistence has advanced, that there are surplus goods, that there may be pressure on land resources, and that organization beyond the primitive is needed. Apparently one way to achieve such organization is to exalt status to a ludicrous degree, fitting everyone into a rank order. The chieftains collect the wealth that shows their prestige and further enhance their prestige by distributing this wealth generously at ceremonies. They thus act as an incipient government, handling certain economic problems that exist when market economics have not developed. They characterize a system that is moving toward social class but has not really attained it. The social system is still kinship based, with at least distant kinship bonds existing between different "classes"; therefore, the word classes can be used only in a special sense. Also, class position is not firmly rooted in property ownership, and, to quote again from White, "It is not until . . . society has become organized upon the basis of property relations and territorial distinctions that true classes of subordination and superordination come into being."[7]

Viewed in this way, only the most rudimentary social class existed among the Northwest Coast Indians, and the class system was mitigated by the cross-

[4]Robert Lowie, *Primitive Society*, Harper Torchbooks, Harper & Row, Publishers, Incorporated, New York, 1961, p. 347.
[5]Ibid., p. 357.
[6]Leslie White, *The Evolution of Culture*, McGraw-Hill Book Company, New York, 1959, p. 202.
[7]Ibid., p. 203.

currents of kinship. The same was true of the Mongols, but among some of the pastoral peoples, especially those who had conquered others, wealth and territorial distinctions became clear and so did subordination and superordination.

INCIPIENT SOCIAL CLASS: Although the Polynesians and the Northwest
THE NATCHEZ Coast peoples had exalted chieftains, the rest of the society was not strictly divided into classes; rank remained individual or at most familial. The Natchez Indians of Mississippi are an important instance of class development. They had an exalted chieftain and also well-marked social classes to which all the people were assigned. Wealth, military power, and esteem for the guardians of their sacred traditions combined to make class important, but even among the Natchez societal kinship resulted in a strange and unusual modification of social class—members of upper classes had to marry members of the lowest class.

The Natchez were probably one of the powerful tribes mentioned by Hernando de Soto in 1542, but they were made famous by the descriptions written by the French, starting with La Salle in 1682.[8] They had a great abundance of game, practiced considerable gardening, and seem to have been militarily superior to the tribes around them. It is possible that they were the last descendants of the Mound Builders, or elements of their culture may have diffused from the Caribbean or from Mexico. The Natchez were sun worshipers, building high temple mounds to the sun so that their chief, the Great Sun, could stand closer to his elder brother, the sun, to whom he made morning sacrifices for the Natchez people. When the Great Sun died, he was buried with great splendor, along with several servants who had the honor of dying with him. His bones were deposited along with those of previous Great Suns in a hut on top of the temple mound. One of the French explorers attended the funeral of a slightly less exalted Sun, the Tattooed Serpent, brother of the Great Sun. According to his description, the favorite wife, the chancellor, the head servant, and the pipebearer of the Tattooed Serpent were all buried with him, as custom required. One of the other noble women, insisted on being buried with him also.[9] Sacrificial victims were first rendered unconscious by a massive dose of tobacco juice and then strangled by their relatives.

[8]Peter Farb, *Man's Rise to Civilization* . . . , Avon Book Division, The Hearst Corporation, New York, 1968, pp. 192–204.
[9]LePage du Pratz, *Indian Tribes of the Lower Mississippi Valley and Adjacent Coast of the Gulf of Mexico,* Bureau of American Ethnology Bulletin no. 43, 1911, pp. 144–149.

The wife of a sixteenth-century Timucuas chief of Florida is carried to an important ceremony. Several southeastern tribes besides the Natchez exalted their upper class with pompous ceremonialism. It is interesting to note, incidentally, that earlier European artists gave American Indians a European appearance.

The Great Sun and his close relatives through his mother's line were all referred to as Suns. Descent was traced through the maternal line among the Natchez, as among many American Indian tribes. The high-ranking female Sun known as White Woman was the mother of the Great Sun. Upon the death of the Great Sun and White Woman, the eldest daughter of White Woman acquired the title and her eldest son became the Great Sun. But the children of the Great Sun himself could not become Great Suns, since males were unable to pass their exalted rank along to their children. In Natchez society, all people of the upper classes had to marry into the lowest class, referred to as Stinkers. Through the female line, high rank was maintained; through the male line, rank dropped one level with each generation. Hence, the great-great-grandson of the Great Sun would be a common Stinker.

There were three noble classes, the Suns, the Nobles, and the Honored People. Children of male Suns became Nobles; children of male Nobles became Honored People; children of male Honored People became Stinkers.

Children of female Suns, on the other hand, remained Suns, even though they were required to marry lowly Stinkers.

At first glance the system seems preposterous, but actually it served a number of functions. An exalted chief and a noble class were provided to symbolize the tribe, uphold its sacred traditions, and give it prestige and importance. The unusual marriage system provided for a generational circulation of elites that may have functioned to prevent an isolated and embittered lower class. The lower class would have diminished in size by constantly marrying upward, but it was replenished by wars in which foreigners were captured and added to the Stinker class. Even the newly absorbed foreigners could eventually marry into the upper classes, which probably mitigated their sense of hostility and helped bring about social cohesion. Moreover, the system provided for other types of upward mobility. Stinkers who distinguished themselves in battle could be elevated to the rank of Honored, although it is not clear whether it was possible to rise higher.[10]

As with any social system, the Natchez upper classes had special rights and privileges. They could tattoo and otherwise ornament themselves as none of the other people could. They were also distinguished by dress, with men of the two top classes wearing black breechclouts and the others white. Houses of the upper classes were larger, and the upper classes engaged in conspicuous consumption of goods drawn from the entire society. The social injustices of class were present, but they were moderate compared with most class systems.

In the majority of societies, social classes marry only their own members and thus perpetuate their positions. The Natchez system can be described as "incipient," or beginning, class, because upper classes had not yet devised a manner of maintaining themselves indefinitely while also assuring the cohesion of the social group.

EARLY CIVILIZATIONS AND AGRARIAN SOCIETIES

Early civilizations and agrarian societies of the preindustrial age developed rigid social classes, although usually not rigid enough to be designated as caste systems. Ancient Sumer in its developmental stage may not have been strongly class structured, but with the growth of wealth and the expansion of power, strong class systems developed. The same pattern occurred in Egypt, in the Indus Valley, and in the civilizations of the New World. During the period before the rise of urban civilizations, many innovations had laid the foundation for

[10]Farb, op. cit., p. 201.

In early civilizations an enormous gulf developed between upper and lower classes, as depicted in this scene of a pharaoh beating captive slaves.

wealthy states: artificial irrigation, the use of animals and wheeled transport, new building techniques, solar calendars, writing, and the first use of metals.[11] V. Gordon Childe shows that progress in new techniques was more rapid in the period before the great urban civilizations developed than afterward and suggests that increased concentration on warfare and greater social class differentiation may have helped to slow inventive progress. New techniques of production, transport, and building had made possible the rise of wealthy governing classes and along with it the debasement of the common people. Peasants and laborers were falling to the rank of serfs. The great building projects of such countries as Egypt and Babylonia undoubtedly employed many people, and the affluence of the upper classes called for new classes of artisans to provide objects of luxury and administrative and merchandising skills. Childe quotes an interesting document from Egypt admonishing the young to learn the skills of the scribe in order to rise above the misery of common labor.

> Put writing in your heart that you may protect yourself from hard labor of any kind and be a magistrate of high repute. The scribe is released from manual tasks; it is he who commands. . . . Do you not hold the scribe's palette? That is what makes the difference between you and the man who handles an oar. I have seen the metal-worker at his task at the mouth of his furnace with fingers like a crocodile's. He stank worse than fish-spawn.[12]

George Orwell once wrote an essay entitled "The Lower Classes Smell."[13] In a modern age when bathing is the custom for all classes, the statement is no longer true, but in ancient civilizations and more recent agrarian societies not only wretched clothes but dirt and odor have separated the lowest classes from those above. Even in certain modern societies, the cleaners of cowhides, the puddlers of iron ore, and the handlers of the dead fall into very low positions. Ancient literature is full of references to rare incenses and perfumes that saved the upper classes from the lower. And contrary to the situation among the Natchez, there were no ties of kinship between the powerful and the lowly.

Since the stratification system of the Aztec Empire of Mexico was still in its developmental stage at the time of the Spanish Conquest, the record of the Aztecs can tell us something of the development of social class in early civiliza-

---

[11]V. Gordon Childe, *Man Makes Himself*, Mentor Books, New American Library, Inc., New York, 1951, pp. 182–183.
[12]Ibid., p. 149.
[13]George Orwell, "The Lower Classes Smell," in Lewis A. Coser (ed.), *Sociology Through Literature*, Prentice-Hall, Inc., Englewood Cliffs, N.J., 1963, pp. 145–149.

tions. The Aztecs were still bound together to some degree by feelings of kinship, and neighborhoods within the city of Tenochtitlán were defined on the basis of both locality and clan. There were hereditary nobility within each clan, and the clan members were ranked in accord with their degree of kinship to the original founder of the clan. Furthermore, some clans were regarded as better than others, and some sections of the city outranked others. Below the Aztecs themselves were conquered laborers, whose position was that of serfs; their service was bought and sold along with the land on which they worked.[14] There were also slaves in Aztec society, among them people who had to enter slavery temporarily to pay off their debts. The social system included a non-hereditary nobility based on military accomplishment, which may have been the basis of the origin of the entire noble class. Merchants formed a special class of their own, traveling widely over the empire, bringing rare goods from great distances, and also acting as Aztec spies. At the top of the society was the royal family and the great Moctezuma, a sacred personage comparable to the Great Sun of the Natchez but with more actual influence on events. The sacred aspects of the culture were also maintained by a well-trained priest class, of exalted status, which made innumerable sacrifices required for rain, for victory, for good harvests, and especially to prevent the death of the great War God.

Despite its elaboration, the Aztec class structure lacked any way of integrating conquered people into the system, which was one of the weaknesses of the empire. Many of the conquered became human sacrifices; most others had permanently degraded status and were restive under Aztec rule. The problem of maintaining class systems without possible rebellion has been greater in some societies than in others. In agrarian societies, peasants occasionally have had considerable military value and have been treated relatively well. Where their services are not needed, their treatment is more severe.[15] In Hammurabi's empire, peasants paid from one-third to one-half of their crops in taxes, and the same was true 3,000 years later in czarist Russia. In China, rents were often 40 to 50 percent of the crop, and during the medieval period of Japanese history, they varied from 30 to 70 percent. The systems were, nevertheless, relatively free of revolution. Tremendous differences in status and awareness of each other separated peasants from aristocrats, and all the military power was on the side of the latter, who alone could bear arms. Furthermore, there was always a class below peasantry and laborers—those whom Gerhard Lenski calls "the expendables"—the beggars and thieves, having no

[14]Farb, op. cit., pp. 218–220.
[15]Gerhard Lenski, *Power and Privilege: A Theory of Social Stratification,* McGraw-Hill Book Company, New York, 1968, p. 275.

place in society and living, if at all, only by wit and stealth. Agrarian societies apparently produced "more people than the dominant classes found it profitable to employ."[16] In this respect, the agrarian societies and the early civilizations had learned to treat human life as expendable in a manner not compatible with the thinking of more primitive peoples. "All aboriginal people accept the theory that every human being has the inalienable right to an irreducible minimum, consisting of adequate food, shelter, and clothing."[17] When the ties of kinship, or at least the feelings of kinship, are broken, the irreducible minimum may be denied. Sometimes the broken ties of kindred feeling also can lead to a particularly rigid system of social class known as caste.

CASTE   References to caste were made in previous chapters in discussing the Indian village of Gopalpur and the pastoralists of East Africa. Caste implies ascribed as opposed to achieved status, social, legal, and religious restrictions against upward mobility, and the avoidance of "pollution" of one caste by another. In the definitive case of India, caste was previously supported by law, and it continues to be part of the social and religious system. The people at the lowest level of the caste system, often referred to in America as pariahs, are more widely known in India as *harijans*, or "untouchables." Although Mahatma Gandhi gave them the name Children of God and despite the fact that according to the Untouchability Act of 1955 they are now considered to have equal voting rights and political rights, the feeling that they are defiling still exists, and most of them sweep floors, clean bathrooms, skin and tan hides, or bury the dead.

The present situation of the *harijans* is quite contradictory. The government insists on giving a quota of civil service jobs to them, making for better *harijan* employment opportunities than in the past. As of 1966–1967, over 130,000 were securing higher education, supported by government scholarships, out of a *harijan* population of about 60 million. At the same time, local custom, especially in rural districts, insists on keeping *harijans* in their place. Use of village wells has traditionally been denied them, and in some cases the use of a common well by untouchables is so strongly resisted by local populations that the government has tacitly recognized untouchability by providing funds for separate wells for the *harijans*.[18]

[16]Ibid., p. 281.
[17]Paul Radin, *Primitive Man*, E. P. Dutton & Co., Inc., New York, 1971, p. 106.
[18]William J. Coughlin, "Caste System Still Operates Inside India," *Los Angeles Times*, July 13, 1969, pp. 1–2.

There are two ways of describing Indian caste, the more common of which starts with the four major divisions of caste according to the laws of Manu—the Brahmans, or priestly caste; the Kshatriya, or warriors and rulers; the Vaisya, or traders and cultivators; and the Sudras, or servants. Below all these come the outcastes, assigned menial and defiling tasks. The major castes actually have a wide range of occupational possibilities, which causes them to break down into hundreds or even thousands of subcastes. The subcastes are so much the social reality, encountered everywhere, that the other way to describe the caste system is to start with them first. As was noted previously in the case of Gopalpur (Chapter Eight), the subcastes, or *jatis*, are largely occupational groupings, although criteria other than occupation influence their ranking. Occasionally a *jati* can gradually improve its status through the generations, thus giving a type of group mobility to a system that has been lacking in individual mobility.

Alan Beals compares the small, local subcastes to clans in the sense that all people belong to one or another caste and both castes and clans are, in theory, kinship groups with common ancestry.[19] However, in the case of castes, kinship has become so attenuated as to no longer be thought of very consciously; therefore, caste members marry within their own caste, whereas clans nearly always marry outside their group. The other difference is that clan members can perform any task, from those of a chieftain down to those of a common peasant, depending upon status within the clan itself. Castes and subcastes, on the other hand, are based on division of labor along traditional lines. Theoretically, the system should work out in such a way that all tasks are performed on a labor exchange system, called *jajmani* in some parts of India. The barber cuts all the hair, the ironworkers make the tools, the cobblers make the shoes, the plowmen tend the fields, and all receive payment in goods and services from the other groups that are served. Such an arrangement is old-fashioned but commonly encountered in villages and illustrates the theory on which the division-of-labor aspect of caste works.

Mason Olcott wrote a description of the caste system as it was in the past, before social reforms and the pressures of an industrializing society began to modify it.[20] His discussion of its origin and its functions is particularly important for understanding comparisons between caste and other class systems. Caste seems to have been molded by a number of factors, including the desire

[19] Alan R. Beals et al., *Culture in Process*, Holt, Rinehart and Winston, Inc., New York, 1967, pp. 86–90.
[20] Mason Olcott, "The Caste System of India," *American Sociological Review*, vol. 9, pp. 648–657, Dec. 6, 1944.

for cohesion among the many small tribes that made up India in the days before the Aryan invasion. The Aryan people from the northwest invaded during the second millennium B.C., bringing with them an already developed class system consisting of a ruling warrior group, the priestly class, and the commoners. The Aryans, wishing to preserve their identity, forbade marriage with the older Dravidian peoples, and they found already-existing avoidance ideas useful for the purpose. As more crafts developed in India, the Aryans with better paying occupations protected their interests and those of their descendants by a system of marriage only within the occupational guild and forced the more menial jobs and the handling of carcasses of dead animals onto some of the other groups. Even before the coming of the Aryans there were many food taboos, believed to have been similar to those of the present animistic Naga of Assam, who taboo alien food. The Naga fear that foreign food has a connection with the soul substance of its producers and might be magically injurious to them. The Indian caste taboos on food might once have had the same kind of explanation.

It would seem that the Aryans, with their supreme warrior class, would have made the Kshatriya supreme in India, and in earlier times they actually did; but the Brahmans, through a near monopoly on learning, religious interpretation, and magic, gained the ascendancy. In the sixth century B.C., Prince Siddhartha Gautama (Buddha) started a new religion opposing caste that temporarily won a wide following in India. However, the influence of Buddhism eventually waned. Hinduism was restored, and the Brahmans remained in their ancient position at the top of the caste hierarchy, partly because the Kshatriya had been decimated by constant warfare and partly by wile. The ancient Laws of Manu, which made the Brahmans' supremacy part of sacred creed, were restored with new vigor. The Brahmans held a monopoly in teaching and also fabricated tales and genealogies to help strengthen their status. In a sense, India emerged with an archaic system in which priestly prestige outweighed that of the rulers, even though the Kshatriya were usually the landowners. The situation only slightly violated general principles of class, however, in that religious and political power and wealth resided in the two upper classes, and those two classes became mutually supporting, each with its vested interest in the system. It is interesting to compare the situation with medieval France, where the clergy also were considered the first estate and the nobility the second. In France, too, most of the wealth and power rested in the hands of the nobility.

Although in some respects caste has always been a system of exploitation, it has also performed certain societal-maintenance functions, which Olcott identifies as reducing internal strife and giving continuity to Hindu learning. The metal workers in their guilds developed and protected high standards, and so did tool makers, potters, cobblers, and all the others. Each caste became something of a corporate group, cooperating for the benefit of its own members. In a way, caste even functioned for the individual, making his position certain and reducing the anxieties of choice and upward striving. It placed all but the very lowest into a vested interest position, giving them a degree of status relative to at least the lowest of the outcastes. Seen in the light of modern democratic values, it was a system of injustice and oppression for those at the bottom of the heap, but for centuries caste attitudes were so internalized as to be little questioned even by the lowly. The religion maintained that those in the lowest positions were inferiors whose souls must live through many more incarnations before they could be born into high status. It emphasized kindness, charitable giving, and respect for animals and for life in general, but gave little impetus to the type of social reform that would disturb caste position. In the material realm of economics, jobs, and industry, however, the caste system has received severe jolts.

What functioned in a nearly unchanging society fails to function in a modern state. More educated people are required than the top castes can supply, so that the door must be opened for a certain measure of competition. Consequently, there are now many cases of inconsistent status, with a well-to-do businessman, a Vaisya, employing a clerk who happens to be a Brahman. In a spiritual sense, the Brahman is still superior, but in material status the Vaisya might actually be more of a subject of envy.

NON-HINDU SYSTEMS OF CASTE   Within India, caste feelings have been so strong that the system draws in non-Hindus as well as Hindus. The Sikhs of the Punjab do not believe in caste, but they are fitted into caste position by their Hindu neighbors. So are the Muslims who remain in India. In nearby Burma, and even as far away as Bali, Indian ideas of caste have spread to a degree, but only as a shadow of the Indian system. When Hindus from India move abroad, they often attempt to upgrade themselves in the caste hierarchy, "passing" as they would never attempt in their own area. The very fact that Indian people in Africa and elsewhere try to move out of their own subcastes shows that the system is almost more social than religious.[21]

Other societies, in no way influenced by India, also have caste, but never quite fitting the definitive Indian case. During Spanish administration of Latin America, four class statuses were given the name "caste"—the Peninsulars

[21]Mita Dhariwal, formerly of Punjab, in interview with author.

(those born in Spain), the Colonials (Spaniards born in the New World), the Mestizos (mixed Spanish-Indian), and the Indians. The system was based on conquest and in two of the four cases involved racial difference. Intermarriage took place, but for Spaniards only marriages to other Spaniards were "right."

Africa has had several castelike states, in which pastoral people form an upper caste and gardeners a lower caste, with mixed breeds sometimes making an intermediate caste. Among the Banyankole, for example, none of the conquered gardening people are allowed to breed livestock or to carry weapons. Generally the upper and lower castes marry only their own members. Mixed children derive either from sexual relations outside of marriage or from concubinage and form an intermediate class. The two major casts are different in appearance, the upper being of tall Nilotic type.[22]

Japan, although not exactly a caste society, has a group of people called the Eta who are in outcaste position.[23] As in India, laws now give them full legal, political, and educational rights, but they continue to be looked down upon. In medieval times they were armor makers and had considerably higher status than they have now. The armor was made of leather, and the Eta have continued to be leather workers, but the trade has fallen to lowly status. In James Michener's novel *Hawaii* there is an excellent description of the deep concern of a Japanese mother for her son in the Hawaiian Islands for fear he might accidentally marry an Eta girl. Overseas the Eta try to pass as non-Eta. The mother warned that if her son married a girl from the city rather than a good farm girl, she would be disappointed but would accept her. If he were to marry a Chinese girl, she would also accept her, reluctantly. But if he were to marry an Eta, he could never again be accepted at home.

UNITED STATES CASTE   One can hardly fail to note that some of the characteristics of caste are similar to traditional racial attitudes in the United States. Such writers as Gunnar Myrdal (*An American Dilemma*) and John Dollard (*Class and Caste in a Southern Town*) have emphasized the point. In the past, it clearly could be said that caste differences were reinforced by differences in racial etiquette, the Jim Crow laws, a strict taboo against intermarriage, and in some cases even by religious attitudes—the myth of the Hamitic curse, for example. As in most of the other cases of caste, the conquest of a people was the beginning of the system; unlike the other cases, chattel slavery was part of

[22]Kalervo Oberg, "The Kingdom of Ankole in Uganda," in E.E. Evans-Pritchard and Meyer Fortes (eds.), *African Political Systems*, Oxford University Press, Fair Lawn, N.J., 1940, pp. 212–262.
[23]Hugh H. Smythe, "The Eta: A Marginal Japanese Caste," *American Journal of Sociology*, vol. 58, pp. 194–196, September 1952.

the background. As in the case of Indian caste, most discriminations are now outlawed, but local custom, occupational and residential patterns, and marriage customs still give racial practices a castelike appearance, more so in some parts of the country than in others.

In conclusion, caste always entails debased occupational status, open or implied rules of social avoidance, and restrictions against intermarriage. It is usually based on conquest, although not in the case of the Japanese Eta. Again with the exception of Japan, caste involves some degree of difference in appearance; even in India, the Brahmans and Kshatriya tend to be taller and lighter in complexion than the lower castes. Finally, it should be noted that caste systems are declining in importance, particularly for competitive, industrial states. Modern economics calls for a maximization of competition for expert knowledge and position, and hereditary restrictions on such competition are an anachronism. Thus caste can be said to function for societal stability but also for stagnation. Turning next to slave systems, we shall see that the production methods of the modern world make them obsolete also.

SLAVERY   Slavery has existed in many parts of the world at more than one level of economic development, but it was most prevalent before the Age of Industrialization and generally occurred in agricultural societies. Although hunting-and-gathering peoples sometimes take war captives as slaves, slavery does not have the same economic meaning to them as to more advanced peoples. Captured children are absorbed into the tribe, and women are taken as extra wives. Captive men are occasionally adopted into the capturing tribes, but more frequently they are killed. There is no way to benefit economically from labor of captives.

A famous study of the Tanala of Madagascar illustrates the development of slavery.[24] The Tanala were hill people who in the past had made their living partly by hunting but mainly by dry rice cultivation, slashing and burning new lands and spreading seed for the seasonal rains to germinate. Rice production was fairly good the first 2 or 3 years, but after 5 or 10 years the land wore out and had to be abandoned. Villages were moved to the sites of new clearings, where the process of soil exhaustion was repeated. Then, approximately two centuries ago, the idea of cultivating wet rice began to diffuse into the Tanala territory, and it gradually changed the way of life. From a pattern of democracy and full equality the society gradually changed to one of social class, individual property ownership, defensive warfare, and slavery. Slavery had been virtually

[24]Linton, op. cit., p. 352.

TRADITIONAL CASTE IN INDIA

OTHER TYPES OF CASTE

FOUR MAJOR DIVISIONS,
INNUMERABLE MINOR
DIVISIONS
RELIGIOUS SUPPORT
IDEA OF POLLUTION
ENDOGAMY IN MAJOR
CASTES
VIRTUALLY NO MOBILITY

JAPANESE ETA
SPANISH COLONIES
BANYAKOLE
BURMA (MODIFIED)
U.S. "RACIAL CASTES"

nonexistent before, but with the new farming system slaves had a value, since wet rice cultivation called for a large amount of backbreaking work. Man was able to become an economic exploiter of his fellow man through the institution of slavery—an institution that remains in many social systems until more efficient means of production develop.

VARIETIES OF SLAVERY   Slavery has not always been as debased a status as it was at its height in the United States and the Caribbean, nor has it always been a lifelong status. In the early days of the United States, thousands of immigrants entered the country as indentured servants, receiving their freedom once they had paid off their indentures. A few of the slaves from Africa were eventually given freedom, but as slavery began to pay better in the heyday of the cotton plantations, the slave status became absolute. Planters rationalized the existence of slavery, pointing out that it had existed in biblical times and that there had been slavery in the very continent of Africa from which the American slaves came. Although much was said about the decent and humane treatment of slaves, the American slave system was of a type that is hard to control by the kinds of normative regulation that have often existed in more traditional slave systems. When slavery exists on a small scale, with a family in charge of one or two slaves, the slaves often take on a status similar to that of the family. When slaves are controlled in large numbers and forced into labor by overseers, their status becomes more debased and the gulf between them and freemen widens. Such was the case with prisoner slaves in the Roman galleys, with impressed workers on great highways, walls, and monumental buildings, and, in much more recent history, with plantation hands. E. Franklin Frazier, in *The Black Bourgeoisie*, shows how the inferior status of field hands tended to carry over long after chattel slavery ended, keeping them and their descendants at the lowest levels of black American society, whereas the descendants of slaves who performed household duties often had knowledge that helped them to achieve a middle-class position.[25] A glance at some sample cases in Africa will show how various the status of slave can be.

AFRICAN SYSTEMS   Slavery has existed in ancient Greece and Rome, in the Far East, in medieval Europe, and also in Africa. It was of only minor importance among the American Indians, except among some of the civilized peoples of Mexico, where captive slaves were used in large numbers for human sacrifices. Since the majority of the peoples of Africa had more highly developed agricultural systems than most American Indian tribes, it is not surprising that slavery was more prevalent there than in the Americas. On a small scale, the African peoples had produced enough surplus goods to enable owners to enrich themselves on the labor of slaves. The European and American slave traders were to multiply this exploitative possibility a thousandfold, but the African systems of slavery are more important for our analysis because they show more variety and had a more usual origin.

Slave status was never an enviable one, even in societies where slaves were well treated. In slaveholding African societies in which kinship ties were very strong, a slave could almost be defined as one without a kinship group to support his interests (with an occasional exception among the Ashanti), and this lack made slave status precarious.[26] In other respects, slave status was not

[25] E. Franklin Frazier, *The Black Bourgeoisie*, The Free Press of Glencoe, Inc., New York, 1957.
[26] Ronald Cohen, "Slavery in Africa: Introduction," *Transaction*, vol. 4, pp. 44–46, January–February 1967.

A Dey king (Liberia) with family and servants. Often in West African households the status difference between kinsmen and servants was not very great, and servants were eventually absorbed into the kinship group.

as debased as in many parts of the world. Generally slaves could own land and other goods, engage in trade, marry, and produce children who would be born free. In Ibo and Ila, and usually in Ashanti society, slavery was eventually terminated by gradual incorporation into the master's kinship group. The favored slave of a high-status monarch or chief sometimes gained great power and prestige. To this day there are people in northern Nigeria who consider themselves slaves, because their slave status associates them with the households of the powerful.

The Kanuri of northern Nigeria, an Islamic people, engaged in wars and captured other people for slaves, usually non-Muslim people. Slave status could be inherited through the father but not through the mother; if the mother was a free woman, the children were free. Slaves functioned as farm workers, as domestic servants, and sometimes as soldiers in warfare. As in ancient Rome, slaves were sometimes used for deadly gladiatorial combat. Women slaves were often concubines. Men who became household servants were generally castrated so that they would not be a danger around the harems. Eunuchs were also used for secretarial duties in royal households. The highest slave status possible was that of *kachella*, military leader in a royal household, and it was this status that some former slaves were unwilling to abandon in recent years.[27]

In the powerful Ashanti society, the word *akoa* was applied to people of low class, but it was also applied to a slave who was considered part of the kinship system. A person could become a slave as the penalty for crime, or he could be sold by his kinsmen if he acquired too many fines and became a problem for them to maintain. One could even sell oneself into slavery temporarily if he had fallen so far into debt as to see no other way out. All war captives became slaves. The slaves had certain special protections; for example, a master could be fined more heavily for adultery with a slave girl than for adultery with a free girl. On the other hand, Ashanti slavery had its special risks; when important people died, slaves were sometimes killed and buried with them as sacrifices. Slaves were used for farming and household tasks and also for carrying cargoes. Many of the Ashanti were wealthy and powerful and could gain prestige and increase their incomes by the ownership of slaves. The one redeeming feature of Ashanti slavery was a modification by the fictive kinship bond. All slaves who were fortunate enough not to become sacrifices were constantly moving in the direction of absorption into households and kinship groups. Occasionally even members of royalty would marry slaves.[28]

There were other variations of African slavery. In Zanzibar powerful Arabic people owned slaves, and a portion of those slaves became plantation workers. For the most part, however, their period of service was not for life and the treatment was rather mild.[29] It was in the New World, where far greater profits were to be made and where the distinction between races was great enough to easily eradicate the feelings of common humanity, that slavery reached its most debased form.

In the New World, however, other forces were at work that were gradually making slavery an archaic system. Contrary to the opinions of the champions of slavery, it was soon proved that agriculture could be carried on with greater efficiency without slavery. In industrial countries, the system of wages became more efficient. It released the owner from responsibility for his workers at times when there were no jobs to be done, but it also brought levels of productivity that would eventually make abundance for all a realizable goal.

[27]Ronald Cohen, "Slavery among the Kanuri," *Transaction*, vol. 4, pp. 48–50, January–February 1967.

[28]David McCall, "Slavery in Ashanti (Ghana)," *Transaction*, vol. 4, pp. 55–56, January–February 1967.

[29]John Middleton, "Slavery in Zanzibar," *Transaction*, vol. 4, pp. 46–48, January–February 1967.

CULTURAL EVOLUTIONARY VIEW OF SOCIAL CLASS

HUNTING AND GATHERING SOCIETIES
VERY LITTLE IF ANY CLASS. EVERYONE ENTITLED TO AN "IRREDUCIBLE MINIMUM"

HORTICULTURE SOCIETIES
VERY LITTLE TO FAIRLY ELABORATE CLASS, OR RANKING. OFTEN REDISTRIBUTIVE AGENTS.

AGRICULTURAL SOCIETIES AND EARLY CIVILIZATIONS
CLASS ALWAYS PRESENT. USUALLY VERY RIGID FREQUENT CASES OF SLAVERY. OFTEN AN EXPENDABLE UNDERCLASS.

MODERN INDUSTRIAL SOCIETIES
GREAT INEQUALITY, BUT CLASSES ILL-DEFINED. MOBILITY GOVERNMENT AS REDISTRIBUTIVE AGENT EXPENDABLE UNDERCLASS OF UNEMPLOYED AND/OR UNEMPLOYABLE.

THE TREND OF SOCIAL CLASS   As has been noted, at the most primitive levels of hunting and food gathering, class systems do not exist. In unusually wealthy hunting societies and in horticultural or pastoral societies, modified types of social class come into existence. Sometimes they are ranking systems, in which chieftains are surrounded with tremendous pomp and ceremony and perform a redistributive function. Sometimes they go beyond individual ranking to systems that fit all people into particular classes, but even then they are usually modified by feelings of kinship among occupants of different class positions. In early civilizations and agrarian societies, feelings of kinship between rich and poor disappear and tremendous economic differences develop. At the top of the society are the holders of landed wealth and power and at the bottom, common peasants and laborers or even beggars and thieves. At intermediate levels are administrators, priests, military men, merchants, and skilled craftsmen, but they make up only a very small percentage of the total society.

240

In a few special cases class has taken on the completely rigid form of caste. Very frequently, even when the system is not completely castelike, there has been an undercaste of slaves, who are much more oppressed in urban civilizations and agrarian societies than in more primitive social orders.

CLASS IN THE MODERN WORLD   In the modern world important changes have taken place in class systems. Slavery has disappeared, superseded by more efficient systems of hired labor. Aristocracies have been undergoing a long decline, even in countries where noble titles still exist. Industrial systems demanding many levels of expertise, managerial and governmental skills, merchandising, scientific research, and professional services have called into existence new types of middle classes, which make up a large part of the population. Labor unions, legislation, and the high productivity of labor have resulted in increased wages in the leading countries of the world. The ownership of wealth has passed into the hands of gigantic corporations, with thousands of investors, ranging from middle-income people to a type of super-rich who could have bought out whole kingdoms of earlier days. To an increasing degree in all countries and almost totally in the communist countries, the management of the great surplus wealth of the society is in the hands of the government.

Ironically, the great industrial societies produce at least as many "expendables" as did the agrarian systems discussed before. Not all potential workers can be used gainfully, and unemployment is a problem. Then, too, there are people whose skills are displaced by new methods; there are some without the ability to learn the skills needed by a technical society; there are some who have not been given the opportunity to obtain skills; and there are always the old, the sick, and the disabled. The new governmental systems act as redistributive agencies and have leveling mechanisms. Their chieftains find that they must dispense vast amounts of wealth, either directly or in public works. They claim to believe in an "irreducible minimum" as a right of all people, just as did their primitive forebears. The new systems also attempt, with a fair measure of success, to allow for movement upward by the people born to the lowliest positions. The new societies face many other problems, but those bearing on social class are really threefold—providing for upward mobility and "circulation of elites," keeping economic systems flourishing so that most of the expendables can be absorbed into productive jobs, and acting successfully as redistributive agencies that will take care of the needs of the underclass.

The followers of Karl Marx have looked upon social class as purely a system of exploitation and have exalted the simple hunting societies that were classless or nearly so. They have written of the virtues of primitive communism—a kind of golden age when land and other resources were held in common. Lowie went to considerable pains to point out that there have always been some kinds of private property, such as tools and weapons and even some types of magic spells and songs; nevertheless, there was far more communal ownership among primitives than there is among moderns. The important argument is not whether Marxists have exaggerated their picture of primitive communism but rather whether they have oversimplified the function of social class. Does class serve only as a means of exploitation, or does it serve useful purposes for an entire society?

The functionalists would argue that social class develops as a need for it develops. As societies become more complex, there is greater need for leadership, and granting deference to the most important offices tends to assure that such offices will be held by capable people. It is easy to point to cases where the function of providing capable leadership miscarries—in cases of simple or mad kings, for example, or of incompetent modern bureaucrats. It also seems questionable whether the gulf between rich and poor needs to be as great as it often is or whether channels of upward mobility should be so often closed. Nevertheless, it is difficult to conceive of a smoothly functioning but completely classless state in the modern industrial world. Apparently social class develops even in Marxist states. The rules for its development have changed from the manipulation of capital assets to scientific and technical competence, or often merely to shrewd political maneuvering, but the fact of social stratification remains.

PART FOUR
THE HUMAN BOND

In the previous section it was found that studying peoples with different means of subsistence is impossible without also considering the social bonds that hold them together. The social bonds were discussed under the generalized heading ''social organization.'' In the course of these discussions, much was said about the importance of kinship, and customs unfamiliar to us were presented—bride price, polygyny, patrilineage, and the like. The great importance of kinship and other forms of organization was so obvious that it seems necessary to pursue the subject further. Can anything be said theoretically about why some types of kinship systems are more prevalent in primitive hunting-and-gathering societies and others in pastoral or agrarian societies? Why is it that in most modern societies it no longer seems important to maintain distant kinship ties or trace lineages? What types of social organization eventually begin to supplement that of family, band, lineage, or tribe?

Family and kinship are of great interest to anthropologists because kinship is the center of social cohesion in societies without complex state or legal institutions. Through understanding the kinship systems, the anthropologist learns much about the interaction patterns of the people, including their loyalties and jealousies, gift giving, celebrations, ancestral observances, family shrines and mythologies, collective efforts, and internal bickerings. Kinship has great importance throughout the human species in creating sentimental ties. Since it is also a system of status and obligation, kinship is just as important in primitive societies in determining rules of obedience, reciprocity, inheritance, and government.

Why do some tribes pay more attention to female descent than to male, and why do the majority trace their descent through the male? Why do some people make no distinction between siblings and cousins but simply classify brothers, sisters, and cousins all together? Why do some societies place very limited emphasis on the nuclear family of mother, father, and their children? Why do some societies become completely absorbed in kinship, joint families, and descent systems? These are some of the difficult questions to be looked at in the following pages.

Finally, we must ask what causes the social system to move past a kinship and tribal base and begin to evolve into the less personal and familistic system known as a state. What are the advantages and disadvantages of the state from the point of view of the common man? In the gradual development from band to state, the law changes. Social control, or the idea of rules and regulations, is always present in human groups but not with the full formality of law. What conditions must be met before generally recognized rules of conduct actually become law? What are the functions of supernatural beliefs in connection with the development of law? How does modern law differ from primitive, ancient, or medieval law? Are we evolving better means of organization and of justice?

The logical starting point for a section devoted to the human bond is marriage and family. These are institutions that hold societies together and give them stability, especially small hunting-gathering or horticultural societies without other specialized institutions. In this chapter we shall look mainly at marriage and the conjugal family in the three major forms—polygynous, polyandrous, and monogamous. In the following chapter, more will be said about extended families that include large numbers of kinsmen.

Family systems are so variable and so important that they have long attracted the attention of anthro-pologists. Many nineteenth century anthropologists, most notably Morgan, thought of the family as an institution that had evolved over a period of thousands of years from pure promis-cuity to group marriage, then to plural marriage systems, and finally to the monogamous family of the Western world. Actually, the evidence does not support such a simple evolutionary development. One of the strongest cases against the theory is that monog-amy is the preferred marriage form among a majority of simple hunting-and-gathering societies. Polygnous families, extended families, lineages, and clans are most elaborated in societies where the family has many tasks to perform. Even such unusual

Chapter Ten
Marriage and
Family

systems as polyandry (one wife with more than one husband), or systems in which paternal responsibilities belong not to the biological father but to the mother's brother, represent adaptations that should be called "specialized" but not "primitive."

How are we, then, to deal with the family in an anthropology book that stresses cultural-evolutionary perspectives? Actually the problem is not insurmountable. Leslie White shows ways in which the basis for choice of marriage partners changes as societies grow from the very small bands of hunting-and-gathering peoples to large, mobile societies. In Chapter Eleven we shall look at Elman Service's analysis of a type of evolution in kinship terminology and at Paul Kirchhoff's view of the growth and decline of what he calls "clanship." In a more general way we shall see that there is a type of evolutionary change if the family is viewed as only one of a number of institutions that provide for social cohesion. In this way it will be seen that the family over the long range of human history has found more and more other institutions supplementing its tasks and that it has lost some of its functions. First we shall look at the wide range of possible marriage and family systems. How have societies generally managed to provide marriage partners for nearly all their members? How have they provided for children? How are the institutions of polygyny and polyandry to be explained? Are there any conditions under which the family approaches the vanishing point? In Chapter Eleven we shall ask under what conditions family systems become extended and how lineage and clan systems usually decline in modern industrial society. We also shall look briefly at some of the complexities of the naming of kinsmen, and finally we shall turn to the trends that seem to be prevalent in family structure as the world becomes increasingly industrialized and urbanized.

PROVIDING
MARRIAGE PARTNERS

In any society there are rules and regulations about who should marry whom. Generally the rules have a certain practicality about them, so that only people of the same generation marry, although there are notable exceptions. Occasionally infant girls are considered married to the men who will later actually be their marital mates and are reared in the husband's household with the idea that paternal affection will combine with a husband's affection to make a good marriage.[1] Among the Siberian Chuckchi there were cases of young women of about twenty marrying two- or three-year-old boys and rearing them till they reached marital age, with the same

[1]For example, see account of a Tupi-Kawahib marriage in Claude Lévi-Strauss, *Tristes Tropiques*, Atheneum Publishers, New York, 1965, pp. 352–353.

idea of having compatible mates.[2] In Tiwi society, where old men attempted to maintain a monopoly on women, girls were married at birth and were expected to perform wifely duties as they reached the age of puberty. Men sometimes also inherited wives from deceased friends or relatives—and such a wife might belong to a man's mother's or grandmother's generation. Inherited wives could help with the tasks of food gathering and were a source of prestige but lacked some of the traits usually desired in wives. Generally marriage has the dual function of providing people with fairly compatible sexual partners and ensuring offspring. Many marriage arrangements were discussed in Part Three, and we have seen that often there are fairly definite rules about whom a person should marry. The rules can be interpreted as restrictions against some types of marriage and as assuring that nearly everyone gets married. The division of labor in primitive societies is based largely on sexual and kinship ties, so that marriage and kinship serve to allocate jobs, property, rights, and duties.

Lévi-Strauss points out the sharp contrast between large, modern societies, where each man has numerous potential mates from whom to choose, and the smallest primitive societies, where the number of possibilities is extremely limited.[3] Therefore, it seems that rules have been developed to assure marriage partners for all people by a method that will avoid too much difficulty. It will be remembered that among the Eskimo there have been frequent fights over women. In many primitive bands the problem of potential quarrels is solved by laying down definite rules as to who has first claim to a particular woman. Often the marriage partner is a man's mother's brother's daughter, or occasionally his father's sister's daughter. There is yet another way to arrange marriages, and that is to divide the tribe into two halves in such a way that each half (called a moiety) exchanges brides with the other half. Occasionally the tribe is further divided into many sections. We ran across one case of Australian aborigines who elaborated tremendously on the rules of marriage, with each of eight subsections of a tribe marrying in successive generations into each of the others. The case makes an interesting illustration of the great complexities that can be calculated by even the most primitive of peoples when the motivation or interest is sufficient. Among the Tiv of Nigeria, a kind of sister-exchange marriage took place.[4] A man with a number of sisters could trade them for the sisters of another man, and thus obtain wives for himself.

[2]Claude Lévi-Strauss, "The Family," in Harry Shapiro (ed.), *Man, Culture, and Society*, Oxford University Press, New York, 1960, p. 273.
[3]Ibid., pp. 278–283.
[4]Margaret Mead (ed.), *Cultural Patterns and Technical Change*, Mentor Books, New American Library, Inc., New York, 1955, pp. 96–125.

Obviously, the system would break down for a family with several sons and only one daughter, so that cousins sometimes had to be substituted, and sometimes an unfortunate man was deprived of any possible "proper" marriage. Even the rules of cousin marriage would run into troubles if the right type of cousin did not exist. Sometimes shrewd negotiations and additional payments make it possible to get a bride anyway.

Although many rules have called for the "right" person for a man to marry, there are also rules that deny the right to certain mates. With rare exception, marriage to sisters has been strictly taboo. Such a taboo could be interpreted as preventing a violation of someone else's prescriptive right; that is, if A's sister is supposed to become the wife of his cousin, then A would be violating another man's rights by marrying her. Kinship theorists, though, do not consider prescriptive rights a major cause of sister avoidance in marriage.

At first glance one might assume that there is a natural revulsion against such marriage, yet it is well known that some exceptions take place. Cases of incest are known in all societies. Furthermore, there have been a few societies in which royal blood was so royal that it could not be contaminated with common blood; in a few such cases, especially ancient Egypt, brother and sister married. The "divine liquid" of the pharaohs was thus kept pure.

EXOGAMY AND THE INCEST TABOO   The rule against sexual relations with very close relatives has so few exceptions that it is referred to as the "universal incest taboo." One's offhand impression might be that close-relative marriage has been avoided by many people because of the fear of biological harm, but there are three reasons for thinking the biological explanation is not the correct one. In the first place, many tribes do not carry the incest taboo so far as to exclude first-cousin marriages, and in the case of royal or sacred lineages, Egyptians, Incas, and Hawaiians all permitted brother-sister marriage. Second, the ill effects of inbreeding are by no means certain and immediately observable. If there are no genetic weaknesses in the heredity of the two mates, none will appear in the offspring. If there are such weaknesses, even in recessive genes, it is true they are more apt to appear in a close-marriage situation; but unfavorable traits are not so common and inevitable that primitive people are likely to have made important discoveries about genetics. Third, psychological and sociological explanations seem to fit the facts better than a biological explanation.

There are psychological objections to the marriage of brothers and sisters, which may be based on a natural lack of sexual interest between people reared together in such a relationship or may exist simply because people are *taught* to regard such relations as abhorrent. There is some evidence that for many people the former, natural-aversion explanation holds true. In the Israeli commune known as the kibbutz, children are reared together as though they were brothers and sisters, even though they are not related. When they mature, they usually choose mates from other communes, not their own. Those who are reared as brothers and sisters seem less attractive as mates than do those reared apart.[5]

A custom that used to occur in rural Chinese families, the marriage of *simpua*, may also cast some light on sexual aversion for siblings. *Simpua* were little girls adopted into a family for the purpose of eventually becoming wives of the sons of the family. The practice helped parents bring up their daughters-in-law in the manner they desired and further strengthened their hand in arranging marriages. Reared in close proximity, the future marriage partners seemed very much like brother and sister, and psychological problems often developed between spouses for this reason,[6] although the marriages were successful enough that the practice continued.

One sociological explanation of the incest taboo has already been suggested in another context. It operates to ensure that marriages are far enough outside the family to provide marriage alliances with other families. This explanation is pursued below under the heading of exogamy-endogamy.

Another common theory of a sociological nature is that presented by Malinowski.[7] His conclusion is that rules against incest were developed to preserve family relationships. A family would exist in a state of chaos if brothers were rivals for their own sisters or if mother-son or father-daughter incest were permitted. All social systems become systems of rights, duties, and obligations and respect for status. The family must function for economic cooperation and the care, protection, and socialization of new members, and respect for status is necessary for these functions. The status of brother, sister, mother, or father is very different from the status of husband or wife and calls for different behavior patterns. In spite of the fact that our primate relatives are often incestuous and although incest occurs not only in myth and legend but in real life, cultures have developed forceful rules against it and severe training about its evilness. In Navaho belief, those who commit incest will be destroyed by fire. In ancient Greek legend, Oedipus blinded himself when he learned of his unintended incest with his mother.

[5]Melford E. Spiro, "Is the Family Universal?" *American Anthropologist*, vol. 56, pp. 845–846, October 1954.

[6]Margery Wolfe, *The House of Lim: A Study of a Chinese Farm Family*, Appleton Century Crofts, New York, 1968, pp. xv, 75–98.

[7]Bronislaw Malinowski, "Culture," *Encyclopedia of the Social Sciences*, vol. 4. 1931, pp. 621–646.

EXPLANATION OF INCEST TABOO

TYPE OF EXPLANATION	REASON GIVEN	COMMENTS
BIOLOGICAL	INCEST WOULD RESULT IN HEREDITARY PROBLEMS	NOT LIKELY PRIMITIVES WOULD LEARN MUCH ABOUT GENETICS
PSYCHOLOGICAL	CHILDREN REARED TOGETHER SHOW LITTLE SEXUAL ATTRACTION	KIBBUTZ AND CHINESE SIMPUA MARRIAGES SEEM TO SUPPORT THEORY
SOCIOLOGICAL	MARRY OUT TO FORM FAMILY ALLIANCES	MORE A MATTER OF EXOGAMY THAN OF INCEST TABOO
	SEX RIVALRY WOULD DISTURB OTHER FAMILY RELATIONSHIPS	THEORY GENERALLY UPHELD BY MARRIAGE RULES BUT THERE ARE A FEW EXCEPTIONS

If, then, mating relations between close kin are to be avoided, why do some peoples permit or even prefer first-cousin marriages? The most common explanation is a matter of social relationships again. Very frequently the cousins who marry are reared in separate households or even separate villages and have had little contact with one another; therefore their marriage does not result in the role contradictions or the in-family jealousies that might otherwise occur. A simple diagram of a family group will help make the point clear. In anthropological diagrams, Δ = male, 0 = female; an = sign stands for marriage, vertical lines for descent, and horizontal lines for sibling relationship.

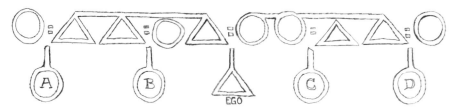

In the above diagram, ego is represented as a male. He has four female cousins, A, B, C, and D. If he belongs to a tribe in which father and father's brother live close to each other in the grandparent's home, the cousin B will seem like a sister to him and probably will not be a potential mate. Sometimes, too, both cousins B and C will be considered a little more closely related than the other two cousins because they are both parallel cousins. "Parallel cousins" are cousins whose relationship is traced through parents of the same sex, that is, through mother and mother's sister or through father and father's brother. Where lineages are important, such cousins are considered very close kinsmen because they belong to the same lineages as ego. Cousins A and D are related through parents of opposite sex, that is, through father's sister and mother's brother. Cousin D is the one most likely to be favored as a marital partner, although not the only possibility. D is a member of the mother's family group, but she is probably reared in a village separate from that of the mother and therefore does not seem like a sister. Cousins A and C would also be reared separately from ego, assuming this is a patrilocal society (one in which sons settle near the household of their father). The reason mother's brother's daughter is often preferred is that a woman's brothers are likely to assume a protective attitude toward her and her children and bestow one of their daughters on her son.[8] It will be recalled that even among the fierce Yanomamö

[8]George D. Homans and D. M. Schneider, *Marriage, Authority, and Final Causes: A Study of Unilateral Cross-Cousin Marriage*, Glencoe Press, The Macmillan Company, New York, 1955.

a woman hoped to receive some protection from her brother. If a man marries his mother's brother's daughter, he is also renewing a marriage alliance with his mother's kinsmen. If he marries his other cross cousin, his father's sister's daughter, he is strengthening ties with his own patrilineage and with the family of his father's sister's husband. In either case, an already-existing tie is strengthened, and the marriage can be said to foster group solidarity.

Relatives on the father's side of the family are called "patrilateral" relatives; father's brother's daughter is therefore a patrilateral parallel cousin. It would seem that in any patrilineal society such a cousin would be reared very close to ego and would seem too much like a sister to be a marital partner. This is usually the case, but the Bedouin Arabs are an exception to the rule. The preferred marriage is between a man and his father's brother's daughter. Probably the factor that makes this a preferred marriage is a greater than average need for solidarity between brothers. The custom has been most marked among the nomadic Arabs, where little government has existed and members of patrilineages have formed extremely close bonds both for protective purposes and for the sake of keeping rights to water sources in the family.[9] Although brothers do in fact quarrel, a cult of brotherhood exists, strengthened by Koranic law. The preferred marriage also meets the previously mentioned function of providing each person with a proper mate. The difficulty with the feeling of a brother-sister bond is modified by the oversheltering of Arab girls. After they begin to mature, they have little contact with boys, even their own cousins. Nothing resembling close brother-sister interaction would exist between the Bedouin Arab girl and her patrilateral parallel cousin.

ENDOGAMY-EXOGAMY   "Endogamy" is defined as the practice of marrying within one's own group, and "exogamy" means marrying outside the group. The group is usually taken to mean a particular tribe or major subdivision of a tribe, but the words endogamy and exogamy can apply to various types of groups. Hence, most marriages are exogamous in some respects and endogamous in others. In the United States, for example, very few people marry cousins, even distant cousins, and in this respect we are exogamous. On the other hand, we nearly always marry members of our own social class and race, and usually of our own religion, and are in these respects endogamous.

For primitive societies, there are usually rules of both endogamy and exogamy. White speaks of endogamy and exogamy as processes.[10] Endogamy

[9]Richard Randolph, "The Palestine Arabs," lecture delivered at the University of California, Berkeley, Summer, 1963.
[10]Leslie White, *The Evolution of Culture*, McGraw-Hill Book Company, New York, pp. 101–105.

is the process of increasing solidarity through marriage within the group; exogamy is the process of gaining new allies for the group by marrying out. The ideal arrangement for a tribe would be to marry out only to a degree that does not break up group solidarity but sufficiently to allow a degree of expansion of the group. White argues convincingly that there has been a type of evolution of marriage in a progression from fairly strict endogamy to more exogamous requirements. Cousin marriage, especially required cousin marriage, is much more common in primitive tribes than in more advanced societies. In modern societies, where kinship solidarity is of declining importance, marriages tend to be much more exogamous. Even at societal levels prior to modern industrialism, such as advanced agrarian societies, the restrictive ties of kin marriage generally weaken. The most notable exception to this rule has been among noble families, who have sometimes become closely inbred in order to cement dynastic alliances. An endogamous tendency can also be noted among old elite families of great wealth, who often find only a few potential mates for their offspring, again the problem of the very small, restricted society.

Marriages are brought about for more purposes, of course, than providing mates and solidifying groups or winning allies. The procreation of offspring and their care is, with extremely few exceptions, the duty of the family and one of its major reasons for existence.

PROCREATION Sometimes in cases of extreme poverty, societies have permitted the killing of babies so that there would be enough food for those already born, and sometimes defective babies have been killed. Infanticide was practiced to some degree among Australian aborigines and among Kalahari Bushmen. According to Elizabeth Thomas, the practice of infanticide was a terrible ordeal for the Bushman mother, but it had to be done if there were more infants than she could possibly support.[11] Some of the Bushmen tried to practice sexual restraint for long periods of time to avoid the possibility of having to kill an infant, for they loved their children. Sometimes the desire for children is a matter of ambition or the need for soldiers or making provision for security in old age rather than just affection, but the desire for children is strong and attested to by many customs. Among the Nuer, for example, if a man dies without any living children, his wife might pay bride price so another couple can marry and bear children to her dead husband's name—his "ghost children." Often

[11]Elizabeth Marshall Thomas, *The Harmless People*, Alfred A. Knopf, Inc., New York, 1959, pp. 88–90.

children are adopted to prevent a line from dying out. The importance of children is also attested by the provision for bride price by most patrilineal groups. If the man's family is to claim the children as its own, it seems only right that a considerable price should be paid for the bride.

Jomo Kenyatta describes the marriage system as it has existed among his Gikuyu (also spelled Kikuyu) people. His description shows the great desire for children and also the importance of bride price, gift exchange, and ceremonial customs that compensate the bride's family for their loss and solidify relations between the two families.

> In the Gikuyu community marriage and its obligations occupy a position of great importance. One of the outstanding features in the Gikuyu system is for every member of the tribe to build up his own family group, and by this means to extend and prolong his father's *mbari* (clan). This results in strengthening the tribe as a whole. . . .
>
> The Gikuyu tribal custom requires that a married couple should have at least four children, two male and two female. The first male is regarded as perpetuating the existence of the man's father, the second as perpetuating that of the woman's father. The first and second female children fulfill the same ritual duty to the souls of their grandmothers on both sides. The children are given names of the persons whose souls they represent.[12]

Thus sentimental, politico-economic, and quasi-religious reasons combine to produce a high birthrate among the Gikuyu. There are other indications of the great importance of procreation. Marriage is assured for all Gikuyu. Since men marry in their twenties and girls at the age of puberty, there are more eligible females than males, so that many men can have more than one wife. According to Kenyatta's account, frequently after the first wife has a child or two, she begins to insist that her husband marry another woman so there will be help in caring for the children and in preparing meals for the husband and his guests and taking care of his house and gardens. If she is a good wife, she will wish the family to grow in size and esteem and will see some advantages for herself in additional wives. She may ask her husband to marry another wife while he is still young and vigorous, saying, *"Mae megotherera matietagerera mondo onyotie."* ("The flowing water of the river does not wait for a thirsty man.")[13] Since the average amount paid for a bride is approximately thirty sheep and goats, there are economic determinants as to how many wives

[12]Jomo Kenyatta, *Facing Mount Kenya*, Vintage books, Random House, Inc., New York, 1936, pp. 157–158.
[13]Ibid., p. 170.

a man can have, and a man's importance can be measured to a great extent in terms of the number of his wives and children. Kenyatta undoubtedly gives a somewhat idealized picture of family relationships, but there is no doubt that in societies accustomed to polygynous marriages there is nothing like the jealousy between wives that a person from the Western world might imagine. The Gikuyu husband is expected to be equally devoted to each of his wives, having been taught always that love should not be exclusive and that the best people can share affection with others. "To live with others is to share and to have mercy for one another; it is witch-doctors who live and eat alone."[14]

The wives occupy separate huts. They cooperate in the gardening, and in the feeding and milking of goats and cows, too, if they are fortunate enough to have cows. The husband helps with the livestock and with the heavier work of clearing land. He also keeps harmony within the compound. A schedule is arranged by which he spends 3 consecutive nights with each of his wives. It is most important that he spend the 3 nights after menstruation has ceased because it is then that his wife desires him most and it is then that she is most likely to become pregnant and to add another child to the family. During pregnancy, for fear of injury to the fetus, sexual relations are supposed to be carried on only with restraint and minimal penetration by the husband.

The idea that the man can love more than one woman is partly complemented by the institution of wife hospitality to certain guests. When members of the husband's age group (those who went through the rites of puberty with him) who live a considerable distance away come to visit, they are invited to spend the night. The wives, under these circumstances, grant their sexual favors to the husband's friends. Any other type of extramarital affair on the part of a wife, however, is regarded as adultery and is punished severely.

Since children are valued, no particular question is raised as to the possibility that one of the children might have actually been fathered by one of the husband's age mates rather than by himself. Sociological or legal fatherhood is what really matters, although it is important for both man and wife to be fertile. If a wife bears no children, she is sometimes permitted to have sexual relations with another man in order to discover whether the failure to conceive is her fault or that of the husband. Corresponding arrangements are made for a man if he has only one wife. The barren wife is of greatly reduced value and may even be returned home to her parents, along with an insistence on return of bride price; but sometimes, if she is otherwise a good wife, she will be kept and children will be adopted. A sterile husband can avoid childlessness by allowing one of his age mates to sire his children. Ideally, the traditional

[14]Ibid., p. 172.

Gikuyu system managed to get everyone married and to make sure that all families produced offspring.

AFFINAL MARRIAGE   "Affine" is the legal word for a relative by marriage. There are two very common cases of marriage to affines in case of the death of one's spouse—"sororate" and "levirate." Although these customs have other functions, they can be interpreted in part as a way of guaranteeing family continuity and, for people who are still young, of allowing procreation to continue. Sororate is the custom by which a man marries the sister of his deceased wife, providing she is not already married. The custom is most common where considerable bride price is paid and the wife's family feels obligated to provide another mate for their son-in-law. Ideally, the new wife should be a young girl, who can fulfill all wifely duties and produce offspring. Her marriage to her brother-in-law will also keep up a tie of friendly alliance between two families, which is nearly always one of the functions of marriage. Occasionally, there will be no sister available, or the sister will be so young that her prospective husband will have to wait for a number of years. Once in a while another woman is substituted, such as the former wife's cousin or niece or even her unmarried or widowed aunt. Even if the new wife is too old to produce children, she can still perform the other duties of a wife.

Levirate is the custom whereby a man marries his deceased brother's wife. Interpreted purely in terms of procreation, it allows more children to be born to the patrilineage of the man and his brother. Levirate also has normative implications. In ancient Hebrew society, levirate was practiced so that widows and orphans would have protectors, and the same idea has existed among many Islamic people. Muhammad himself was never in a position to practice levirate, since he had no widowed sisters-in-law; but he followed the normative ideal that is often implied in levirate rules. Two of Muhammad's four marriages were to widows of his generals who had fallen in battle. Koranic law allows a man as many as four wives, and they do not have to be widows; however, marriage to protect the widow and orphan has always been looked upon as the ideal. Levirate is much more easily instituted in a polygynous society than in a monogamous society, where the living brother might already be married to the only wife he is permitted.

In societies where bride price is paid, the custom of levirate can also be looked upon in economic terms. If a father and mother paid considerable bride price for a wife for their elder son, it seems only fair that when he dies his dearly purchased wife should belong to another of their sons. Largely for this reason, levirate is most common in patrilineal societies, where bride price is most common. It should be said, incidentally, that the purchase of a wife is not thought of as belittling to her; one can interpret bride price as a sign that women are valued. Many people among whom this custom is practiced would see our paying nothing for a wife as a sign of stinginess and as an insult to women.

The student of European history is more familiar with levirate as a forbidden custom than as a preferred one. It will be recalled that the legal ground on which Henry VIII sought an annulment of his marriage to Catherine of Aragon was that she had once been betrothed to his elder brother, Arthur. King Henry became convinced that the marriage was incestuous and had not been blessed with living male issue for that reason. Regardless of whether one is convinced of King Henry's sincerity (it has more plausibility than most people would think), the case is interesting from the point of view of the rights and wrongs of levirate. A custom practiced by the ancient Hebrews was outlawed by the medieval church, but undoubtedly the church officials knew that the custom had once been permitted. The explanation for the change of custom is probably closely associated with our general observation that marriage customs tend to fit other folkways and norms of the society. The abandonment of polygyny made levirate a less practical custom than it had once been, but there are also normative problems involved in levirate. If a man's brother's wife is looked upon as a potential mate, might there not be jealousy in the family or even a temptation to regard her as an actual wife? As noted earlier, among American Indians, "anticipatory levirate" was actually practiced in a few cases. Since a younger brother might inherit his sister-in-law, he was allowed sexual rights to her, at least until such time as he acquired a wife of his own. Carrying the dangers of levirate to their ultimate, we can think of the plot of *Hamlet*, in which Hamlet's uncle is believed to have murdered his own brother in order to inherit the kingdom and marry Hamlet's mother.

POLYGYNY Polygyny has been mentioned so often in this chapter and elsewhere that its meaning is probably obvious. It would be well, though, to clear up a little terminological confusion about multiple marriages. Polygyny is the word used in anthropology to refer specifically to a family with one husband and more than one wife. The commonly used word "polygamy" can refer to polygyny or to the opposite practice of "polyandry," in which a wife has more than one husband. "Bigamy" refers specifically to a person's having two mates instead of one but is not adequate to describe the polygynous or polyandrous family.

The many cases of polygyny that have been mentioned so far make it clear that polygyny is by no means an unusual family system. As a matter of fact, more societies known to anthropologists permit polygyny than forbid it. Nevertheless, polygyny is not as frequent a marriage pattern as monogamy for the simple reason that there are usually not enough women available to allow all men to have extra wives. Usually only a few men have polygynous households and the majority get by with only one wife. In old Chinese families, wealthy men sometimes had additional wives, but the poor peasant seldom had more than one. In Islamic countries, Koranic law permits extra wives only to men of means and high standards.

A number of arguments can be made in favor of polygynous marriages, even though they fall on deaf ears in Western societies. If it is a societal ideal that all women should marry, then it would seem wise to permit at least a few men to have extra wives, since there are usually slightly more women than men. An old-fashioned male moralist could argue, as some do, that unmarried women may be tempted into extramarital affairs and even prostitution, causing the morality of the society to decline. Some people have even made a genetic argument for polygyny based on the theory that the stronger and abler males would have more mates and more offspring and the less competent would be less likely to perpetuate their kind. Occasionally polygyny has become a real necessity because of a shortage of males. In this respect, Baganda society once constituted an almost ideal case for polygyny.

BAGANDA POLYGYNY   In the old days of the Baganda kingdom, in the present African state of Uganda, several pressures operated to keep down the number of males in the population relative to the number of females.[15] As in many societies, considerable warfare killed off some of the young men, and occasional internecine struggles of rebellious chiefs against the powerful king had the same effect. Offenses against the king were often punished by execution, and priests sacrificed human victims, mainly male. There was also a much less common practice that cut down on the male population—male infanticide. If the firstborn child of a chief was a male, he was considered an ill omen for the father. In such a case the midwife strangled the baby and told the chief it was stillborn. The consequence of such customs was that in the late nineteenth century there were about 3 times as many women as men in the Baganda kingdom, with as many as 100 wives for the king, large numbers for the chiefs, and 2 or 3 for commoners.

---

[15]The material in this section is based on Stuart A. Queen et al., *The Family in Various Cultures*, J. B. Lippincott Company, Chicago, 1952, pp. 66–87.

A polygnous family among the Bakhtiari
of Iran. As in many societies of the
Near East, polygyny is limited mainly to
men of means and high status.

As in many cases where polygyny is not confined to the wealthy class, wives were an economic asset. The people lived largely from gardening, with plantains being the most common food. Although men did some hunting and fishing, helped clear the land, and wove the mats from which the neat houses were made, the majority of the gardening was done by the women. The Baganda were a diligent people, especially the women, and a man with two or three wives could live well.

First marriages began at a very young age, about thirteen for a girl and fifteen for a boy, although it often took an additional year for the boy to raise enough bride price for the marriage to be approved. Second and third wives were usually less costly than the first, and little ceremony surrounded their marriages. Especially when the couple were very young, they were not expected to rear their own children after the age of weaning (about three years) but were to give them to an older brother of the father. The older brother, it was felt, would know more about how to take care of the children and would be less likely than the parents to overindulge them. A child was named after a deceased ancestor and, at the time of the naming, acquired the soul of that ancestor. During the same ceremony, a test was made to make sure the child was legitimate. The umbilical cord, which was saved for ceremonial purposes, was dropped into a mixture of beer, milk, and water. If it floated, the child was legitimate; if it sank, he was considered to have been born in adultery and could not be considered a member of the clan.

As is the usual practice among African pastoralists, wives occupied separate huts, so that the polygynous family really consisted of a series of conjugal units, each with the same male. In this respect, the polygynous family, although it can contain many members, is quite different from the joint households to be described later.

The Baganda have been selected as an example of polygynous societies mainly because of the universality of polygyny among them in earlier days. It must be emphasized, though, that many societies without anything like such an uneven sex ratio also practice polygyny. Since polygyny differs widely in function, it cannot be summarized as belonging to only one type of society. Recall that among the Washo, parents sometimes tried to get their son-in-law to marry another of their daughters if they thought he was a particularly good man. The most likely reason for polygyny among the Eskimo was similar: a man capable of supporting two wives could have two, if there were extra women around. In East Asian societies, extra wives were more likely to be a luxury afforded by the rich, a situation slightly comparable to the keeping of mistresses by wealthy European and American men. Most frequently polygyny becomes a practice for common men only when women are an economic asset.

In present times polygyny is a declining institution. Modern urban societies make it difficult to establish the large house that could accommodate a number of wives or to maintain separate establishments for them. Countries that once had many polygynous families and now pride themselves on modernization, Turkey and Iran for example, are ending the practice. Although the Western prejudice against polygyny as debasement of the status of women is greatly exaggerated, it seems that movements for equality of women are often accompanied by a decline in polygyny, as in Turkey. In China, the Communists' efforts to establish economic equality and female equality combine against the practice. Also, the overpowering desire for male progeny to carry on the family line, which once was a reason for taking concubines, is less important in the less family-centered modern world.

POLYANDRY   Whereas polygyny has been permitted in a majority of human societies, the opposite practice of polyandry is extremely uncommon. Once in a a while polyandry occurs in Eskimo society if there is a shortage of women. Occasionally it occurs in a society where bride price is so high that two brothers can afford enough for only one wife. And the anticipatory levirate sometimes allows a younger brother to share his older brother's wife. None of these are cases, though, in which polyandry is thought of as the right and proper form of marriage. The best-known cases of societies in which polyandry is, or was, the common practice are those of the Toda and the Tibetans. Of the two societies, the Toda have been studied the more thoroughly by anthropologists.

TODA POLYANDRY   The Toda are a very small tribe of people living in the Nilgiri Hills of southern India. Their economic life centers around their sacred buffalo.[16] Polyandry among these people consists in the fact that when the elder brother in a family marries, his wife becomes the wife of his brothers as well. Often marriages are arranged in childhood, and the preferred marriage is to one of the cross cousins. Marriage to cross cousins is so much the expectation that such cousins are referred to as "husband" and "wife" even in childhood.

Several problems present themselves as non-Toda people look on the family system. One might first ask what happens to the extra women. It would seem that if one woman has several husbands, others would have none. In the old days, this problem did not arise because of the frequent practice of female

[16]The material in this section is based on Queen et al., Ibid., pp. 18–43.

A polyandrous Toda household. The wife is the elderly woman seated on log at right. Daughters, near center, are grinding grain, one of the main tasks of the women. Husbands and sons are grouped around the house, and one is standing by the smaller building, a "dairy temple" for the sacred cattle.

infanticide. More recently, with quite a number of women available, younger brothers sometimes marry as well and bring their wives into the household of the older brother. The result is a kind of group marriage not part of the earlier system of Toda marriage but far from uncongenial to it. Even in the older days, it was possible for one of the brothers to take a mistress, provided she was a member of one of the clans with which he could not actually marry. She could live in her lover's household as a wife, but her children would not belong to his family group because the marriage would not be considered legal. If she had a legal husband, the children would be regarded as his regardless of who actually sired them. Similarly, it was possible for one of the younger brothers to move in with another man and share his wife, provided adequate gifts were given and consent was granted.

The problem of which of several brothers is the actual biological father of a child is of little importance and is determined ceremonially by a "presenting of the bow." In about the seventh month of pregnancy, one of the brothers, usually the oldest brother first, makes a bow and arrow out of twigs and grass and before witnesses presents it to the wife. By so doing, he becomes recognized as the father of the baby. Another reason that paternity is not much of a problem is that inheritance is patrilineal, so the household will eventually be inherited by the same group of boys regardless of which brother is the actual father. The desire that the inheritance be kept in the paternal line and that it not be divided is one of the possible explanations of Toda polyandry. The other explanation is that since the men herd their buffalo over a fairly large territory, one or more of the men of a family must be away with the animals at any one time, but with polyandry at least one can be at home to protect the household and live with the wife.

POLYANDRY IN LADAKH AND TIBET   Many of the Buddhist people of Ladakh in Tibet also practice polyandry. Justice William O. Douglas visited Ladakh and Leh in 1951 and found the practice of polyandry scorned by government officialdom but still widely practiced by the common people and supported by the lamas.[17] Polyandry in Ladakh is in some ways similar to the practice in the land of the Toda; it is fraternal polyandry, that is, that marriage of a woman to a group of brothers, and it serves the purpose of keeping inheritance in the patrilineage and avoiding the division of lands and households in an inhospitable area where only small plots of good land could be developed. The younger sons are provided for to a degree, because they share the wife, the house, and the sheep and goats, but they cannot increase the population unreasonably by each having wives and homes.

Along with polyandry Ladakh has the institution of *magpa*, designed to accommodate families without male heirs. In *magpa*, a man with daughters but no son chooses a promising young man to marry his daughters with the understanding that the son-in-law will adopt the family name and carry on its tradition. Thus a fortunate man may find himself in possession of a house, flocks, land, and wives for the minor price of changing his surname. *Magpa* amounts to complementing polyandry with an occasional polygynous household. Yet another arrangement must sometimes be used to make the system of polyandry work. Since infanticide is not practiced, or at least not enough to be evi-

[17]William O. Douglas, *Beyond the High Himalayas*, Doubleday & Company, Inc., Garden City, N. Y., 1952.

dent in an uneven sex ratio, there are extra women. Some extra women become prostitutes, but many of them marry into Muslim households in the vicinity.

Besides the family property argument for Ladakh polyandry, several other explanations have been offered. As with the Toda, much herding of animals is done, and one or more of the men has to be away part of the time. It is sometimes said that it takes more than one man to support a woman and her children. Another explanation is that polyandry has the backing of the lamas and the lamaseries. (We are speaking of the period before the Chinese Communist takeover.) There are two theories regarding lama support of the system. One is that since the lamas collect fees from the peasants and therefore live well, they prefer to see a system in which population is held down so that the people will not become increasingly impoverished and rebellious against the well-fed lamas. The other is that the lamaseries require a system in which quite a few men will be discontented with family life and will therefore enter monastic life. As a matter of fact, some men do find family life difficult, especially if the wife favors one of the brothers and has little to do with the others, but many families are harmonious. However, since very similar polyandrous families developed among the Toda, in spite of no comparable monastic system, it seems very dubious that polyandry results from the presence of lamaseries. The lamas support the system, possibly to recruit members, as suggested by Douglas, but very possibly just because religious orders tend to be conservative and oppose major changes in custom.

MONOGAMY   Monogamy is the most common form of marriage, in spite of the fact that a majority of the societies known to anthropologists permit other forms, especially polygyny. For fear of merely reflecting ethnocentric attitudes, one must be cautious in stating the advantages of the type of marriage system preferred by one's own culture. Obviously, polygynous marriages have worked very well in many societies and polyandrous in a few, but in the modern world both systems seem to be giving ground before the practice of monogamy, the marriage of one man to one woman.

The most obvious advantage of monogamy is that unless a society engages in such practices as infanticide or incessant raiding and feuding to thin out one sex or the other, monogamy works out well mathematically; that is, it assures about the same number of males as females, so that everyone should be able to find a marriage partner. Economically, monogamy is quite well adapted to urban societies, where houses are relatively small and where there are no chores for extra wives to perform even if it were feasible to provide extra houses for them to live in. Monogamy also fits the equalitarian norms of modern countries, both in the sense that each woman is conceded to have the right to a spouse of her own and in the sense that not even the richest of men are believed to be entitled to the favors of extra wives.

One can hardly examine any of this reasoning, though, without finding certain exceptions to it. For one thing, no totally modern monogamous societies actually have an equal number of men and women. In all cases, there are a few more women than men among the elderly, because women, on the average, live longer than men. Sometimes wars exterminate large numbers of young men, as in Germany and Russia in both World Wars, so that mates for all women could be assured only if a fairly large number shared the same man in a polygynous marriage. It is also true that in modern urban societies there are men of enormous wealth who could easily support a number of wives, all in one compound or in separate houses. The advantages listed, then, are only generalities. It can be argued that in a few cases polygyny would be advantageous. Why cannot cultures make exceptions in such cases?

Actually, cultures do make some exceptions to rules, but not officially. The exceptions to rules come in the form of "norms of evasion"—practices that are known to occur, and may even secretly be boasted about, but are still defined as contrary to the rules. In Europe wealthy men often keep mistresses. The same custom occurs in the United States, but less frequently. The more common American practice is to divorce one wife and marry another, sometimes repeating the process in rapid succession. In all countries, of course, a certain amount of prostitution also takes place, often officially denied. Even when the marital norms are supposedly puritanical, both premarital and extramarital sexual relations are fairly common.

The problem of why Western societies wink at a number of norms of evasion but would not consider legalizing polygyny is illustrative of the essential nature of cultural norms. A culture insists on the sacred or semisacred nature of its norms, including norms about marriage. The norms may be broken, but they cannot be denied or repudiated. They especially must be upheld by such normative leaders as clerics and public officials, or reputations can be ruined. When the norms finally change, they do so in a gradual and unofficial manner. At present in the United States, for example, we have a number of experimental communes, some of which are quite conventional in marital matters but some of which believe in free love. Our newspapers carry tales about wife-exchange clubs. We also have a rising divorce rate and considerable numbers of young mating partners who refuse to go through the legal process of marriage. The monogamous marriage, like all other forms of marriage, obviously has its strains, especially in times of rapid change. In an age when a high reproduction rate is no longer a norm, when mates are no longer forced by economic necessity to stay together, when family business enterprises are few and inheritances relatively unimportant, the older family ties weaken.

MINIMAL FAMILY   In a few instances of polyandry, where brothers are married to one wife but some of the younger brothers bring extra women into the household, the simple conjugal unit known to us virtually disappears. Even in these cases, though, there are socially recognized, legal spouses. In some family types, however, marriage ties are of no importance or are postponed for a long period of time. To these we apply the term "minimal family," referring to a minimization of the conjugal unit but not necessarily of lineage or the extended family. One of the extreme cases is the Nayar system.

THE NAYAR TARAVAD   The Nayars are a matrilineal people, living in Kerala in southwestern India, whose family system of earlier times completely separated the sexual role from marriage.[18] Following Hindu law, the women married, but they remained with their husbands for only 3 or 4 days. After that they were free to accept visiting lovers from their subcastes, or occasionally they were fortunate enough to have a liaison with a younger son of one of the Brahman families. The Brahman men could not marry Nayar women, since the Nayars were below them in caste, but they could have mating relations with them. The women continued to live in the households of their mothers, bearing their children in that household, sometimes receiving gifts from their lovers, but not holding the sires of their children responsible for their rearing. The mother's brothers were the men of the household and took responsibility for the children. The characteristic of the society that made the system work in the past (the system is no longer practiced) was that the Nayars were a military caste, whose men were often away on military duty. One or two of the brothers might be present in the maternal household, but none of them had the responsibility of being nearly always present, as is expected in more common types of families. The Nayars were a high caste group, with servants, which was another factor helping to make the otherwise minimal family work.

The Nayars are one example of the frequent relationship between the minimal family and the military society. Though Masai and Chagga of Africa recognized family in a way the Nayars did not, young men of military age did not marry but simply had sexual relations with unmarried girls until they outgrew young warrior status. One of the warlike tribes of Brazil, the Caduveo,

---

[18]E. Kathleen Gouch, "The Nayars and the Definition of Marriage," *The Journal of the Royal Anthropological Institute of Great Britain and Ireland*, vol 89, pp. 23–34, 1959. Reprinted in James P. Spradley and David M. McCurdy (eds.), *Conformity and Conflict: Readings in Cultural Anthropology*, Little, Brown and Company, Boston, 1971, pp. 126–144.

An important contemporary example of a minimal family is that of the kibbutz of Israel. Economic support, socialization, and education of children are the responsibility of the commune as a whole, not of the parents.

once had a similar type of minimal family.[19] Although the women married, the common girls often went off with the warriors to serve them as mistresses and tried to avoid the duties of bearing children. Noble women, too, could have affairs, and they also tried either by abortion or by infanticide to avoid the usual family role of rearing children. The children reared by the Caduveo were mainly captive children. Even the children who were accidentally born to the Caduveo nobles were brought up by foster families.

THE KIBBUTZ   The kibbutz (pl. kibbutzim) is a type of commune that has operated successfully for as much as three generations among a small minority of the people of Israel. It presents a special case of minimal family of considerable importance in an age of experimental communes. The founding of the first kibbutzim was a matter of idealism combined with protest against the traditional Jewish family.[20] The kibbutz places a high value on hard work, communal ownership, cooperation, equality, and individual liberty. The unusual family characteristic is that, although couples tend to mate fairly per-

[19]Lévi-Strauss, *Tristes Tropiques*, pp. 162–164.
[20]Queen et al., op. cit., pp. 116–117.

manently, they are not directly responsible for the rearing of their own children. The children are brought up by the commune itself, with the women most adept at caring for children taking over that function, while the parents are left free to clear land, cultivate crops, carry on the other work of the commune, and, when necessary, serve in the armed forces. Although the motivation for founding the kibbutzim was not military, it is interesting to note that again the minimal family has served to free parents for military duties. We must not assume, however, that military societies always result in minimal-family systems or that military duties are the only requirements that erode family functions. In a previous chapter we noted that the matrilocal Zuñi, although a peaceful society, had a family system in which most of the functions of father were performed by mother's brother and in which marriages were extremely brittle. Oscar Lewis shows that in modern societies the father often disappears from the most impoverished families.[21] In the days of slavery, the social role of the father was often made impossible for the black American family. Finally, as we shall note in the next chapter, there may be characteristics of all modern industrial societies that are leading the family in a direction that can be called "minimization."

[21] Oscar Lewis, "The Culture of Poverty," *Scientific American*, vol 215, pp. 19–25, October 1966.

In Chapter Ten we examined the important family concerns of marriage and reproduction and the contrasts between monogamy, polygyny, and polyandry. We also looked at an exceptional case or two in which the basic conjugal unit declined in importance or was not readily recognized in terms of more usual family systems. Several questions were left unanswered, though. What conditions account for joint households with several families living under one roof or in close proximity? What are the varieties of lineages and clans encountered in societies, and what seems to account for such varieties? How do systems for naming kinsmen reflect attitudes toward nuclear families and toward lineages? Finally, what changes of a cultural-evolutionary type can be found that have a bearing on lineages, clans, kinship terminologies, and the general position of the family in society? What happens to the joint or extended family in modern societies?

Chapter Eleven
Kinship and
Lineage

THE JOINT FAMILY   One of the last family types described in Chapter Ten was that of the Nayar taravad. It was included to illustrate a minimization of the role of the biological father in some types of family systems, but it could also have served to illustrate another variation on family life—the joint family. The Nayar taravad was a lineage group of descendants of a common ancestress, owning property jointly and inheriting through the mother's line. Daughters and sons belonged to the taravad, but not the mates of the daughters; the homes of such "husbands" continued to be with their mothers and sisters. The property was controlled by the *karanavan*, who was usually the oldest male member of the household.[1] Thus it can be seen that important roles were held by males, although not in the capacity of biological father. It is also obvious that the nuclear unit of mating pairs was of little sociological importance; the larger kinship group was responsible for the nurture, socialization, and economic care of the family.

OTHER MATRILOCAL JOINT HOUSHOLDS   The Nayar system was in some respects unique, but it was not the only joint family of a matrilineal type. The Hopi and Zuñi also live in a mother-centered household of matrilineal descent in which the husband is a mere sojourner, feeling that he really belongs in the household of his mother and sisters. Although actual marriages do take place, the individual marriage unit is less important than the total matrilineal household. The man's paternal role relative to his sister's children is more important than his role relative to his own.

The matrilocal joint family has a stability about it that is uninterrupted by divorce. The brother-sister bond remains even if the husband-wife bond is broken. It would seem possible that the brother-sister bond might be too close under such circumstances and possibly lead to cases of incest. Actually, there is fear of incestuous relations in certain societies in which mother's brother has the protective role toward his sister and her children. Trobriand society, although patrilocal instead of matrilocal, gives the protective role to the mother's brother. Consequently, brother and sister practice avoidance throughout their lives, addressing each other only with the greatest formality, not playing together even as children, and expected to have no knowledge of the feelings or love life of the other.[2]

---

[1] A. R. Radcliffe-Brown and Daryll Forde (eds.), Introduction to *African Systems of Kinship and Marriage*, Oxford University Press, New York, 1950, pp. 72–75.
[2] Bronislaw Malinowski, *The Sexual Life of Savages in Northwestern Melanesia*, Halcyon House, Garden City Books, New York, 1929, pp. 519–523.

PATRILOCAL JOINT FAMILIES   Patrilocality is the rule by which the wife moves into her husband's parental household or its immediate vicinity. A patrilocal joint family, then, is one most frequently consisting of an elderly couple, their married sons and daughters-in-law, and their grandchildren. Sometimes even more relatives might be included, as long as they are in the male line. The old patriarch might have a brother or two, who, along with their children, are also part of the household. As seems apparent, a family with a high rate of reproduction can easily outgrow the joint household system after a few generations. Interpersonal relations can also become strained, so there is always a practical limit to how large the joint family can grow. Essentially, the joint family is a combination of several conjugal units, each having its own importance but in many respects subordinated to the good of the larger group. Although the polygynous family often approximates or even exceeds the joint family in size, it is not the same thing. In the polygynous family, the same male is the mate in each conjugal unit; in the patrilocal joint family, each subordinate unit consists of a married pair and their children. Such households are found occasionally in India and were common in China in precommunist days. A few such households existed in earlier days in Russia, known as *bratsvos*, in Yugoslavia (*zadrugas*), and in France (*maisnie*). The joint family exists most commonly in an agricultural society in which the labor of many family members can be employed to their mutual advantage. Ralph Linton's description of the joint family of the Tanala of Madagascar illustrates well its function for some types of societies.

THE TANALA JOINT FAMILY   The joint family is the most important social unit among the Tanala.[3] The unit starts with a man and his wife and children and eventually includes also his daughters-in-law and his grandchildren. Among one of the Tanala tribes, the Imerina, the symbol of family unity is a joint tomb, built by the family head; and no man can hope to head a family until he has amassed enough wealth to build such a tomb. Since ancestors are held in reverence, the tomb is an appropriate symbol, calling to mind the authority of the past and of the elders. The oldest male is supreme in the joint family, has control of all property and income, and supervises work in the rice fields. Since clearing of land requires cooperative effort, the joint family is well fitted to the necessary economic enterprises. The conjugal units making up the joint family are assigned their own allotments of land on an equalitarian basis to avoid jealousies and frictions. If such a family grows to great size, internal dissension can develop, but there are devices for the maintenance of family disci-

[3] The material in this section is based on Ralph Linton, *The Study of Man*, D. Appleton-Century Company, Inc., New York, 1936, pp. 189–195.

pline. The member whose conduct is so bad as to bring disgrace to the family can face the very severe punishment of disownment, in which case he is cut off from his living family and from his ancestors. His soul will find no rest or home in the next world. The stated reason for disownment is that the ancestral spirits are horrified by such crimes as disobedience to parents or incest and will bring plagues or crop failures upon the people unless the crimes are punished. In practice, the belief greatly strengthens the family head.

In spite of precautions to keep the family united, the size eventually becomes impractical. Families break up eventually, often with two brothers forming separate households that, it is hoped, will grow to include many members.

THE CHINESE JOINT HOUSEHOLD   In precommunist China, the family was an extended institution taking in large numbers of kinsmen, but not always in a joint household. The large household was the ideal, and sometimes members lived together under one roof for many generations. In the days of the Manchu Dynasty, it was a criminal offense for sons to break away from their parental household without the consent of the elders.[4] Family esprit de corps was maintained by recording all honors won by the family, keeping up family shrines and tombs, and observing ritual honors to the ancestors.

Besides maintaining family honor and pride, the family system depended upon extremely close father-son identification, a gradual increase in status as one reached old age, and a strong sense of living under the constant supervision of the ancestral spirits.[5] Romantic love had to be downgraded, as is often the case in situations where the maintenance of the family is far more important than the emotional fulfillment of any of its young members. Women moved into their husbands' households upon marriage, often without ever having seen their husbands before. To maintain the system of parental control over marriage, precautions were taken to avoid erotic expressions of any kind in public behavior, so much so that Francis Hsu uses the expression "estrangement between the sexes."[6] In spite of this attitude, marriages often turned out to be quite satisfactory. The young bride was a stranger in a strange home needing affection; the husband was usually a vigorous country youth who had never been allowed any intimacy with the opposite sex before. For these reasons, the couple usually became very fond of each another.[7] It seems that at

[4]Francis L. K. Hsu, *The Ancestors' Shadow: Family and Religion in China*, The Natural History Press, Garden City, N.Y., 1967, chap. 9.

[5]Ibid., p. 244–245.

[6]Ibid., p. 241.

[7]Martin Yang, *A Chinese Village, Taitou, Shantung Province*, Columbia University Press, New York, 1945, Chapter 6.

least in some parts of China there were popular myths of a semiromantic type backing up the ideal of parental selection of mates. The wife of an important Chinese official was asked what would have happened if her parents had not made a good selection of a husband for her. She seemed almost offended by the question. Of course they would choose the right man. She proceeded to explain: "Every couple that ought to marry is tied together with an invisible red string. So when parents make arrangements, fate leads. Matches are made in the moon, so it is always right. Fate makes one certain man for each woman."[8] Socialization into such an expectation of parental wisdom undoubtedly helps to make the system work in the great majority of cases. Probably the hardest part of the system in the past was that for the unhappy wife there was little recourse.

Whatever the interpersonal relations, as long as the joint family could be maintained, a large cooperative unit could manage the land and perform the additional tasks of maintaining irrigation ditches and roads and repairing buildings. If the family was in the vicinity of a city, some members could work for wages to be contributed to the economic maintenance of the group, although city life tends to undermine the joint family.

JOINT FAMILIES AND SOCIAL EVOLUTION

Small families and small bands without joint families or lineages are typical of hunting-and-gathering societies. Extended families occur much more commonly in advanced agricultural and pastoral societies. M. F. Nimkoff and Russell Middleton see three economic variables as the determinants of the size of family groupings: "size of food supply, the degree of spacial mobility involved in subsistence activities, and the kind and amount of family property."[9] Hunting peoples must travel too widely in search of food to allow for larger groupings than small bands throughout most of the year and have little family property. Pastoral peoples usually travel less, are assured a more constant food supply, and have slightly more family property. Settled agricultural peoples have the advantage in all three respects and are most likely to be organized around extended families. Statistics from 549 societies indicate that societies in which agriculture and animal husbandry are co-dominant have extended families in 88.9 percent of the case; societies com-

[8]David Mace and Vera Mace, *Marriage East and West*, Dolphin Books, Doubleday & Company, Inc., Garden City, N.Y., 1959, pp. 143–144.
[9]M. F. Nimoff and Russell Middleton, "Types of Family and Types of Economy," *American Journal of Sociology*, vol. 66, pp. 215–225, 1960.

bining agriculture and fishing have extended families in 77.8 percent of the cases. In societies based on animal husbandry alone, 51.2 percent have extended families, but only 16.7 percent of hunting-and-gathering societies have them.

The Nimkoff and Middleton data also show that extended families become more common as the degree of stratification increases. In India the joint family occurs more frequently among higher than among lower castes. In precommunist China, the families with large amounts of land were the most extended families, sometimes even adding to their numbers by adoption in order to hold and manage more land in a situation where hired labor was not available. In modern industrial societies, on the other hand, few families own land or engage in enterprises in which family labor can add greatly to income, holdings, or family prestige. Anything resembling a joint family exists only in a few agricultural areas, where sons occasionally establish farms near the parental homestead, but even such types of family farms are becoming increasingly rare.

LINEAGES AND CLANS   In the joint families just considered, lineage is of major importance, but it must not be assumed that lineage is important only in joint families. The royal houses and aristocracies of Europe, with titles, lands, and powers to inherit, have been vitally concerned with lineage, and sometimes wealthy families without titles of aristocracy have also been greatly concerned with it. In many of the societies studied by anthropologists, though, lineage is not confined to a few upper-class families but is a part of social organization. It is often the center of social control, determining who owes duties and obligations to whom, ensuring support in a dispute, determining the inheritance of property, and making the rules, regulations, and necessary provisions for marriage. Sometimes lineage becomes very complex, but usually it simplifies the problem of descent and inheritance by adopting a unilineal principle, rather than a bilateral principle.

UNILINEAL DESCENT SYSTEMS   Patrilineages trace descent strictly through the father's line, and matrilineal systems trace descent through the mother's line. In either case the system is much simpler than the bilateral principle that most Americans use in tracing their family histories. A bilateral system becomes too burdensome to follow after several generations, because it tries to take all ancestors into consideration, with the number doubling with each ascending generation, as in the diagram below.

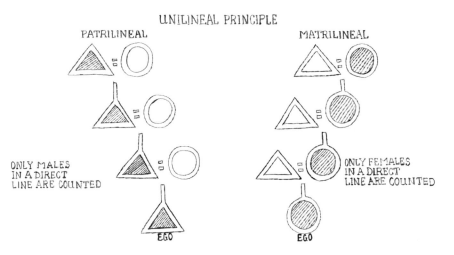

BILATERAL PRINCIPLE

ALL ANCESTORS ARE COUNTED

EGO

A much simpler system is to trace descent through only one side, so that there is only one significant ancestor in each generation. Such a pattern can be illustrated easily for either patrilineage or matrilineage, as follows:

UNILINEAL PRINCIPLE

PATRILINEAL

MATRILINEAL

ONLY MALES IN A DIRECT LINE ARE COUNTED

ONLY FEMALES IN A DIRECT LINE ARE COUNTED

EGO

EGO

In either system there will be large numbers of descendants of a lineage founder, but not so many as in the case of the bilateral system. They will have a greater sense of social solidarity based on the lineage tie and will be sure which kinsman to support in a dispute. The two lineages shown above cover only four generations, so they can be thought of as short lineages or "minimal lineages." A group of minimal lineages related through a more distant ancestor will be referred to as a "maximal lineage." Clans are descent groups of the same type as lineages, but whereas the lineage is able to trace its descent from

279

a known ancestor of the historical past, clans trace descent from very remote and unknown ancestors or even mythological ancestors. Clans also incorporate several different lineages into one descent group.

Matrilineages are much less common than patrilineages but occur fairly often among hoe-agriculture societies where much of the income depends upon gardening done by the women. Even where matrilineages exist, they are sometimes modified by the placing of considerable authority in the hands of the mother's brother, who is the only elder male able to teach a young man all the lore he should know about his matrilineage. In Trobriand society chieftaincies were passed through the matrilineage but were vested in males. Thus a chieftaincy was inherited by a man through his mother's line but would go to his sister's son, since his own son would not be part of the matrilineage. The very frequent rule of marriage to a patrilateral cross cousin (father's sister's daughter, in this case) helped to keep the chieftaincy in the father's family. As in the diagram below, it can be seen that although the chief's son could not inherit his position, the marriage of his son to his sister's daughter would ensure the chieftaincy for his grandson. Thus a type of "intermittent patrilineal succession goes on through a framework of matrilineal system."[10]

A TROBRIAND MARRIAGE SYSTEM FOR RETAINING CHIEFTAINCY IN FAMILY

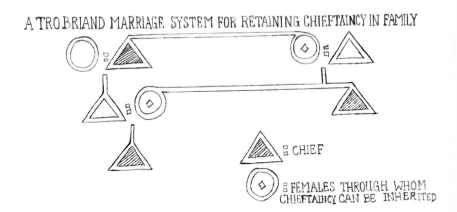

= CHIEF

= FEMALES THROUGH WHOM CHIEFTAINCY CAN BE INHERITED

DUAL DESCENT SYSTEMS   Several African tribes have a system of dual descent, and there are also cases of dual descent in India, Australia, and Melanesia.[11] A small tribe in southeastern Nigeria, the Yako, described by Daryll Forde, is typical of dual descent systems. At first glance the tribe appears to be patrilineal, featuring compounds composed of a group of brothers and their wives and

[10]Raymond Firth, *Human Types*, Thomas Nelson & Sons, New York, 1957, pp. 177–119.
[11]George P. Murdock, "Double Descent," *American Anthropologist*, vol. 42., pp. 555–561, 1940.

children, all belonging to a descent group called an *eponama*. The members of an *eponama* decide on the distribution of farms and houses and palm-tree clusters within their own area but are subject to the control of a patrilineal clan called a *kepun*. The *kepun* holds feasts, maintains shrines, and regulates land ownership among the *eponama*. But there are also matrilineages in the social system, known as *yajima* (singular *lejima*), and through the *yajima* most kinds of movable property are inherited, especially cattle and currency. The *yajima* also have clan elders, with the power to excommunicate offenders, but the punishments must be approved by the priest of the *yose*—a fertility spirit. The *yajima* are primarily religious clans, each with its own special fertility spirit and shrines. Thus the individual is born into a system of membership in two clans, both of which have a protective role toward him and to both of which he owes loyalty and good behavior.[12] Dual descent systems vary, but it is fairly common for landed property to descend through the male line and for other kinds of property to be inherited through the female line. In the Yako case, passing landed property through the male line is necessitated by the practice of patrilocal residence.

MOIETIES AND PHRATRIES   Sometimes tribes are divided into two halves, with each half providing marriage partners for the other, and often performing a number of ceremonial duties for the other. Such halves are called moieties. Many American Indian tribes were divided into moieties, often named after natural dualities, such as earth and sky or water and land. The six major tribes that made up the Iroquois nation—Seneca, Mohawk, Onandaga, Tuscarora, Oneida, and Cayuga—were divided into clans. In some cases the clans themselves were divided into moieties. In the Seneca tribe, the Bear, Wolf, Turtle, and Beaver clans made up one moiety and the Deer, Snipe, Heron, and Hawk clans the other.

Sometimes clans are grouped into more than two tribal divisions, in which case the groups are referred to as phratries. The Tlingit Indians of the Northwest Coast are divided into three matrilineal phratries, the Wolves, Eagles, and Ravens, and each phratry is exogamous. The Aztecs were divided into four exogamous phratries, and the Hopi are divided into twelve. When a society is divided into a number of exogamous phratries, with specific rules as to which phratry receives women from which, the system becomes very confusing to a person not accustomed to kinship complications. There are arrangements with four generational circularity, in which group A gives its

[12]Daryll Forde, "Double Descent among the Yako," in Radcliffe-Brown and Forde (eds.), op. cit., pp. 285–320.

women to group B, which gives its women to C, which gives its women to D, which gives its women to A. In Chapter Five an even more confusing, eightfold Australian system was mentioned. The function of such systems seems to be to keep up friendly ties through recurring marriage bonds, but the reasons for the extreme complications of some Australian kinship systems are not clearly understood.

CLANS IN CULTURAL-EVOLUTIONARY PERSPECTIVE Clans have been an extremely widespread phenomenon and were functional organizations among the Scottish and Irish and the Yugoslavs until fairly recent times. The ancient Hebrew patrilineages were very similar to clans. The Roman *gens* was a group of households tracing patrilineal descent from a common ancestor, often very remote, and Roman household (*pater familias*) was of an extended type. Anglo-Saxons took great interest in tracing descent but contrary to the usual practice in clans, they traced descent through both male and female lines. In China, clans have been of major importance throughout of all but the recent communist phase of history. Many of these historical cases of clans have been studied less by anthropologists than the clan systems of Africans, American Indians, and Oceanic peoples. Paul Kirchhoff contends that the view of clanship has been too narrow and that the institution falls into developmental order only if we take into consideration all types of societies in which clanship was once a prominent part of the social order.[13]

Kirchhoff uses the word "clanship" somewhat loosely, lumping together important lineages and clans. He speaks of the disappearance of clanship as the dominant form of social organization and its replacement by an increase in social stratification as a significant turning point in history. Clans have served to give stability and continuity to societies that are not organized on a state basis, and even to add to the stability of many state systems. They take on this function, just as do joint families, at the more advanced stages of economic development—to some degree in horticultural and fishing societies, but even more in pastoral and agricultural societies.

Kirchhoff sees two basic types of clans, the first being more archaic than the second but not necessarily leading to the second. The first type of clan is characterized by unilineal descent, exogamous marriage, a strong feeling of kinship among all members, and equality of the families making up the clan. The system is one that assures each individual his place in a primary group,

[13]Paul Kirchhoff, "Principles of Clanship in Human Societies," in Morton H. Fried (ed.), *Readings in Anthropology*, Vol. II, Thomas Y. Crowell Company, New York, 1968, pp. 370–381.

takes care of its own, and controls and disciplines its members, but within a family context.

The second type of clan is characterized by increasing degrees of inequality within. Early Indo-European and Semitic clans were of this type, and so were many of the clan systems of the Polynesians, Gaels, Germans, and Romans. Families had different standings based on degree of relationship to founding fathers. It could even be said that there were different degrees of membership within the clan—a characteristic previously noted in discussing the Northwest Coast tribes. Members of such clans eventually become what Kirchhoff calls "ambilateral," tracing descent through either the paternal or the maternal line, depending on which has the higher prestige. Another departure from ordinary clan rules also often develops in clans of the second type, especially for the noble core of the clan, and that is marriage to relatives in order to keep wealth and prestige in the family and the noble blood pure. Eventually the upper and lower families of such clans drift apart until kinship feelings are dropped and aristocratic classes become fully separated from lower classes. It should be added, too, that sacred beliefs and ritual activities help to keep up the ties of clan solidarity, but in the full development of class systems the manner of worship and the sacred cults often become separated along class lines. Priests represent the official, upper-class religion, and unofficial holy men, magicians, and soothsayers flourish in larger numbers at the lower levels.

Another characteristic of the second type of clan is that it continues to benefit the aristocrats more than the commoners. In the case of some of the Igorot tribes of the Philippine Islands, upper and lower classes still belong to the same clans and are even united under a mutual oath to come to each other's assistance. In real fact, the aristocrats can enforce the oath against the commoners much more easily than the commoners can against the aristocrats.

Since the poor do not often have the wealth needed for traditional funerals and weddings, they sometimes have to pawn their land to a rich man in order to get the required money or pigs. Thus the system contributes to a further intensification of differences in property holding between classes. The unequal types of clans lack the harmony of the equalitarian types but seem to be a step in the direction of urban, stratified societies.

KINSHIP TERMINOLOGY In the previous chapter it was noted that many people make distinctions between parallel and cross cousins, although such a distinction is seldom made by Americans. It was also noted that the distinction had an importance in societies in which a parallel cousin was thought of as almost the same as a brother or sister and a cross cousin was not. In other words, the system by which a people name their kinsmen usually relates to the way they regard various types of kin. People who seem to have very similar kinship status are often called by the same name, or classified together. In American kinship terminology, many kinds of aunts and uncles are classified together because they are very much alike in perceived status, whether they are on the mother's or father's side of the family, and even whether they are consanguine relatives or in-laws. Some people carry the classification principle much further than we do and others, not nearly as far. A system in which all degrees of kinsmen are given different titles is a "particularizing" system. Most frequently, kinship terminology is a combination of classificatory and particularizing principles, but as a general rule a greater amount of classifying is done by simple hunting-and-gathering societies than by advanced agrarian societies. The early point of view of Morgan was that differences in terminology reflect stages in cultural evolution of the family. Although Morgan's theories had wide acceptance at the time, Kroeber, in 1909, wrote an essay contradicting them.[14] In Kroeber's opinion, kinship terminologies reflect language and patterns of thought more than contrasts between primitive and advanced social systems. Kroeber concluded that eight different principles can be deduced from known kinship terminologies, some of which are stressed in one society and some in another. Summarized briefly, and with a few explanations, his principles are the following:

1   Generational differences as between children and parents. These are almost universally stated in kinship terminologies—and in some societies are stressed to the exclusion of other principles.

2   Lineal versus collateral relatives, for example, the distinction between father and uncle. This distinction is by no means always made.

3   Age differences within a generation. If this principle is followed, there are different terms for elder and younger brothers.

4   The sex of the relative. In English, the distinction is not made in the word "cousin." Kroeber tells us that in many kinship systems the distinction is not clear for large numbers of relatives.

5   The sex of the speaker. Often relatives are called by one term by a man and by a different term by his sister—a distinction not made in European languages.

6   The sex of the person through whom relationship exists. This distinction

[14]Alfred L. Kroeber, "Classificatory Systems of Relationship," *Journal of the Royal Anthropological Institute*, vol. 39, pp. 77–84, 1909.

is not clear in English and has to be clarified by such terms as "my maternal uncle" or "my paternal grandfather."

7   The distinction between blood relatives and relatives by marriage (affines). In English, the words "uncle" and "aunt" do not make this distinction. In some languages they do.

8   Whether relationship is traced through the living or the dead. Sometimes in American Indian languages a distinction is made between a nephew by a living brother and an orphaned nephew, for example, especially if the difference carries a sociological importance.

In comparing Indian languages with English, Kroeber found that English expresses smaller numbers of categories but expresses them more completely. For example, we do not express any of categories 5 through 8 above, but we make distinction number four in all cases except cousins, and we always distinguish between brother and sister and cousins.

The argument over the connection between social systems and kinship terminology has continued through the years, especially as a number of very difficult systems, such as Omaha and Crow (to be explained below), have been discovered. The student might wonder why so much attention is paid to kinship by anthropologists. Admittedly, to some degree it seems an interesting puzzle, and it is possible to become completely absorbed in the puzzle. Another reason is that kinship questions are easy ones for anthropologists to ask the people they study and are good ways to get to know them. Furthermore, as we have seen, kinship is tremendously important to tribes without very much formal government, with kins and lineages taking over many governmental roles. Kinship is a center of both social organization and sentiment, and its rules tell the investigator who takes sides with whom in a dispute, what some of the sources of friction may be, who will be the mourners at funerals, who will be the recipients of inheritances, near whose household a new couple will settle, and many other details that make people from very different worlds understandable to one another. Finally, there are intriguing questions from a theoretical point of view—whether kinship terminology merely reflects language, whether there is something about it basic to human thought patterns, whether there is a type of cultural evolution reflected in kinship systems, and whether kinship terms reflect mainly sentiment or status. A glance at the best-known kinship systems will help to explore at least a few of these questions. Below, four types of descent groups are diagramed and discussed.

GENERATIONAL SYSTEM   No distinction is made between lineal and collateral relatives in the generational system. All aunts and uncles are called by the same term as mother and father. All cousins are called by the same term as brother and sister, and this cousin terminology is known as "Hawaiian." The system is very common in bilateral descent groups, especially among hunting-and-gathering bands.

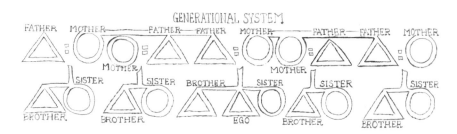

LINEAL SYSTEM The lineal system is essentially that of the United States. Aunts and uncles are classified under the same terms but are separate from father and mother. The accompanying cousin system is referred to as "Eskimo." All cousins are called by the same term but are separated from brother and sister. Lineal systems are less common than generational systems but are also associated with bilateral descent.

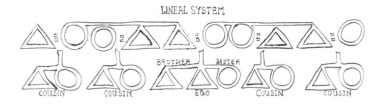

BIFURCATE-MERGING SYSTEM "Bifurcate" means to divide in half, and "merge" means to pull together, and the bifurcate-merging system is based partly on each principle. Father and father's brother are merged in that they are called by the same name, and the same is true of mother and mother's sister. Father's sister and mother's brother are called by terms equivalent to our words for aunt and uncle. Parallel cousins are merged with brother and sister; cross cousins are called by other terms equivalent to cousin, not brother and sister. The cousin terminology is of the "Iroquois" system and very similar to the "Crow" and "Omaha" systems. Bifurcate merging is more common than any other system, especially among unilineal descent groups.

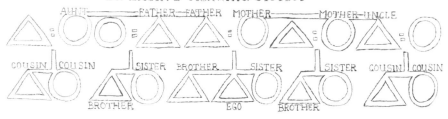

BIFURCATE COLLATERAL   In the case of bifurcate-collateral kinship systems, separate terms are given for each type of aunt and uncle and for each type of cousin. The cousin system is known as "Sudanese." In one sense this system is rare, since it exists among only a small number of societies; however, some extremely large societies use it, in China, India, and Southeast Asia. The example given below follows the description of an Indian informant from the Punjab.

A BIFURCATE COLLATERAL SYSTEM OF THE PUNJAB

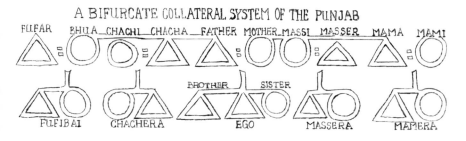

A BIFURCATE-COLLATERAL SYSTEM OF THE PUNJAB   In the above bifurcate-collateral system, father's brother is more important then the other relatives from the point of view of family continuity and inheritance. Other aunts and uncles are thought of as having slightly different roles and therefore have different designations. The same is true with the four classes of cousins. Generally, social relations with mother's kinsmen are a little more relaxed and informal than with father's kinsmen.

OMAHA AND CROW SYSTEMS   Much more baffling than the above-described kinship terminologies are those referred to as Omaha and Crow. The Omaha system is found not only among the Omaha Indians but among several other patrilineal tribes, including the Winnebago and a few tribes of Africa and New Guinea. The Crow system is found among several American Indian tribes, including, besides the Crow themselves, the Hopi, Cherokee, and Tlingit; there

287

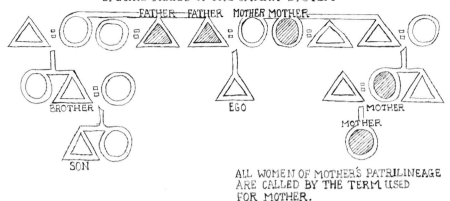

ALL WOMEN OF MOTHER'S PATRILINEAGE
ARE CALLED BY THE TERM USED
FOR MOTHER.

are also a few rare cases of the Crow system in Africa and Melanesia. Both systems are essentially bifurcate merging, but they include peculiarities of their own.

Special traits of the Omaha system   In the Omaha system, mother and mother's sister are merged under the same term, as one would expect, and so are father and father's brother. The children of "mothers" and "fathers" are called brothers and sisters, as in any other bifurcate-merging system. Going a step further than usual to emphasize the patrilineage, an Omaha will not only call his father's brother's son "brother" but will apply the word "son" to the son of that particular type of brother. Apparently in an effort to give some recognition to the mother's line also, the name applied to one's mother will be extended not only to the mother's sister but also to mother's brother's daughter and even to mother's brother's son's daughter. Stated another way, the name by which the mother is called is applied to any woman of the mother's patrilineage. Note that the word would not apply to mother's sister's children because their kinship is traced through a woman rather than a man. It is helpful to visualize the system by imaging that the word for mother is comparable to a genetic trait that appears only in females but must be passed through the male line.

Special traits of the Crow system   The Crow system is matrilineal rather than patrilineal, so many of the naming details are reversed. A group term is used for males of the father's matrilineage, including father, father's brother, father's sister's son, and even father's sister's daughter's son. All are called by the name *birupxe*. *Birupxe* is most easily conceptualized if one compares it with a genetic trait inherited by father and his male relatives, but only if passed through females. Another interesting point in the Crow system is that all males called *birupxe* will refer to ego's mother as "wife," because they all stand in a position to inherit her through rules of levirate, even men of younger generations.

It can be seen that both Omaha and Crow systems keep genealogies straight, emphasizing one lineage, but give at least some recognition to the other. However, there is no satisfactory explanation of why a few unilineal tribes use systems of these kinds and the great majority do not. As was mentioned in the previous chapter, family systems and terminologies do not fit neatly into an evolutionary plan. It is true that classificatory terminologies for cousins are more common among hunting-and-gathering tribes than in more advanced societies, but to go much beyond that observation calls for looking at other types of status terms besides those of kinship.

EVOLUTION OF STATUS TERMS   Elman Service suggests a scheme for thinking of kinship terminology in cultural-evolutionary terms in spite of the fact that the systems discussed above show little or no indication of evolutionary sequence.[15] He first points out that kinship terms are only partly indications of biological relationship and only partly matters of kinship sentiment. To a great extent they are expressions of status relationship, and if they are seen as such, they are part of a general order of status terms that change as society evolves. In the first level of society, practically all status terminology is that of kinship, centering in one or a very few families of a band. In the second level, "sociocentric-familistic" terms are added, referring to larger social groups such as lineages, moieties, clans, and age sets. In the third level—the level just before modern industrial society—new status terms are added, which Service refers to as "egocentric-nonfamilistic." By this he means status terms designating a personal relationship but not one based on kinship. His examples include "m'lord," "my servant," "his coachman," "our slave." Previous status words are not dropped, but the new ones become prevalent and characteristic of the society. Finally, in industrial societies, there is a much greater prevalence of "sociocentric-nonfamilistic" terms—mister, doctor, accountant, judge, workman—indicating the greater impersonality of the society. Although the old kinship terms do not disappear, they occupy a smaller part of total status terminology and become more specific. Even titles of address of older kinsmen are sometimes dropped; Uncle Charles becomes simply "Charlie," and even mother and father are called by first names. However, as Service allows, kinship terms per se do not evolve, because they relate basically to the parts of society where face-to-face relationships persist, but they recede in importance as more secondary relationships emerge and the family becomes "dethroned."

[15]Elman R. Service, "Kinship Terminology and Evolution," *American Anthropologist*, vol. 62, pp. 747–762, 1960.

KINSHIP TERMS BECOME LESS COMMON, MORE SPECIFIC.

NONKINSHIP STATUS TERMS BECOME MORE NUMEROUS
RELATIVE DECLINE OF KINSHIP

Admittedly, Service treats kinship in an unfamiliar way by emphasizing the status aspects almost to the exclusion of the genetic and sentimental aspects, but he points out important trends, showing kinship declining from virtually the total of human relationships to a much smaller proportion. Other anthropological and sociological comments on family change are similar. The small family unit becomes more isolated in modern society, and kinship linkages decline. Family and clan shrines and rituals disappear, and a larger part of the care of children is taken over by public institutions. The decline of parental and lineage involvements, of anxiety over continuance of lineages, and of the contracts implied in gift exchange and bride price all testify to the same diminution of the family role. Along with the decline of familism goes greater individualism and liberty but also the threat of greater emotional isolation. There are, however, other associations and institutions besides those of kinship that involve the individual emotionally. The solidarity that once resided in the band or the clan is now sought for in other meaningful groups, especially the state, which must be described next.

Descriptions of a variety of cultures in Chapters Five through Eight demonstrated that the cohesion of tribal groups does not depend upon types of government with which the Western world is familiar. The bond of unity was strong among Ituri Pygmies, Eskimo and Australian bands, and among many of the horticulturists and pastoralists, but the bond was that of family and kinship, not formalized government and state. In the preceding chapters on family and kinship, it became clear that lineages and clans often perform most of the functions of government. It is also clear that no people live in a state of total anarchy and that all are regulated by recognition of rights and duties relative to one another, with those rights and duties generally based on real or mythical kinship. In the cases of the Northwest Coast Indians and many Polynesians and Turko-Mongolian pastoralists, the kinship ties were loose enough to permit large differences in prestige and leadership, but the myth of kinship was never entirely abandoned. On the other hand, several peasant societies were described, and in such societies there were both kinsmen and nonkinsmen even in rural districts, and in distant cities lived people who seemed of a

Chapter Twelve
From Tribalism
to State

different kind, strange and antagonizing. Yet all these people make up a cohesive group relative to other societies. They defend one another in times of war, pledge loyalty to the same kings or other rulers, and observe the same rituals of unity. Clearly, a great transition has come about, expanding both the political base of social organization and the sentiments supporting that political base.

In investigating the transition from tribal society to the types of states prevalent in most of the modern world, we must answer several questions about the natures of the tribe and the state. What are the characteristics of tribal society? The word "tribe" is widely used, sometimes applied to small bands of Eskimo or Bushmen and also to such vast aggregates as the Ashanti people of Ghana, numbering in the millions. How widely can societies vary and still be referred to as tribes? How does the tribe differ from the state? What are the possible transitional steps leading from tribe to state? Do all the advantages belong on the side of the modern state, or are there sentiments about tribalism that are hard to replace? How does the state attempt to cope with the erosion of feelings of kinship and common identity that occurs as social organization grows to include millions of people? Finally, is the state the ultimate in possiblities for human organization, or might the future hold other alternatives? All these questions need examination in an anthropological attempt to describe social variety, survey the course we have covered, define our present place in time, and make educated guesses about the future.

CHARACTERISTICS
OF TRIBAL SOCIETY

Tribal societies and modern nations have at least a few traits in common. The Frenchman, Italian, or Spaniard speaks the same language as other people of his country and is strongly aware of the difference between compatriot and foreigner, even though he may be divided from other of his countrymen by considerable differences in local customs and accents. The same sense of common identity holds for members of tribes. They may be organized in separate villages, segmental lineages, clans, or moieties, but they recognize the similarity of their people in contrast to the outsiders who speak different languages, dress differently, observe different rituals, and honor different gods. The feeling of common identity is strongest among members of family and minimal lineage, and it weakens as it embraces more and more distant people, but there is still a boundary line that separates fellow tribesman from foreigner. Among such quarrelsome people as the Yanomamö, alliances are made and raids are perpetrated on people known to be of the same type—fierce people, Yanomamö. But today's enemies may have to be taken in as allies tomorrow, and even if they remain enemies they are still part of the same system, playing the same deadly game, interpreting behavior by the same rules.

The Yanomamö have been deliberately used as an example to show that the word tribe does not always denote internal harmony. It usually does, but not always. The tribe differs from the state in that there is no supreme authority that can enforce peace within. Marshall Sahlins, whose analysis of tribes is being followed here, strongly emphasizes the point that much of the energy of the tribe is turned to types of diplomacy that help to keep peace within[1]—a feat best accomplished by more culturally organized tribes than the Yanomamö. The seventeenth century social philosopher Thomas Hobbes used a frequently quoted phrase to describe the condition of man before the coming of state power, saying the life of man was "solitary, poore, nasty, brutish, and short." The statement is a vast exaggeration, but Sahlins credits Hobbes with pointing out an important problem of tribalism—it must develop mechanisms for maintaining peace or life can almost fit the Hobbes description.

GIFT, TRADE, MARRIAGE, AND PEACE   In certain East African languages, the word for "trade" and "barter" also means "peace." In the English language, the word for "kindred" derives from the same root as "kindness." Among the Nuer, the word for "kinship" is also the word for "peace." In Fijian, the expression "living in peace" is rendered "living as relatives."[2] Anything that promotes gift exchange, trade, or the extension of kinship through marriage is seen as working toward peace, both within the tribe and in attempts to bring about friendly relations with outsiders.

Among the Plains Indians, much trade was disguised as gift giving. The most admired man was the one who gave generously. Prized possessions circulated through the village, because no one family was expected to keep them long and passing them along to others helped establish friendly relations. In the great chieftaincies of the Northwest Coast, goods of the kinship group were bestowed upon chiefs for ceremonial purposes, but they in turn acted as agents of redistribution, giving generously. Gift giving and reciprocity are major means for maintaining internal harmony.

In trade between tribes, or between separate branches of the same tribe, the idea of reciprocity was equally strong. The most famous anthropological example of gift exchange accompanied by actual trade is that of the Kula Ring

[1]Marshall D. Sahlins, *Tribesmen*, Prentice-Hall, Inc., Englewood Cliffs, N.J., 1968.
[2]All examples from Sahlins, op. cit., p. 10.

of the Southwestern Pacific, as described by Malinowski.[3] His lengthy description includes magic and ceremonialism and pragmatic trade, but above all an intertribal exchange system that helped promote peaceful relations between trading partners in the island groups just to the east of New Guinea. White shell arm bands, objects of great ceremonial value, were traded for red shell necklaces, one class of objects moving around the islands in a clockwise direction and the other in a counterclockwise direction. Other types of objects were also traded, were of more commercial value, and were haggled over in pricing, but the ostensible reason for the trade was to keep up gift exchange in ceremonial shell necklaces and arm bands. The Kula Ring is only the most famous of innumerable cases of the connection between primitive trade and harmonious relationships. Although we sometimes think of trade and friendship as incompatible, the Melanesians do not. Throughout Melanesia trade partnership is common, and the trade partner is a friend who can guarantee hospitality and safety.[4] As is the general case in tribal society, however, harmony depends upon the decisions of each individual, which are structured to a degree by custom, habit, and norm but not imposed by an undisputed authority.

THE HYDRAHEADED NATURE OF TRIBALISM   Although many tribes have a titular chief, real authority is likely to be vested in local leaders, so that the tribe has as many heads as the mythical Hydra. The multiplicity of limited authorities exists in governmental matters and in other areas of life as well. Lineage heads have their areas of influence, and they in turn are under the higher authority of clan chiefs. There may be a tribal chief who on an organizational chart appears to hold supreme authority but who is actually too remote from local matters. In many African tribal systems there are well-ordered courts of justice, but more frequently members of kinship groups are responsible for seeing that justice is done for wrongs against members of their families, making feud a deadly possibility.

As for religion, local villages have their rituals and special observances, and so have households and lineages, with their own ancestral spirits and special protectors. The cleansing of the village from defilement, its protection against ghosts, and attempts to heal its sick are generally local religious matters. On the higher organizational level there may be a superior priest whose office is vested in a particular clan and who will conduct ceremonies for the

[3]Bronislaw Malinowski, *Argonauts of the Western Pacific*, E. P. Dutton & Co., Inc., New York, 1961 (originally published 1922).
[4]Dorothy Hammond, *Associations*, McCaleb Module in Anthropology no. 14, Addison-Wesley Publishing Company, Inc., Reading, Mass., 1972, p. 6.

INTENSE LOYALTY TO FAMILY
AND LINEAGE ; DECLINING
LOYALTY TO OUTER CIRCLES
OF TRIBE.

DIVISIVE FORCES : RIVAL
LINEAGES AND CLANS ; MANY-
HEADED POLITICAL AND RELIGIOUS
ORGANIZATION.

UNITING FORCES : GIFT
EXCHANGE , TRADE , MARRIAGE ,
CEREMONIAL AND ECONOMIC
RECIPROCITY.

GENERALIZED INSTITUTIONS,
CENTERING IN KINSHIP.

entire tribe to the more powerful gods; but the gods or spirits of most constant concern are the local ones.[5]

Moral responsibilities are also segmented. Clyde Kluckhohn has said of the Navaho that many of their moral attitudes are particularistic rather than general. The same is true for many tribesmen. There is one code of conduct for kinsmen, another for more distant members of the tribe, and a very different one for strangers. In fact, a type of particularism about rights and wrongs exists even in modern societies to a degree, but particularism is especially strong where kinship loyalties are overwhelming. In their dealings in Southeast Asia, American officials have found that the honorable man takes care of his kinsmen first, giving them special favors in governmental treatment that would be condemned in Western societies as nepotism.

[5]Sahlins, op. cit., pp. 16–20.

Often the kinship systems of tribes are crosscut by other types of associations, including associations of a fraternal nature, military clubs, and age grades, all of which demand degrees of loyalty from the individual that could compete with his duties to a state. These loyalties, too, are particularistic.

In contrast to its particularism regarding moral obligations, tribal life generalizes institutions. There is no clear separation between religion and government, between government and family, between economics and social relationships. Government, religion, law, justice, economics, protection, education are all segments of kinship responsibilities and not separated into formal institutions.

THE TRIBE IN HISTORY   Sahlins speaks of tribalism as the great development of Neolithic times, during which the first domestication of plants and animals took place.[6] The Paleolithic, in contrast, was dominated by small bands of hunters and gatherers, too small and separate to be called tribes. Even before the Neolithic, a few fishing peoples, and hunters in lands of great abundance, probably were capable of expanding into large tribes with segmental organization. But it took the development of horticulture to make tribal life dominant in the world and able to infringe upon the lands of the less organized hunting-and-gathering peoples. Tribalism remained dominant until the development of urban civilizations with a propensity for organizing into powerful states.

Naturally, such a wide-ranged view of the developments of thousands of years leaves out many details, but it does put tribalism into perspective. One of the variations on the tribal pattern has already been noted—clans and tribes with a pyramid of rank, in contrast to the equalitarian type of clan. Other contrasts include a close approach to statelike unity on the one hand and a constant state of internecine conflict on the other. Among the important variations in tribal attempts to deal with problems of government were confederacies. One of the most famous was the League of the Iroquois, which serves as a good example of what could be accomplished under tribalism and also of the gap between well-developed tribal leagues and actual states.

TRIBAL CONFEDERACY: THE LEAGUE OF THE IROQUOIS   The weaknesses of tribal organization can be partly surmounted by the formation of alliances. One of the most famous and long-lasting tribal alliances was that of the League of the Five Nations, composed of the Iroquoian-speaking Mohawk, Seneca, Oneida,

[6]Ibid., pp. 2–4.

Onandaga, and Cayuga and later including also the Tuscarora.[7] The Iroquois were a matrilineal people, many of them living in long houses accommodating several related families. According to Iroquois custom, the houses belonged to the women and were their domain. The forests were the domain of the men. According to legend, a prophet by the name of Deganawidah appeared in about 1570 and dreamed of a great tree reaching to the heavens. The tree had five roots, which to Deganawidah symbolized the five tribes, and its leaves and branches symbolized strength and peace among the people. Deganawidah and his friend Hiawatha traveled to the five tribes, teaching the message of unity and finally persuading them to join into a great confederacy.

A kind of check-and-balance system of government was worked out, with each tribe represented by a number of sachems who together made up the Council of the Iroquois. The sachems were men, but they were selected by women from particular matrilineages. The system was not entirely democratic, since only certain family members could become sachems. The five nations were not represented quite equally in the number of sachems chosen, but the inequality mattered little since each nation had to approve any decisions made, and the sachems of each nation voted as a bloc. As a further precaution against disunity, clans cut across tribal lines, proclaiming at least fictive kinships of people from different tribes.

Since the Iroquois were surrounded by enemy Algonkian tribes and by other Iroquoian-speaking people who were not part of the league, they were incessantly at war. Their confederacy held together for centuries, although its power was broken by the end of the War of 1812. Probably the incursion of white men during the century after the formation of the league helped to make it a necessity and to continue its development. Whatever the case, the early French explorer Samuel de Champlain made enemies of the Iroquois, much to the later regret of the French. At times the Iroquois served as allies of the British and thus had an impact on the course of colonial history.

The Iroquois were noted for their ferocity and for their practice of torturing prisoners, although they were not much worse than Europeans had been in the treatment of prisoners and heretics. Probably a reason for their ferocity was that incessant fighting resulted in an escalation of hatred and fright. Furthermore, their reputed ferocity served as a device of psychological warfare, helping to dissuade potential enemies from attack.[8] By unity and ferocity, the league became a force to be reckoned with, but it was never strong enough to

---

[7] The material in this section is based on Peter Farb, *Man's Rise to Civilization* . . . , Avon Book Division, The Hearst Corporation, New York, 1968, pp. 126–144.

[8] Ibid., p. 139.

bring peace to its part of the world. Despite its strengths, the league had certain weaknesses inevitable in tribal organization.

The council of sachems had no power to interfere in internal affairs of any of the tribes. It had no power to pass uniform laws or to handle matters of justice within tribes. The sole function of the council was to decide intertribal matters, mainly to decide on matters of war and peace. There was no power of enforcement against component tribes, which made unanimous decisions absolutely necessary for the league to survive. The sachems, then, were comparable to the diplomatic staffs of states represented at an international conference, not to a true governing body. The Iroquois system represented a remarkable advance over the isolated tribe, but it fell far short of meeting the criteria of a sovereign state, which must be described next.

CHARACTERISTICS OF STATES States have existed in the world since the founding of the first great urban civilizations in the valleys of the Tigris-Euphrates, the Nile, the Indus, and the Hwang Ho and the building of the cities of Mesoamerica, central Mexico, and Peru. Some states have been only city-states of very limited size, and others have been empires. States have ranged in form of government from monarchies and aristocracies to republics, theocracies, and fascist or communist dictatorships, but they have always differed in important respects from the tribes just discussed. When the state emerges in its completed form, the "king's peace" is maintained; there is order throughout the realm. When the state attains its full functions, there is no longer a hydraheaded control of society, but only one final authority. Early anarchists denounced the state as organized violence; Marxists have seen it as institutionalized support for exploitation of the poor by upper classes. Social scientists describe it simply as a social system in which there is a monopoly on the legitimate use of force. In Lawrence Krader's words:

> In the organization of the state, man concentrates his power over man in a single office. The monopoly of physical force by the office is absolute. It may channel its power by specifically delegating it [but] the power remains at the disposal of the central authority.[9]

The state is a formidable power center. Small wonder that some groups—including our own ancestors—have attempted confederacies instead and have looked for constitutional, representational, and legal guarantees against its full

[9]Lawrence Krader, *Formation of the State*, Prentice-Hall, Inc., Englewood Cliffs, N.J., 1968, p. 9.

CHARACTERISTICS OF STATES

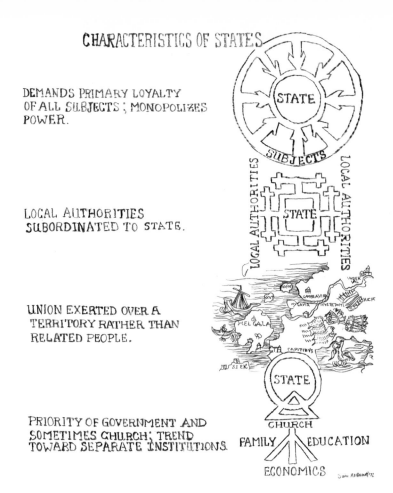

DEMANDS PRIMARY LOYALTY
OF ALL SUBJECTS ; MONOPOLIZES
POWER.

LOCAL AUTHORITIES
SUBORDINATED TO STATE.

UNION EXERTED OVER A
TERRITORY RATHER THAN
RELATED PEOPLE.

PRIORITY OF GOVERNMENT AND
SOMETIMES CHURCH; TREND
TOWARD SEPARATE INSTITUTIONS.

potential weight. Krader adds that in addition to organization the state develops its own "mystique of power"—its religion or ideology.

As in the old tribal days, there can be important local authorities and lineage heads within incipient states, but they can no longer exert power in their own right. On the religious level, there can still be local gods and rites, but they are subordinated to the god or gods of the state. On the moral level, particularism wanes, especially if it interferes with the supreme duty of the citizen to the state. In the old tribal society total equality was not always attained, but it was a possibility. In the state there is a dominant group, a "power elite" in the phrase of C. Wright Mills, even if the state has its roots in a democratic philosophy. So great is the unity of the state politically and religiously that White speaks of the "state-church," which he views as one entity.

"The special coordinative, integrative mechanism of political control in civil societies is everywhere marked by a civil, political, and military aspect, on the one hand, and an ecclesiastical, clerical, and theological aspect, on the other."[10] Such a description may sound exaggerated in the modern secularized world, but in times of crisis the state looks to religion or to the newer magico-religious mystiques of racism, communism, fascism, or extreme nationalism to rationalize its existence.

Besides its supreme authority, the state has a definite territory, and it sees itself as sovereign over that territory. People of a multiplicity of tribal origins can live within the territory, but they are all subject to the will of the same state. The rule is over the land, not over a tribe of people. Sir Henry Maine expressed the idea thus: "the 'King of the Franks' becomes instead the 'King of France.' "[11] Ideally, the state not only rules over all its subjects but has first claim on their loyalty. This criterion is not always met in a state; nearly all large nation-states have restive minorities, but the centrifugal forces must be controlled or the state ceases to exist. A number of historical states have been so torn with internal dissension as to disintegrate rapidly once a strong external challenge was able to exploit their internal weakness. Such was the fate of the Austro-Hungarian empire and the empire of the Ottoman Turks, and at the end of World War I it nearly became the fate of Imperial Russia. In the New World, the Aztec empire is a case in point. The military power of the Aztecs was very great, but they achieved no method for integrating their empire and assuring the loyalty of the conquered tribes. Consequently, the empire was ripe for dissolution once the foreign forces of Spain were able to form a rallying point for its destruction.

All states have had their problems, and few have approached the model of total unity described above. Some have come closer to fitting the model than others, and the differences may be partly a matter of differences in origin. What are the possible transitions from tribe to state?

TYPES OF
STATE DEVELOPMENT

Explanations of the origin of states follow several theoretical lines—development from associations, development from divine kingships, development resulting from the control of river valleys, and development resulting from conquest. Krader examines all these possibilities.[12] He first considers an idea of Robert Lowie's—the associational theory of states.

---

[10]Leslie A. White, *The Evolution of Culture*, McGraw-Hill Book Company, New York, 1959, p. 303.
[11]Quoted in Sahlins, op. cit., p. 6.
[12]Krader, op. cit.

ASSOCIATIONS AND THE STATE   Only a little has been said about clubs, age groups, military fraternities, and other associations in primitive life. We have noted briefly the Yoruba Ogboni (Chapter Six) and the age sets of the Masai and Barabaig (Chapter Seven) and the Gikuyu (Chapter Ten). Age sets are most prominent in societies in which there is a strong need for close cooperation among males regardless of family ties, for example, the societies mentioned in Chapter Ten in which the family was a very limited institution because of the military requirements placed upon young men. S. N. Eisenstadt theorizes that age sets are most prominent in societies in which universalistic principles must take precedence over familistic principles.[13] In such cases, he points out, more than average attention is given to the rites of puberty that initiate boys into manhood. Rites of puberty, often including instruction in the sacred ways of the tribe, tests of endurance, circumcision, and tatooing or scarification, are very common in the primitive world, and they are generally most severe in tribes that are wrenching boys from strong family ties in order to transfer their loyalty to larger social groups. In the case of such people as the Masai, Nandi, Nyakusa, and Barabaig, military sets of young men are important to the tribe and definitely compete with lineage groups for the loyality of the men, but such arrangements have not ordinarily led to states. In fact, fully developed age sets that remain corporate groups for life exist only in societies without centralized government.[14] The only African age-set societies that developed into states were those in which age groups were important only in the early years of life. Chaka, the great military leader who made the South African Zulu a powerful force in the early nineteenth century, subordinated age-graded regiments to his rule. In his case, and also in the case of the fairly centralized government of the Swazi, older men did not continue their age-group organizations.[15] The Zulu use of youth has been likened to Hitler's mobilization of a youth movement and to youth groups under communist regimes.

The Hidatsa, Crow, Pawnee, Blackfeet, Dakotas, and other Great Plains Indians had chiefs who were only first among equals and councils of renowned warriors who also had but little authority over the people. In the absence of centralized authority, military societies performed certain ceremonial functions, especially in healing and minor governmental services. In the case of the Crow, there were eight such associations, directing the communal buffalo hunt, providing military defense, and providing mutual aid to members. Although

---

[13]S. N. Eisenstadt, *From Generation to Generation: Age Groups and Social Structure*, The Free Press, New York, 1964.
[14]Hammon, op. cit., p. 11.
[15]Ibid.

they were associations that cut across kinship lines, it is hard to see how they could have constituted the beginnings of statelike unity, since they were often rivalrous and even disrupted the internal peace.[16] None of the Great Plains societies achieved a statehood with stable political order and territorial integrity.

Secret societies   Many African societies have other types of associations that cut across kinship lines and appear to be possible nuclei for state development. The Kpelle of Liberia and Guinea, for example, were a patrilineally organized people with district chiefs and a king. In name, the king was owner of all the land, ruler, and supreme judge; in actuality his power depended very much on his diplomatic ability, especially in his relations with the most important of the secret societies, the Poro. The Poro society had social, religious, and political functions. It was the organization to which all important men belonged. Its secretly elected head was a man of great prestige, around whom a myth of immortality was built, so that his death was always kept secret as long as possible. The women also had their secret society, the Sande, which all girls joined at puberty. The head of the Sande was a woman endowed with the power to bring fertility to the people and the land.

Spreading beyond the lands of the Kpelle was the Leopard society, prominent also in Guinea and Sierra Leone. Leopard society worship included human sacrifice, with the victim executed by a Leopard member dressed in a leopard skin. At times the Leopard society worked with the Poro and gained ascendancy among the Kpelle and nearby tribes. During much of the societies' period of development, the leaders acted as countervailing forces against the power of the king. These societies could, then, be interpreted as forces actually retarding development of the state by preventing power from concentrating in a central office, but encouraging it insofar as they separated loyalties from a purely kinship base.[17] Another interpretation is that they enforced the power of the king more frequently than they opposed it, in a manner comparable to the usual support of church and state for each other. There were periods of rivalry, but both worked in the direction of forcing respect for power structures beyond the kinship or village level. At the same time, such societies would be a problem for a truly supreme ruler. In Dahomey, where the most centralized of the West African kingly states developed, secret societies were suppressed.[18] In summary, it seems that some further ingredient besides association, going

[16]Krader, op. cit., pp. 34–35.
[17]Ibid., pp. 38–50.
[18]Hammond, op. cit., p. 14.

A mask of the secret Poro society.
Although secret societies sometimes
collaborated with kings, they were a
potential rival to centralized power and
were outlawed by the powerful kings of
Dahomey.

beyond age grade, military fraternity, or secret society, was needed in each of the associational societies.

BIG MEN AND CHIEFS: POLYNESIAN APPROACHES TO STATE POWER   Sahlins illustrates how an evolution in the direction of the state took place in the islands of Polynesia.[19] In New Guinea and other parts of Melanesia, the role of leader was usually vested in a Big Man, not a chief. The Big Man was a type of self-made man, gaining a following on the basis of his ability as a fighter, cajoler, and manipulator. Always his position depended on his personal ability to hold a following of people who would contribute to his wealth so that he could be a dispenser of gifts and hence add prestige to his group and to his segment of the tribe. He was a vulnerable leader, however, whose influence would decline rapidly if he asked too much of his followers without gaining new prestige or booty for them. He was always vulnerable to another primitive politician of a similar type, trying also to be a Big Man.

In contrast to the Melanesian Big Man was the Polynesian chief, whom we have already met in our discussion of wealth and social class in Chapter 9. The Polynesian chief was the head of a high-ranking branch of a clan. So great was his magico-religious power that he could place taboos upon objects and render them too sacred for the commoner to touch. In the smaller and more primitive societies, the chief's powers were mainly ceremonial, but in the larger societies, particularly those of the Hawaiian Islands and Tahiti, he was surrounded by military and other officials. His power of taboo made it possible for him to reserve crops and commodities for the public domain, so that his wealth and economic power could grow. Conspicuous consumption not only served the pleasure of the chief but widened the social distance between him and the lesser people and made him a subject of awe and reverence. Unlike the Big Man's power, the chief's power came, not from his personal achievements, but from his office; and his office devolved upon him because of the divine nature of his lineage. The hereditary nature of his office gave it a stability the Melanesian system never attained.

The power of the chief was such that he could call for the labor and goods of his people, and subchiefs constituted a bureaucracy that helped to enforce his power. Such economic power made it possible for him to build temples, impressive storehouses, and irrigation works and to marshal manpower for war. He could entertain lavishly, which helped his position in negotiating with other chiefs. In Tahiti and Hawaii, the chief had physical force in the form of

[19]Marshall D. Sahlins, "Poor Man, Rich Man, Big Man, Chief: Political Types in Melanesia and Polynesia," in James P. Spradley and David W. McCurdy (eds.), *Conformity and Conflict, Readings in Cultural Anthropology*, Little, Brown and Company, Boston, 1971, pp. 318–332.

a body of executioners, and his courtiers depended upon him for support. In this way, says Sahlins, his position was the reverse of that of the Big Man of Melanesia, who had always to depend upon his followers for support. The Big Man gathered goods from his retainers to make presents and buy the loyalty of more distant groups; the chief assessed all the people for the funds with which to buy the loyalty of his armed retainers. Nevertheless, stable, long-lasting regimes among the Polynesians were rare. Although in the cases of Hawaii and Tahiti most of the criteria of the state were met, kingdoms tended to come and go. What probably still weakened the state institution among the Polynesians was that chiefs' reigns were essentially kinship based. Sahlins adds another and perhaps more important limitation to state growth in Polynesia: "progressive expansion in political scale entailed more than proportionate accretion in the ruling apparatus, unbalancing the flow of wealth"[20] In other words, the system became administratively top-heavy and expensive in terms of the productive potential of the society, causing periodic unrest and decline of chieftaincies.

What had evolved in Polynesia, especially in the extensive kingdom of Hawaii, was a system that centralized power and gave the state a religious mystique of its own and a possibility of continuity. In certain other societies, which were able to marshal the energy of their people more fully, the state achieved greater stability. Egypt was one such society, and most of the early social systems that evolved into states shared certain traits with Egypt.

EGYPT AND THE THEORY OF ORIENTAL SOCIETY   Upper and Lower Egypt were combined into a unified kingdom in the period from 3400 B.C. to 3200 B.C., but state development had come about before unification.[21] In Neolithic times, similar cultures evolved in many places along the valley of the Nile. Early evidence shows little social stratification or centralization of rule, but these traits gradually developed along with monarchy as internal conquest was achieved. There is some skeletal evidence suggesting that foreign people invaded Egypt during the fourth millennium B.C., but by the time of unification all Egypt had a common language and fairly common culture. Another factor making for state growth was an easy territorial delimitation, with the fertile lands restricted to a narrow band along the Nile. Contrary to the case with the smaller chiefdoms of Polynesia, the Nile Valley produced the abundance needed for supporting all the trappings of monarchy and the bureaucracy generated by it.

[20]Ibid., p. 330.
[21]Krader, op. cit., pp. 52–63.

During the long period before unification, local villages were drawing together into larger complexes. Village rulers, *saru*, were probably clan heads, but villages were eventually ruled by kings, to whom the *saru* may have had the status of vassal. As kings grew in power and became reduced in numbers, the power of clan and tribe declined. The village clusters (*spats*) that had once been tribal centers gradually changed status and became districts or provinces of an empire. Tribes sometimes absorbed other tribes, and tribal gods were blended with other tribal gods. Eventually gods of the entire empire arose, including the pharaoh himself.

In historical legend, the first ruler was Menes, a king-god with supernatural powers who is said to have redirected the course of the Nile. He was the culture hero, the bringer of all the gifts of Egypt, and had gone to join the

Ramses II, wearing the crowns of upper and lower Egypt, symbolizes the absolute power of the pharoah—king, living god, and fountainhead of all political power.

other gods. His descendants, the rulers of Egypt, were also divine, combining secular and spiritual power. The pharaoh was possessed of divine spirits. At the time of his birth, he was Horus, the sky god, symbol of power; when he died he became Osiris, the god identified with the seasonal cycles of flood and drought and with the continuity between life and death. As has been the case with other divine kings, a disabled or senile pharaoh had to be put to death, since he was the earthly manifestation of divinity and could not be allowed to ail or falter. In theory, the pharaoh was the owner of all the land and the people, and the people labored for his glory. The biblical story of Joseph is perhaps an Israelite myth about how the pharaoh acquired such powers. According to the story, upon Joseph's advice, the pharaoh saved up grain and foodstuffs during bad times as a guarantee of abundance during later years of famine. When the people were hungry, they came to the pharaoh for grain, but to obtain it they had to give all their wealth and land and finally to sign themselves over to the pharaoh. The reality was not nearly as grim as the tale. Actually Egypt was a fairly tranquil land throughout much of its history, and a land of extensive division of labor, even providing paths to upward mobility for the skilled physician or scholar. There were powerful priests, military men, and bureaucrats, but all were "subjects" of the pharaoh, not citizens. So august was the pharaoh that his name and his title were seldom spoken. The word "pharaoh" means "great house," and that was the term by which his divine presence was known.

To say the pharaoh was divine, absolute, and awe inspiring, however, does not mean that there were no considerations to restrain him. A society is always more than a mere power pyramid; it is the conveyor of a culture, a total way of life including custom and a sense of right and wrong. Even the divine ruler is restrained by the cultural norms that become an ingrained part of him. There were also occasional problems with district governors, with palace intrigue, and with the priests of Ammon. But primarily Egypt was one of the world's first and longest surviving examples of a fully developed, monarch state. The state had been formed mainly by internal developments. Tribalism had vanished. Pharaoh was not "ruler of the Egyptians," but "ruler of Egypt." "The ethnic identity of the Egyptian people emerged out of the political identity of the Egyptian state."[22] The pharaoh could easily have made the statement attributed to Louis XIV of France—"*L'etat, c'est moi!*" ("The state, it is I!")

Other states developed as the late Neolithic merged into the age of urban civilizations. The great city-states of Mesopotamia date back at least as far as

[22]Ibid., p. 60.

the cities of Egypt. Cities arose also along the Indus River during the millennium after the uniting of Egypt. At about the same time, urban civilization emerged along the Hwang Ho in China, and state power arose. Karl Wittfogel, in an important essay that first appeared under the title "The Theory of Oriental Society," maintains that river valleys were necessary for the early development of state power and that the states developing along river valleys were, of necessity, powerful and autocratic.[23] The control of rivers to ensure irrigation and prevent flooding calls for the marshaling of populations in a manner not achieved in other parts of the world, according to the theory. Priests and godlike kings are believed able to control the rise and fall of rivers and ensure the welfare of the land, and military leaders work in harmony with them. Not only do powerful states arise, but the major cities that accompany them tend to be primarily centers of administrative bureaucracy rather than centers of free trade and commerce. The result is what Wittfogel calls the "stagnant society," one that persists for long ages but changes little. In Egypt, dynasties came and went for nearly 4,000 years, but the essential system remained as eternal as the Nile. Similarly, in China, dynasty followed dynasty—very often foreign dynasties—but the new rulers were absorbed into the system. Foreign conquerors were changed, not China.

Wittfogel's "theory of Oriental society" would not, of course, account for every type of state development or every close approach to it, such as those described in West Africa and Polynesia. It does not account directly for the later development of states in Europe, which Wittfogel sees as illustrating a different principle. European agriculture depended mainly upon rainfall, not on the control of great river systems. Consequently, there was no central, uniting principle. The emergence of states was slower, and their forms showed more variety. Generally speaking, local lords were gradually made subservient to central monarchies, but aristocracies long contested the power of kings. In later years, newly emerging commercial interests also contested for power within the systems, making concentrations of power and bureaucracy more difficult and making the state less "stagnant."

While civilizations and states formed along the great river valleys, ruder peoples from the country and the hills came to trade or plunder. We have already discussed some of these peoples in terms of their ways of life and their patterns of conquest. It was mentioned in Chapter Seven that the pastoral peoples, such as the Mongols, experienced difficulty in keeping their conquest states together but that they had at times conquered the most extensive empires

[23]Karl August Wittfogel, "The Theory of Oriental Society," in Morton H. Fried (ed.), *Readings in Anthropology*, vol. II, Thomas Y. Crowell Company, New York, 1968, pp. 179–198.

known to history. Let us next examine conquest as a means of state development.

CONQUEST STATES   Conquest states are encountered in many parts of the world and are very common, although evidence from ancient Egypt and Mesopotamia points to internal development as the earliest model. In fact, Krader's extensive work on the Turks and Mongols suggests that agricultural civilization is required for the growth of power among the peripheral peoples—pastoralists and mounted warriors.[24]

The Mongols and early Islamic states   The early peoples of central Asia turned to agriculture for an existence only if they were far removed from China, but remained nomadic pastoralists as long as they were close to the great productive centers of China, where they could trade for Chinese foodstuffs and such luxury goods as silk and jewels. China became dependent on the nomads for horses, camels, and other animals, for meat and leather, and for such luxury goods as ermine and sable pelts. The relationship between the two sides was partly governed by political and military considerations. In all negotiations the stronger side spoke first—usually China, but occasionally the Mongols.

When the Mongols reached their greatest periods of strength and conquest, their social system served well for expansionism, as has been shown in the chapter on pastoralism, but in the long-range task of ruling over foreign people, a weakness developed. The Mongol and Tatar hordes were organized on a fictive kinship basis, which helped to promote unity and subordination within but made it impossible to incorporate Chinese, Russians, Persians, and Hindus. Yet the state had to depend upon local populations for administration of its policies. Conquered people were subjects of their conquerors, but in a different sense than that in which the people of Egypt were subjects of the pharaoh. The Egyptians were subjects of their own god-king; the people conquered by the Mongols were subjects of a foreign power.[25] However, the difference disappeared with the passing of time. The Mongols could rule China only through Chinese officialdom, and they inevitably took on Chinese customs and Chinese values. Within three generations they were merely another Chinese dynasty, but a dynasty of rather short duration.

A very similar fate awaited the Arabic conquerors of the period after Muhammad. The Arabs, as they spread the message of Islam and conquered in

[24]Krader, op. cit. See also Lawrence Krader, *Social Organization of the Mongol-Turkic Nomads,* Indiana University Publications, Uralic and Altaic Series, vol. 20, published by Mouton and Co., The Hague, 1963.
[25]Krader, *Formation of the State,* p. 97.

the name of the Prophet, found themselves in possession of the empires of the Near East. They were forced to take over the administrative machinery of the previous states, and "within two or three generations their tribal chiefs had become Oriental monarchs."[26]

Dispersal of power   All conquest states must face first the problems of ruling and exploiting and eventually the problem of doing so without the hatreds that make the state vulnerable to dissolution from within. Linton suggests that two basic patterns have been used for the control of conquered people, one the technique of dispersal of rulers and the second the technique of the concentration of rulers and the apparatus of the state.[27] The invading tribes that conquered Europe as the Roman Empire came to an end ruled by the method of dispersal, with noblemen setting up their feudal headquarters in many places among the conquered people. Holding a monopoly on arms and backed by religious institutions, they maintained their high status, but in their identity they began to merge with the people over whom they ruled. There was a weakening of the esprit de corps of the original invading peoples, and many Visigoths, Vandals, and, later, Norsemen lost their identity. Even where a strong state was established, as in Norman England, the invaders could not remain a separate ruling people but eventually merged into the larger society, becoming Englishmen and Scotsmen, depending on where they lived.

Concentrated control   Linton suggests that the opposite conquest model, that of concentrating control at power centers, was typical of most of the early civilizations of the Near East. Here his ideas are in considerable agreement with those of Wittfogel. Control through central bureaucracies came about, but such administrative bureaucracies were sometimes preceded by the mere use of armed force to terrorize the subject people into paying tribute. The central bureaucracy was a more sophisticated development and grew most rapidly in the irrigated river valleys.

Many techniques were used to try to gain the loyalty of subject peoples. Rome was particularly adept in this respect, having adopted the policy of extending citizenship to conquered peoples. In other societies, children of the conquered were sometimes adopted into the royal court so that they could serve as links between rulers and subjects. Chinese emperors often presented Chinese concubines to chiefs of tribute-bearing societies, hoping to buy their loyalty and also to place in their courts women of both beauty and brains who could fill a diplomatic role. A more brutal technique of control was to capture

[26]Ralph Linton, *The Study of Man*, D. Appleton-Century Company, Inc., New York, 1936, p. 244.
[27]Ibid., pp. 244–251.

tribes of people, move them from their land, and award their lands to more loyal subjects—an excellent "divide-and-rule" policy. The Babylonian captivity of the Hebrew people is one of the best-known examples. The Ottoman Turks used yet another technique, similar to but not the same as the policies mentioned by Linton. The Ottomans imposed a "blood tax," which took a number of boys from conquered villages to be brought up in Turkey and become members of the elite Turkish military corps, the Janissaries. The boys so chosen were considered by the Turks to be highly honored. Christian subjects were horrified over the custom, fearing for the souls of their sons, who would be taken to a foreign land and probably converted to Islam.

Finally, the possibility of creating a caste system bears repeating at this point. The full development of caste makes a conquest state virtually immune to overthrow. If those in depressed status completely internalize caste attitudes, they begin to accept their inferior position as inevitable and as heaven willed. A few of the caste societies of East Africa approached this solution; India became the only fully developed case.

PERSISTENCE OF TRIBAL SENTIMENTS   It is obvious that state development has taken many forms. Possibly the river valley civilizations were the models and the nuclei for the development of other states. Many of the conquests actually started at the tribal level, with conquering tribesmen mastering the people near them but themselves becoming captives of the cultural systems they had seized. Always the state was faced with problems of control. Always the true state rose above kinship principles in organization, but was there not always a lingering desire for kindred feeling? In Linton's words, "The most successful states are those in which the attitudes of the individual toward the state most nearly approximate the attitudes of the uncivilized individual toward his tribe"[28] The modern state attempts to achieve this tribal feeling, often by granting citizenship and participating rights to all its people. It frequently uses the trappings of pageantry, such as flags, parades, national songs, and other symbols of collective identity, and it even retains the shadow of what White called the state-church in public prayers and dedications and in its certainty that God is on its side in any conflict. In a few cases the tribal mystique has taken on a pathological character never quite approached even in the older types of tribes, as when imperialist nations have spoken of their "manifest destiny" or the "white man's burden." New heights of such statist psychopathology were reached in Hitler's ravings about the German soul and the thousand-year reich. Like the divine king of the Shilluk or the alafin of the Yoruba, he attempted to personify the tribal soul. In a more normal way, any great political leader out-

[28]Ibid., p. 252.

standing enough to become a hero of his nation becomes a symbol of unity almost analogous to the divine ruler.

BEYOND THE STATE States impose supreme authority over their people and prevent feud within, but relative to one another they may remain comparable to the feuding branches of a tribe. Much of the effort of statesmanship is aimed at keeping peace—in the old days by interdynastic marriage alliances reminiscent of tribal times. In the age of imperialism, states simulated tribal gift exchange by allowing one another to acquire territories from those parts of the world that were characterized as "backward." (Such areas included some of the world's oldest and most highly developed civilizations.) States signed alliances but still watched one another as warily as two adjacent Yanomamö villages. At present they exchange ambassadors and goods, stage Olympic games, invite students to visit, honor visiting dignitaries, and give sumptuous banquets; but still they fight. Frequently the life of modern man, like that of Hobbes' savage, becomes "poore, nasty, brutish, and short."

In fairly recent years some observers thought they detected a trend toward alignments based on ideology rather than nationalism. International communism was expected to hold together in a condition of "monolithic unity." In reality, the older idea of the nation-state has reemerged, and states linked together in ideology (particularly Russia and China) have found conflicting national interests much stronger than unity of political and economic philosophy.

Attempts are made to link the nations of the world into grand international organizations, such as the United Nations. Such organizations have so far had all the weaknesses and none of the strengths of the League of the Iroquois. All the sachems have to agree before a decision can be made in the Security Council, but contrary to the Iroquois case, such decisions are not made.

Another struggling attempt at unity is that of a modern "Kula Ring," in which goods are exchanged without tariff on the basis of national trading partnerships. The outstanding example is the group of Common Market countries of western Europe, whose mutual involvement in one another's economies may become so strong that they can no longer afford to fight. This situation occurred in at least one historical case, when in the middle of the nineteenth century the many quarreling states of Germany were united into a trading partnership called the Zollverein and soon thereafter became politically united.

The merging of states into superstate trading areas is economically desirable and probably a growing trend. There is, though, the specter raised in

Whether the nation-states can be united into a new kind of political and economic order is an issue still in doubt. The United Nations, like the League of the Iroquois, can act only if all the "sachems" agree.

George Orwell's description of the world of the future, in which a number of superstates hold the loyalty of their people by maintaining a constant state of fright and war threat. Gloomy though Orwell's picture is, it imagines a future in which the rulers of the superstates dare not actually go to war. They know war is an impossibility. Human technology has made possible the total destruction of the earth, and in Orwell's imagination, that threat will bring an end to actual military confrontation between the major powers.

But real peace depends upon more than mutual fear. When primitive man first developed systems of gift exchange and mutual obligation and later moved on to the ideas of trade and mutual benefit, he had started one of the processes of peace. His later descendants continued that process by uniting into systems of political unity. The processes of survival have been discovered; man's next task is to expand them to meet the needs of the world of tomorrow.

313

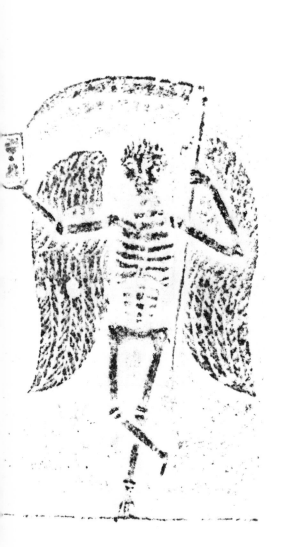

Chapter Thirteen
The Rule of Law

Societies cannot function without normative rules that grow out of the lives and customs of the people. Such normative rules are not exactly the same as laws, but there is a relationship between norms and laws. Laws are generally in line with a culture's definition of rights and wrongs; laws that are not in line with such definitions are difficult to enforce. There are complications, however, to the analysis of law in terms of customs and normative rules. In the first place, societies differ greatly in their beliefs about right and wrong. In one society, the killing of deformed or unhealthy infants seems the right way to ensure survival and strengthen the stock; in another, such a custom is looked upon with horror. Another complication is that the very concept of law might not be applicable to all societies. How formalized must rules become before they can be called laws? Does a public enforcement agency of some type have to come into play before law exists? In one of his best-known books, *The Call of the Wild*, Jack London used the expression "the law of club and fang." Was he really talking about law, or merely about the rule of might?

Another interesting and extremely important question about law is how people conceptualize it. Are laws conceived to be the will of the people, growing out of their lifeways and their sense of justice, or are they believed to be imposed from without? The first type of explanation comes very close to the concept of common law or customary law in British and American thinking. The second, that law is imposed upon the people, can pertain to law made by elected representatives or in less palatable form, law imposed upon a people by their conquerors. Both conceptions are encountered in anthropology and also a third one—that law is given to the people by the divine will of god or the gods. What kinds of societies conceive of the law in these differing ways and what are the functions of such views? What changes in legal practice take place as we move from simple hunting-and-gathering societies to early civilizations and to modern societies? What kinds of courts develop? What rules of evidence? Finally, are there any discernible trends in the law?

THE ESSENTIALS OF LAW   Law, strictly defined, must meet several criteria: (1) It must derive from and be executed on the basis of legitimate authority, and (2) universal enforcement must be intended. (3) It must define rights and obligations of people relative to one another, and (4) it must carry the threat of sanctions for violation.[1]

Considering these criteria in more detail, it can be seen that legitimate authority can be of many types, but it must be publicly recognized as having the right of enforcement. Directly or indirectly that right stems from group opinion and tradition, although the law is often attributed to ancient wise men or to the gods. The important point is that the authority is looked upon as "right," regardless of what explanation is given to sanctify it. As for the second criterion—universal enforcement—there seem at first glance to be exceptions to the rule. It is impossible to catch all offenders in any system; but all that is required for law to exist is that a serious attempt be made at universal enforcement. Some legal systems allow laws to be enforced much more severely on some classes than on others, as in the distinction between slaves and freemen or nobles and commoners. Such regulations are, nevertheless, law if they apply universally to members of particular categories of people. They may seem unjust by the standards of modern societies, but justice is differently defined in different cultures.

Law involves definitions of rights and obligations. Some of these definitions are based on kinship. For example, parents must assume certain respon-

---

[1]Leopold Pospisil, "The Attributes of Law," in Paul Bohannan (ed.), *Law and Warfare: Studies in the Anthropology of Conflict*, The Natural History Press, Garden City, N.Y., 1967, pp. 25–41. (Excerpted from Leopold Pospisil, *Kapauku, Papuans and Their Law*, Yale University Publications in Anthropology no. 54, 1958.)

sibilities for their children, and children owe obligations to their parents. Relations between ruler and ruled are defined, between employers and employees, between men and women. Finally, a rule is a mere custom or norm unless its violation holds the threat of punishment. The punishment may be anything from a small fine or public humiliation all the way to ostracism or even death, but there must be some kind of threat and someone to carry out the threat. In simpler societies, the punishment is often carried out by relatives of an injured person. Such enforcement is spoken of as "private law," but it is law as long as the relatives have a recognized right to punish and will not be interfered with in that right. In more complex societies, with state power, all criminal law becomes public law, enforced by officially chosen agents.

Since by no means everything regarded as law meets all the above requirements, it can be argued that there are degrees of law. We speak of "international law," for example, although it consists only of customs, traditions, and signed conventions that members of the Family of Nations make but a bare pretense of abiding by. We know that violations can go unpunished and that there is no authority for execution of the laws' provisions. There are cases in international disputes in which a degree of concern is shown over the weight of world opinion or over the possible alienation of allies or trade if international policies become too high-handed and arrogant. There is also the threat of war in international affairs, which is almost the exact equivalent of the threat of feud in societies based on clans or lineages. We could call international law a primitive type of law, because the signatories of international conventions are all sovereign states of the type discussed in the last chapter, all hold territories over which they are supreme and recognize no superior power to which they must bend.

Robert Redfield analyzes primitive law in a manner very similar to the above comparison with international law. He points out that not all attempts made by societies at social control can be called law or the subject of law will expand to include religion, moral tales, methods of child rearing, and everything remotely concerned with normative systems. Law, then, is only an aspect of social control—but it is the aspect having to do with threat and legitimate enforcement. However, the analysis of law in the strictest sense would lead to the conclusion that "there is no law in primitive society and that therefore there is nothing to talk about."[2] Redfield's solution to the dilemma is to admit developmental stages of law, including as law the rules of primitive

---

[2]Robert Redfield, "Primitive Law," *University of Cincinnati Law Review*, vol. 33, pp. 1–22, Winter 1964.

tribes that "by their formal or systematic or coercive nature foreshadow our law and seem to illustrate the simpler modes of conduct out of which a law such as ours might develop."[3]

LEGAL ATTITUDES: ENFORCEMENT, CRIMINAL MOTIVE, WERGILD

Just as there is some justification for speaking of degrees of law, it can be argued that there are gradations in policies about enforcement, about the importance of proving criminal motive, and about what types of crime can be settled by payment. Paul Radin makes a very strong distinction between primitive societies and modern civilizations regarding the agency of enforcement of law.[4] Occasionally, in primitive societies, violations of law are believed to bring their own punishment, or they are punished by ostracism or by unbearable ridicule from the social group. Many offenses are considered private affairs and are handled by the family itself or by quarrels between families that sometimes result in feuds. Among the Winnebago Indians, the legal power to make rules and insist on their enforcement was only an emergency power, belonging to the war chief and used only during war. After the war, quarrels were again private matters. In nearly all societies attempts are made to bring about private settlement of a majority of interpersonal disputes, but the violations defined as crime become public matters in most modern states.

Such crimes as murder were public matters among the Plains Indians, but the procedure for their settlement was very different from that of modern courts. Occasionally there was violent revenge, but often violence was avoided. The Winnebago chief was expected to be a man of fairness, judgment, and patience. His lodge was a place of temporary refuge for the offender. His duty was to mediate disputes, representing the feeling of outrage of the group but also their feeling of need for harmony and reconciliation. The chief would work always in the interests of reconciliation, even humbling himself before the offended family in behalf of the culprit and trying to arrange recompense in gifts, horses, and other payments.[5]

Among the Cheyenne, the same attempt was made at maintaining harmony.[6] So numerous were the rituals emphasizing the importance of unity and "Cheyenneness" that feuding became impossible within the tribe. The part

[3]Ibid., p. 6.
[4]Paul Radin, *The World of Primitive Man*, E. P. Dutton & Co., New York, 1971, pp. 220–230.
[5]Ibid., p. 228.
[6]E. Adamson Hoebel, *The Cheyennes: Indians of the Great Plains*, Holt, Rinehart and Winston, Inc., New York, 1960, pp. 49–56.

of law that was public law was concerned with the regulation of hunts and the prevention of killing of one Cheyenne by another. When murder occurred, the offender was ostracized, no longer allowed to eat with the people, to take part in ceremonies, to smoke the ritual pipe, or to receive assistance in time of need. The Cheyenne word for "murder" is the same as the word for "putrid," meaning the murderer is one who rots internally and whose putrescence can afflict the tribe. An elaborate Renewal of Arrows ceremony had to be performed if such an offense occurred within the tribe to renew and purify the land and the people. It was also a principle of Cheyenne law, however, that no ostracism or banishment need last forever. The time would come when the offender seemed contrite, reformed, ready to make recompense and receive forgiveness. The ostracism might last for many years, but it was not automatically for life.

CRIMINAL INTENT   Another feature distinguishing attitudes about law is the importance of criminal intent. In our society we distinguish between first degree murder, committed with full intent and premeditation, and other types of killing, such as involuntary manslaughter. Intent makes a very great difference. Some people do not distinguish between the two types of offenses. For example, a Hupa child was accidentally killed in a fire built by a woman heating water for washing. Although the accident was not her fault, a demand was made for the death of her child as recompense.[7] It is not unusual for an equivalent relative to be taken in retribution rather than the accused. On the other hand, the Ifugao of the Philippines, whose legal system was in some ways quite primitive, made a very great distinction between crimes of intent and mere accidents—with one interesting exception. If one of the rich men staged a sumptuous feast that ended in a brawl, any damages done were his fault and the fault of the priest who presided over the affair. It cannot be said categorically that all primitive people fail to take intent into account and that all civilized people do, but there is at least a tendency in that direction.[8]

WERGILD   There are also wide differences among societies in attitudes concerning the degree to which crimes can be absolved by the payment of wergild. "Wergild," meaning "blood money," is derived from an old Germanic word for the payment made in compensation for a man's life. The amount paid differed on the basis of the victim's rank. The custom was in force among

[7]Robert H. Lowie, *Primitive Society*, Harper Torchbooks, Harper & Brothers, New York, 1961, pp. 400–402.
[8]Ibid., pp. 401–402.

THE RULE OF LAW

RUDIMENTARY	INTERMEDIATE	ADVANCED
DEFINING RIGHTS AND WRONGS:		
CUSTOM MORE THAN LAW	FORMAL LAW, UNDERSTOOD BUT NOT WRITTEN	FORMAL LAW WRITTEN
ENFORCEMENT:		
BY KINSMEN OF OFFENDED PARTY	BY COMMUNITY ACTION	BY FORMAL ENFORCEMENT AGENT
SANCTIONS:		
PRIVATE REVENGE	COMMUNAL REVENGE (EYE FOR EYE)	MORE COMPLEX DEFINITIONS OF JUSTICE
CRIMINAL INTENT:		
SOMETIMES IRRELEVANT	CONSIDERED	CONSIDERED
WERGILD:		
MAY EVEN ABSOLVE MURDER	MAY ABSOLVE CRIMES OF UPPER CLASS	ONLY IN ACCIDENTAL OFFENCES

ancient Germanic peoples and also among the Slavic people to the east. Among many of the Plains Indians, compensations were often made in horses and were sometimes sufficient to prevent blood revenge. The ancient Kirghiz demanded 100 horses or 1,000 sheep as payment of blood money. The much more ancient laws of Hammurabi, to be discussed below, also called for compensation for life and limb. The major difference among societies regarding wergild is whether it will be accepted in cases of murder or only in cases of accidental deaths. In the ancient kingdoms of the Near East, murder always called for blood. Among the Ifugao it usually did. The Plains Indian family was more likely eventually to settle the matter by accepting compensation, and the Samoans were usually able to prevent further bloodshed by the same device.[9] Blood money is particularly useful in societies without strong enough court and police systems to prevent possible blood feuds. In such cases wergild prevents protracted bloodshed and chaos.

The following newspaper article relates the sharp contrast between British tradition and New Guinea tradition in handling a case of involuntary manslaughter. It will be noted that the Australian magistrate found no guilt. To the Jiga tribe of New Guinea, however, a death was a death and had to be paid for; consequently, relatives of the deceased gathered to back their claim.

> Peter Howard, from Cambridge, England . . . owns a plantation 10 miles from Mt. Hagen in the western highlands of New Guinea. His troubles with the Jiga tribe began October 29 when his car struck a tribesman who died later that day in a hospital.
>
> A few hours later, he was attacked by the dead man's kinsmen, knocked unconscious and severely bruised.
>
> Howard was charged with manslaughter but a magistrate found he had no case to answer.
>
> Four Jiga tribesmen were charged with assaulting him and causing bodily harm. One was acquitted last week in the supreme court and the others released on bail.
>
> While white man's law was still running its course, the Jiga tribe, in accordance with customary law, demanded $3,000 and 28 head of cattle in compensation for the death.
>
> Howard told reporters: "I asked what the alternative was. They told me it was to be killed. Neither the police nor the administration could guarantee my safety if I refused to pay."
>
> However, he managed to coax them down to $1,000 and four head of cattle.

[9]Ibid., pp. 402–404.

At the gathering of the tribesmen, Howard told them he was paying them compensation in accordance with their laws. He argued that under the same laws he was entitled to compensation for the beating they had given him.

Tribal elders at first disagreed. But after long arguments and many conferences among themselves, the Jiga have tentatively suggested payment of $20 and a pig.[10]

RUDIMENTARY LAW   Although we have previously noted that in small band-type societies headmen have little authority, there are nevertheless cases of incipient legalism. In Australian society, a group of distinguished old men usually constituted authority that would seldom be violated. Among the very primitive Yaghan there was more than mere group pressure. "There is never a shortage of men who because of their old age, spotless character, long experience and mental superiority, gain such an extent of moral influence that it is equal to a peculiar domination."[11] The situation is similar among the Kapauku. Kapauku society of New Guinea is one that has been described by Westerners as having no one in authority and hence no law. Yet Leonard Pospisil, during his study of the Kapauku, found that there were men of accomplishment, prestige, and respect, called *tonowi*, who attempted to impose legal authority and usually succeeded. Of 176 cases of clashes of interest, 132 were settled by the *tonowi*, 41 were settled by other types of negotiation, and only 3 were settled by a fight.[12] The forces for settlement were not as strong as those backed by court systems, but, consisting of moral suasion and respect for official position, they were stronger than mere group opinion.

THE ESKIMO SONG DUEL   Eskimo law illustrates the wide variation in types of offenses that are considered matters of legal concern.[13] Because of the hardships of their lives, Eskimo bands have practiced both infanticide and senilicide, especially when times were bad and survival of the family was in doubt. The marriage system also was not encumbered by many rules and regulations. Nevertheless, a man's wife was his property, and wife stealing was a serious crime. Quite a number of cases of wife stealing took place, and they sometimes led to deadly fights. If all such cases were settled by a fight to the death, with

---

[10]By permission of Reuters, Ltd., Feb. 7, 1972.

[11]Pospisil, op. cit., p. 27.

[12]Ibid., p. 38.

[13]The material in this section is based on E. Adamson Hoebel, *The Law of Primitive Man*, Chapter 5, "The Eskimo: Rudimentary Law in a Primitive Anarchy," Harvard University Press, Cambridge, Mass., 1954.

no public intervention or institutionalized means for determining the merits of the case, no law can be said to have existed. If, however, there were routinized ways of settlement aimed at preventing bloodshed and eliciting the concern of the band, then it can be argued that the first rudiments of law were present. Actually, there were such alternatives to a fight; one was a wrestling match, and the other was a song duel.

The song duel in some ways almost resembled a court case in which the argument goes to the side that shows the greater eloquence in its plea. Each of the two angry men would in turn beat out a rhythm on a drum and make up words to go with the rhythm, upholding his own case and denouncing the opposition. A wife stealer would be denounced as a thief and a liar and not enough of a man to get a wife of his own. The injured husband would be accused of being unable to satisfy his wife and of being a brute and a fool. All embarrassing situations of the past would be retold in ribald language. Putting all the denunciations into rhythm called for great skill, and the better songster was greatly admired by the audience that would eventually make the decision. E. Adamson Hoebel points out that, in a sense, the audience was a court hearing a case. There is a little ambiguity about the matter of justice, because the decision was supposed to be based on the quality of the insult song rather than the merits of the case. However, it is likely that the audience also thought in terms of the justifications involved. In any event, the winner found the audience increasingly reacting to his drum and words, perhaps even repeating the taunts he threw at his opponent. The loser would be "sung into the ground;" his humiliation would be unbearable. He might even go into self-imposed exile for a time because of his inability to face public humiliation. Whatever the justice of the situation, a deadly fight would have been avoided and a decision made. In modern American courts the order of precedence theoretically is reversed; that is, we are supposed to make a decision on the merits of the case rather than on how good a "song" the lawyers bring forth, but there is a degree of resemblance. In both cases a type of court has rendered a decision—in the Eskimo case the court of public opinion.

Eskimo customs called for a type of legal control in yet another respect. If one man murdered another, the kinsmen of the victim could take revenge, but counterrevenge from the relatives of the original offender was not permitted; feud had to be avoided. Informal legal customs also protected the group against a dangerous man and even designated a law-enforcement agent. In one case a man went berserk and killed members of the village. The brother of the killer was selected by the group to execute him. In this way the matter could be settled without any possibility of retaliation from kinsmen.

Eskimo at Point Hope, Alaska, at a whaling feast sing and beat drums of a type formerly used in song duels.

The final example of Eskimo law enforcement is of a type left to the angakok, the practitioner of religion and magic who was able to contact the spirit world. The person who broke sacred taboos was even more of a danger to the group than was the insane killer, because violation of taboos could cause animals to desert the territory so there would be no food or could cause disasters to occur at sea. When hunters had a run of bad luck, a meeting was held in which the angakok elicited confessions from taboo violators who had committed such offenses as holding evil thoughts, eating forbidden foods (many food taboos were placed on women), smoking a pipe without permission, having sexual relations just before a whale hunt, and many more. Ordinarily to confess was to be forgiven, but not unless the culprit agreed to correct her errors. (Women were thought to be the most likely violators of taboos.) One woman continued to eat caribou and seal meat together and finally had to be exiled, because the two meats are ritually incompatible, one representing land and the other water. Occasionally the angakok would exploit his magical position, as often happens with the specialist in the spirit world. He might rule that the best way for a woman to make atonement for her violations would be to have sexual relations with him!

In summary, the Eskimo illustrate several points about primitive law. They found devices that could settle disputes without bloodshed and ways of preventing bloodshed, when it did occur, from turning to feud. They believed in a responsibility of the individual to the group that carried into the spiritual realm. As with the Cheyenne, an individual offender could bring contamination to a group. The angakok, in his manipulations, illustrates one of the possibilities of legal corruption, especially when legal and magical principles blend.

IFUGAO LAW   The Ifugao of the Philippines were quite advanced in farming techniques, but like the Eskimo they had no official court for enforcing law, although they were tremendously interested in law.[14] The Ifugao were energetic people, growing rice in extremely hilly terrain that called for tremendous amounts of work in terracing. They were interested in trade and wealth and were given to long bouts of haggling over debts, even minor ones. Since they prided themselves on the ability to win a dispute, their quarrels were not easily settled and sometimes resulted in bloody feuds. In an attempt to avert feud, two quarreling families would hire a go-between, called a *monkalun*, to attempt to mediate the dispute. As soon as he took up his duties, he placed the two families in a state of isolation from each other, separated by magical taboo as much as by hostility. The *monkalun* would go from one family to the other, warning of the strong points in the case of the opposition and of the enemy's power to make war, thus trying to get the two sides to come to terms. He was well compensated if he succeeded. If he failed, feud was likely, because there was no governmental machinery to enforce law; the Ifugao had not developed a state.

Besides hiring a *monkalun*, there were a few other Ifugao devices for averting bloodshed. Litigants sometimes resorted to duels with eggs, but often the person hit with an egg retaliated with a rock, and then his opponent used his spear. Usually, though, violence was avoided, either by such devices as the egg duel or by the *monkalun*. In addition, the high-ranking men of the society, known as *kadangyangs*, were expected to exert their influence in behalf of peaceful settlement.

THE TIV: DRUMS AND INSULTS   The Tiv of Nigeria were a more numerous and politically advanced people than either the Eskimo or the Ifugao, but they

---

[14]The material in this section is based on R. F. Barton, *Procedure among the Ifugao*, University of California Publications in American Archaeology and Ethnology, vol. 15, no. 1, pp. 92–109, Feb. 19, 1919.

sometimes used a type of song contest reminiscent of the Eskimo.[15] Paul Bohannan tells the story of a bitter quarrel over an attempt to get a refund on bride price. The contestants, both Tiv of separate lineages, became increasingly angry. Finally the first man got his drum, late at night when all was quiet and none could fail to hear him, and drummed and sang his denunciations of his enemy. Since his antagonist was not good at song, he hired a professional to help him, which was perfectly legal, but costly. Tiv rules made it legal to say anything about a person that was true or that was so impossible that it could not really have happened and therefore didn't actually constitute bearing false witness. One song told of how one of the men turned himself into a boar hog at night and menaced every sow in the village.

The songs went on every night for 3 weeks, until finally the local official, the *mbatarev*, intervened and told the two men to present their case before him. The men and their supporters arrived, giving a last great song contest and presenting their cases. In the Tiv contest, the quality of the songs did not sway the court; the poorer of the two drummers won the decision on its merits.

The resemblance between the Tiv case and the Eskimo case is in some respects only superficial. Unlike the Eskimo, the Tiv had a legal official to bring disputes to trial and a court for hearing the case. In many of the court systems of Africa legal procedures are advanced well beyond the most primitive levels.

LEGAL SYSTEMS IN AFRICAN KINGDOMS African societies have been more interested in litigation than most of the Indian tribes of the Americas, and they present many interesting legal patterns. Those whose organization was a matter of segmentary lineages without strong unifying controls were inclined toward occasional feuds, although sometimes systems were developed for a type of ritualized combat that would avoid all-out war.

ZULU RITUALIZED COMBAT In the early development of the Zulu, before they became a unified, formidable fighting power that slowed down the white occupation of South Africa, they had had frequent internal disputes that were settled by a regulated form of combat.[16] When legal disputes arose, the litigants and their supporters took sides at a prearranged place and hurled javelins at

[15]The material in this section is based on Paul Bohannan, "Drumming the Scandal among the Tiv," in Paul Bohannan (ed.), *Law and Warfare: Studies in the Anthropology of Conflict*, The Natural History Press, Garden City, N.Y., 1967, pp. 263–265.
[16]Keith F. Otterbein, "The Evolution of Zulu Warfare," *Kansas Journal of Sociology*, Winter 1964, pp. 56–63.

A Dahomey chief and entourage. Much protocol surrounded the courts of Africa, with chiefs and kings often playing a role—a great advance over legal systems of primitive hunters.

one another. The javelins were relatively ineffective, and the defense weapons were excellent rawhide shields, so few were wounded, but the side that fled first lost the dispute and also had its cattle and women raided. After powerful leaders, most notably Chaka, united the tribes, disputes were settled by adjudication in the courts. The Zulu case bears a resemblance to the trial-by-combat method frequently used in medieval Europe and to be discussed later.

BAROTSE LAW Barotse law featured a more highly developed court system than any discussed so far.[17] The Lozi, who live in the region of the Zambezi River, are the dominant people of Barotseland. According to myth, they were created by the god Nyambe. The son and daughter of First Man founded a kingdom and developed Lozi law, which has been in effect ever since. Following the lead of its original founders, Barotseland was long ruled by a king at the northern capital city and a princess at the southern capital. Under the monarchs was an elaborate system of courts dedicated to securing justice and

[17]The material in this section is based on Max Gluckman, *Order and Rebellion in Tribal Africa*, Cohen & West Publishers, London, 1963, pp. 178–206.

tranquillity. Opposite each royal palace was a council house where important trials were held.

Trials were long and involved and usually included much material that our courts would consider "irrelevant and immaterial to the case." There were two reasons for this: (1) Each litigant was expected to be able to tell his story in such a way as to defend his reputation as a reasonable man who had acted as he had only because of wrongs; and (2) because of lack of the modern instruments for determining guilt, it seemed necessary to make a thorough character analysis of the litigants before the case was decided. Above all, the person on trial and the person making the accusation wished to prove themselves "reasonable and customary men," carrying out their roles and duties in the way prescribed by Lozi custom. If such a conclusion could be made about one's character, then one's chances of winning the case were enhanced.

The power to cross-question was in the hands of councilors (*indunas*), the most powerful of whom was described as "another kind of king." The king himself often attended the trials and had the final power to decide. The decision process, however, was not as arbitrary as the king's position makes it sound. The lowliest ranking *indunas* gave their judgments first, followed by the others in order of rank. The king was likely to intervene only if there was uncertainty in the decision. Witnesses and kinsmen were called in to testify. The whole system is highly praised by Max Gluckman as an orderly procedure, aimed at justice and free of threat or corruption.

Among the Lozi there was a certain divinity to law, since the law ultimately derived from the founding king, who was very close to the creator god; but the reasonable element in law and evidence was more important even than the divine. In some of the African states, however, divine intervention was depended upon more than among the Lozi. In some respects this was true of the Ashanti legal system.

THE ASHANTI OF GHANA   The Ashanti of Ghana, West Africa, are a numerous people and had established a strong kingdom long before the period of European influence in West Africa.[18] The king was a man of very great prestige, a kind of king-of-kings, with district and local chiefs at different levels below him in the power structure. The Ashanti did not have the clearly limited territory mentioned in the previous chapter as a criterion of state, but their court system clearly showed state supremacy. Any troublesome disputes were to be

[18]The material in this section is based on R. S. Rattray, *Ashanti*, Oxford University Press, Fair Lawn, N.J., 1923.

settled amicably by the disputants themselves, and long quarrels were a disturbance to the king's peace. If men could not settle their own quarrels, it was possible to take the risky alternative of going before the courts. The way to take a matter before the courts was for the contestants to swear an oath on the forbidden name of one of the gods. Such an oath was an offense against the kingdom, as is often the case with acts that disturb the supernatural.

The trial process was especially interesting from the point of view of evidence. As in the case of the Barotse, there were no detectives, no fingerprints or wiretaps. It is well known in all legal systems that litigants do not necessarily tell the truth and neither do witnesses. The problem of honest witnesses was solved by the Ashanti, however, by making the witness swear on the Great Forbidden Name that all he said was the truth. After that he dared not lie because divine punishment would be upon him if he did. The gods did not always punish immediately, but in the long run there could be no escaping them.

Several traits of Ashanti law are of importance because they are commonly encountered and their equivalents are found at high levels of state development. Many courts ask witnesses to swear "so help you God," the implication in more sacred times having been that falsehood would thereby become an offense against God. Ashanti law also had the characteristic of making individual disputes the concern of the state and making the trial process uncertain and dreadful enough to force most people to settle their disputes out of court. The two contestants were always arrested and chained to a log, both treated as guilty until the truth was determined. The official verdict was always death for the person found guilty of taking a false oath. In actual practice, the guilty party was usually allowed to "buy his head," that is, prevent decapitation by paying a heavy fine to the court. Verdicts could be appealed all the way to the royal court, but an appellant was less likely to be able to buy his head if he carried the case that far and lost. Nevertheless, there *was* a right of appeal, and there was a system for keeping the witness honest. The method was believed in so strongly that only one witness was called.

DIVINE LAW When kings become divinities, or even when they rule "by the grace of God" and such descriptions are taken literally, the law becomes divine law. Barotse law approached such a definition but was modified by the requirement of reasonableness. Ashanti law also had certain aspects of divine sanction. But probably the most definitive examples of divine law come from the ancient Oriental societies (see Chapter Twelve) or from conquest states. When conquerors rule over a number of people with different norms and customs, it is helpful to enunciate laws that have divine sanction. Such expressions as "the divine right of kings" and "the king can do no wrong" are familiar in European tradition. In the ancient Near East, one of the most important legal documents known is the Code of Hammurabi, the great king of Babylon and the surrounding Mesopotamian Valley of circa 1700 B.C.

Ancient stone carvings picture a god handing a code of laws to King Hammurabi, although the text states the matter differently.

> I have not withdrawn myself from the men whom Bel gave me, the rule over whom Marduk gave me; I was not negligent but made them a peaceful abiding-place. I expounded all difficulties; I made the light shine upon them. With the mighty weapons which Zamama and Ishtar entrusted to me, with the keen vision with which Ea endowed me, with the wisdom that Marduk gave me . . . I am the salvation-bearing shepherd.[19]

Such were the credentials of Hammurabi, and he issued his laws "by the command of Shamash, the great Judge of Heaven and Earth."

There are dangers in viewing laws as divine, but Hammurabi must be given his just place in history for bringing a more uniform type of justice than had existed before. His code made it impossible for law to depend upon the mere whim of a local lord. In his words:

> That the strong might not injure the weak, in order to protect the widows and orphans . . . in order to bespeak justice in the land, in order to settle all disputes . . . I have set upon these my precious word, written upon my memorial stone, before the image of me as king of righteousness.[20]

Another important aspect of the Code of Hammurabi is that it represents a triumph of public law as opposed to private law, which is an important step in development of the state. Private enforcement, which can sometimes break into feud, cannot be tolerated in the fully developed state. Keeping of the king's peace is the concern of the king, his subjects, and the gods.

In looking over the actual laws, several important characteristics can be seen. First of all, the laws are extremely severe, enunciating the principle of revenge, or *lex talionis* ("an eye for an eye"). For example: "If a man strike his father, his hands shall be hewn off." "If a man has borne false witness in a trial . . . that man shall be put to death." This principle was to be pronounced

[19]Lewis Browne, *The World's Great Scriptures*, The Macmillan Company, New York, 1946, pp. 17–26.
[20]Ibid.

many years later in the laws of Moses. For example: "Whoever strikes his father or his mother shall be put to death" (Exodus 21:15). "You shall not permit a sorceress to live" (Exodus 22:18).

Second, Hammurabi's code was class structured. For example: "If anyone strike the body of a man higher in rank than he, he shall receive sixty blows with an ox whip in public." For offenses punishable by fine, the partrician had to pay more than the plebeian, but if the latter was unable to pay, he might be killed or mutilated.

Third, the law permitted trial by ordeal, with the assumption that heavenly forces would protect the innocent. "If one accuses another of having placed a nerti ['death spell'] upon him, he shall take the test of the sacred river." Apparently the river would drown the guilty and save the innocent, although in medieval Europe it was assumed that only innocent bodies would be received by water and therefore sink. In the later Mosaic law there is a similar attempt to determine guilt or innocence by appealing to divine judgment. If two men dispute over a breach of trust, they may, in some cases, "come before God; he whom God shall condemn shall pay double to his neighbor" (Exodus 22:9).

Finally, there is a strange anomaly met in the ancient laws. In some ways they are cruel; in other respects they seem merciful and enlightened. In Hammurabi's law, for example, if a man should be robbed by a highwayman who could not be caught, he would "state an oath what he lost, and the city or district governor in whose territory or district the robbery took place shall restore to him what he has lost." The powerful ancient state seemed to take strong responsibilities. Recall, too, that the code begins, "That the strong might not injure the weak, in order to protect the widows and orphans. . . ." Centuries later, Moses was to bring the following command:

> You shall not wrong a stranger or oppress him, for you were strangers in the land of Egypt. You shall not afflict any widow or orphan. If you do afflict them, and they cry out to me, I will surely hear their cry; and my wrath shall burn, and I will kill with the sword, and your wives shall become widows and your children fatherless. [Exodus 22:21.]

As in so much law, kindness is interspersed with cruelty, because law, in its zeal to protect the group, wishes to stamp out all sources of threat. In the last quotation from the Bible, even kindness to the widow and orphan is to be enforced by a wrath that burns.

Not only are gentle and harsh principles interspersed in the Hammurabi Code, but so are the principles of evenhanded justice and class-structured justice and those of the natural search for evidence and the supernatural search for evidence. Belief in supernaturalism as a means of solving difficult legal cases is so common as to require some investigation as to its motives, explanations, and consequences.

FINDING EVIDENCE   The Ashanti, it will be recalled, were able to assess the merits of a case on the testimony of a single witness, on the theory that he so feared the god on whose name he had sworn that he could take no other course than to tell the whole truth. Most court systems, including our own, use the method of oath taking. For strong believers in the powers whose names must be appealed to, the oath is a good precaution; but there are always people who will perjure themselves. For many courts there is a way out of the most difficult cases: leave the decision up to divine intervention. Decisions of the spirit world can be learned in three ways, which are not always distinguishable in practice: divination, ordeal, and combat.

DIVINATION   Divination is the art of foretelling the future or of finding hidden truths by supernatural means. The Ovimbundu diviner could tell who had caused a man's death by hanging the corpse of the deceased from a tree and studying the way it swung. Ancient Roman diviners read secrets from the entrails of animals, and many modern-world diviners use crystal balls, in which the images of the truths they are seeking are said to appear. Divination is used by many people for ferreting out witches or pronouncing guilt or innocence regarding other misdeeds. Sometimes the diviner takes a concoction that causes him to have seizures and dreams in which the truth appears to him, frequently explained as being learned from a spirit that possesses him. Sometimes poison is fed to a chicken, and its survival or death will determine whether the accused is guilty. Another possibility is to give the poison to the accused, but this procedure is described better as trial by ordeal.

TRIAL BY ORDEAL   Ordeals were used in the ancient world from the time of Hammurabi or before, and they have also been very common in European and African history. In European theory, the ordeal by boiling water was one of the best, because water represents the Great Flood, with which God passed judgment on the earth, and fire represents the judgment of Hell. When water is heated to the boiling point with fire, the two elements of judgment are combined.[21] In the medieval period of European history a frequent test of guilt was

[21]William J. Tewksbury, "The Ordeal as a Vehicle for Divine Intervention in Medieval Europe," in Bohannan (ed.), op. cit., pp. 267–270.

West African witch doctor entering state
of trance. When possessed of a spirit,
the magician is believed to divine truth,
detect guilt, and foresee the future.

to have the accused reach into a cauldron of boiling water to remove a pebble from the bottom. After 3 days (a sacred number), his hand was examined, and the condition of the wound determined whether he was innocent or guilty. An alternative ordeal, in which water became the judge, was to throw the suspect into a river or lake. Since water is an element of great purity, it rejects the polluted and impure and therefore causes the guilty person to float on its surface and thus convict himself. The innocent sink. William Tewksbury says that attempts were made to test the validity of the ordeal, but they often seemed to malfunction. "Witches would sink like rocks, while leading members of the community, offering themselves to the rigors of the ordeal to test its validity, would float, often not sinking at all, even with the efforts of the officiating executioner."[22]

Finally, the judgment of God could be ascertained by having the suspect eat dry bread and cheese or some other comestible that is hard to swallow without liquid. In theory, the guilty person would have much more trouble swallowing the food than would the innocent. There is probably a physiological principle at work in favor of this kind of ordeal, because great nervousness restricts saliva flow and hence restricts the ability to swallow. One wonders, though, whether even the innocent might not be nervous under the circumstances. Tewksbury says that this method was used most frequently when investigative sources of evidence failed; it was a case of "passing the buck to God."[23]

Similar procedures have been used in many parts of the world. Esther Warner tells of a case in Liberia in which a woman accused of crime underwent an ordeal by poison called a "poison oracle."[24] She gulped down a large cup of poison, sufficient to have killed anyone, but threw it up immediately and remained unharmed, thus proving her innocence. The surmise is that a person less sure of innocence would have swallowed too slowly, allowing the poison to enter the blood stream. Another type of Liberian ordeal is similar to one described for Europe, except that boiling oil is used instead of boiling water. There is also an ordeal by cutlass, in which a heated blade is stroked across the backs of all suspects. Only the guilty party is supposed to be burned.

It is plain that some of the ordeals described are subject to manipulation. How hot is the water? How strong is the mixture of poison? Among the Nzkara of the Central African Republic, ordeals by poison are used for divining guilt. Formerly the poison was given to people; now it is given to chickens. If the

[22]Ibid., p. 268.
[23]Ibid., p. 270.
[24]Esther Warner, "A Liberian Ordeal," in Bohannan (ed.), op. cit., p. 272.

chicken lives, the accused is innocent; if it dies, he is guilty. The diviners, though, seem to manipulate the case by varying the strength of the poison, with the result that persons favored by the authorities are usually found innocent and others guilty. Despite their cheating, the diviners consider their work very important for finding sorcerers.[25] As with so many elements of the legal processes of the primitive world, such manipulations have had their counterpart in Europe. Rarely if ever was a witchcraft suspect or a heretic found innocent, even the now-sainted Joan of Arc. But in many cases the method of trial by combat was used in Europe, and it was peculiarly given to miscarriages of justice.

TRIAL BY COMBAT   Early medieval Christendom found a biblical justification for trial by combat: just as David's triumph over the giant Goliath was attributed to the intervention of God, all righteous people could expect divine intervention in their behalf if faced by uneven combat.[26] Even to this day, many people are convinced that God comes to the rescue of the righteous in warfare. Trial by combat was widespread in Europe, so much so that the practice must

Medieval trial by combat. In theory, God settled the case by granting victory to the innocent, just as He had made David triumphant over Goliath. No amount of evidence could stand up against the verdict of combat.

have even predated Christianity, but Christian theologians were able to rationalize its continued use. Among the Burgundians, combat superseded all evidence, even the most obvious. At times in parts of Germany and England, so much credence was given to trial by combat that a convicted person was permitted to challenge the judge to a duel to prove his innocence. In such courts, only the most distinguished duelists became judges.

Bowing to reality to a limited degree, medieval authorities realized that women and children might not be the equals of men in combat, so knights were expected to nobly champion their causes if they were believed to be unjustly accused. The custom of allowing champions, however, degenerated, until nearly everyone followed the practice, and many of the worst ruffians and cutthroats of Europe hired out as champions to people accused of crime. A custom that had once given special favors to well-armed and well-trained aristocrats now began to favor rogues. Eventually laws were changed so that the champion could be killed for losing his case or could at least have a hand or an ear cut off. In 1150, Henry II of England outlawed the hiring of champions, but, ironically, it was so hard to prove whether a champion was really hired or was acting merely as a friend that the only solution was to have a secondary combat to prove the worthiness of the champion to represent the accused.[27] Not only was the system ludicrous, but it was a powerful weapon in the hands of the strong against the weak and of the rich against the poor. Whatever its faults, however, the custom continued well into the thirteenth century. Even ecclesiastical communities had to hire champions if they became embroiled in civil cases.

THE TREND OF THE LAW The examples given in this chapter make it clear that to some degree law is a part of all societies, but in those societies that have not yet achieved state-type organization there is always the possibility of law breaking down into feud. Formalization of rules into written codes is not necessary for law, but there must be some kind of publicly enforced procedure that prevents the rule of mere brute force. In the primitive levels of development, there is usually the belief that law grows out of the lives and experiences of the people and that most types of law belong to the natural rather than the supernatural world.

[25]Anne Retel-Laurentin, *Oracles et Ordalies chez les Nzakara*, pt II, Ecole Pratique des Hautes Études, Science Economiques et Sociales, Étude XXXIII, Mouton and Co., The Hague, 1969.

[26]The material in this section is based on Henry Charles Lea, "The Wager of Battle," in Bohannan (ed.), op. cit, pp. 233–253. Extracted from Henry Charles Lea, *Supersitition and Force: Essays on the Wager of Law—the Wager of Battle, Ordeal, Torture*, Lea Brothers & Co., Philadelphia, 1892.

[27]Ibid., p. 252.

SOME TRENDS OF THE LAW

PRIMITIVE

KINGLY STATES, ARCHAIC AND MEDIEVAL

MODERN

SUPERNATURALISM

CUSTOM AND SACRED TABOOS, DIVINATION SOMETIMES USED	DIVINE RULERS AND DIVINE LAW, OFTEN TRIAL BY COMBAT, ORDEAL, OR DIVINATION	MAN-MADE LAW, NATURAL EXPLANATION, MATERIAL EVIDENCE

LEGAL SUPREMACY:

POORLY DEFINED; POSSIBILITY OF FEUD	CLEARLY DESIGNATED AUTHORITY	CLEARLY DESIGNATED AUTHORITY

REVENGE:

REVENGE BY KIN, BUT NOT ALWAYS REQUIRED. POSSIBILITY OF WERGILD.	LEX TALIONIS "EYE FOR EYE" REVENGE AT HANDS OF STATE	PENALTY DETERMINED BY STATE SLIGHT DECLINE IN THEORY OF REVENGE

However, even among hunting-and-gathering peoples there is a feeling about the violation of taboos that enters into supernaturalism. The Eskimo feared taboo violation would bring consequences directly connected with the well-being of the group and their means of livelihood. The Cheyenne believed it necessary to remove contamination from the land and the people if murder had been committed.

At a more highly developed level of organization, chieftains or kings begin to embody the supernatural aspects of law, representing the tribal soul and the rights and wrongs connected with it. Supernaturalism becomes more prominent in the theory of origin of laws and in the pursuit of evidence. Powerful monarchs in conquest states find a supernatural explanation of law to be of value to their reigns, and the idea of divine law is given more outward expression than before. Sometimes divine powers are even called upon to determine guilt or innocence.

Behind all the absurdities of imputing the work of man to the gods, however, certain problems of law were being solved. First of all, the supremacy of legal authority was established, reducing the possibility of feud or societal dissolution. Enforcement became universal or nearly so; rights and obligations were clearly defined, and law violation carried the threat of sanction. Whatever the crudity of the operation of law and the rules of evidence, a legal order was achieved.

Once the supremacy of the state and its laws is established, the appeal of supernaturalism becomes less necessary. In modern secular states the closest approach to supernaturalism is found in the form of ideologies that define political crime, and these are most common in states whose foundations are still insecure.

Even in secure modern states the problems of law and justice remain difficult. Many laws become outdated but remain on the books, and the treatment of offenders lags behind modern knowledge of psychology, sociology, and criminology. But the old dictum of "eye for eye, tooth for tooth, limb for limb, wound for wound, burn for burn, and stripe for stripe" is no longer upheld by popular views of divine sanction. The law is secure enough that it need not be enforced by terrorism or revenge. Already a number of modern nations are experimenting with rehabilitation rather than punishment of law violators, seeking to bring law out of its tradition of retribution and into an age of rationalism and empiricism.

PART FIVE
EVOLVING VIEWS
OF THE WORLD

Parts Three and Four have both been concerned with magic, religion, and views of the world. In the descriptions of many peoples in Part Three, it will be recalled, world view was always an important part of total style of life. In Part Four, world view was again emphasized, as it related to ancestors, to the sacred nature of tribal rites and important personages, to law and the finding of evidence, and to the personification of the people through sacred chieftains and kings. For all the peoples so far described, views of the world and of man were not merely naturalistic but contained important elements of supernaturalism. Now, in the modern world, many phenomena that were once subjects of religious reverence and awe are given purely natural explanations. What changes have come about in the view of the world as the human being has moved from a more primitive state to ancient civilizations, to industrial civilizations, and finally to an age of science? Have systems of writing, which facilitate greater accumulation and diffusion of ideas, had their influence on changing views of the world?

The world is viewed quite differently among the major existent religions, and there is an even greater difference between their views and those of the surviving religions of the primitives. In Chapter Fourteen we shall describe many of these differences, some of the puzzling details of human diversity in belief. In Chapter Fifteen we shall attempt to bring these belief systems into some kind of order and to provide explanations and analyze trends. Is it merely the ethnocentric point of view of modern men that causes us to place such widespread religions as Christianity and Judaism, Buddhism, Taoism, Confucianism, and Islam in a separate category from the religions of the more primitive peoples? Are there similarities in religions at various stages of cultural development? Are styles of religion compatible with other aspects of styles of life?

It will be noted that communication is included under the general subject of evolving world views. The contention here is that the ability to extend communication over wide ranges of time and space ultimately affects perception of the world, making it much more possible than before for each generation to know the conclusions of the previous generation and build upon them and to make it possible for religious, philosophical, and scientific ideas to spread to all parts of the world. Not only do such ideas accumulate and spread, but each has the possibility of stimulating new thought in many parts of the world. The writing systems that started with the first notations and the first attempts at art must be placed, along with the technologies to be considered later, among the major factors that have changed the world.

For nearly all of mankind the view of the world has included both the natural and the supernatural. The natural order is that of the seen, the ordinary, the commonplace; but there is an unseen realm beyond the natural and observed, hidden from common sight, mysterious and unobservable. The supernatural has been used to account for uncommon happenings, eerie sights and sounds, sudden disasters, good fortune and bad fortune, and fertility and infertility of people and animals. The supernatural is believed to work in ways that are hard to discern, through spirits and unseen forces, through magic incantations and group rites. Societies develop theories as to how the supernatural can be influenced or controlled, as well as specialists in the manipulation of its forces.

A belief in the supernatural is sometimes thought of as a psychological necessity for man, to comfort and reassure a creature aware of his own mortality and able to speculate about death and the unknown. At the same time, concepts of the supernatural have peopled the world with beings of a dreadful nature and increased human anxieties in many ways rather than always alleviating them. Questions arise as to why supernatural beliefs should have the function of producing fright just as much as

Chapter Fourteen
The Awesome Spirits

that of reassurance. Attempts to answer this basic question will be left until the next chapter. At this point we wish only to examine the nature of the awesome spirits that are believed to exist in heaven and earth and how the spirit idea arose.

Can spirits or other types of supernatural power be manipulated into doing the bidding of magicians, shamans, and sorcerers? How do people become witches, and what societies are most likely to be worried about witches? And what about ghosts? Are they conceived of merely as spirits of the dead? Do we all become ghosts eventually? Among some of the best-known religions of the world, it is considered possible that the spirits of the dead will go to a distant heaven or transmigrate into another form on earth or even become protective ancestors. How can all these ideas be reconciled with the more primitive belief (but one held by many moderns) of wandering, frightening ghosts? In short, what are the alternative explanations of what happens to the dead? After studying examples of beliefs about all the above questions, we shall, in another chapter, turn to an analysis of attempts to fit belief systems into a theoretical framework. For the present, we shall simply examine beliefs in the awesome spirits and other supernatural phenomena.

SUPERNATURAL SPIRITS AND POWER To the modern world, the distinction between natural and supernatural is fairly clear. We often speak poetically of the "miracles of nature," but as long as they are the results of perceived natural law, they are not miracles. In modern thinking miracles are events that seem to occur outside the natural order, in a separate category of their own, if they do, indeed, occur. Such categorizing, however, is not common to primitive concepts. Nature and supernature are both total realities, and the rules of the one are little different from the rules of the other. There are contradictory premises, though, as to how supernatural forces act—whether they are comparable to vital, purposeful beings or whether they are the consequences of some mysterious, impersonal force operating through various objects and people. The first of these positions was explained by Tylor[1] and is the basis for his theory as to how supernatural and religious concepts first came about.

THE GHOST-SOUL AND ANIMISM Tylor's theory about animism contends that the concept of the dualities of body and soul arose from the dream life. Dreams are often disturbing phenomena even for people living in a supposedly scientific society. To the primitive, Tylor reasoned, they must have been much

[1] Edward B. Tylor, *Primitive Culture: Researches into the Development of Mythology, Philosophy, Religion, Art and Custom*, John Murray (Publishers), Ltd., London, 1871.

more disturbing. If a person dreams at night that he is in some other place, might it not be possible that some part of him, some strange and unseen spirit, has left his body and traveled in the course of the night? And why is it hard for him to awaken in the morning? Obviously, because his wandering spirit has to return. And what about the dead? Death could easily be accounted for as resulting when the spirit leaves the body and fails to return. The possibilities of animistic interpretation expand into the idea that all moving things are animated by spirits of their own. Dogs can be observed to dream; they growl in their sleep. Do their spirits also wander, and are they visited by the spirits of other animals in the night? This second possibility seems very likely, for people are visited by other people in their dreams. Furthermore, the living are often visited by dreams of the dead. Isn't it possible, then, that the spirits that have crossed over into the land of the dead are capable of returning and that they actually do visit their old friends and enemies in dreams?

If people and animals have spirits, what about other moving and apparently living things? Trees? Moving water? The winds that moan chillingly in the night? The clouds racing like ghosts in front of the moon as a storm gathers? What about volcanoes? The ocean? The earth itself, which changes its mood in all seasons? Does the earth possess a female spirit that bears new life in the spring and accounts for the fertility of the soil? The imagination can race on to populate all of nature with spirits, both benevolent and malevolent, calm and turbulent, predictable and capricious.

What we are not quite sure of is that primitive man actually reasoned about the phenomena of dreams and of nature in the way suggested by Tylor. His theory seems highly plausible but is hard to subject to proof. Some researchers have argued over whether small children actually do animistic thinking, attributing reason and purpose to inanimate things. Jean Piaget found that till a certain age they actually do, with a display of such reasoning as blaming chairs for hitting them or blocks on the floor for tripping them.[2] Even adults have been known to fly into a very personal rage against such objects when thinking becomes purely emotional rather than rational. Such comparisons do not answer the question, however, because primitives are not mentally childlike, nor are they comparable to a person in an irrational fit of anger. They concentrate their attention very differently from the way sophisticated moderns do, but their reasoning, nonetheless, can be subtle and far removed from childlike simplicity. Many of their folk tales seem to be "the stuff that dreams are made of," but so are ours. Some might even arise out of dreams.

[2]Jean Piaget, *The Child's Conception of the World,* Harcourt, Brace and Company, Inc., New York, 1929, pp. 215–220.

There are many literary references that show how seriously our own ancestors have interpreted dreams, and there are some present-day or recent cases of primitives who place great emphasis upon dreams. The Iroquois were almost pre-Freudian in their feelings about responsibility for their dreams and the necessity to relate strange dreams to other people to relieve themselves of guilt feelings. The Great Plains Indians sought dream experiences, expecting, after a period of fasting and privation (and sometimes the cutting off of a finger), to see a vision of an animal spirit that would give them the power to become great hunters. The Ghost Dance of the late nineteenth century, which aimed at restoring the vigor of Indian culture and even bringing the ghosts of the dead back to join their people, was conceived in dreams. Innumerable people have sought psychic phenomena by taking some drug that would bring on vivid dreams, especially of things spiritual. The Jívaro Indians are especially involved in a long series of drug rituals for the contacting of the "real" world that is revealed to them only through their drugs.

Nor is the interest in dreams limited to the primitives. Muhammad and Buddha had visions, as did St. Paul and large numbers of Christian saints. In the Middle Ages, knights sought the Holy Grail; and quite a number managed to see it. However, none of these instances of the importance of dreams to people casts much light on whether the idea of duality of body and soul first started as dream phenomena. Furthermore, there are types of supernatural belief, generally described by the words "mana" or "animatism," that do not flow naturally from the theory of spirits.

ANIMATISM AND MANA   Animatism is a belief in some mysterious force or power that attaches itself to things and places, and mana is the Melanesian name for that force, brought into the English language by Malinowski after his studies in the Trobriand Islands. The idea is by no means unique to Melanesia or to primitives in general. People who believe in good luck charms, if they try to rationalize the matter at all, probably conclude that some power attaches to the charm rather than that the lucky piece actually has a little spirit dwelling inside it. Our feeling of awe and mystery at particular shrines may be comparable and also the superstitious dread of certain places, as in Coleridge's

> A savage place, as holy and enchanted
> As e'er beneath a waning moon was haunted
> By woman wailing for her deamon lover.

Whatever the comparisons to our own modes of thought, as Malinowski analyzed mana, it is a power possessed by some people and not by others. Mana belongs to sacred personages and individuals of great power, and they can transfer mana to objects and thus make them taboo to ordinary people. In other parts of the primitive world, quite similar ideas arise. In Chapter Six it was mentioned that the Gururumba world view perceives man as struggling for the possession of certain powers emanating from himself—a very similar idea. Among the Tiv of Nigeria, the mysterious power comes only to people who are born of a proper marriage, and it can grow as a result of the right cere- monial observances and also increases with age. "Old age is 'tsav,'" they say.[3] One wonders whether mana might not also be employed, craftily or innocently, to strengthen the position of elders, priests, and chiefs, thus merging the super- natural with the political facets of society. Whether supernatural beliefs attach to mana or spirits or gods, they result in a group of people who are specialists in control of the supernatural, the manipulators of magic.

MAGIC, SCIENCE, AND RELIGION   In a book entitled *Magic, Science and Religion*, Malinowski develops an analytic comparison of three modes of dealing with problems of human survival.[4] Malinowski separates magic and religion much more than they should be separated for most of the primitive world, because in actual practice the two blend together; nevertheless, his analysis helps espe- cially with an understanding of the nature of magic and some of the reasons for its existence. All people, says Malinowski, have their magic, their science, and their religion. Even his simplest Trobriander, when planting yams, had enough knowledge of practical science to know what to plant and when to plant and that yams needed weeding and care. Similarly, in fishing, the Trobriander had enough science to make a serviceable boat and fishing equip- ment and to know where to fish and the most favorable times for fishing. Nevertheless, he did not always harvest a good crop of yams, nor did he al- ways catch fish. Science failed. It needed supplementing by another ingre- dient—magic. Consequently, the Trobriander would never think of planting his yams or going fishing without first pronouncing the right magical incantations and ritually guaranteeing success. Even then failure could occur, but it would not destroy his belief in magic. Failure could be explained as a consequence of someone with stronger magic working against him. In Dobu, according to Ruth Benedict, it is believed that yams can be made to travel underground from one person's yam patch to another's if strong enough magic is used.[5] So there

[3]Margaret Mead (ed.), *Cultural Patterns and Technical Change*, Mentor Books, New American Library, Inc., New York, 1954, pp. 96–125.
[4]Bronislaw Malinowski, *Magic, Science and Religion and Other Essays*, Anchor Books, Doubleday & Company, Inc., Garden City, N.Y., 1955, pp. 17–87.
[5]Ruth Benedict, *Patterns of Culture*, Mentor Books, New American Library, Inc., New York, 1946, pp. 120–159.

is a secret world of magic and countermagic, with explanations completely impervious to doubt. If a deadly curse does not kill a man, it is because it was not performed right or stronger forces intervened. If healing magic fails, it may have been applied too late or by a wizard whose power is not as great as that of the evil spirit inside the sick man.

In his explanation of the functions of magic, Malinowski constantly re-emphasizes the idea that magic always enters where there is a gap between strongly felt desire or need and scientific means of obtaining results. Since no human desires are completely solved by science, all people have magic. He further hypothesizes that, whatever the ills and illusions of magic, man might not have survived without it. It gives him the psychological feeling that, in the most dire emergency, something can be done or at least tried. Even modern men under combat conditions will mutter magic incantations or develop their own superstitions about the efficacy of luck charms or corps insignia. One researcher found a group of paratroopers that believed strongly in the importance of never losing the first pair of wings issued and also of avoiding flights with a man who has turned out to be a "jinx."[6] In the old days, when life at sea was dangerous, seafarers had many magical means of ensuring safety.

Malinowski does not touch on the problem of the anxieties that arise from magic, such as the anxiety of suspecting that one's enemy has access to stronger magic than one's own. We could say, though, following Malinowski's reasoning, that what is functional in some cases becomes dysfunctional in others, but not sufficiently to obliterate the psychological boost provided by magic belief.

Religion is given a very restricted definition in Malinowski's analysis. As he sees it, religion, in its pure form, does not pretend to be a formula for obtaining results but depends only on faith. Although he does not use these examples, the words "Thy will be done" or "the Lord giveth and the Lord taketh away, praise ye the Lord" seem to express his conception of religion in contrast to magic. Magic is a formula for getting results; religion enters the picture when there can be no certainty of results. Thus death and survival beyond the grave have to be the realm of religion; no magician would risk his reputation trying to bring the dead back to life. In fact, in the Trobriand and adjacent islands, there are no rituals for curing people with diseases known to be incurable. Magic plays its role in areas where results are possible but not certain. Rites to cause rain or increased production of game for hunting are, by this definition, magic. It is at this point that most anthropologists would not agree with Malinowski. His definition relegates prayer for rain to magic rather

[6]Milford S. Weiss, "Rebirth in the Airborne," *Transaction*, vol. 4, pp. 27-31. May 1967.

than religion, although practically all religions countenance such observances. Certainly the contrast between magic and religion narrows at several points, as will be demonstrated in considering contagious magic and its relation to sacrifice.

THE TYPES OF MAGIC   Just as no primitive medicine man would analyze the difference between magic and religion, none would provide a theory to explain the functioning of magic. It is performed in the same manner as planting yams, sharpening arrows, or tracking animals; it is part of the means of survival, and one need not concern oneself with the theory of how it works. Malinowski did try such theorizing, however, and spoke of "will magic" and the casting of the spell. Apparently his Trobriand magicians, especially in casting an evil spell, would work themselves into a frenzy, repeating in a rising crescendo of fury, "I twist, I burn, I destroy." The actual words, the emotional passion, and certain secret utterances constituted the spell. The emotional tones make such a type of magic understandable as will magic; something has to happen because it is willed so strongly. Another idea connected with magic is simply that of imitation. The Trobrianders sometimes made a smokey fire and blew the smoke in a particular direction to try to get the wind to blow that way. The more familiar example of imitative magic is making a waxen image of one's enemy and sticking pins through it.

A third type of magic is repetitive magic—the idea that things that have occurred under particular circumstances once will probably occur in the same manner again. If a tragic event has happened on Wednesday, one must always be careful about Wednesdays. If one has suffered bad luck after seeing a black cat cross one's path, then he must beware of black cats in the future. Probably many of our own superstitions are remotely based on the idea of repetitive magic. Believers in palmistry are inclined to employ the type of memory that that reinforces such magic belief by remembering the predicted events that materialize and forgetting the many more that do not.

The final type of magic, and the one emphasized throughout Sir James Frazer's *The Golden Bough*, is contagious magic. The idea is that objects that have been in close association physically bear some spiritual or manalike association that continues. On the basis of contagious magic, a witch might put a curse on a lock of hair that once belonged to an individual and hence make him sick. In a description of some of the problems of Western hospitals, Mead mentions primitive people's fear of a place in which death occurs, because death might have a contagious essence.[7] There were also complaints about hospitals not

[7]Margaret Mead (ed.), op. cit., 205–206.

being careful about secret disposal of lochial blood and the placenta. If a witch were to get possession of the blood, a curse could be placed on both the mother and the child.

In Frazer's analysis, contagious magic goes much further in its implications, sometimes reaching the borderland between magic and religion. To him, the idea of sacrifice was based on contagious magic. Even the scapegoat ceremony of the Bible states that the sins of the people shall be vested in the goat and he shall be sacrificed for their sins. In other words, a contagion has passed from the people to the goat. In the case of sacrificial human beings, the same idea holds. *The Golden Bough* relates many cases of sacrifice—of the high priest, the sacrificial king, the sacrificial maiden of the Maya, and many more—always with the conclusion that they contain enough of the magical essence of their people to be able to sacrifice in their behalf. Naturally, he implies that the same idea exists behind the sacrifice of Jesus for mankind, or at least that the sacrificial god is a very similar phenomenon. Certainly Frazer has demonstrated very clearly that the idea of a sacrificial god is not unique to Christianity, as was once supposed, and we have already noted examples of the killing of high priests or kings because their spiritual identity with the people is so close that they cannot be allowed to grow feeble with age. In other contexts, Frazer's conclusion is questionable. Often the idea expressed in sacrifice is that the sacrificial animal or person is a messenger or a link between the material world and the spiritual world. The Ainu take this attitude in their bear sacrifice. The Aztecs sacrificed human victims to Huitzilopochtli because he could subsist only on human blood and their future depended upon keeping him well and happy. Since sacrifices were usually war captives, not Aztecs, it is hard to see how they could have been of the same magical essence as the people for whom they were being sacrificed. In many cases, such as the Mayan, however, sacrificial victims were greatly honored and were expected to receive some reward for their sacrifice on behalf of the people, with their souls joining the gods.

THEORIES OF THE SOUL   Aldous Huxley once wrote an essay entitled "Squeak and Gibber." He took his title from Shakespeare's lines about the night Caesar died. "The graves stood tenantless and the sheeted dead/Did squeak and gibber in the Roman streets" (*Hamlet*, act 1, scene 1). According to Huxley, the idea of ghosts making demented sounds was quite common in the ancient Roman world and is believed in by many people today. He even mentions spiritual séances in which the ghosts seem to make little sense and proceeds to contend, at least half seriously, that the "squeak and gibber theory" is one of the common theories of the disposition of the soul. In contrast to it, he mentions the traditional Christian theory, which he calls the "harp and scream" theory. One either goes to heaven and plays a harp or goes to hell and screams.[8] Seen in a cross-cultural perspective, the "harp and scream theory" is a minority view, although not unique to Christendom. Another very common theory is that of transmigration of the soul from one form to the next, and less common theories hold that the ghost eventually fades away.

THE PLACE OF CONTINUANCE   Many people have pictured an afterlife as a place of reward or at least of continuance. Often among hunters the theory is that the other world has more game in it than this one. Most of the Plains Indians subscribed to this view. For the Trobrianders, the souls of the dead went to the Island of Baloma, not very far away, and there they continued to live much as they had in this world. For other peoples, the question of the continuance of the soul became involved with ethics. The ancient Egyptian had to answer to the Judge of the Dead before entering a heaven, and the idea is present also in Islam and Christianity. It will be recalled that the villagers of Gopalpur, although believing in transmigration of the soul, also felt that the souls of the wicked would suffer tortures before being reborn.

JOINING THE ANCESTORS   In the ancient Orient, especially China, the ancestral spirits were expected to remain around as a benevolent, protective force, and after death one went to join the ancestral spirits. There were also harmful ghosts around, who were probably the ghosts of foreigners or of people who died without offspring to keep up their family shrine and honor their memories.[9] In Manus, the protective ancestral ghost eventually gave out in its protectiveness and had to be replaced by a more recently deceased relative. As we have seen, among the Gururumba the recently dead were very harmful and evil ghosts, but the remotely dead were protective ancestral spirits.

TRANSMIGRATION   The idea of transmigration of the soul is usually thought of as Indian, but it is encountered in many parts of the world outside of India. The Eskimo, in spite of an inconsistency in their fear of the dead and of ghosts, seem to think that the spirits of the dead are born again. These people are very gentle with young children because they actually contain the spirits of people who have passed through this world before.

[8]Aldous Huxley, "Squeak and Gibber," *Music at Night and Other Essays*, Chatto & Windus, Ltd., London, 1931, pp. 99–108.
[9]Francis L. K. Hsu, *The Ancestors' Shadow: Family and Religion in China*, The Natural History Press, Garden City. N.Y., 1967, Chapter 9.

The Australian aborigines also believe in the survival of the soul and its reentry into the world in another form. In Arunta belief the soul becomes either another human being or else his totem animal and will continue through endless cycles of existence. In India, belief differs considerably, but practically all Hindus agree on the idea of transmigration of the soul. In the Hindu religion, the condition of the soul is linked to ethics; one has to have followed righteous paths in order to make progress in one's next incarnation. In Burma, a predominantly Buddhist country, life is seen as a struggle for storing up merits toward a better incarnation in the next life. Buddhism offers an ultimate release from the cycle of existence, but it also holds to the view that we return to the world for many lives.

DETERIORATION OF THE SOUL   In Manus society the soul loses its power with the passing of time.[10] A newly deceased ancestor's head is placed in a shrine box in front of the house to protect the household. Although all the dead are perceived as becoming ghosts, this particular one is the honored ghost for whom gifts of food are made. If the honored ghost is properly protected, he can bring great benefits to the household. If, however, a lot of bad luck occurs, then it is clear that the honored ghost is no longer doing his duty. The head is thrown out and a new one is placed in the shrine box. Eventually the ghost so disposed of will wander off to sea. There he will be a menace to boats for some time, but eventually he will sink into the sea and become a sea slug.

The Jívaro Indians of the eastern slopes of the Andes Mountains also seem to believe in a type of eventual decomposition of the soul.[11] The Jívaro are dangerous head shrinkers, cutting off the heads of enemies on raids. The heads are not actually shrunk, but all the flesh is peeled off the skull, tanned into a leathery state, and then sewn back together and shaped up to look like the actual shrunken image of its former possessor. The lips are sewn so that the soul cannot escape, because a major purpose in acquiring the head is to gain an extra soul that will give added ferocity and long life. Souls, then, can be captured, but they will eventually be released again, though not until they have deteriorated beyond all possible power and danger.

The Jívaro actually believe in three souls. One type is an *arutam*—a type of spirit of some remote ancestor that wanders around freely through the forests but can be caught by the right ceremony. The ceremony consists of taking strong drugs that sometimes cause convulsions, then falling asleep by a waterfall. In the middle of the night an apparition will appear, usually in the form of

[10]William J. Goode, *Religion among the Primitives*, The Free Press, New York, 1964, p. 65.
[11]Michael J. Harner, "Jívaro Souls," *American Anthropologist*, vol. 64, pp. 252–272, 1962.

Jívaro shrunken head. The lips are sewn
so the soul will not escape. A captured
soul strengthens its new owner and
prolongs his life.

two struggling animals, jaguars or anacondas. The soul seeker must reach out and touch them, in which case he receives an *arutam* soul. The owner of an *arutam* is immortal, but it is possible for someone else, most likely a shaman, to induce it to leave him. Thus, if a man with an *arutam* dies, it can easily be explained that he had already lost his *arutam* soul. Even a man who has lost his *arutam* will nevertheless have a *muisik* avenging soul. Possessors of *muisiks* are the men whose heads must be handled with the greatest care, because an escaped *muisik* can turn into a giant water snake and capsize its enemy's boat when he is crossing a stream or can turn into a great tree and fall on its enemy when he is walking down a jungle trail.

Finally, there is the true soul. The true soul survives after death and can at first be quite powerful and dangerous, occurring often in animal form. The only trouble with souls is that they are always hungry, since all they really eat is air—spirit birds and spirit animals, which really have no substance. The result is that eventually the souls turn into butterflies and moths. Finally their wings are ruined in the rain and drop to the earth, from which they eventually rise in the form of mist.

GHOSTS   In connection with nearly all the societies discussed in Chapters Five to Eight, ghosts were mentioned, because most people believe in ghosts. Even people who have a fairly well-developed theory that runs counter to ghosts nevertheless are haunted by ghosts. In Christianity there is a confusion about whether the spirit immediately departs for the Pearly Gates or whether it waits for Judgment Day. At the same time many people from Christian countries believe in ghosts. Similarly, Eskimo who believe a spirit will be born again are constantly haunted by ghosts. The Navaho Indians, because of ghost fear, often abandon the hogan (the earth-covered house) in which a person has died. Sometimes ghosts can be visited and appeased by a successful shaman. Among the now nearly extinct Tapirapé of the Amazon rain forest, shamans believe themselves capable of wandering off and associating with ghosts and other types of supernatural monsters.[12]

The ghosts and monsters (called * açunga*) encountered by the Tapirapé shaman are of different types and categories, but all are extremely terrible and repulsive. Some of them have sharp chins, which they jab into the necks of their victims. Some have enormous penises, with which they rape people and kill them. All of them drink blood and eat entrails and are so hideous that

[12]Charles Wagley, "Tapirapé Shamanism," in Morton H. Fried (ed.), *Readings in Anthropology,* vol. II, Thomas Y. Crowell Company, New York, 1968, pp. 617–635.

the sight of them would kill anyone but a very capable shaman. However, the shamans can converse with them and persuade them not to do harm to the people. One famous shaman even exterminated certain types of *açunga* years ago, and another one managed to get them to call off the disease that was attacking the Tapirapé people. There is no clarity in the Tapirapé account as to whether all dead people become loathsome *açunga*, but the implication is that only a few of them do.

DISPOSAL OF THE DEAD   In many societies the method of disposal of the dead is believed to have an important effect on the soul. Funerals are of great importance for several sociological reasons. As Durkheim noted, society requires that its members mourn, even if mourners have to be hired, because the act of mourning is an act of group solidarity. Funeral observations can also be rites of intensification, heightening the sense of cohesion among the relatives or tribesmen who remain and providing collective reassurance about the hopeful disposition of the soul. Sometimes the body must be buried in a particular manner, or the grave must be trampled after the burial, or the body must be burned. Among the Parsis, dead bodies were left atop the buildings known as Towers of Silence, where they were consumed by the vultures but not brought back into contact with the earth. Among most Hindus, bodies are cremated, preferably at the sacred city of Benaras. Some of the Congolese people smoke the bodies of the dead in order to destroy the blood, which they consider the center of the soul. Once the blood has dried, the soul cannot return. The ancient Egyptians were the most famous mummifiers of the dead, but many other peoples have tried mummification with differing degrees of success, especially in Polynesia. Many American Indians, and also Stone Age and Bronze Age people of Europe, performed secondary burial, recovering the bones after the flesh had rotted away and burying them in skins, pots, or other containers. The Polynesians practiced secondary burial in the belief that the soul could not rest until the bones had been cleaned; others seem to have honored the bones in this manner merely as a final form of respect.[13] In chieftaincies and kingdoms, important personages had far more elaborate funerals than commoners, and often servants had to be killed to accompany them to the next world. In parts of tropical South America endocannibalism (the eating of the flesh of the dead) was practiced. Through this practice the soul of the deceased was reincorporated into the social group.

[13] William Howells, *The Heathens: Primitive Man and His Religions*, Natural History Library, Garden City, N.Y., 1962, pp. 150–156.

Ever since Malinowski introduced the word "taboo" from Melanesia, it has been associated with animatism or mana. Things possessing too much mana are taboo, at least to many categories of people, such as women and children, and sometimes to anyone not specializing in the sacred. One volume of Frazer's *The Golden Bough* is entitled "Taboo, and the Perils of the Soul," indicating that taboo violations are matters of more than ordinary human regulation, but somehow imperil a person's standing in the supernatural world. Although taboos are often thought of as having supernatural connotations, there are also social taboos, but even the latter can be very powerful forces of social control. Strict etiquette regulates interrelations between the lowly and the powerful, and violation is almost as bad as a violation of the gods. Taboos are group norms, and their observance unites members of the society. Those who violate taboos are outside the social system.

Taboo may have originated as a means of making some people sacred and elevated in status, and in this respect it may be closely connected with the preservation of social control. Another indication that taboo is an agent of social control is the fact that certain acts are rendered taboo—sexual relations between people reckoned as very close kinsmen, for example. The Ten Commandments and the "thou shalt nots" of other religions are sometimes categorized as taboos. Most of them plainly can be seen as attempts to enforce the social order and the supremacy of the god or gods of a particular people. Other kinds of taboos are more puzzling, however, and may be more closely associated with people's conceptions of reality than with the types of moral rules that are meaningful to modern societies. Nevertheless, they too have the effect of cementing social unity around ritual acts and avoidances.

DIETARY TABOOS   Dietary taboos were imposed on the Eskimo and the Nootka before going to hunt whales. Similar taboos are placed on pregnant women, and occasionally they are placed also upon the fathers of babies at the time of birth or during the period before birth. Such rules function as special precautions to be taken at times of peril, and many taboos are of such a type.

Sometimes, though, there are food taboos that cannot be explained in this manner. Totem animals are often taboo because of their spiritual relationship with the people to whom they are a totem. But sometimes animals are tabooed even though they are in no way totems. The Shoshoni Indian, regardless of how hungry, would not have eaten a coyote. Some people will not eat fish; a few have tabooed all meat. In the case of tabooing of meat, the reason might be a philosophical one of avoidance of killing. Often, though, the reason defies easy explanation. Many of the dietary rules of the Old Testament, found mainly in Leviticus, are of this type and have given rise to confused explanations.

The dietary rule of Leviticus that is best known and most widely observed is the rule against the eating of pork, but it is only an insignificant part of the list of taboos. Many people attempt a scientific explanation for the avoidance of pork, such as the fear of trichinosis. However, Leviticus gives absolutely no such reason, no mention of sickness or ill health. The only thing wrong with the pig according to the dietary restrictions is that it does not chew its cud. Further taboos, not as well known, are those against many kinds of birds and creatures of the sea and many, but not all, insects. Mary Douglas has an explanation that seems to fit all cases of the ancient dietary taboos and that may well be relevant to other types of food taboos encountered in the world.[14]

Rather than dwelling on particular types of animals, Douglas turns first to the notion of ritual purity among the ancient Hebrews. Blemished animals were not fit for sacrifices; blemished persons with physical defects lacked sufficient "holiness" to enter the temple. It was not that such people were evil, but they lacked the qualities called for by the Lord. The perfect specimen, running true to its kind, was preferred, and those deviating too far from the model were "an abomination unto the Lord." This idea leads rather naturally to a categorization of animals. What land animals are the model—the "best" type, the ones that all good animals should resemble? Obviously, the best animals of those days and the ones depended upon for food were cattle, sheep, and goats. They possess a cloven hoof and chew the cud, and so do certain other acceptable animals such as antelope. The camel, however, does not "part the hoof" and therefore is unclean even though it chews its cud. The swine "parts the hoof" but does not chew its cud and is therefore unclean. The rock badger and the hare are specifically excluded on one or the other of these grounds.

So far as the creatures of the waters are concerned, those that have fins and scales are edible; others are abominable. It is as though the "proper" type of marine animal is the most common type of fish, with scales and fins. No statement is made as to scavengers and nonscavengers, and the fins-and-scales criterion would not make such a distinction; the important point is whether the species conform "according to their kind." Similarly with the birds of the air. The model bird should have two feet and wings and, judging by the list of exclusions, should not be a bird of prey. The long list of exclusions (Leviticus

[14]Mary Douglas, *Purity and Danger*, Frederick A. Praeger, Inc., New York, 1966, pp. 41–67.

DIETARY RULES ACCORDING to LEVITICUS

DOMESTIC ANIMALS   **SEA CREATURES**   **INSECTS**

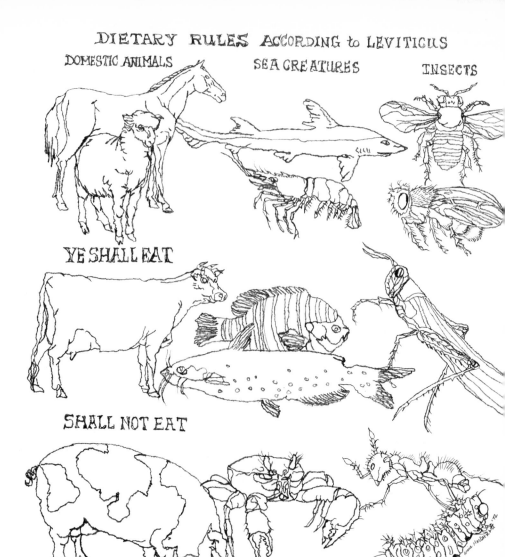

YE SHALL EAT

SHALL NOT EAT

POSTULATE : ABOMINABLE ARE THOSE THAT DO NOT
FOLLOW THE RULES "ACCORDING TO THEIR KIND."
DOMESTIC ANIMALS: SHOULD CHEW CUD AND HAVE CLOVEN HOOF.
SEA CREATURES : SHOULD HAVE FINS AND SCALES.
INSECTS: SHOULD CREEP AND LEAP.

9:13-17) consists mainly of birds of prey and diving birds. The latter mix elements of water and sky and therefore are not true "according to their kind."

Finally, there are the insects. Locusts, crickets, and grasshoppers are specifically listed as suitable for food, but virtually all other "swarming things" are omitted. It seems plausible that the large numbers of locusts, crickets, and grasshoppers in the biblical lands were sufficient to create a meaningful category of proper insects. A proper one both creeps and leaps; but "that that creepeth and leapeth not, that ye may not eat." If Douglas's explanation is correct, it demonstrates a possibility of taboo being placed not only on the strange and forbidding, but upon things lying outside the range of the proper as constructed in human classification systems.

WITCHCRAFT   Witch fear is an extremely widespread phenomenon. In many parts of Africa, Melanesia, and Amazonia practically all deaths are attributed to witchcraft, unless the cause is obviously old age, death in combat, or some accidental tragedy. E. E. Evans-Pritchard tells us that among the Azande even an accidental death can easily be attributed to witchcraft. If a man wanders into the forest and is killed by an elephant, the reason is obviously witchcraft. If he had not been bewitched, the elephant would not have hurt him.[15]

AZANDE WITCHCRAFT   Evans-Pritchard's account of the Azande (sing., Zande) and their witch beliefs is an anthropological classic that demonstrates wide differences in thinking about the cause of witchcraft. In the European tradition, witches were believed to have sold their souls to the Devil. Among the Azande witch explanation is quite different. Some people are born with witchcraft, believed to be caused by a small growth in the stomach or intestines, a blackish swelling, sometimes said to be lined with hair. Sons of male witches and daughters of female witches always inherit witchcraft, which would seem to throw suspicion on all members of a witch's family. Family members always try to claim that the witch in the family is really illegitimate so that other members are above suspicion.

The Zande witch is able to send out *mangu*, an unseen substance that captures souls or bits of soul matter. The soul matter is eaten in secret by the witch, and when all of a person's soul has been devoured, he dies. Witchcraft can also be seen traveling at night in the form of a light or ball of fire sent out by the witch and directed by him against his victim. One who sees an unac-

---

[15]E. E. Evans-Pritchard, "Witchcraft among the Azande," in John Middleton (ed.), *Studies in Social and Cultural Anthropology*, Thomas Y. Crowell Company, New York, 1968, pp. 196–246.

counted-for light moving around in the darkness is sure he has seen witchcraft at work, and he must investigate to see who is being bewitched and who is working the evil. The treatment for witchcraft is to consult a witch oracle to discover the witch. The witch is then negotiated with and made to promise to cease and desist. He is made to blow water on a chicken's wing, which removes curses from intended victims. The Azande realize that some people cannot help being witches, and the sense of blame and horror is not as great as among many other people. The explanation is similar to the attitudes of some people toward the evil eye. Among the Barabaig and the Tuareg, certain men, especially foreigners, can give the evil eye, placing a hex on people by merely staring at them; but the act must be done with ill intent. In certain southern European countries, on the other hand, some people are naturally possessed of the evil eye without meaning to be. They are the bearers of ill fortune and must be avoided, but, like the Azande witches, they cannot be blamed as though they were entirely free agents.

NAVAHO WITCHCRAFT   Navaho witches closely resemble the witches of European tradition.[16] They are disgusting creatures practicing many types of loathsome and forbidden rituals. They hold secret meetings, witches' sabbaths in which they commit incest and other perversions; they practice cannibalism; they eat filthy things. Initiations are held in the secret meetings, and one must murder one of one's close relatives in order to be initiated into the witches' cult. As in earlier Christian belief, much of the witch ceremony is a perversion of religious ritual. After initiations and revolting ceremonies, witches have the power to do evil to people, making them ill or causing their horses to run away or their sheep to die. Practically all illness is attributed to witchcraft, and so is death. All people fear illness, but it is a much more overriding concern in the lives of people without knowledge of modern medicine who attribute their ills to powerful and malevolent supernatural causes.

WITCHCRAFT EXPLANATIONS   Although the great majority of people have believed in some form of witchcraft, witch belief is much more a preoccupation in some societies than in others. Evans-Pritchard concludes that it is most prevalent in societies without well-defined methods of obtaining justice. The man who cannot obtain justice either by combat or court may be tempted to wreak vengeance on his enemy by witchcraft. Evans-Pritchard also contends that Azande witchcraft might have its normative aspects. The fear of witchcraft

[16] The material in this section is based on Clyde Kluckhohn, *The Navaho*, Natural History Library, Garden City, N.Y., 1962, pp. 184–192.

Medieval witch drawing milk from the handle of an ax. European witches were believed to have sold their souls to Satan. Many other explanations of witchcraft involve evil forces, loathsome acts, and perverted rites.

causes people to be very careful not to do harm to others and make enemies. Clyde Kluckhohn found that the Navaho who claimed to be victims of witchcraft were nearly always people of low status, unhappy and neurotic and in need of attention and sympathy. The witch was also a neurotic individual, full of enmity but taking it out through magical hocus-pocus rather than by committing outright aggression. Witchcraft is often very prevalent in societies under stress, as has been the case with Navaho society during all the time it has been studied by anthropologists.

In the early days of Christendom in Europe, witch belief served to an unusual degree the function of enforcing orthodoxy.[17] Members of pagan cults, which the Christians were trying to eliminate, were believed to be worshipers of evil beings. Pagan beliefs were equated with Satanism, and their followers were equated with witches. At times in medieval history, similar theories existed about the Jews.[18] Although the fear of witches seems to have declined after the complete triumph of Christianity, it was revived again by unfortunate

[17]Howells, op. cit., pp. 104–108.
[18]Joshua Trachenberg, *The Devil and the Jews*, Harper Torchbooks, Harper & Row, Publishers, Incorporated, New York, 1968, pp. 124–139.

events. The failure of the Crusades and the disorganization of Christendom by the Protestant Reformation caused a revival of witch fear. Special courts were established for the trial of witches, and learned clergymen became specialists in demonology. The episodes of witch trials in Salem, Massachusetts, came after much of the furor was declining in Europe, but they were not the only witch trials to occur that late in history. According to Homer Smith, the last European witchcraft burning took place in Poland in 1793,[19] but in England in 1865 a wizard died as a result of an ordeal by water. In 1900, two Irish peasants attempted unsuccessfully to roast a witch.

European beliefs in witchcraft had some traits in common with witch belief in many parts of the world. Many other people have believed in secret meetings, witch initiation, loathsome ceremonies, and generally evil intent. The European concept of Satanism and of a particular Prince of Darkness as the ultimate source of witchcraft is much less common. More frequently, witches are seen as manipulators of spirit forces—the converse of medicine men and shamans, who can use their power to dispel evil spirits and cure disease.

HEALING THE SICK   In the primitive world there is much anxiety about sickness and early death; morbidity rates are much higher than in societies with modern medical practice and even the explanations of sickness and death are more frightening. The Azande are by no means alone in thinking that evil witches can steal and eat souls and thus cause death. The soul-theft idea is widespread, and so are other ideas about the penetration of the body by evil spirits or by foreign substances introduced by magic.

MEDICINE MEN   The medicine man is the healer. He is called by different names in different parts of the world. In Siberia, the magico-religious practitioner is known as the shaman. Among American Indians, the term medicine man is more common. Often the African specialist in cures and other forms of magic is called the witch doctor. Similar healing procedures range widely over the world. A very common practice is for the medicine man to go into a trance to determine the cause of disease or ill fortune. The Siberian shaman is particularly good at having epileptic seizures or putting on an act closely resembling epilepsy. In such a state he is possessed of a good spirit that helps him to find the source of the trouble and determine a cure. A very frequent remedy for pains in any particular part of the body is the sucking cure. The medicine man sucks on the sore spot, drawing out the substance that has caused pain—

    [19]Homer W. Smith, *Man and His Gods*, Little, Brown and Company, Boston, 1952, pp. 294–295.

often bits of stick or rocks or small lizards. By sleight of hand he somehow inserts such things into his mouth so that he can spit them out and demonstrate they have actually come out of the afflicted patient.

When the reason for illness is perceived as possession by an evil spirit, other types of cure are in order. Eating something vile tasting may offend the evil spirit lodged in one's stomach and cause it to leave the body by way of regurgitation. The Marquesans use an overripe *moni* fruit, which has such a nauseating odor that no evil spirit could endure it.[20] The Ga of West Africa take every precaution to make the patient uncomfortable, thinking the spirit might be equally uncomfortable and therefore leave him. Sometimes they even give the patient a sound beating. A Maori doctor, knowing that evil spirits come up from the underworld through flax stems, learns how to divine which stem the evil spirit used. He then plucks the stem and hangs it over the patient, at the same time casting a spell that causes the spirit to go back to its stem. The ancient Chinese were among many people who reasoned that loud, disturbing noises might cause an evil spirit to take flight. The Marquesans were more drastic, sometimes building a fire under the patient, it was hoped not hot enough to kill him but sufficient to drive out the evil spirit. Even ancient practices well known to the Western world have had their origin in spirit beliefs. Many people believe that contaminating spirits may enter the blood and that bleeding the patient can get rid of the evil. The widespread art of trepanning (cutting a small hole in the patient's skull), found all the way from ancient Egypt to Melanesia and to the Peruvian and Colombian civilizations of America, was practiced for the purpose of letting bad spirits out of the brain. The operation required a high degree of skill for primitive surgery but must have succeeded occasionally or it would have been abandoned.

Sometimes evil spirits are induced to enter some other object and leave the patient alone. Bantu medicine men manage to imprison evil disease spirits in anthills. Sometimes such spirits are removed from a man and given to animals.[21] In the Book of Mark there is an account of Jesus curing a man possessed of many devils. He orders the devils to come forth; they do so, but enter a herd of swine instead. Folk cures for mental illness have often worked on the theory of possession by evil spirits, with maltreatment of patients considered a good way to get rid of the possession.

On the other hand, some perfectly beneficial practices have come from the ancient and primitive worlds. Occasionally the right herb was found. Trepanning occasionally worked. Medicine men learned to set broken arms and to

---

[20]Marquesan and following examples are from Howells, op. cit., pp. 92–93.
[21]Ibid., p. 94.

Many magical rites are psychic medicine. In Canyon de Chelly, Arizona, a masked Navaho, representing a god, drives the evil spirit of sickness from a patient. Nearby, two women representing goddesses initiate a boy, giving him the spiritual strength for manhood.

knock out broken teeth. At the present time a great amount of interest has been awakened in the ancient Chinese art of acupuncture, which actually seems to work, although no one has an adequate explanation of why. Yet the great majority of medical practice, based on it was on ideas about troublesome spirits, derived from false hypotheses and certainly should have done more harm than good. Why, then, were such practices continued?

EXPLAINING THE CURES   One reason medicine men have often succeeded is a mere matter of mathematical probability. Most people become sick a number of times, but, like Caesar's brave man, "never taste of death but once." The odds are in the medicine man's favor. Secondly, medicine men are crafty about what cures they will try. Albert Schweitzer, during his long years of medical work in Gabon, found that many local witch doctors regarded him as a fool for attempting to cure people who they knew could not be cured. A good medicine man preserves his reputation against such folly.

Another reason for magical cures is that a fair amount of illness is of a hysterical type. A study of the Canadian Cree Indians is interesting in this respect.[22] In the summer months, when jobs are available, young men leave their reservation to work on farms and in town. Being strangers in a white

[22]Alice B. Kehoe, "Psychosomatic Reactions to Stress as a Factor in Persistence of American Religions," paper presented at the American Anthropological Association convention, San Francisco, November 23, 1963.

world, they often develop nervous symptoms, including stomach pains, headache, and a general feeling of weakness and malaise. White doctors' medicine does no good, since the sickness is one of loneliness and unhappiness. Returning to the reservation, they find the medicine man able to effect an immediate cure by his ancient ceremonies. His is obviously medicine of the spirit, and it is undoubtedly this function of primitive medicine that accounts for its hold on people. The patient is surrounded by tradition, by kinsmen, and by feelings of faith. The functions of magical and spiritual faith are as strong in healing ceremonies as at funerals. They are the functions of magic that prompted Malinowski to say:

> Looking from far and above, from our high places of safety in developed civilization, it is easy to see all the crudity and irrelevance of magic. But without its power and guidance early man could not have mastered his practical difficulties as he has done, nor could man have advanced to the higher stages of culture. Hence the universal occurrence of magic in primitive societies and its enormous sway. Hence do we find magic an invariable adjunct of all important activities. I think we must see in it the embodiment of the sublime folly of hope, which has yet been the best school of man's character.[23]

In the next chapter we must turn to the question of what changes have come about in magical thinking and conceptions of the spirit world as man approaches the higher levels of civilization. The contrast will not be absolute, because a wide gulf remains between man's desires and his knowledge of how to fulfill those desires. New types of solutions emerge—religions, philosophies, ideologies—but often they seem to express a nostalgia for the old world of magic and enchantment that has dissolved in the crucibles of modern science.

[23]Malinowski, op. cit., p. 90. The essay "Magic, Science and Religion," from which this extract is taken, originally appeared in Joseph Needham (ed.), *Science, Religion and Reality,* published by the Society for Promoting Christian Knowledge.

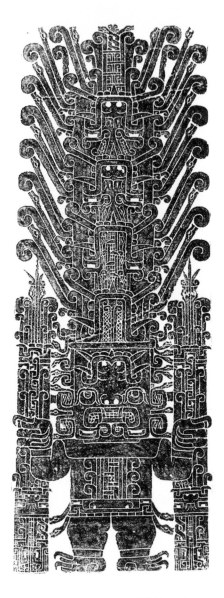

Chapter Fifteen
The Growth
of the Gods

The previous chapter examined many supernatural beliefs, explained Tylor's theory about the origin of supernaturalism, discussed the meaning and functions of magic, and gave examples of different concepts of survival, ghosts, taboos, witches, and healing by supernatural means. It was noted that all people have their magic, science, and religion. Brief mention was made of the idea that belief in supernaturalism has been reassuring to man but that it has also been frightening. The terrors of the supernatural world are often so elaborated upon in the imagination as to become much more dreadful than those of the natural world. What are we to say, then, about Malinowski's praise of magic as a necessity for survival?

The title of the present chapter seems to imply that there is a growth of the gods, or, less poetically, a growth of human concepts about gods. Is this really true? If so, what conditions would cause man to pay heed to more powerful gods and to a high god superior to all others? Mythologies usually account for creation, man's place in nature, and the mysterious forces of nature itself, as well as many social themes. How do the symbolizations of myths change in emphasis as levels of technology and social organization advance? Do changes in types of mythology indicate that primitive man thinks less clearly than civilized man, or do the changes merely reflect differences in problems to be coped with through mythical conceptualizations?

What happens when social orders are undermined, when small tribes are submerged in the movements of the technological world and their supernatural beings are powerless to help? Can the religions of the conquerors bring the reassurance of worth that was supplied by older faiths? Finally, what are the consequences of the rapid shrinkage of that part of reality that is still explained in supernatural terms? Are we to live eventually in what Max Weber calls "the disenchanted world"?

REASSURANCE AND FEAR The paradox of magic as an important source of reassurance and also an important source of anxiety led to a conflict of interpretations between Malinowski and Radcliffe-Brown. Malinowski's emphasis of the ritually reassuring aspects of magic has already been dwelt upon, but not enough has been said of the frightening, anxiety-creating aspects of magic. In reply to Malinowski, Radcliffe-Brown contended that magical rites do much more to instill fear than to relieve fear. In fact, there are cases where "if it were not for the existence of the rite and the belief associated with it, the individual would feel no anxiety."[1] Drawing on examples from his long study of the Andamanese people, he gives several instances of anxiety states created by the taboos of society. Why does the Andamanese father undergo food taboos when his wife is about to have a baby? He would feel great fear of sickness or misfortune if he did not, and he would offend his social group. Rituals express the tribal sentiments of what is proper for the occasion, especially an occasion that could be fraught with danger. The explanation of food taboos for both father and mother is closely related to other types of food taboo, and it can also elucidate such a custom as couvade. "Couvade" is the practice of having the father feign illness and go through the same periods of avoidance as his wife at the time of childbirth. Seen in terms of biology, it is nonsense. In psychological terms, it is very important, helping to protect husband, wife, and infant against evil forces. The practice has what Radcliffe-Brown calls "ritual value"—the value of reassurance of personal and social welfare.

The much more common custom of mourning at funerals has the same implications of ritual value. A person may mourn because he is truly sad, but

A. R. Radcliffe-Brown, *Taboo*, The Frazer Lecture, Cambridge, 1939. Reprinted in William A. Lessa and Evon Z. Vogt (eds.), *Reader in Comparative Religion*, Harper & Row, Publishers, Incorporated, New York, 1965, pp. 112–123.

it is possible that he mourns simply because society *expects* him to grieve. Furthermore, a failure to show the sentiments required by society could be a threat to the society itself. Magico-religious acts are not performed simply because the individual feels anxiety, but because the society also feels anxiety. Social rights and wrongs are enforced, then, by the fears and anxieties induced in the individual who violates ritual. Although Radcliffe-Brown does not imply that the depths of such fears were as great among the Andamanese people as they are among societies that fear hell fire, the function is similar. People are held in line by the compulsive nature of social acts, and that compulsive nature is religious, not merely a matter of habit or magic.

It is commonly said that in more advanced religions, the rules turn more to general principles of good conduct toward others than to elaborate ritual. There are many examples that support the contention, and "golden rules" will be commented on later. In connection with the present perspective, though, it must be pointed out that many modern religions pay very great attention to ritual forms of prayer, food taboos, etiquette toward saints and divine beings, pilgrimages, christenings, and the like. Radcliffe-Brown notes that the reformer Mo Ti, in the fourth century b.c., tried to teach a simple religion of brotherhood and goodwill, love and altruism, free from elaborate ritual. Years later his opponents, Hsun Tze and other Confucian scholars, answered that the rites might have no utilitarian value but called for the proper expression of proper sentiment and thus gave cohesion to the social order.[2]

George C. Homans attempts to resolve the controversy between Malinowski and Radcliffe-Brown by showing that both interpretations of magic and ritual are correct.[3] The magic that allays one's fears of being drowned at sea is of the reassuring type. The ritual of food taboo allays no primary fear but can induce fear if violated. Homans would call the fear of taboo violation a "secondary anxiety" and the fear of drowning a "primary anxiety." The secondary anxieties can be felt whenever the traditions of society are not properly upheld. Rites to prevent primary anxiety are reassuring to the *individual*; rites to prevent secondary anxieties are reassuring to the *society*. The first kind of rite is often related to the external world; the function of the second kind of rite "is not related to the world external to the society but to the internal constitution of the society."[4] Such an analysis would help to answer questions not answered by Tylor: Why is religion not merely an individual affair if it arises out of the

[2]Ibid., p. 119.
[3]George C. Homans, "Anxiety and Ritual: The Theories of Malinowski and Radcliffe-Brown, *American Anthropologist*, vol. 43, pp. 164–172, 1941.
[4]Ibid., p. 171.

dream life? Why have societies, with rare exceptions, absolutely insisted that everyone follow their religious rituals, that all people at least display the outward forms of religion? The answer, obviously, is that society feels threatened by nonbelievers who will not perform its rituals and follow its sacred rules.

Another person to have answered questions about the functions of religion in a manner similar to that of Radcliffe-Brown was Durkheim, who postulated an extremely close identity between society and its gods. In *The Division of Labor in Society* he argues that all social orders depend upon some degree of consensus about moral values. What one society sees as moral another may consider completely immoral, but in their own definitions societies are, in Durkheim's view, moral systems, conforming to their sacred beliefs and their gods.[5]

THE GODS AND SOCIETY   In Durkheim's opinion, developed in *The Elementary Forms of the Religious Life*, religious emotions arise out of the rites and ceremonies of the people.[6] The performance of acts is not merely a consequence of religion but a source of religion, because religion is above all else a sentiment of social solidarity. It is a commonplace in our society to observe that "man creates gods in his own image." To Durkheim, the idea was not that man creates gods in his own image, but rather that he creates gods in the image of his *society*. The gods reflect the social system in the supernatural world. To the primitive Australians, on whose customs Durkheim's book on religion was based, the objects of veneration were ancestral and animal spirits, represented by sacred objects, especially the sacred stones called churinga. Ceremonial and ritual care of sacred objects, dramatic enactments of the sacred events of the past, initiation ceremonies of the young, and sharing the great tribal secrets of existence were the emotional centers of religion. The ceremonies and sacred symbols of a people are its "collective representations," the things that unite the people into a social system. For more advanced peoples, these representations are gods; for some primitives they are sacred places or objects or sometimes zoomorphic spirits (animallike spirits). A very generalized confirmation of Durkheim's view has been suggested in previous chapters, where it was frequently found that animal spirits are of particular importance to hunters. Such half-man, half-animal gods as Thoth of ancient Egypt may represent a transition to more

[5] Émile Durkheim, *The Division of Labor in Society*, trans. George Simpson, The Free Press, Glencoe, Ill., 1947.
[6] Émile Durkheim. *The Elementary Forms of the Religious Life*, The Free Press of Glencoe, Ill., Chicago, 1954, pp. 416–425.

anthropomorphic (manlike) gods of early urban civilizations.[7] Rain gods and sun gods are of major ritual importance in many agrarian societies. As seen by Durkheim, religion brings unity to a people. In modern history there have been many cases (especially during the Protestant Reformation) in which religion divided societies, but even then the particular religious denomination united its followers in opposition to the outsider. In modern, secular society, it is surprising to what degree people can rally behind their god in times of war, as if God is peculiarly the god of only one people. Religion can still be the symbol of unity, and there can still be truth in Durkheim's phrase that "God and society are the same thing."

If God and society are the same thing, even in a figurative sense, then we would expect the type of social system to have a considerable bearing on the conceptualization of God or the gods and spirits. For example, modern Americans generally think of the Christian religion as implying a democratic governmental system. Medieval man saw Christianity as an intellectual support for aristocracies and kingdoms. Each age interprets its gods in terms of its social systems.

Guy Swanson has tried to put the idea of "sociomorphic" religion to a test in a study based on fifty religions, carefully chosen to represent the major culture areas of the world.[8] His conclusions generally support the idea of a strong relationship between social systems and religions. Although his data present religion in a functional perspective (serving the function of backing up the ways of a society), they imply a certain evolution of religious ideas insofar as such ideas reflect the social systems in which they are found. On the average, more highly organized and technically advanced societies are found to have different god concepts from those of simpler societies.

Swanson finds a significant correlation between levels of social organization and the numbers and powers of gods. Superior deities, powerful gods controlling forces of nature, correlate with more complex societies. Moreover, when social classes are prominent and many occupational or regional groups have a measure of sovereignty, gods are more likely than elsewhere to exist on different levels of power. Simpler societies often have capricious spirits to be appeased, but no hierarchy of gods.

For many years there has been an anthropological interest in the high god concept. Tylor speculated that belief in a high god came about only with in-

[7]Leslie A. White, *The Evolution of Culture: The Development of Civilization to the Fall of Rome*, McGraw-Hill Book Company, New York, 1959, p. 274.
[8]Guy L. Swanson, *The Birth of the Gods: The Origin of Primitive Beliefs*, The University of Michigan Press, Ann Arbor, 1960.

Shrine in mausoleum of Ieyasu, Nikku, Japan. Reverence for ancestors and national heroes is one means of linking religion and society together.

creasing intellectual sophistication. In later years, Andrew Lang established the fact that many primitive people believe in a kind of high god, but usually one remote from the immediate affairs of man.[9] Wilhelm Schmidt of Austria had noted the same fact and came to a conclusion precisely opposite to that of Tylor.[10] In his opinion, all simple societies started with a belief in a high god, which he considers necessary for satisfying human psychological needs. As societies became more complex, with rival clans and social groups, they began to invent other gods of more particular function, including lineage deities and nature deities. Swanson's data contradict Schmidt's idea, and they lead to the conclusion that whether a high god is of any importance to a people is determined largely by the complexity of their social structure. A high god concept is "positively related to the presence of a hierarchy of three or more sovereign groups in a society."[11] Thus the Iroquois, with their clan, tribal, and league levels of organization, attached ritual importance to a great, superior god; most Indian tribes with similar ways of life were interested mainly in

[9]Andrew Lang, *The Making of Religion*, Longmans, Green & Co., Ltd., London, 1909.
[10]Wilhelm Schmidt, The Origin and Growth of Religion, H. J. Rose, New York, 1935.
[11]Swanson, p. 81.

lesser spirits. Ancient civilizations often had many gods with differing degrees of power and frequently one superior to all others, a king of the gods.

Swanson also tested the hypothesis that societies with sovereign kinship groups (important clans and lineages) are likely to believe in ancestral spirits and make them an object of veneration. Once again, and not surprisingly, a significant relationship was found. Similarly, a belief in witchcraft was found to correlate with societies in which people must "interact with one another on important matters in the absence of legitimated social controls and arrangements,"[12] a conclusion reached by other investigators as well.

A more subtle type of difference in thinking was put to the test regarding the immanence of the soul. "Immanence" refers to the idea of the soul being part of the substance of the person rather than something transcendent. If the soul is considered immanent, there is less perception of a duality between the physical and the spiritual than if the soul is considered transcendent. It might, consequently, be expected that if the soul is considered immanent, its essence can be captured with the capture of the body and ritualistic cannibalism would give the cannibal some part of the soul substance of the victim. The Jívaro idea of capturing a soul by cutting off a head and carefully preparing it would indicate a belief in the immanence as opposed to the transcendence of the soul. Swanson's findings were that belief in the immanence of the soul is most common among groups whose units of settlement are very small, whose kinship units are small and self-governing, and whose society is not highly integrated. His description, in short, is mainly of societies not advanced beyond the level of primitive horticulture.

The idea of possession—that a person can be possessed of the spirit of a god—is frequently found in many of the more prominent of the world's religions. Many Christians, for example, believe in possession by the Holy Ghost; but the idea is not the same as immanence. Salvationist religions may feel that one is possessed of a divine spirit, but the spirit is, nevertheless, not one with the flesh, but transcendent to it.

Always the religion of a people is explained by a large body of myths about origins of people and animals, about cultural heroes who bring gifts to the people, about gods and spirits in many forms, often part human and part animal or even vegetable. Sometimes there are moral tales, but many of the spiritual beings are of dubious morality, even base and lascivious. Family-type plots appear in mythologies, taboo violations, murders, swallowings by serpents or eels, miraculous births and rebirths. How are such myths to be interpreted?

[12]Ibid., p. 151.

THE INTERPRETATION OF MYTH   If concepts of gods bear a relationship to social realities, then it would seem likely that so do other types of mythological themes. Unfortunately, the interpretation of mythology is a subject of much controversy. Mythologies are artistic rather than scientific interpretations of reality and, like all art forms, have a multipersonality, with possibilities for many interpretations. Often they exist on the level of the common tale, but behind the narrative there is, perhaps, allegory or social reality. In Malinowski's view their major function is that of validating social systems—explaining why particular families are superior to others, why old people should dominate, and, in patriarchal societies, why women should obey their husbands. Others see additional meanings in myths. The story of the death of a father-type deity might be interpreted as a symbolic statement that all things must die or it might be interpreted in Freudian terms as a death wish centered about the father figure. A story that conveys a moral lesson to one person is seen as pointless and crude by another. In a short summary regarding the analysis of myth, probably the best that can be done is to relate the most common themes and to show that some of them occur more frequently at one societal level than at another and then to glance briefly at the type of analysis presented by a prominent modern anthropologist.

COMMON THEMES IN MYTH-MAKING   In an analysis of fifty societies, Kluckhohn noted the most common themes in mythology.[13] Creation myths are nearly universal, but are infrequent in Melanesia. In all societies, however, even if there is no myth of creation of the earth, there are myths about the creation of man. Often the first parents are the earth and the sky or the sun and the moon. In one version of Polynesian mythology, for example, out of primordial chaos arose the principles of sexual opposition, from which emerged the female Earth (Papa) and the male Sky (Rangi). They gave birth to gods who separated them from their close embrace, allowing room for light and forests, birds, animals, and people; but Rangi still rages in storms over the separation.[14] In North America, the Pima, Mojave, and Yuma Indians had a very similar myth of creation.[15] Early Chinese mythology also postulated a male principle of the sky (Yang) and a female principle of the earth (Yin).

[13]Clyde Kluckhohn, "Recurrent Themes in Myth and Mythmaking," *Daedalus: Journal of the American Academy of Arts and Sciences*, vol. 58, pp. 268–279, 1959.
[14]A. M. Panoff, "Oceania Society and Tradition." in *Larousse World Mythology*, G. P. Putnam's Sons, New York, 1965, pp. 492–494.
[15]Susan Feldman (ed.), *The Story Telling Stone: Myths and Tales of the American Indians*, Dell Publishing Co., Inc., New York, 1965, p. 16.

Destruction of the earth. Sumerians, Babylonians, Assyrians, and Hebrews all had similar stories of a great deluge. Other mythologies tell of how the earth has been destroyed many times by flood, fire, and other disasters.

Kluckhohn finds that the most common origin of man is the shaping of a creature from clay. Human beings also frequently emerge from the earth, very much as vegetation does, and at first they cannot walk straight.

Another common theme in mythology is that of renewal of the world after a great calamity. The Aztecs claimed the earth had been destroyed by cataclysms of the great winds, the jaguars, fire, and flood and eventually would be destroyed again. In parts of Amazonia there was a belief in seven cycles of destruction. The familiar tale of destruction by the Great Flood is found very commonly in the Near East, probably derived from a more ancient Babylonian tale, which in turn comes from an earlier Sumerian story of Gilgamesh and the flood. There are many flood tales in that part of the world, because there have been many floods, but in the oldest known story—that told in the epic of Gilgamesh—even the gods were frightened by the fury of the flood. Ulnapishtin, the friend of Gilgamesh, made a great boat in which he was saved, and he took all the species of animals aboard so that they too could be saved. Even the dimensions of the boat are similar to those in the later account of Noah, and in both stories birds were sent out to see if the waters were receding.[16] Obviously, two principles are at work in many of the ancient myths—diffusion and a fascination with the same problems.

Other themes that Kluckhohn found to be very common will not be elaborated upon, but they include the bringing of fire to man (the Prometheus tale), the first occurrence of death, illness or death as the result of introducing noxious substances into the body by magic means, were-animals, a connection between incest and witchcraft, sibling rivalry and even fratricide, father-daughter and mother-son incest, and castration fears. Of these latter themes, Kluckhohn concludes that they "suggest the interaction of a certain kind of physical world with some inevitabilities of the human condition [for example, helpless infancy, parental dominance, sibling resentment] bringing about regularities in the formation of imaginative productions."[17]

Other kinds of myths, not included in Kluckhohn's analysis, are apparently related to developmental steps in human societies. The myth of the sun god is so common that Max Müller regarded it as a universal, although his position is now considered exaggerated.[18] The sun god undoubtedly played a major role in the development of calendrical rites and calendars. The Egyptian pharaoh Ikhnaton attempted to make the sun god the one and only god and was the first prominent advocate of complete monotheism. The sun god Shamash was almost as important in Mesopotamia as was Amen-Ra (later called Aton) in Egypt. In an earlier chapter we discussed the Great Sun of the Natchez, and he may have been only a derivative of the greater sun gods of the Aztecs and Toltecs. Sun gods are generally believed to be prominent among agricultural peoples, who must pay close attention to seasons, but Alexander Marshack suggests that an interest in the calculations of seasons and solar and lunar records greatly predates established agriculture.[19] Whatever the case, the sun god takes on great importance in many early civilizations, and so does the moon, usually a goddess. Other people, not advanced to the stage of urban civilization, must have had very great interest in the sun and moon, for example, the builders of Stonehenge in England.[20] Other prominent themes, centering especially in particular periods of cultural development, include certain types of dying and reviving gods, such as Osiris of Egypt. In agrarian societies they often relate to spring and renewal, but at times they merge with

[16]N. K. Sandars (ed.), *The Epic of Gilgamesh*, Penguin Books, Inc., Baltimore, 1966, pp. 105–110.
[17]Kluckhohn, op. cit., pp. 271–272.
[18]Richard M. Dorn, "The Eclipse of Solar Mythology," *Journal of American Folklore*, vol. 68, pp. 393–416, 1955.
[19]Alexander Marshack, *The Roots of Civilization*, McGraw-Hill Book Company, New York, 1972, pp. 27–32.
[20]Gerald S. Hawkins, *Stonehenge Decoded*, Dell Publishing Co., Inc., New York, 1965.

heroes and saviors—a theme to be discussed later. For the present, let it be noted that mythological themes bear great resemblances to one another the world over, as though there were only a limited number of constructs from which to draw. Lévi-Strauss in particular concludes that the threads of mythology are limited, appearing over and over again in changing combinations and reflecting a surprising mental depth in the symbolic solution of philosophical problems.[21]

STRUCTURAL ANALYSIS OF MYTH   Lévi-Strauss breaks myths into component segments, looking for the symbolic meaning in each and linking them into systems of opposition or conflict resolution. For example, the famous Oedipus myth and the later story of his daughter Antigone break down into two opposing propositions concerning kinship. Oedipus marries his mother, Jocasta; and Antigone buries her brother Polynices in spite of the law of her uncle Creon, the king. These episodes represent an "overevaluation" of kinship. In two other episodes, Oedipus kills Laius, his father; and Eteocles kills Polynices, his own brother. These represent the oppositional elements of underevaluation of kinship.

The story also represents two other themes in opposition. Cadmus kills the dragon, and Oedipus kills the sphinx. The dragon is a chthonic being (infernal and belonging to the earth) "which has to be killed in order that man can be born from the earth. The Sphinx is a monster unwilling to permit men to live."[22] The opposition is one of monsters versus men, but several men in the story are deformed or have trouble walking. The name Oedipus means "swollen-footed"; his father's name, Laius, probably means "left-sided," and his grandfather's name, Labdacus, means "lame." The solution to the symbolism, then, according to Lévi-Strauss, is that the two monsters represent a denial of the autochthonic (born out of the earth) origin of man, whereas the slaying of the monsters affiirms such an origin, but at a cost. Lévi-Strauss cites a number of mythologies in which man is born out of the ground, but in all cases he is at first unable to walk. The Pueblo mythical hero, Muyingwu, who leads men up out of the earth, is lame "bleeding foot." The Koskimo of the Northwest Coast Kwakiutl tribe were swallowed by a chthonic monster and emerged lame, limping forward or walking sidewise. The final resolution of the Oedipus myth, then, is that "the overrating of blood relations is to the

[21]Claude Lévi-Strauss, *Tristes Tropiques*, Atheneum Publishers, New York, 1965, p. 160.
[22]Claude Lévi-Strauss, *Structural Anthropology*, Anchor Books, Doubleday & Company, Inc., Garden City, N.Y., 1967, p. 211.

underrating of blood relations as the attempt to escape autochthony is to the impossibility to succeed in it."[23] The myth seems to be dealing with an attempt to prove that man was born out of the ground in spite of the knowledge that man must be born as the result of the union of male and female and that his continuance depends on proper kin relationships. Although Lévi-Strauss does not say so, it seems logical that since the episodes involving kinship are tragic, the oppositional autochthonic birth theme must also be tragic.

From the Oedipus myth, Lévi-Strauss advances to a careful analysis of Zuñi myths. The Zuñi, like the ancient Greeks, had a theory that human life sprang from the earth, in a manner analogous to the growth of plants. The major themes of the Zuñi emergence myth involve the resolution of agriculture versus hunting, peace versus war, and life versus death. Agriculture, by the growing of annual plants, alternates between life and death; hunting provides food for life but is similar to war in that it causes death. In a mythological war, the defeated people use a sinew string on their bows, denoting hunting; the victors use fiber string, denoting gardening. The latter, equated with the Zuñi, eventually find salvation for their tribe by finding the center of the earth. Death is integrated into the system, but out of death comes life. One of the themes occurring in the Zuñi myth is that of sacrifice of a brother and sister, in one case to gain victory, in another to avoid a flood. It appears that the resolution of the life-death dichotomy calls for sacrifice of life to death that other life may survive or be renewed.

The idea of oppositions of pairs and of a third element partially resolving the opposition is very strong in the Lévi-Strauss type of analysis. Thus the trickster of American Indian mythology is frequently either Coyote or Raven. Both eat carrion and thus are intermediate between hunting and agriculture—like agriculturists, seldom actually killing, but, like hunters, eating meat. Since they seldom kill but eat the dead, they also stand midway as resolutions of the life-death dichotomy. Like many personages of myth, they are sympathetic characters, generally likable, but they pull many tricks; hence it might also be argued that they stand at the mediation point between good and bad, although Lévi-Strauss deals with the good-bad dichotomy elsewhere.

In looking at the very intriguing, but still controversial, analysis of myth found in the works of Lévi-Strauss, we cannot conclude that there is an evolutionary progression from simplistic to advanced thinking. The progression, he says, is from working with one type of material or idea to working with another. It is impossible to say a steel ax represents better workmanship than a stone ax; the difference is in the materials used. Similarly, the difference

[23]Ibid., p. 212.

between mythical thought and scientific thought is not in the quality of the thought processes but in the nature of the knowledge dealt with. "The difference lies, not in the quality of the intellectual process, but in the nature of the things to which it is applied."[24] If Lévi-Strauss is right, we must look, not to the processes of myth-making, but rather to the materials dealt with, if we wish to put mythology into cultural-evolutionary perspective. Do different types of spirits, gods, and forces appear at different levels of cultural development, and is the myth-making facility turned to the resolution of different problems, or of the same problems in different ways?

EVOLUTION OF RELIGIOUS CONCEPTS Swanson's studies indicate that conceptualizations of the gods change with changes in the organizational complexity of social systems. The gods grow with the society. A few examples of myth indicate that the points of emphasis vary also as social systems change. At the same time, there is a certain persistence of older ideas. It can be said, for example, that such prominent religions of the modern world as Christianity, Buddhism, Islam, Hinduism, Confucianism, and Taoism are all universalistic and emphasize the brotherhood of man; but that does not mean all their followers show such breadth of mind and vision. All kinds of ethnocentric beliefs still persist; not only that, but many of the followers of the modern religions continue to be haunted by ghosts and ill omens and to carry good luck charms and amulets to ward off such evils. Consequently, when speaking of an evolution of religion, we can speak only of an evolution of the prevailing opinion of society at various periods. The older, persistent ideas may be what Tylor characterized as "survivals"—leftovers from earlier times, analogous to vestigial organs of the human body; or they may live on because they still serve important psychological functions for at least some segments of modern societies. Regardless of which explanation is accepted, it should not be forgotten that none of the religious forms that a twentieth-century American thinks of as passé are really gone. People still believe in ghosts, witches, animism, mana, poltergeists, werewolves, and many other kinds of debris of the past.

Robert Bellah, in developing an analysis of religion in evolutionary perspective, takes cognizance of all the above points but tries to analyze the most characteristic changes at several levels of societal development.[25] The first three

[24]Ibid. p. 227.
[25]Robert Bellah, "Religious Evolution," *American Sociological Review*, vol. 29, pp. 358–374, 1964.

stages he analyzes are particularly pertinent for our purposes: primitive religion, archaic religion, and historic religion.

PRIMITIVE RELIGION   Bellah's description of primitive religion includes all that can be gleaned from the distant past as well as a generalization from hunting-and-gathering peoples and primitive horticulturists of today. Using particularly Australia for a model, he concludes that there is a hazy, ill-defined character to the spirit figures of the primitive world. In Australia they are spoken of as belonging to the Dreamtime or simply the Dreaming. Among many other primitive peoples, characterizations of the founding ancestors, the bringers of cultural gifts, and creation figures are not clearly defined; and the tales change character as related by different informants. In another sense, though, the religions are precise. There is a detailed account for all the features of the physical world, for all the animals and plants, for each clan and its founders, and for fairly specific linkages between men, animals, and locations.

Another characteristic of primitive religion is that its mythology is acted out, sometimes in rather routine ways and sometimes in ecstatic rites. Human actions symbolize offerings, destruction, transformations, communion with the spirits, maledictions and benedictions. Organizationally, the most primitive religions are little separated from everyday life. Despite Malinowski's analysis of magic, science, and religion, in the thoughts of primitive people there is no analytical distinction. One casts a spell with the same feeling of precise knowledge one has when planting yams, and one's religious explanations of linkages to eternity are just as matter of fact. Religion may have its shamans, but there is no organization or insitutionalization, and there is seldom a high god, nor is there a separation between religious days and weekdays. Religion at the primitive level reinforces group solidarity, and it does so without strain or argument. All the people of a particular social group see themselves as the products of the same supernatural forces, as distinct from the not-quite-human people beyond their borders. At more sophisticated levels of societal development, the distinction is not always so clear; lower classes do not share the religious orientation of upper classes, and conquered subjects attempt to cling to their faiths in opposition to the official religion of the country. Sometimes, too, sectarian divisions such as those of Catholic versus Protestant can arise in more advanced societies, but not in primitive tribes.

ARCHAIC RELIGION   Bellah's next description is of what he calls archaic religion, existing at or before the dawn of recorded history but in regions of the world developing urban civilizations. The system of symbolism differs from that of the primitives, with mythical beings more actively and willfully in control. Archaic religion centers in the superior gods found in Swanson's study of societies with multiple levels of administration. Although the rule is far from perfect, there is a greater tendency toward anthropomorphic gods at the archaic level, as opposed to the zoomorphic gods of the more primitive level. The archaic gods are more definitive and more clearly conceived than the primitive gods, and the symbolic structure is more stable—that is, there is more agreement regarding the gods and the myths. At the same time, the gods remain part of nature, just as are the more primitive spirits; they are not remote and transcendent.

Sacrifice in the more primitive religions had been a symbolic representation of myth, with plants or animals or even people being sacrificed so that more would arise. In archaic religions the same types of sacrifice continue, but the motive more frequently becomes one of communication between worlds. On the organizational level, cults with complexes of gods and with sacrifice and priests or even priest-kings are common. Socially, the archaic societies present the possibility of rival cults with rival deities or of a dichotomy between the political leadership and the religious hierarchies. They are also characterized by underground cults, more shamanistic in leadership and clinging to earlier beliefs.

HISTORIC RELIGION   The third level designated by Bellah, and the last of his examples to be followed closely here, is what he calls historic religion, belonging to the early periods of recorded history. The symbolization of the deities changes in emphasis again, with powerful gods or even ultimate gods. In Hindu thinking, Brahma is the eternal and immutable, the origin and destiny of all things, transcending them all. The god of the Hebrews in the later chapters of Isaiah becomes a god who "hath measured the waters in the hollow of his hand, and meted out heaven with a span . . . and weighed the mountains in scales" (Isaiah 40:12). In Egypt, Ikhnaton declared the supremacy of the sun god, Aton, and sought to make him the one and only god.

Many of the historic gods are no longer embodied in nature, no longer specific to volcanoes or seas, to trees or mountains, but transcendent and belonging to an order over and above nature. The doctrine of transcendence replaces that of immanence. Thus the duality of nature and supernature takes on new meaning, helping to divide the world more fully into two distinct realms— a division that Weber considered a forerunner to modern rationalism and secularization. Some areas of life were no longer as pervaded by religion as before.

TRENDS IN RELIGIOUS DEVELOPMENT

PRIMITIVE RELIGIONS (PREURBAN)	ARCHAIC RELIGIONS (SEMILITERATE STATE OF URBAN DEVELOPMENT)	HISTORIC RELIGIONS (LITERATE CIVILIZATIONS, APPROXIMATELY 500 BC- 600 AD)

RELIGIOUS SYMBOLISM:

VAGUE ANCESTRAL FIGURES, MAGIC, SPIRITS, NO MAJOR GODS	CLEARER MYTHICAL BEINGS, WILFUL CONTROLLING FORCES	GODS AS MAJOR OR EVEN ULTIMATE BEINGS. FREQUENT PROPHETS AND SAVIORS.

RELATION TO NATURE:

MYTHS RELATED TO PRECISE DETAILS OF NATURE, CLANS, PLACES	DIFFERENTIATED GODS CONTROL NATURAL FORCES, BUT STILL PART OF NATURE, NOT REMOTE	GREATER DUALISM; TRANSCENDENT GODS AND POWERS, SOMETIMES REMOTE

STABILITY OF MYTH:

CHANGING MYTHS, RESHAPED BY DREAMS AND DIFFERENT INFORMANTS	SYMBOLIC STRUCTURE MORE STABLE, AGREED UPON	AUTHORITATIVE THEOLOGIES, LEARNED AND POWERFUL PRIESTS

PURPOSE OF RITES:

SYMBOLIC REPRESENTATION THROUGH DRAMATIZATION OF MYTHS AND EVENTS	SACRIFICE AS COMMUNICATION BETWEEN WORLDS MORE THAN SYMBOLIC REPRESENTATION	FREQUENT REJECTION OF THE WORLD; ACTION CENTERED ON INDIVIDUAL SALVATION

COMPLEXITY:

NO SEPARATE ORGANIZATION OF RELIGION; NO SEPARATION FROM EVERYDAY LIFE	SPECIAL CELEBRATIONS, CULTS, PRIESTLY ORDERS	GROWING DIFFERENTIATION BETWEEN SACRED AND SECULAR, POSSIBLY OPENING DOOR TO SCIENCE. SPECIAL HOLY DAYS

SOCIAL IMPLICATIONS:

REINFORCES SOCIAL SOLIDARITY THROUGH MAGIC, TABOO, AND RITUAL OBSERVANCE	DIFFERENTIATION IN SOCIAL CLASS, PRIESTLY ORDERS, POSSIBLE RIVAL CULTS	RELIGIOUS HIERARCHIES, SOCIAL CLASS, BUT RELIGIOUS MESSAGE IS OFTEN OF BROTHERHOOD- UNIVERSALISTIC APPEAL

The theologies became even more authoritative, explained and elaborated upon by learned priests.

The aim of religious action itself gradually changed. In the primitive state, religious action aimed at ensuring game, offspring, abundant food, health, and the perpetuation of the tribe. In historic religion the aim became more typically that of individual salvation. The salvationist theme might have reflected to a degree the longings of people in the more powerfully organized kingdoms of historic times for the freedom of earlier days. Certainly it appealed to many people over scattered parts of the world.

Egypt   Possibly the prototype of the savior gods originated in Egypt in the form of Osiris, who had been killed and cut into many pieces by the wicked god Set. Isis, the loving wife of Osiris, herself an earth goddess, wandered throughout Egypt finding the remains of Osiris for proper burial, and when they were assembled, behold, the dead Osiris revived! In his early days Osiris might have symbolized merely the return of vegetation in the spring, but eventually he became an important god in the cult of salvation, the Judge of the Dead. To enter the blissful hereafter, a person had to be able to say to the Judge of the Dead that he was free from sins. Among other statements, he had to say:

> I have done violence to no man.
> I have not committed theft.
> I have not slain man or woman.
> I have not made light the bushel.
> I have not acted deceitfully.[26]

Persia   The road to the heaven of Osiris depended on good deeds, but it also depended on many magic charms and incantations. The later hero gods in many cases combined the two elements of magic formulas and moral principle, but not all the heroes were entirely objects of myth. Some of the historic religions were founded by prophets, appearing mainly in the time span from 600 B.C. or 800 B.C. until the coming of Muhammad in the seventh century A.D. Zoroaster of Persia was probably the oldest of the teachers, telling of a struggle between good and evil in which man must choose sides. Man's path to salvation lay through following the good god, Ahura Mazda, who was supported by his six vessels: Good Thought, Right Law, Noble Government, Holy Character, Health, and Immortality. Like the later Jesus, Zoroaster overcame

[26]Homer Smith, *Man and His Gods*, Little, Brown and Company, Boston, 1952, p. 43.

the temptations presented to him by the god of evil. In a portion of his doctrine, he seems almost a prelude to what Weber called the "Protestant ethic" of salvation through hard work. Every morning, said Zoroaster, the demon of laziness whispers in one's ear to sleep on, but we must rise and work. "He who sows corn, sows religion."[27]

India   In the sixth century B.C., two great religious teachers appeared in India, the first, Mahavira, asking men to follow his way to total abolition of desire as the road to union with the Eternal. He was the *jin*, "the conqueror," who had learned to conquer all desire in order to attain salvation. Contemporary with Mahavira was the greater teacher, Prince Siddhartha, or Gautama Buddha, The Enlightened One, who also promised individual salvation through freeing the self from desire and possessions. His message was one of self-knowledge and of love for all created things. The cult of the more mythical Krishna, said to be an avatar (an appearance in human form) of the god Vishnu, also emphasizes a mystical type of salvation. It teaches that whoever worships Krishna with utter devotion "dwells in Me, whatever be his course in life. They who worship Me devoutly are in Me; and I am also in them. Be well assured that he who worships Me does not perish."[28] The idea of spiritual interpenetration was to be found later in Christian symbolism.

China   In China there appeared two great sages, Lao-tzu and K'ung Fu-tzu (Confucius), in the sixth century B.C. Lao-tzu, the earlier of the two, wrote the *Tao Te Ching*, explaining the great mysterious force of eternity, the Tao, and teaching people how to live serenely. "To them that are good, I am good, and to them that are not good, I am also good; thus all get to be good."[29] Confucius wrapped his teaching in much ritual and protocol, but behind it all was the same theme of helping man in how to live. "With whom should I make fellowship save with suffering mankind?" "Do not unto others what you would not have done to you."

Greece   In Greece a series of mystery cults, often based on the idea of a dying and reviving god of the type of Osiris—Orpheus, Dionysus, Attis, or Osiris himself, whose cult spread from Egypt—promised immortality to their followers. Shortly before the beginning of the Christian era, Mithras, an offspring

---

[7]Lewis Browne, *This Believing World*, The Macmillan Company, New York, 1937, pp. 205–206.
[8]Quoted in Robert E. Hume, *The World's Living Religions*, Charles Scribner's Sons, New York, 1959, p. 30.
[9]Browne, op. cit., pp. 169–182.

Krishna, eleventh avatar of the god
Vishnu, loves both animals and people
and brings a message of faith and
progress for the soul. The teaching of
charity as a path to salvation is typical
of the historical religions.

of the teachings of Zoroaster, was introduced into the Greco-Roman world. Mithras was a god identified with the sun and with eternal light and fire and salvation, able to give eternal life to his followers. Not only that, but Mithraism promised high status rewards for even the lowly if they would but follow the way. Mithraism was made the state religion of Rome for a brief period during the reign of Aurelian (A.D. 270-275);[30] but the followers of another savior, Jesus, were making converts even more rapidly by that time, and they eventually destroyed the temples of Mithras. The new religion was equally salvationist and had even greater appeal to the lowly, with its message of "Blessed are the meek."

In the seventh century A.D. came the last of the great teachers of the historic period, Muhammad, less an advocate of retreat from worldly affairs than some of his predecessors, but also pointing the path to salvation for those who would follow him to the paradise of Allah. As with the other historic religions, Islam's principles were universalistic, promising brotherhood to all. The universalistic messages continued through the years, but centuries after the coming of the great teachers, all the promised paradises seemed to fade in importance in favor of the material world.

DISENCHANTMENT AND ITS RESPONSES

Oddly enough, the very changes that in ways seemed to be leading people to salvation in another world rather than to a concentration on the world of the here and now ultimately may have had the opposite effect. For one thing, there were always those of little faith or those willing to follow the advice of Omar Khayyám: "Ah, take the cash and let the credit go, Nor heed the rumble of a distant drum." But there were more important implications to changes in religious emphasis than the ignoring of the prophet's paradise. Bellah, in another article, has drawn the contrast between a religion based on prescriptive rules and one based on general principles.[31] The latter, he points out, frees man from heavy ceremonial duties, so that he can better pursue worldly ends. Weber and Durkheim held similar views. To Durkheim, the new types of society freed man from the need to follow tradition with the precision of earlier times. A moral order in society had to remain, he said, but it was less demanding.[32] Weber studies the great scope of human history looking for the changes in ideas that made possible modern rationalism

[30] Smith, op. cit., pp. 130-131.
[31] Robert Bellah, "Religious Aspects of Modernization in Turkey and Japan," *American Journal of Sociology*, vol. 64, pp. 1-5, July 1958.
[32] Durkheim, op. cit.

as opposed to older supernaturalism, the modern urge toward material production, and the triumph of modern science and bureaucratic organization.[33] He found his answers in the shifting of religious attitudes. The separation of the natural and supernatural worlds had contributed to the change, and so had the shift from overly taxing prescriptive rules to general principles. Both Bellah and Weber place too exclusive an emphasis on Christianity for our purposes here, but they conclude that the rational-scientific-material trend that started in northwestern Europe and the United States was able eventually to spread over the world, changing the emphasis of the older religions. Even the Western, scientific world often feels nostalgia for its more sacred past, but its problems are only a mild reflection of the spiritual problems it has exported to the primitive and underdeveloped parts of the world.

RELIGION IN CRISIS   When cultures succumb to other cultures and must undergo drastic changes or perish, a spiritual crisis occurs. If the gods and spirits are symbols of the tribe but are powerless to save their people, then new rationalizations must be found. Sometimes these rationalizations are met through syncretism—joining together elements of the old order and the new. Sometimes the response comes in messianic movements or in cargo cults, and sometimes the response is such a total retreat from the world as to approach oblivion. All these alternatives have occurred many times over in human history, but a few examples belong to the present or the very recent past.

SYNCRETISM   Religious ideas have constantly spread from one part of the world to another. Prophets of one people have inspired prophets to arise among others. Sometimes there are superficial resemblances between religious beliefs that make the adoption of elements of one religious system by another fairly easy. Slaves taken from Africa and converted to Catholicism were able to equate their old African gods with many of the Christian saints. The *vodun* ceremonies of Dahomey became the voodoo ceremonies of the Caribbean islands, particularly Haiti.[34] The god Legba of Dahomey, who stands guard at entrances to temples, villages, and compounds, is often equated with Saint Anthony, because he bears a slight resemblance to pictures of Saint Anthony. Others think he is really Saint Peter, because it is Saint Peter who stands at the gateway to heaven. Damballa, the rainbow-serpent deity, is identified with

[33]Max Weber, "Science and the Disenchantment of the World," trans. H. H. Gerth and C. Wright Mills, reprinted in Dennis H. Wrong and Harry L. Gracey, *Readings in Sociology*, The Macmillan Company, New York, 1972, pp. 214–219.
[34]Melville Herskovitz, "African Gods and Catholic Saints in New World Religious Belief," *American Anthropologist*, vol. 39, pp. 635–643, 1937.

The ghost dance among the Dakota Sioux, 1890—a revitalization movement destroyed by the massacre at Wounded Knee.

Saint Patrick, who is pictured as driving serpents before him. Saint John the Baptist is a powerful nature spirit who controls thunder and lightning. The goddess Gran' Erzilie is the Mater Dolorosa. In Brazil the syncretism is similar, but the gods' names are different, having come more typically from Nigeria. Several gods are celebrated on religious festival days along with the Christian saints. In an earlier chapter, mention was made of syncretism in Mexico, where the Aztec goddess Tonantzin became the Virgin of Guadalupe. Such blending of religious beliefs lessens the shock of transition from one cultural world to another. There are differences in belief, but behind them all are similarities in the conceptualization of the supernatural.

REVITALIZATION MOVEMENTS: GHOST DANCES AND CARGO CULTS   Among American Indians there were large numbers of messianic characters at different periods in history. A ghost dance originated among the Western Paiutes in the 1870s and was revived some years later by the great messianic leader Wovoka, who had a vision of a great future for the Indians. The ghosts of the dead would return, and all the buffalo, the Indian lands would be restored, and there would be no more sickness. Ceremonies spread from tribe to tribe, differently interpreted but always with a revitalization spirit.[35] The ghost dance continues in some tribes as a healing ceremony, one that restores the spirit as much as the body, but its original hope was quickly dashed. Fearing that the Sioux might be about to start an uprising, the American Seventh Cavalry descended upon them at Wounded Knee, South Dakota, killing 300 men, women, and children in an unprovoked attack and burying their bodies in a common grave, and with them the last hope of revitalization.[36]

In other parts of the world as well, messianic ideas have arisen as a response to contact with the overwhelming civilization of the white man. Many prophets have appeared, foretelling the return of ancestral spirits and relating the gifts they would bring. Some of the most famous examples of these messianic ideas are the so-called cargo cults of Melanesia. The cults are named from the belief of many New Guinea people that the white men (whom some of them call "red men") perform feats of magic that cause cargoes to come from overseas. Since white men are never seen to do any work to produce the cargoes, it only stands to reason that they must produce them by supernatural means. White missionaries have taught that the end of the world is at hand and that there will be a second coming of their great messiah. It just happens that parts of New Guinea also have a hero, old Mansren, who created their people and their islands and the vegetation on them. He was also able to restore himself to youth and is, therefore, something of a reviving god.[37] The cargo cult beliefs take many forms, but they often center around such a god and the observation that the European people have all the cargoes. In at least one version of cargo cult belief, Mansren will return again, and the cargoes that belong by rights to the people of New Guinea will be restored to them. "The last shall be first and the first, last;" the white men will turn black and the black men, white, and those that hunger shall be filled.

Obviously, cargo cults cannot produce their cargoes, and the long wait for the ships and airplanes that will deliver them eventually comes to an end. Now the New Guinea people, more wise to the ways of the world, attempt political and labor union action to gain their fair share of the cargoes. Probably the next phase will be a type of antiforeign nationalism, arising as another response to the disruption of old ways and old beliefs by the encroachment of the outside world.

[35] Ralph Linton, "Nativistic Movements," *American Anthropologist*, vol. 45, pp. 230–240, 1943.
[36] Dee Brown, *Bury My Heart at Wounded Knee: An Indian History of the American West*, Bantam Books, Inc., New York, 1972.
[37] Peter M. Worsley, "Cargo Cults," in James P. Spradley and David W. McCurdy (eds.), *Conformity and Conflict: Readings in Cultural Anthropology*, Little, Brown and Company, Boston, 1971, pp. 308–315.

The Peyote Way, or the Native American Church, is in some respects a case of syncretism, since it puts Christian concepts into a form plausible to many American Indian tribes. It can also be thought of as a retreatist religion, since it gained followers after the more messianic ghost dance waned as an influence and also because a psychedelic drug is taken as part of the service. Peyote, a spineless cactus, produces a drug similar to, but not nearly as strong as, mescaline, but for most people it is very hard to take, often inducing vomiting on the first trial. The ceremonies consist of prayer, singing, taking peyote, and contemplation. The white man gains his knowledge through reading; the Indian gains it through the peyote. One Comanche told J. S. Slotkin, "The white man talks *about* Jesus; we talk *to* Jesus."[38] Users of peyote claim to have greater sensitivity to one another and more spiritual visions. The claims are similar to those of other types of drug cults of recent years. Since peyote is relatively mild and is used only on religious ceremonial occasions, it is probably not particularly harmful. The peyote cult, though, is obviously one of quietism and surrender, not the messianic cult of revival and activity. Marxians have called religion "the opiate of the people." It would not be far wrong to reverse the statement and say opiates had become the religion of the people, helping to make bearable an outcast status in a world that would otherwise have no enchantment and no spirit.

THE DISENCHANTMENT
OF THE WORLD   "The fate of our times," said Weber, "is characterized by rationalization and intellectualization, and, above all, by the 'disenchantment of the world.'"[39] No longer need one look for magical means to solve the problems of existence; the method has become intellectual and scientific. No longer must man deal with forces that are mysterious and incalculable; all forces are weighed and measured and, if not understood, are at least considered within the range of investigation. Whatever is tragic about dealing with unembellished realities is at least compensated for, in Weber's opinion, by the advantages of calculability. Hewing to rationalization, one is in the service of "moral forces," in the sense of bringing about clarification and self-responsibility. There are strong compensations to a world rooted in the here and now, the seen, and the calculable.

Even Weber realizes, though, that many people cannot bear the fate of living in times of disenchantment. For them "the arms of the old churches are

---

[38]J. S. Slotkin, "The Peyote Way," *Tomorrow,* vol. 4, pp. 64–70, 1955–1956. Also reprinted in Lessa and Vogt, op. cit., 513–517.
[39]Weber, op. cit., p. 217.

opened widely and compassionately."[40] Bellah's theory bears repeating: although there is a dominant trend in the development of the magico-religious world, no period of the past is completely superseded. Among the remaining primitives of the world, there are those who plant their yams with the ceremonies of old, who bury their dead with magical incantations to ward off the evil of ghosts and to avoid the taboo violations that are dangerous sacrilege. The archaic religions also remain, with their sacrosanct priests and their restorative rites that keep up the rhythm of the world and the return of life and spring. The historic religions are still strong in all parts of the world, even among the proud, but for the humble of the earth they have their greatest appeal. Their followers stare off into the distance, waiting much as the New Guinea natives have waited for their magical cargoes or as others have waited for the return of the great culture hero. The number of gods has declined with the passing of so much of the primitive world, but the late-found savior gods and their prophets continue to flourish in many forms, and many more will undoubtedly appear. They assure those who are crushed in the material world that there is yet a world for them, and that the cargoes men should seek are those of human dignity and hope. Therein lies the power of religion even in a secularized and disenchanted world—a power well described by the late Lewis Browne.

> Strange potency, this thing we call religion! It has made men do barbarities quite beyond the reaches of credence. . . . Yet for it also men have done benevolences such as transcend the benevolence of angels. If men have killed and died for religion, men have also lived for it. Not merely lived for it, but by it. . . . That cowering Yemenite Jew slinking in the shadow of the archways sloughs off his terror and becomes a king when he enters the synagogue. His bent shoulders straighten, his sagging knees become firm, and the blessedness of peace lightens his eyes. . . . That blind Arab beggar, a mere frame of bones hung over with smelling rags, becomes a sultan when he stands at prayer in his mosque. He stands healed there of his ailments; he becomes a changed man with a vision reaching through his world to Paradise. . . . That dark-eyed Syrian girl, poor trull whose lips have caressed the flesh of twenty races, becomes clean once more when she kneels at the feet of the virgin. Strength floods into her tortured bones, healing comes to her flesh. Life, so long a hell of lust and lechery, becomes now wondrously clean and worthy. She feels saved—saved! Strange potency, this thing we call religion![41]

---

[40]Ibid., p. 218.
[41]Browne, op. cit., pp. 22–23.

We do not know how long the human species has had the gift of language. We know only that all human societies have complex, highly developed languages, adequate to their needs. The major difference between primitive and advanced societies in linguistic respects is merely a reflection of total cultures and the vocabularies needed at different cultural levels. The other differences are those of notation and writing and the transmission of messages and information.

Mankind is a communicating species, with many forms of communication in addition to language, ranging all the way from a sigh or a groan to the most exquisite of the arts, but language is the most important communicative gift. Language not only makes communication possible, but it helps in the development of ideas and even in the perception of reality. Each word used is a symbol, and language is the major form of symbolic communication. Just what is the meaning of symbolizing, and what forms does symbolizing take? In most respects, speech is superior to other forms of symbolic communication, but, unlike some of the arts, it lacks permanence. How was art able to convey more permanent messages? What were the steps by which speech was turned into written language so it could be recorded

Chapter Sixteen
Extensions of
Communication

permanently? What part was played by stylization of artistic expression? Were there parallels in the development of writing in Mesopotamia, Egypt, China, and Mexico? How did pictographs and ideograms gradually change form, taking on phonetic traits and in a few cases becoming alphabets? Once invented, what purposes did writing serve? How has writing combined with other means of communication to widen knowledge, ideas, and perceptions and to aid in the transformation of the world?

THE FORMS OF COMMUNICATION Speech is a rare gift, belonging only to the human species. Although other animals can make sounds that convey emotions and warnings and some can learn to recognize a number of words, none of them use all the elements of human speech. They cannot use abstract and arbitrary expressions, or tell what heppened in the past or in distant places, or give warnings about the future. Although many animals teach their young, they must do so by examples, signs, and warning cries, not by careful explanation. Consequently, cultural development among the lower animals is extremely limited, so much so that only the term "protoculture" is applied to the lifeways of even such advanced primates as chimpanzees and macaque monkeys.

CHARACTERISTICS OF SPEECH The gift of speech makes possible the transmission of learning from generation to generation. It makes possible the formation of new words as new artifacts and ideas enter into a culture. It becomes a vehicle not only for expression but for the formation of thought and perception. It adds greatly to emotional as well as intellectual life, accompanying drama and music, constructing illustrative tales and mythologies, adding forceful voice to anger, exhaltation to the mighty, vocal magic to the spell and the prayer, and expressing love and compassion with poetic beauty. Words are invented to name all things, to classify the objects of nature and personify the unseen forces behind them. Each style of speech evolves its own more-or-less logical rules of grammar to which all speakers must conform in order to be understood. Human speech conveys the simplest of ideas and also the most abstract. It often conveys its messages on more than one level, employing metaphor and enigmatic proverb as well as matter-of-fact statement. Such an expression as "for the golden bowl is broken, and the silver cord is loosed" does not really refer to bowls or to cords, but to death. This very ambiguity of language makes it possible to substitute one type of symbol for another and was undoubtedly useful in substituting pictorial symbols for spoken symbols.

Any one thing that suggests or represents another is a symbol. All words are symbols, because the words themselves have no existence and no meaning except that assigned them by their users. To symbolize is to think in terms of the symbols that represent things, whether those symbols are words, pictures, road signs, banners, hand signals, or melodies. Each culture creates its own largely symbolic view of the world.

COMMUNICATION AND THE ARTS   To some degree, most art forms are types of symbolic communication, but usually they are not as precise as language. Music is communicative and, like speech, varies from society to society. To the initiated, a particular type of music can convey moods of love, ecstasy, or sadness. It can accompany important occasions and ceremonies, such as weddings, coronations, or funerals, and as such an accompaniment it conveys meaning. Dances and dramas are also means of communication, as well as all other arts, and are studied more extensively in more specialized branches of anthropology. Such arts certainly intensify emotional experience, promote group solidarity, and aid in conceptualization, especially of the supernatural world. Arts of many kinds are universal among societies and are clearly expressions of human needs. In some respects they all fall short of the communicative capacities of speech, being less clear and precise. Certain of the arts, though, have the advantage of permanence, which speech lacks, and therefore have been seized upon since Paleolithic times to aid in the processes of communication.

PALEOLITHIC ART
AND NOTATION   Drawings, carvings, and decorations have other purposes than merely making speech more permanent. Man has a need for artistic expression as well as communication, to work off inner tensions, to give vent to desires, and to fill the same kind of urge as that conveyed by a shout of triumph or a wail of pain. The cave art of late Paleolithic times (ca. 30,000–10,000 B.C.) undoubtedly also had its magic functions, but in a sense the magic was communicative, conveying messages to supernatural forces. The late Henri Breuil in particular interprets much of the art of the cave painters of southern France and Spain as of magical significance.[1] Pregnant animals, so common in the cave art, are believed to have been painted to ensure more game in the future; animals penetrated with spears probably helped to ensure success on the hunt. The many statuettes of pregnant females are often referred

[1]Henri Breuil, *Four Centuries of Cave Art*, trans. by Mary E. Boyle, Centre d'Etudes et de Documentation Prehistoriques, Montignac, Dordogne, France, 1952.

to by anthropologists as goddesses of fertility or earth mothers, on the assumption that their meaning was the same as that of similar art work of living primitives. Late Paleolithic carving emphasizes no other theme more than pregnant females, depicted with grossly exaggerated abdomen and mammaries and in a case or two in the process of giving birth.

Paleolithic art may also have had the function of concentrating the attention of people on objects of veneration, or what Radcliffe-Brown would have called "objects of ritual value." Such objects are clearly means of communication, conveying ideas throughout the tribe. Sacred places and objects probably called for strong emotional response, as the spirit centers of the Australian aborigines have in recent times and as sacred shrines do for the devotees of the world's major religions. Such shrines can serve as focal centers not only of social solidarity but also a society's view of the world. In these respects, the arts could have served the same expressive functions as language.

CONFLICTING INTERPRETATIONS   One of the leading authorities on cave art was the Abbé Henri Breuil, who concentrated his attention mainly on the paintings on cave walls and only secondarily on carved bone, horn, and other smaller objects. Partly for this reason his attention turned largely to animals and the hunting and reproductive magic implied in their representation.

Along with the animal paintings in the caves of Europe are a number of abstract symbols whose interpretation is uncertain. Henri Breuil interpreted the markings in this photograph as a warning of a dangerous passage ahead.

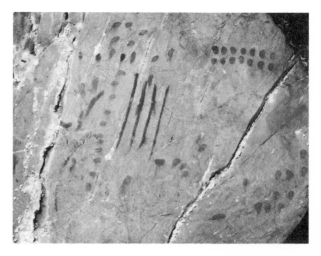

	OVAL	RECTANGLE	KEY SHAPE		HOOK	BARB	DOT
NORMAL							
SIMPLIFIED							
DERIVED							

Leroi-Gourhan believes many symbols to be derived from male or female figures or sexual organs, but in their latest stages the forms change so greatly as to be unrecognizable as such.

Breuil, however, was aware of other markings as well. One figure in Trois Frères cave is believed to represent a shaman, having a human body with an animal mask. Much more abstract drawings are also found—rows of red and black dots, parallel lines, clublike signs, and rectangular drawings (in contrasting colors) that have sometimes been interpreted rather fancifully as banners. Breuil speculated little about such signs, but assumed some of them conveyed messages. For example, he said of the markings shown on the opposite page, "I believe these signs are topographical, to help the brave explorers of the Reindeer Age to find their way on the visits to the Sanctuary."[2] They occur just before a steep ascent makes the path dangerous if not impassable.

In more recent years the leading authority on cave art has been André Leroi-Gourhan,[3] who has turned his attention to dating the sequence of art forms and also to the problem of interpretation of the abstract symbols. His arrangement of artistic sequences seems very reasonable and shows a progression in ability to represent anatomical details and sometimes even to convey a sense of life and motion. (See figure on following page.)

Leroi-Gourhan also places the abstract symbols in chronological order and arranges them all in male and female categories. The earlier and simpler symbols seem to clearly represent male and female figures or sex organs, but

[2]Breuil, ibid., p. 195.

[3]Andre Leroi-Gourhan, *Treasure of Prehistoric Art*, trans. by Norbert Guterman, Henry A. Abrams, Inc., New York, 1967, pp. 136–138.

André Leroi-Gourhan has found developmental sequences in cave art. The later style (top) shows greater attention to detail and proportion and even conveys a sense of life and movement.

the later developments are much less clear and leave questions unanswered (see page 395). Why is there such a profusion of rows of dots? Couldn't the symbol that resembles a stalk of grain actually denote a stalk of grain? Would not the Paleolithic artists have other ideas to convey besides the endless repetition of male and female symbols?

There is a possibility that art was becoming more of a direct means of notation and communication than has previously been thought. Alexander Marshack[4] is convinced that such is the case. After years of making careful, microscopic studies of large numbers of paleolithic art objects, mainly from France in the period of 30,000 to 10,000 years ago, he has found what he regards as good evidence that much carving was being done for reasons of notations of time, of keeping track of lunar months, and recording seasons and the rites and ceremonies that had to accompany changes of seasons.

Consistent with Marshack's reasoning, it is clear that the female "goddess of fertility" shown in the figure on page 398 illustrates a possibility of several interpretations. First, there is little doubt that she is a symbol of fertility. Second, she holds in her hand a horn that may well have further symbolic significance. The horn itself is marked with thirteen straight lines that Leroi-Gourhan would call male symbols. But isn't it possible they are some kind of notation of days or events? Couldn't the horn symbolize the crescent moon and the lines indicate the days of a celebration? This is mere speculation, of course, but much of Marshack's research would make it seem plausible.

Marshack has found what he believes to be human notations on stones and bones of the Upper Paleolithic. Much of what he believes to be lunar-type notations are made with simple notches but frequently grouped in rows of 29 or 30. A lunar month is almost exactly 29.5 days, so it would seem quite logical to represent 1 month as 30 days and the next as 29. Such interpretations are controversial, but they are given indirect support by the fascination the constantly changing moon has held for both primitive and civilized people.

The figure on page 399 is taken from Leroi-Gourhan's work because Marshack's illustrations are not yet released for general reproduction. Particularly, in the bottom row of dots in the figure are several of a type commented on by Marshack—dots that are not round but look rather like phases of the moon. Some positions show very light, outlined circles, possibly denoting the dark of the moon. At the top left is a circle of dots around a center, which could be interpreted as a moon cycle around the earth. Although it is impossible to be sure about the interpretation of such notations, a lunar explanation seems a little more likely than simply assuming that all the dots are male symbols.

[4]Alexander Marschack, *The Roots of Civilization*, McGraw-Hill Book Company, New York, 1972.

The carved female figure is probably a
goddess of fertility, but it is likely that
the horn or crescent she holds also has
symbolic significance. Possibly the lines
carved in the horn represent days or
some other type of notation.

Could some of the dots represent the moon orbiting the earth? Close examination shows that dots in lower groups are crescent shaped, as though they might represent phases of the moon—a possibility raised by Marshack's new interpretations.

Some of Marshack's material is a bit more convincing than the illustration shown here, especially a series of circles imprinted on a bone plaque, arranged in a series of 29, and many in crescent shapes that reverse direction, as the moon does in successive phases.[5]

The second of Marshack's well-developed ideas is that of the recording of seasons. He even speculates that some of the great caves of the Late Paleolithic were visited seasonally for certain rites and that the large number of pregnant animals may indicate that the time of most important rites was in the spring. A series of carvings on a much smaller scale than the cave paintings, however, is presented as his best evidence of the recording of seasons, probably in connection with seasonal rites. A baton found approximately 100 miles inland in southern France and dating from Magdalenian times (the last phase of the Upper Paleolithic) shows an interesting composition of seals, a salmon at spawning time, budding plants, and two snakes, probably at mating season. All are signs of spring, and the fact that all are carved together shows an intense interest in the season.[6] Marshack has also found contrasting carvings of a similar type that he believes denote autumn and winter as well as scenes seeming to show ceremonies of sacrifice.

The Paleolithic artists made advances in communication in many ways. Even their most naturalistic drawings communicated desires for game and reproduction. Some of the more abstract symbols were probably male and

[5]Ibid., p. 45.
[6]Ibid., p. 171.

female, as Leroi-Gourhan suggests. Whether Marshack's conjectures are entirely correct or not, it seems likely that many of the notations had more meaning than mere decoration. The men of the Late Paleolithic were grappling with the problems of communications that would last through long periods of time.

THE WEDDING OF
LANGUAGE AND ART

The late Paleolithic in Europe came to an end with the retreat of the last glaciation and the extinction of the woolly mammoth, woolly rhinoceros, bison, and other great animals of the Ice Age. The succeeding period is referred to as Mesolithic, the time between the Old and the New Stone Age. Cave art declined, but carvings on bone, stone, and ivory continued, often reduced in size and more stylized than the previous art work.

"Stylization" here refers to a departure from nature in a manner characteristic of a particular time and culture. The grotesquely exaggerated fertility goddesses of the Paleolithic were stylized to a degree, but recognizable. Stone Age anthropomorphs (manlike figures) are stylized further. In a few cases, cattle are recognizable only by a pair of horns. In such a type of stylization, the principle of *pars pro toto* (the part stands for the whole) is used.[7] This principle is obvious in the stylized eye idols of ancient Sumeria (ca. 3000 B.C.) (see the following figure) and in many of the Egyptian alphabetical symbols to be presented later.

Eye idols of Sumeria, 3000 B.C. The eye idols illustrate the idea that the part can stand for the whole, an idea useful in the development of writing systems.

Artistic stylization bears a slight resemblance to abbreviation in writing. If carried too far it can lack much of the ready comprehensibility of more naturalistic art, but it gains in economy of expression. The style can become increasingly abstract, until, like words in a language, it has no meaning whatever except that conferred upon it by the culture that produces it. Many Mesolithic markings seem to be of this type, possibly symbolizing ideas or objects of nature, but with meanings hidden to us or given to varied interpretations.

Nearly all art is stylized to a degree. Even modern artists, struggling for originality and uniqueness, tend to develop recognizable styles, identifiable by periods. Primitive artists are less concerned with originality than moderns, even though they may think of their own art as better than that of others. They stay within guidelines of style and can readily tell the art product of their own people from that of others. The differences in artistic styles may help to account for the great differences in writing styles that developed in Mesopotamia, Egypt, China, and Mesoamerica.

In the settled villages that emerged in the Mesolithic and grew more numerous with the Neolithic development of agriculture and animal husbandry, the need for records increased. The only one of the early civilizations not to have developed a writing system was that of the Incas, and even they developed a means of sending messages by knotted ropes. Seasonal observances were, if anything, more important for agricultural peoples than they had been for hunting peoples; in this respect the Incas were no exception. In many parts of the world, the need to record events connected with gods and kings became almost obsessive, and often the notational systems had a touch of magic about them. Trade increased, and along with it a need for records and accounts of fields and crops and trade items. Some of the very earliest attempts at writing related to such records (see illustration, page 402).

CUNEIFORM WRITING   Ancient Sumer, located near the mouth of the Tigris-Euphrates, was developing an incipient writing system early in the fourth millennium B.C. The Sumerians had simple stylized pictures, or pictographs, for a number

[7]M. E. L. Mallowan, *Early Mesopotamia and Iran*, McGraw-Hill Book Company, New York, 1965, p. 60.

The earliest Mesopotamian writing used pictographs and abstract symbols, stamped in clay as were the later cuneiform writings.

of words—sheep and cows, human heads, walking, agricultural implements, and temples, for example. They also had old symbols that had long been used on their pottery. An eight-pointed star ⚹ stood for god or heaven or high. ⚴ stood for water, ⬭ for earth, and ⚶ for the deep. Often symbols had a number of related meanings. The symbol for leg also meant "to stand," "to go," and "to carry off." In one or two cases, sound values were attached to symbols, but generally the symbols were either of abstract nature, as in the earth symbol shown above, or were pictographic; nevertheless, the more nearly alphabetical writing of the later civilizations of Mesopotamia began its evolution in Sumer. Sumerian writing, like later Babylonian and Persian, was stamped in clay with a wedge-shaped stylus—a type of writing called "cuneiform."[8]

DECODING CUNEIFORM   In the latter part of the sixth century B.C., King Darius I of Persia faced a series of uprisings and challenges to his right to the throne of the Persian empire. He won decisive victories over his enemies, and to commemorate his victories and discourage ambitions on the part of any new rivals, he ordered that a message be carved onto a high cliff, attesting to his greatness and power. It was duly carved in Persian cuneiform and in two older languages,

402   [8]Ibid., p. 62.

Elamite and Assyrian, so that all could be aware of his power and take warning.[9] The great stone cliff is now known as the Behistun stone and lies on what was once the main route from the old Persian capital at Ecbatana to Babylon.

The Persian empire perished, and the winds of 2,500 years sandblasted the great inscription, but it remained mainly intact. Wandering shepherds saw it and were curious, and so were Arabic scholars of later centuries and the handful of Europeans who chanced to pass through that part of the world. As so often happens in invention and discovery, productive study had to await a moment when such cultural developments as linguistic knowledge had readied scholars for the task. By the early nineteenth century many European scholars were prepared to struggle with the enormous task of decipherment. The best known of these scholars was the Englishman George Rawlinson, who, combining ingenuity with athletic skill, repeatedly climbed the perilous cliff on which Darius had had his message inscribed.[10] Clinging to ropes and improvised scaffoldings, he paper-traced all the cuneiform characters, even those at the top of the cliff, which turned out to be Assyrian. So great was the interest in the mysterious writing that the decipherment task turned into a race, with rivals from France, Germany, and Ireland publishing the first results just as Rawlinson was readying a more thorough and accurate translation. From studying the writings of Herodotus, the linguists learned the words for the

[9]P. E. Cleator, Lost Languages, Mentor Books, New American Library, Inc., New York, pp. 67–70.
[10]Ibid., pp. 90–97.

Well-developed cuneiform writing from Ur, 1900 B.C. The words are simplified and no longer resemble pictographs. Cuneiform writing was useful for business, law, and records as well as for sacred writ.

403

Achaemenid Dynasty and for Kings Darius, Xerxes, and Hystaspes. Eventually the Persian script succumbed to the work of the translators, then the Elamite. The ancient Assyrian turned out to be much more of a problem, being much less alphabetical than either of the other languages. The decipherment was eventually accomplished by Rawlinson, in this case unquestionably first to make real progress. A knowledge of names and the frequent repetition of the word "king" helped to make the task of translation possible.

The translation of the Behistun stone was only the beginning, however, for in the following years more and more Mesopotamian languages began to rise from the dead. A great library housing thousands of clay tablets had been built by the powerful Assyrian king Ashurbanipal, and the ruins of this library were eventually found. Among the tablets were records that seemed untranslatable, even to those who had learned the many varieties of cuneiform writing already disclosed. Messages mentioned such places as Sumer and Ur and Uruk and Eridu, and there were found legends of a people who were said to have emerged out of the Persian Gulf and erected cities at the mouth of the Tigris-Euphrates many ages before the rise of Babylon. Eventually the ruins of such cities were found and with them the knowledge of the Sumerians who first began to change pictures into wedge-shaped marks. Like that of the Egyptians, their written language often depended upon ideograms (combinations of symbols to convey new ideas), as in the following example.[11]

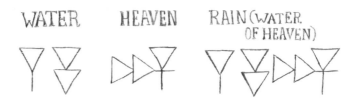

The early cuneiform symbols were cumbersome compared to modern alphabets, and even when they became alphabetical, they omitted vowel sounds. Nevertheless, a very useful writing system had developed and from early times was used by both priests and laymen. Cuneiform tablets recorded wills and documents, business transactions, tax records, weights and measures, historical events, sacred myths, and bits of philosophy and poetry. Man's ability to communicate probably made its first practical advance in Sumer, although the better-known hieroglyphics of Egypt rival the Sumerian accomplishment in antiquity.

[11]Ibid., p. 103.

Nowhere was picture writing more highly developed than in Egypt. Animal paintings on rocks occur in Upper Egypt well before the beginning of the Egyptian kingdoms, and findings from El Gerza in Lower Egypt also date from a period before the First Dynasty. Even in Gerzean times (probably 5000 to 3500 B.C.), Egyptian tomb art showed a combination of methods of recording and communicating. Animal-god symbols occurred along with pictures of the things of everyday life—boats and oxen, shepherds, spears, arrows, pottery. Before the dynastic period of Egyptian history, which starts around 3100 B.C., hieroglyphic writing was developing, using pictographs, ideograms, and phonograms.[12]

"Pictographs" are symbols conveying messages with abbreviated pictures. "Ideograms" fit pictures together to create new ideas, as in the cuneiform example above. "Phonograms" involve a different principle, that of depicting sounds rather than objects or ideas, which is the essence of syllabaries and alphabets, to be discussed later. Much of the earliest tomb art was pictographic, and as such it was able to convey direct meaning even before the language was deciphered. It is interesting to note that when Thor Heyerdahl attempted to build a reed boat of Egyptian type in which to cross the Atlantic, he had but to study Egyptian tomb art to learn all the details of the building and equipping of such a boat.

However, Egyptian writing developed far beyond its early pictographic beginnings, contrary to the beliefs of earlier times. It eventually became largely alphabetic. Egyptian writing took three forms. The carvings on temple walls and on the walls of tombs, nearly always made for sacred purposes, are known as "hieroglyphics." Almost as ancient was a cursive script, known as "hieratic," written on papyrus with a reed pen and also used largely by the priests. Much later, during the Twenty-fifth Dynasty (ca. 600–500 B.C.), a much more rapid, abbreviated form of writing developed, called "demotic" and used more for secular purposes. During the final dynasty of Egypt (the Thirty-first or Macedonian Dynasty), Greek characters also were used considerably.[13]

THE ROSETTA STONE Since the Macedonian descendants of Alexander the Great's conquest were foreigners to Egypt, they had difficulty being accepted as legitimate rulers. To assure acceptance, they gained the support of the priests of Amen-Ra, who set up obelisks proclaiming the legitimacy of the Mace-

---

[12]Cyril Aldred, *Egypt to the End of the Old Kingdom*, McGraw-Hill Book Company, New York, 1965, pp. 21–30.
[13]Cleator, op. cit., pp. 29–35.

donian kings and their status as gods. In 238 B.C., one of several of the Macedonian pharaohs by the name of Ptolemy had such a stone erected at the Rosetta mouth of the Nile, with an inscription in Greek, demotic, and hieroglyphic. Seven centuries later, the Christians triumphed in Egypt and closed the old temples that had trained the priests in hieroglyphic writing, and the ancient language lay dead. The Rosetta stone lay buried for over 1,000 years and was chipped and defaced considerably in the long interval.

In 1798 Napoleon's army was in Egypt on an indirect strike at the British, who had interests there. Some of the French soldiers discovered the old Rosetta stone. Since the Greek text was readable and it was assumed that the other texts carried the same message, the Rosetta stone immediately drew the attention of the scholarly world, but for many years no progress in translation was made. The hieroglyphic text was partly destroyed and later proved to be only an approximate rendition of the Greek. The grammars and orders of words in sentences were very different, and there was no certainty as to which way Egyptian characters ran. As a matter of fact, those on the Rosetta stone ran simply from left to right, but others have been found to run from right to left or up and down or even in circular patterns to fill spaces attractively. Some scholars in the early nineteenth century even questioned whether the hieroglyphics were anything but decoration.

The first progress toward interpretation was made by several researchers who noted that some of the characters were surrounded by a circle that looked something like a noose of rope and is now called a cartouche. They postulated, correctly, that such characters were names of important people or gods. Then a Cambridge scholar, Dr. Thomas Young, studied more diligently, came to the conclusion that the language was actually alphabetical, and correctly deciphered five or six letters.[14] Subsequently, in the 1820s, a young French scholar, Champollion, who had already dedicated his life to the task, made much more

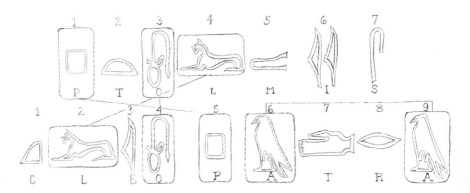

progress in decipherment.[15] From another stone he found what he guessed to be the name Cleopatra. He compared it with what Young had guessed was the name of Ptolemy, with startling results (see illustration, page 406).

Identification of the letters that corresponded in the two names meant that all the other letters were known. Then another name was found—one that had to be Alexander.

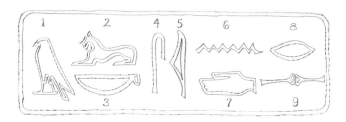

Just as it seemed that an Egyptian alphabet was unraveling and that it would be the clue to the entire hieroglyphic system, Champollion discovered other names that seemed to rest on different principles. One consisted of the following symbols:

The first symbol denoted the sun god, Ra; the final symbol was already identified as standing for an *s* sound. In the middle was a character that seemed to have no phonetic meaning but that Champollion interpreted as an abstract symbol meaning "son of." Hence, the name meant "Son of Ra" or Rameses. A similar type of character made up another name:

Since the god Thoth was represented as a bird, the name was easily interpreted as Thothmes, or "Son of Thoth."[16]

[14]Ibid., pp. 41–43.
[15]Ibid., pp. 43–45.
[16]Ibid., p. 51.

Obviously, Egyptian was not purely alphabetical, but in some cases combined pictographs and abstract symbols into ideographs. There were also specialized symbols denoting male and female, singular and plural, and ends of statements, so that much more had to be learned. Nevertheless, it was clear that, during 3,500 years of dynastic history, Egypt had succeeded in wedding sound to carved or written symbol sufficiently to develop a very useful writing system. In a more distant part of the world, a similar beginning of pictographic inscriptions developed in a different manner.

THE CHINESE
CHARACTER SYSTEM

The civilization of China, because of the obvious antiquity and brilliance of many of its arts and crafts and because of the early development of its writing, was once believed to be older than those of the Near East; but at present the issue is in doubt. Legends of the unification of China begin with the date 2852 B.C., but much of the legend is plainly mythological. Chinese astronomers recorded a solar eclipse in 2186 B.C., during the still unauthenticated Hsia Dynasty. Decorated pottery goes back to 3000 B.C or earlier, and fairly authentic records start with the Shang Dynasty, circa 1500–1027 B.C., the beginning of the Chinese Bronze Age.[17]

During the Shang Dynasty, divination was practiced to foretell the future and to answer important questions. The method of divination was to heat the shoulder bones of cattle until they cracked in the fire and then to read the mysterious messages conveyed by the pattern of cracking. The questions posed to the bone oracle were painted with a brush on the bones and are the earliest known Chinese characters.[18] Many of the characters are the names of kings; some are undecipherable, but of about 5,000 ideograms of Shang times, about 1,500 can be interpreted. Even in those days, Chinese was a monosyllabic language, and it depended on word order rather than tense for making time sequences clear. Often in the oldest form of the written language, pictographic origin is evident. In the modern equivalents, stylization has progressed so far that the pictographic origin is no longer recognizable.

The written language of China, then, gradually became one in which the characters are words in themselves. Occasionally it can be seen how characters combined to make up new ideas. For example, the Chinese word for happiness combines the characters for woman and son, with the implication that any woman with a son is happy. It is only rarely, however, that such clear origins can be found. In the thousands of years of use of the Chinese written language,

[17]William Watson, *Early Civilization in China*, McGraw-Hill Book Company, New York, 1966, pp. 11–15.
[18]Ibid., pp. 58–60.

it has not evolved into an alphabetical system. In one respect, however, sound elements have been brought into it. Many characters in Chinese are made of two parts, one of which gives a hint of the pronunciation and the other the exact meaning. The words for "red," "quarrel," and "quicksilver" are all pronounced "hung." One part, which we might call the "phonetic hint," is the same in each word; the other part is different. "Hung" meaning "red" combines with the character for "silk." "Hung" meaning "quarrel" combines with the character for "word." "Hung" meaning "quicksilver" combines with the character for "water."

A few of the characters, then, seem almost like a puzzle. What sounds like "hung" but can be said of silk? What sounds like "hung" but relates to words? What sounds like "hung" but is something like water? The answers are, respectively, red, quarrel, and quicksilver.[19]

The Chinese language did not die out as did the other ancient languages mentioned so far. It has continued as a difficult but very usable form of writing, harder to learn than alphabetical systems. Chinese governments in recent years have tried to simplify it; and Japanese, based on old Chinese, has been simplified more successfully. Through thousands of years no basic changes had been attempted, partly because of habit, partly because of China's relative isolation from other systems, but largely because the system served its purpose extremely well. Scholars could learn it, keep records, write exquisite poetry and philosophy, relate myths, stories, and dramas, give instructions, describe distant places and people, and invent new characters when necessary. The fact that it was too difficult to be learned by many of the common peasants mattered little until recent times.

Many other writing systems remained too difficult to become common knowledge among the people. This had been true of the older forms of Egyptian and of the languages of the Hittites, Assyrians, and Amorites. Far away from either China or the Near East, another expansion of communication into writing took place. It will be referred to here as the Mayan system, although parts of the system probably originated elsewhere, among the little-known Olmecs to the north of Yucatan.

MAYAN NOTATION AND WRITING The Mayan writing system has attracted very wide attention for several reasons. First of all, it shows a peculiar concentration on notation of dates, based on a solar calendar, a lunar calendar, and another dating system called the "long count." The Mayan numeral sys-

[19]Holger Pedersen, *The Discovery of Language*, Indiana University Press, Bloomington, Ind., 1962, pp. 143–145.

tem is unique and the only one besides our so-called Arabic system (actually derived from India through Arabia) to use decimal placing. The system has a fascination also because it seems to have been the greatest literary achievement of the American Indians. Finally, the very difficulty of decipherment has helped turn attention to the language.

There has been no Rosetta stone for the Mayan script, and all but three of the Mayan books were destroyed during the Spanish conquest; but one Spanish priest, Diego de Landa, copied large numbers of the glyphs and made an attempt at decipherment. His records have helped, although he added confusion to later efforts by his largely erroneous assumption that the glyphs represented alphabetical sounds.[20] His information about the calendrical and numerical systems was correct, and the writings having to do with those systems are the most easily deciphered.

The numeral system was vigesimal; that is, it worked on a base-20 system. A shell-like sign ⬭ was a zero; a dot • represented 1, and a bar ▬ represented 5.[21] However, placement in upper levels multiplied values by 20. Hence the number shown below would be read as 57, since each dot in the upper level counts for 20, and in the lower level each bar counts for 5 and each dot 1.

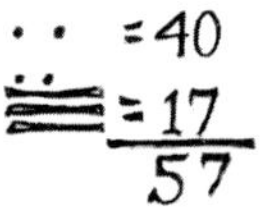

$$
\begin{array}{r}
\bullet\bullet = 40 \\
\equiv\equiv = 17 \\
\hline
57
\end{array}
$$

A bar in the upper level counted for 100 (20 × 5). A dot in the third level represented 20 × 20, or 400, and one in the fourth row (not shown) represented 20 × 20 × 20, or 8,000. The date 1975 could be conveniently written as follows:

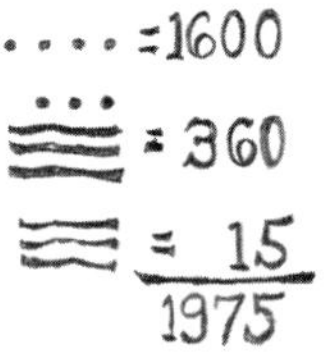

$$
\begin{array}{r}
\bullet\bullet\bullet\bullet = 1600 \\
\equiv\equiv = 360 \\
\equiv\equiv = \ \ 15 \\
\hline
1975
\end{array}
$$

However puzzling it may seem to us, the system worked well enough to be used by merchants as well as by priests and is far better for computational purposes than the old Roman system that had no zeros or placements.

[20]Michael D. Coe, *The Maya*, Frederick A. Praeger, Inc., New York, 1966, pp. 166–167.
[21]Ibid., pp. 156–159.

Although the numeral system was reasonably simple for the Maya, the calendrical system presented additional complications. The system still used a base 20 but also had to use an 18 in order for the year to approximate reality.

```
20 days   = 1 uinal
18 uinals = 1 tun (360 days, or a "vague year")
20 tuns   = 1 katun (7,200 days)
20 katuns = 1 baktun (144,000 days)
```

One tun equaled approximately a year, but the Maya realized there were 5 more days, and they had a dread of those 5 days that failed to come out even—days called the *uayeb*.

There was also a much more puzzling cycle of 260 days, called the long count, or the *tzolkin*, formed by multiplying the magic number 13 by 20. A *tzolkin* of 260 days multiplied by 73 equals 52 years of 365 days each, meaning that every fifty-second year the two systems meshed, making the fifty-second year a portentous time. (The Aztecs also dreaded the fifty-second year, which happens to have coincided with the arrival of Hernando Cortes.)

The Mayan year left out the extra quarter day that is accounted for in our calendar. The Maya were aware of it but did not figure in fractions. Their calculation of the moon cycle is enough to convince us of the precision of their work. The moon completes its phases in an uneven number of days, between 29 and 30. The Maya concluded that 149 moon cycles equal 4,400 days. The calculation is accurate to within three ten-thousandths of a day! The Maya also knew the likely times of lunar and solar eclipses, and they calculated the year of Venus as 584 days, missing it by only eight one-hundredths of a day.[22]

THE WRITING SYSTEM   Enough of the Mayan writing system has been deciphered to make it possible to relate events during the reigns of particular kings and to note the rise and fall of Mayan cities. Early researchers concluded either that de Landa was right and the Mayan system was indeed alphabetic, or that it was totally ideographic, or that it was merely decorative. As we have seen, most early writing systems combine principles, and, according to the very able Russian epigrapher, Yuri Knorosov, this is true of the Mayan.[23] The script has about 287 signs—far too many for an alphabet and far too few for a system in which each sign represents a distinct word. The script, then, must combine ideographic and phonetic principles. The glyphs that are known to date seem

[22]Ibid., pp. 161–162.
[23]Ibid., pp. 166–168.

A page from one of the few remaining Mayan books. Although not fully deciphered, the writing is believed to be partly ideographic and partly phonetic.

to fit Knorosov's theory. Several have been identified in recent years, and the feeling now exists that decipherment will eventually be accomplished.

SYLLABARIES AND ALPHABETS It is obvious from the foregoing illustrations from many parts of the world that certain of the same problems develop in writing systems and that solutions to those problems take some of the same turns. In nearly all cases, simple, stylized pictures are the first step, the step called pictographic. Nearly always the next step is ideographic—applying the picture in a way that relates to ideas not directly illustrated, as when the symbol for foot takes on also the meaning of walking, standing, or even carrying a burden or when the picture of an eye stands for God (the all-seeing eye). Ideograms are difficult to work with, however, and usually an easier method is found, using similar sounds to convey a variety of meanings. In many cases writing systems depended mainly on using such sound designations, with each one becoming a syllable. In such cases, large numbers of sound symbols, each denoting a syllable, were the major part of a writing system. The older Egyptian hieroglyphics were largely syllabaries, and many of the cuneiform systems of Mesopotamia were based on syllabaries instead of true alphabets, especially the Hittite, a few examples of which are shown below.[24] An ancient

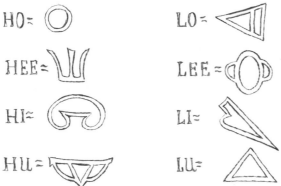

script of Cyprus has been found, still only partly deciphered, that is basically a syllabary. The Japanese, whose language differs greatly from Chinese in being multisyllabic, use syllabaries as well as some of the older Chinese ideograms. The great Cherokee leader, Sequoia, developed a written language for his people that is basically of a syllabary type and was able to teach reading very rapidly with it. Syllabaries reduce greatly the number of characters that must be made to convey meanings, but they still require far more memorization of symbols than do alphabets.

[24]Cleator, op, cit., p. 125.

The examples given from the Rosetta stone and from the Behistun stone make it clear that both the Egyptian and the Sumerian-Babylonian-Persian traditions were moving in the direction of alphabets but that Egyptian still retained some characters of a different type and that cuneiform letters were very complicated. Both writing forms left out vowel sounds, except in a few cases of very late Egyptian.

Besides the Semitic people of Mesopotamia, there were other Semitic-speaking peoples in the ancient world—the Phoenicians, Hebrews, and Aramaeans. Some of the Semitic peoples were among the first to see the utility of a simple phonetic script, and possibly as long ago as 1800 B.C. they began to convert syllables (several of them Egyptian) into consonant sounds. The result was the old Semitic alphabet, developed in its most practical form by the widely traveled commercial people, the Phoenicians, and consisting of twenty-four letters. One of those letters was an ox-head symbol that stood for a glottal stop in Phoenician. A glottal stop is not used in English. It is an unvoiced pause made at the back of the throat that can be approximated by saying such words as "little" and "bottle" without pronouncing the *tt*. The Greeks had no glottal stop, so when they appropriated the Phoenician alphabet, they changed the old ox head into an A, turning the symbol upside down and giving it a vowel sound. Most of their vowels were made of old Phoenician symbols for which they had no sound equivalent. One of the interesting consonants was the D, which took its form from the shape of the delta of the Nile.

From Greece the Semitic-Phoenician alphabet traveled northward into the Balkan Peninsula and eventually into Russia in modified form. To the west it traveled to Etruria and then to Rome, where it underwent other slight modifications to become the Latin alphabet, which eventually spread northward to most of the rest of Europe. The old Semitic alphabet was so good that it did not have to be invented again. Other systems of writing persist, but all alphabetical systems derive directly or indirectly from the old alphabet developed partly from the Egyptian by the Phoenicians and taken from them by the Greeks.[25]

OF MAKING BOOKS
THERE IS NO END   Along with a description of the development of writing, quite a bit has already been said about the use of the writing. In its earliest days writing was used primarily in connection with magic and for lunar and seasonal notation. In societies whose religion could be termed archaic, much of it was used mainly for priestly inscription, the lauding of

---

[25]Harry Hoijer, "Language and Writing," in Harry L. Shapiro (ed.), *Man, Culture, and Society,* rev. ed., Oxford University Press, New York, 1971, pp. 268–295.

priest-kings, and the perpetuation of tradition. Often writing consisted of sterile reproductions of what had gone before. It is tempting to speculate that the rather iconoclastic author of the Book of Ecclesiastes was thinking of the sterility of the writing of his time when he wrote, "Of making books there is no end, and much reading is a weariness of the flesh" (Ecclesiastes 12:12). Whatever the case, man the talking species had become man the writing species. Sometimes his old books, relics of the past, seemed a dead weight on his shoulders. A famous historical character who felt this way was the Chinese emperor Shih Huang-ti (259–210 B.C.), and he ordered the classic writings of China burned in order to escape the authority of their tradition.

Men with very different ideas from those of Shih Huang-ti attempted to stamp out other books. The great library of ancient Nineveh, with its 200,000 clay tablets assembled by Ashurbanipal, was destroyed. Many centuries later the Library of Alexandria was burned for fear its writings did not agree with holy writ. In the Age of Exploration, nearly all the Mayan books were destroyed. Centuries after that, Hitler's government made bonfires of books that collided with Nazi ideology. But the writers of books would not be silenced. Obviously, books did much more than preserve records and pass along traditions. Many of them became challenging and even threatening.

The scholars of India and Greece began to teach men to think logically, and they passed their thoughts along to later generations. The thoughts of the Greeks helped to stimulate the thoughts of such Arabic scholars as the brilliant ibn-Khaldun (fourteenth century) and the Renaissance scholars of Italy, France, Spain, and other parts of Europe. Conversation and oral teaching have always been means of stimulating thought and widening perspectives, but the written word could bridge the gaps between distant countries and centuries of time. The thoughts and knowledge available to the human mind expanded interminably. So far as anyone knows, the human mind has in no way increased its potential through tens of thousands of years, but it now has so much more cultural accumulation on which to build that modern men have often thought of their progenitors as childish and simple. Actually, those very progenitors were laying the groundwork for modernity; they had, over millenniums of time, accomplished the greatest single intellectual achievement of the human species by turning the spoken word into the written word.

The story of written communication has no end. The Chinese invented block printing as early as the sixth century A.D. The idea was known to the Islamic world but was rejected on the grounds that it would be sacrilege to produce the holy Koran by any means but handwriting. Then Johann Gutenberg, in the mid-fifteenth century, invented printing from movable type, and the presses have never stopped since that day. They have been supplemented, instead, by all the media of communication—radio, television, news bureaus, satellites—and even by the computational devices that speed the processes of human thought and solve problems that their maker, unaided, could not solve. New symbols and new systems of logic have evolved, as far from the common man's grasp as were the priest's hieroglyphics from the common layman of antiquity; but their aim is different. The new priesthood of the machine does not hide its secrets in an attempt to preserve tradition but releases them, shattering tradition in ways both exciting and frightening.

Not all historians and anthropologists would go quite as far as the previous pages have in interpreting writing as the watershed between primitive and nonprimitive or between civilization and precivilization. No one would deny its importance, but some will point out that tremendous cultural achievements were possible before writing was invented. In the final section of this book, we must turn to an analysis of the technological side of human development and also to a consideration of how the technical deed and the written word have combined to transform the world into a planet of entirely new problems, unnerving in many ways but probably maintaining the same proportion between human problems and human potential as has existed since the time of the first chipped tools of man's stone beginnings.

PART SIX
THE QUICKENING
PACE
OF CHANGE

Since the perspective of this book has been one of evolving social systems, social change has been a dominant theme throughout. We have looked at the consequences of change in subsistence systems, from hunting through agriculture, and at the frequently accompanying changes from band or village to tribe, state, and empire. We have seen how changes in world view have tended to correspond with other changes in human cultures. Among these changes have been population growth, increased trade in goods and ideas, and sometimes the mingling of social systems, religions, and technologies as people form alliances or invade and conquer one another.

In the discussion of subsistence systems in Part Three, a certain amount of attention was given to technology, but the brief comments made require much supplementation. In fact, a tradition of anthropology is to view man primarily as a tool maker. Such a point of view would provide grounds for starting the discussion of mankind with technology as the moving force in cultural evolution, rather than leaving it to the last. The major reason for postponing the discussion of technological developments is that they, more than any other cultural trait, symbolize today's changing world and lead naturally to a discussion of the present height and plight of human accomplishment.

It is impossible to give a full history of man's technology, but there are a few major developments behind all the detailed inventions that must be mentioned. Some of these are the evolution of transportation, means of organization of manpower, nonhuman sources of energy, exploration, and time- and precision-centered systems of production.

Unfortunately, the types of technological changes that have occurred at an accelerating pace, particularly in the last phases of history, have brought their problems. Systems of social organization and of normative rules and regulations lag behind in the process of change, and the entire world is thrown into a state of imbalance as the technologically advanced societies tend to overwhelm the more traditional societies and force them to react strongly or to fall into a state of relative decline. What are the possible consequences of such changes in the world?

Man has always interfered to some extent with his own evolution, frustrating the natural-selection process by the development of protective cultures and technologies. Will the long-term result of technical and scientific development be the emergence of a human type more fully in charge of its own evolution? What would be the dangers in man playing God to such an extent? What are the reasons for believing, alternatively, that the long process of natural selection and experimentation will continue indefinitely? If the future were slave to our will, what would we yet need to know before we could determine what course to pursue?

We have previously noted the long, slow struggle of man's ancestors from their australopithecine beginnings to their attainment of fully human form and intelligence. We have noted the gradual progression of social and economic systems from the hunting stage to the stage of agriculture and urbanism and from tribalism to state. Along with these changes, we have noted changes in man's perception of the world and his ability to increase rapidly his fund of knowledge by writing his records, his thoughts, and his new findings and stimulating other minds of his own and future generations. The ability to record and to spread the writings of the scribes is not enough, however, to account for the constantly speeding pace of change that has been the legend of the last 4,000 or 5,000 years. New discoveries and inventions were also of vast importance—so much so that at least one prominent cultural evolutionist, Leslie White, would start the story with technical change rather than with the economic, social, and ideational changes that have been stressed so far. There is no question that both types of change advance side by side, one stimulating the other, and that it is very difficult to say which is the prime cause.

Chapter Seventeen
From Stone
to Steel:
Technological
Evolution

New ideas in social organization, systems of exchange and distribution, and systems of government are spoken of as "social" or "nonmaterial" inventions. New techniques in tool production or the harnessing of energy are called "technical" or "material" inventions. These are the kinds of inventions that usually come to mind first when the word "invention" is used. Usually the word also brings to mind intricate mechanical devices or scientific laboratories. Actually, the foundations of invention are much simpler. Malinowski, it will be recalled, emphasized the idea that all people have their science—their practical, and often experimentally learned, means of coping with the material world. In the long processes of trial and error, new tools, new weapons, new materials, new physical and chemical processes, building techniques, and sources of energy have been found.

What are the basic technical inventions that have moved mankind from an age of stone to an age of steel and plastics? How and when were new materials discovered to replace the earlier implements of stone, bone, and wood? What were the roots of the transportation of goods that would eventually extend trade routes, conquer the seas, and change man from a plodding being to one with supersonic speed? What inventions had the effect of speeding up the pace of man's mental life, turning him into a restless, hurried being unlike his mammalian relatives? How did he learn to tap more and more sources of energy and increasingly bend nature to his will? How have all these mechanical changes interacted with his systems of organization and ideas to change his numbers from a mere handful, struggling to survive, to his present swarming billions? In the final chapter we shall examine some of the appalling problems that have resulted from man's conquest of the earth, but for the present we shall examine only the anthropological and historical details of how the task was accomplished.

THE MATERIALS OF CHANGE
The change from Stone Age to modern technology is such a long, complicated story that only a few highlights can be considered. Some of the most important changes are in the general areas of materials, transportation, speed, and energy. These areas of invention overlap to such a degree that it is hard to consider one without the other. However, one of the first steps in technical change had to be change in the materials with which people could work. Eventually the materials would become iron and steel, refined in gigantic furnaces, plastics for the thousands of utilitarian objects of everyday life, and reinforced concrete for building purposes. In the beginning, though, the first steps were merely improvements on the age-old

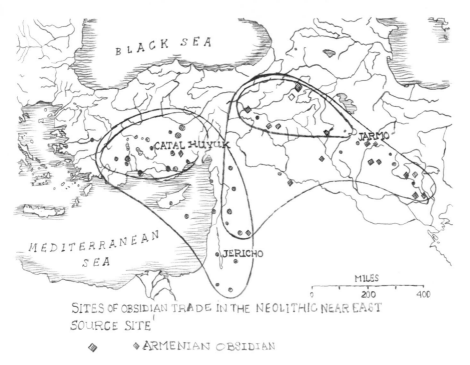

SITES OF OBSIDIAN TRADE IN THE NEOLITHIC NEAR EAST
SOURCE SITE

◈   ◈ ARMENIAN OBSIDIAN

●   ● ANATOLIAN OBSIDIAN

HEAVY LINE SURROUNDS A NUCLEAR ZONE WITHIN EACH TRADE AREA-
THEY DESIGNATE SUPPLY ZONES.

The obsidian trade. In both the Old World and the New, the best stone for tools was sought for and traded over long distances. Obsidian spread from its source in Anatolia to many parts of the Near East.

materials already at hand—bone, shell, and wood, and particularly stone. A brief illustration or two will show how even the search for the right kind of stone constituted a type of science and promoted the trade and exchange of ideas so important to social change.

THE OBSIDIAN TRADE   By the end of the Paleolithic there was a great variety of stone and bone tools—spears and spear throwers, harpoons, chisels, drills, sandstone blocks for polishing, and stone bowls for holding animal fat for fires. Great skill was used in the shaping of spear points and other tools and also in the selection of materials used for their manufacture. Flint, chalcedony, diorite, and any other very hard stone that flakes into sharp points and edges

425

were sought after. Particularly valuable for flaked and polished stone knives, spear points, and arrowheads was obsidian, or volcanic glass. It occurs in places in the Sierra Nevadas of California, and obsidian from such sources has traveled widely, probably traded by mountain Indians for other materials from the valley and seacoasts.

The same type of trade for obsidian took place in the circum-Mediterranean region and the Near East from the early Neolithic until the Age of Metals. Probably such trade was common in many parts of the world, but it has been successfully documented for the Mediterranean and Near Eastern regions. A team of researchers developed techniques for analyzing trace minerals in obsidian so as to be able to trace the point of origin of obsidian tools.[1] They found that the beautiful obsidian knives and mirrors of a 5,000-year-old civilization of Malta came from an island just off the Italian coast 150 miles away. The ancient civilization of Crete obtained its obsidian from a tiny Greek Island close to Rhodes. One of the oldest towns ever uncovered is that of Jarmo, in the north of the Mesopotamian Valley, close to the Anatolian highlands where obsidian is found. By 8000 B.C. obsidian tools were very common at Jarmo. Over 500 miles from the same source of obsidian was the even more ancient town of Jericho, by the Dead Sea in Palestine. Only small amounts of obsidian are found there in as early a period, but by the end of another thousand years obsidian began to spread rather generally throughout the Near Eastern region, even to places very distant from the supply. The trade in obsidian continued to grow until the Age of Metals after 4000 B.C.

The significance of the obsidian trade is not merely in the beauty of obsidian implements found in Palestine, Anatolia, Mesopotamia, and Egypt, but in the search for materials that was obviously in progress and in a growing knowledge of materials. The same growing knowledge is evident when we turn to the very ancient uses of mud and clay for building and for pottery.

CLAY AND POTS   Large numbers of pots and potsherds are found in Mesopotamia dating back to a period of around 5000–4000 B.C., but there is every indication that the first making of pottery is considerably older than that. For example, a large number of brick kilns are found in Mesopotamia by 4000 B.C., and brick kilns are not ordinarily an early development in the making of pottery. It must be assumed that pots were first fired by cruder methods and were not as well made. The earliest Mesopotamian and Egyptian pottery sites usually indicate the use of different kinds of clay and also the use of sand,

[1]J. E. Dixon. J. R. Cann, and Colin Renfrew, "Obsidian and the Origin of Trade," *Scientific American,* vol. 218, pp. 38–55, March 1968.

stone, or organic materials for strengthening and for spreading the heat during firing. Mixtures of clay were different, probably so pots could serve different purposes. The techniques are too advanced to be rudimentary, but the important point is that they seem to show a propensity for experimenting with materials and mixtures.

Recently findings of fragments of pottery dated at more than 7000 B.C. have been made at Spirit Cave near the border between Tailand and Burma.[2] Even this pottery, which along with a variety of grains such as rice and soybeans may indicate greater antiquity for agriculture in Southeast Asia than anywhere else in the world, also shows a considerable degree of sophistication. It is decorated with different designs made by different tools. Some of the pottery is highly polished, indicating good firing techniques that must belong to a tradition that had been long in developing.

The potter's art also developed in Egypt at a very early age, and along with it an attempt to make a type of glaze resembling lapis lazuli, a very rare, vivid-blue mineral highly prized among the Egyptians. In this attempt the Egyptians may have been the first people in the world to synthesize materials. Talc stone was powdered with an ore of copper, probably malachite or azurite, and then heated until the surface resembled blue glass.[3] To produce the effect and to melt the copper ore, a much higher heat had to be attained than was usually needed for pottery, and probably a method of blowing into a closed crucible had to be used. Later small beads resembling lapis lazuli were made by heating sand and soda until the sand particles fused and were covered with the desired blue color. The fusing of sand and copper ore, called Egyptian faience, may have been the first case of fusing in the world's history. Its major significance lies in the heating and melting of bits of copper ore—a first step in the direction of metallurgy.

METALLURGY   Small nuggets of gold were found back in the remote beginnings of urban civilization in the Near East, and the gold was pounded and shaped into jewelry. There are even a few examples of ancient bits of silver, although silver is more rarely found in free form. Occasionally, rather primitive people also have found metals in usable form and pounded them into shape, as in the cases of the Copper Eskimo and of the use of raw iron ore among some of the Indians of the Great Lakes region. True metallurgists do not think of this use of metal that occurs in free form as metallurgy, because no smelting, refining, or

[2] William G. Solheim II, "An Earlier Agricultural Revolution?" *Scientific American*, vol. 226, pp. 34–37, April 1972.
[3] Henry Hodges, *Technology in the Ancient World*, Alfred A. Knopf, Inc., New York, 1970, pp. 62–64.

mixing is done. In many cases, though, it is an obvious step in the direction of metallurgy and shows a growing interest in exploiting more of the materials at hand.

The metal that is most important in the line of development toward modern metallurgy is copper, not gold or silver. Like gold, copper occasionally occurs in nugget form. Raw copper is attractive and malleable, so it can be shaped into jewelry. Copper's first use was probably in eastern Turkey, near sources of copper ore. Later copper was found on the island of Cyprus, from which it gets its name. Another possible first region for the use of copper is at Non Nok That in Thailand, where a copper tool has been tentatively dated at the fourth millennium B.C. Not only had the copper been smelted, but it contained traces of arsenic and phosphorus, which might imply some attempt to use other minerals to harden the metal.[4] In the Near East, the first step toward metallurgy was the annealing of copper, that is, heating it till it becomes soft enough to work and to cause nuggets to adhere to one another.

By 2000 B.C. tin ore was being mixed with copper to harden it. Soon after that, tin was successfully melted from its ore and mixed with copper to make bronze. An active trade in bronze centered around Crete and Cyprus, and later ancient ships sailed to far-off England for tin ore.[5]

In the New World in both Mexico and Peru metallurgy began in a manner similar to the beginnings in the Old World. The oldest evidence of the use of metal is from Peru, around 500 B.C., where the first metal used was gold. By the time of the arrival of the Spaniards, however, the Peruvians made cylindrical furnaces of terra-cotta, called *huairas*. In Peru, Mexico, and Colombia, copper was extracted from ores by smelting. "Metallic tin was also smelted from cassiterite, and lead from galena. In spite of the rudimentary methods used the metals recovered were surprisingly pure."[6] In quality of workmanship, the gold objects made in the New World rivaled anything found in the Old World.

Iron was a more difficult metal to extract than copper, gold, or tin, but its utility for tools and weapons was much greater. The melting temperature of iron is too high for the furnaces of the ancient world, so the early method of use seems to have been to heat it into a spongy mass and then pound it. Iron was available for swords by about 1500 B.C. The Hittites are the first people known to have used iron, and they supplied it to others, but there is no certainty that they were the original inventors. Their early use of iron made the

[4]Solheim, op. cit., p. 41.

[5]Hodges, op. cit., pp. 141–143.

[6]Dudley T. Easby, Jr., "Early Metallurgy in the New World," *Scientific American*, vol. 214, pp. 73–81, April 1966.

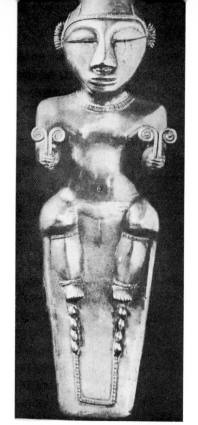

Well before the arrival of the conquistadores, Mexico, Colombia, and Peru had made many advances in metallurgy. The quality of workmanship rivaled anything produced in Europe, as in the case of this gold figurine from Colombia.

Hittites militarily dominant over a vast empire. By about 1000 B.C. the use of iron for tools as well as for swords was fairly common.[7] Eight centuries later an improved draft furnace was developed in China that made it possible to keep a steady flow of air on the molten metal and thus remove much of the carbon from it, making it far less brittle than before. The result was more malleable iron and its gradual replacement of bronze for most types of tools.[8]

So much was learned about new materials during the period of development of urban civilizations that the use of the word "science" does not exaggerate the case. "No one today would any longer think of attributing these enormous advances to the fortuitous accumulation of chance discoveries. . . . Each of these techniques assumes centuries of active and methodical observation," says Lévi-Strauss of developments in agriculture, building, and technology.[9] Henry Hodges says of the metal objects found in the Sumerian tombs

[7]Hodges, op. cit., pp. 144–146.
[8]Ibid., p. 267.
[9]Claude Lévi-Strauss, *The Savage Mind*, The University of Chicago Press, Chicago, 1966, pp. 13–14.

that "the smiths had made considerable technical advances. . . . It is quite clear from the chemical composition of some of the weapons and ornaments that the smiths had been experimenting quite extensively with various alloys."[10] The Age of Iron was on its way, and the uses of iron and steel were to continue to grow for the next 3,000 years.

WHEELS, WAGONS, CHARIOTS

The invention of wheeled transport is generally believed to have occurred in Mesopotamia or near there, but wheeled transport was widely distributed before 2000 B.C. Wheels from that date, or clay models of wheels indicating a knowledge of either wagons or chariots, are found in the Kalmyk steppes of Russian Turkestan, on the lower Dniester River, in tombs in the Georgian U.S.S.R., in Azerbaĭdzhan, eastward to Iran and India, throughout the Near East, throughout the Caucasus region, and in far-away Poland, Germany, and the Netherlands.[11] The first wheels were probably made during the fourth millennium B.C. At first their construction appeared awkward. Wagon wheels were of solid wood and were hewed out of three pieces, held together by struts. Such wheels were adequate for early two-wheeled carts and wagons pulled by oxen. The wheels were not permanently attached but were tied by leather straps so that the cart could be disassembled easily if the terrain was too rough for travel. This kind of construction was widespread in the early days of wagons, suggesting that the idea was copied from a central point of origin. Probably oxen were the first beasts of burden used for pulling carts, but donkeys are shown in a Mesopotamian limestone relief of 3000 B.C.

In Egypt, too, oxen were the preferred beasts of burden at an early date and were used for pulling plows. Ancient tomb carvings show oxen pulling plows without harness, but by means of ropes tied around the horns. In the early period of pyramid building, wheeled transport was not yet in use in Egypt. The giant building blocks were floated down the Nile on rafts and transported in sledges over well-prepared tracks, pulled by large teams of men with towropes.[12] Sometimes, but not always, the sledges were pulled over log rollers to make the task easier. There is no evidence, though, for concluding that the use of rollers led to the use of wheels; it seems possible, but the distribution pattern of wheels suggests that the idea was imported from Mesopotamia. In Mexico and Peru, log rollers may have been used for moving large blocks of

[10]Hodges, op. cit., p. 92.
[11]Stuart Piggott, "The Beginnings of Wheeled Transport," *Scientific American*, vol. 219, pp. 82–93, July 1968.

[12]Hodges, op. cit., p. 99.

The earliest war chariots used heavy wooden wheels and were pulled by donkeys, as shown in this copper model from Tell Agrab, Iraq, approximately 2800 B.C.

stone; but if they were, they did not lead to the development of wheeled transport. Wheeled toys have been found in Mexico, but the wheel for transport was not developed, probably because of the lack of beasts of burden.

Many advances were needed before the ox-drawn, heavy-wheeled cart or wagon could give rise to the war chariot of later times. The earliest known war chariots continued to use solid wooden wheels. The use of wheels probably diffused to the north into the Asiatic steppes, and it is very likely that the same area was the first place of domestication of horses. The nomadic people who drifted southward and moved into the mountain areas to the north of Mesopotamia combined their knowledge of horsemanship with Mesopotamian craftsmanship and soon learned to build much lighter, more maneuverable vehicles for war. Great skill was shown in selecting the hardest wood for making light frames. Wheels became spoked rather than solid. Warfare was revolutionized, and the new devices served the conquering armies of the Hittites and the Assyrians. Egyptian chariots are pictured in the tomb art of about 1500 B.C., but chariots were in use to the north before that time and probably also in China. Later, more changes were made. Metal wheels replaced wooden ones, and new types of harness came in from central Asia or China. There were probably times when the military peoples to the north of the Tigris-Euphrates Valley, equipped with chariots and improved arts of war, had the effect of cutting the Mesopotamians off from their supplies of copper and tin in the mountains of Anatolia and Armenia, which may have had an impact on the development of overseas trade from Lebanon to Cyprus and Crete.[13]

[13]Ibid., p. 137.

Many primitive peoples have been fairly adept at seafaring. In Chapter Three comments were made about the skill of the peoples of the South Pacific, especially the Polynesians. With their knowledge of winds, clouds, currents, and stars and their netlike bamboo charts and rope knots for distance notation, they were far more skillful than the ancients who started the boat-building traditions that were to lead finally to extensive international trade and the Age of Discovery.

In the period before 3000 B.C. commerce moved down the Nile by raft, but also by boats made of bundles of reeds tied together, curved upward fore and aft, and strengthened by tying the ends together with heavy rope. The boats were light and of shallow draft, propelled by oars, and good for negotiating streams. Very similar boats were built on the Tigris and Euphrates Rivers and are still used by the Marsh Arabs at the mouth of the Euphrates. By 3000 B.C. wooden boats as well as reed boats are shown in Egyptian art, built in a very similar shape, with no keel, still of low draft, still relying mainly on oars, but also using a single square sail, probably of linen, supported in the frail craft by a bipod mast.[14]

One thousand years later pictures on Cretan artifacts showed boats of essentially the same shape; the main hull probably was hollowed out of a log, with plank sides added, but still with only one square sail and no keel. Such boats were rowed by from five to ten men. By 1000 B.C., commerce in the Mediterranean was growing more extensive, and the Greeks and Phoenicians were becoming more prominent in shipping. The Phoenicians introduced keels, giving boats greater strength and stability and making them easier to steer. A stone relief found at Nineveh shows a Phoenician warship, with sharpened prow, a high deck carrying soldiers, and at least twenty oarsmen.[15] Far more Phoenician ships were built for trade than for war, and the Phoenicians surpassed the other peoples of the ancient world as seafarers. In those days there were no adequate systems of navigation, and ships sailed from island to island or from promontory to promontory, losing sight of land as little as possible. Although much was known of astronomy and star positions, taking an accurate position by measurement of the apparent elevation of stars was extremely difficult. The North Star was helpful then as now, but far more reference points were needed before a position could be determined on the uncharted open ocean. The ancient Egyptians, Greeks, and Phoenicians made only a bare be-

---

[14]Ibid., p. 98.
[15]G. H. Crone and Alan Kendall, *The Voyages of Discovery*, G. P. Putnam's Sons, New York, 1970, pp. 12–14.

Nile boat from the treasure of Tutankhamen, ca. 1350 B.C. Boats of the period used a single sail, no keel or rudder, and depended on oars for both steering and supplemental power.

ginning at star navigation. The Phoenicians sailed past the Pillars of Hercules out into the open ocean as far as the British Isles. Later the Romans were to do the same, but explorations beyond that point were out of the question, except down along the African Coast where land could be kept in sight. It is believed that the Phoenicians sailed as far as the Gulf of Guinea.

CARTOGRAPHY   The old Egyptians learned some of the skills of surveying and land measurement, as well as a limited use of the stars, in determining locations. The Greek philosopher Thales used such knowledge for working out a system of triangulation for measuring the distance to ships at sea. His contemporary Anaximander (611–547 B.C.) is believed to have been the first map maker and is given credit for inventing the astrolabe—an instrument for measuring the elevation of celestial bodies.[16] The art of map making improved in the ancient world of the Greeks and Romans until the Mediterranean and Black Seas were quite successfully outlined, although Italy continued to be shown extending too far eastward.

[16]Hodges, op. cit., pp. 183–184.

During the Middle Ages, the art of cartography was largely lost. The Greeks had recognized the proper shape of the earth and Eratosthenes had even measured the distance around the earth by observing the elevation of the sun at different latitudes and solving the size of the sphere by trigonometry. Medieval maps, in contrast, showed a flat earth, covered mainly by Europe, Asia, and Africa, with small areas of water around the fringes. Christian belief compounded the many errors of the map makers. According to Christian belief, Jerusalem was at the center of the earth, and the world could be represented as a great wheel with the Holy City at the center.[17] Legends of lands of giants, boiling seas, rivers of gold, the kingdom of Prester John, oceanic whirlpools, and ship-devouring monsters did nothing to relieve the confusion. However, a return to science began before the end of the Middle Ages. Geographical and astronomical knowledge began to drift into Europe from the lands of the Arabs, along with knowledge of rudders and an interest in using the stars for navigation. Prince Henry the Navigator of Portugal opened a school of navigation, collected all the geographical knowledge available, and started his captains on the search around Africa for India. The three-masted caravel with fore and aft booms replaced the old oar-driven galleys of the Mediterranean, and the Age of Discovery was at hand.

The first map projection was devised by a Dutch geographer, Gerhardus Mercator, in the sixteenth century. The Mercator map has confused school children ever since, because it distorts sizes in high latitudes; but it nevertheless had many advantages for navigation. Its primary advantage lay in spreading the world out on a grid system in which all parts could be described in terms of latitude and longitude. The use of the prime meridian did not develop until centuries after Mercator's death, so that not all countries started numbering longitude from the same reference point, but scientific navigation was well under way.

SCIENTIFIC NAVIGATION   During the days of Henry the Navigator, much better methods of map making were devised, and the magnetic compass, first used in China, became standard equipment. An awareness of prevailing winds helped navigators to ride the trades and avoid the doldrums. Much navigation continued to be largely "by God and by guess," however, and few of the explorations of the great Age of Discovery could be called scientific in the modern sense of the word. Precision in navigation awaited standardized mapping, a sextant for measuring the stars, a mathematical system for tracing the azimuths of stars on a map, and extremely accurate timepieces. Ships' clocks were of

[17]John R. Hale, *Age of Exploration*, Time-Life Books, New York, 1966, p. 31.

tremendous importance because the sun, moon, and stars all appear to move across the sky diurnally and to change their positions seasonally. Approximate knowledge of the locations of heavenly bodies and the time of night was of some help, but finding exact locations called for near perfection. Navigation was only one of many developments that has made the measurement of time, and even attitudes about time, important to modern man—and psychologically almost enslaving.

TIME AND PRECISION   As was observed in the previous chapter, notations of time have fascinated many cultures, particularly time as measured in lunar and solar cycles. In the case of the Maya, it will be recalled, time was measured with notable precision, especially the phases of the moon and the year of Venus. Much of the work of early civilizations has shown extreme precision in other directions. For example, the largest of the pyramids is perfectly aligned by the four compass points. It is 755 feet on each side, and the dimensions of the sides differ by less than 8 inches. Some of the blocks of stone, the largest of which weighs 50 tons, are set together with seams of 0.0001 inch.[18]

Much of the concern of the ancients over accuracy in calculations of sun and moon had to do with a dread of eclipses. The fact that an eclipse of the moon can occur only when the moon is full and in the path of the ecliptic, just opposite the sun, has been known since ancient times by Babylonians, Chinese, and Mayans, among others. The builders of Stonehenge must also have been aware of this fact. An astronomer, Gerald S. Hawkins, has found that the fifty-six holes (called Aubrey holes) on the outer circle of Stonehenge correspond to a lunar eclipse cycle for the period 1600–1450 B.C.[19] Any year in which the northernmost winter moonset was over one particular stone (as seen from the center) would witness an eclipse of the harvest moon. This would happen at slightly irregular intervals of 19, 19, and 18 years, adding up to 56 years, which would be the only number giving regularity to the series. If Hawkins is right, some types of astronomical calculations achieved astounding accuracy for people who were in most respects quite primitive. Whether the conjecture is entirely right or not, it is true that Stonehenge shows large numbers of alignments with reference to summer and winter solstice, spring and autumn equinoxes, and the extreme northerly and southerly positions of moonrise and moonset.

[18]Lewis Mumford, *The Myth of the Machine: Technics and Human Development*, Harcourt, Brace & World, Inc., New York, 1962, p. 196.
[19]Gerald S. Hawkins, *Stonehenge Decoded*, Dell Publishing Co., Inc., New York, 1965, pp. 132–148.

The sun rises over the heelstone of
Stonehenge on the longest day of the
year—one of many alignments worked
out by the early inhabitants of England
around 1700 B.C. Many early civilizations
showed remarkable accuracy in years,
lunar months, and other calendrical
calculations.

Accurate astronomical knowledge is very important to a knowledge of time and to navigation by sun and stars, but a more important and much later development was that of precision in calculating the hour of the day. Sundials and water clocks are extremely ancient but have certain drawbacks. Sundials can work only while the sun is shining, and water clocks can freeze in cold weather. Sundials also need corrections for seasons of the year, which were first made by Anaximander. If we try to compare time by a sundial with time as calculated by a clock, there will be certain differences. The most obvious one is that a clock is set by standard time, whereas a sundial follows true solar time for the place in which the dial is located. There is also a less commonly known problem, and that is that the apparent path of the sun through the sky is not uniform at all seasons of the year—a reflection of the fact that the earth moves more rapidly in some parts of its orbit around the sun than in others. Many globes have a figure-eight-shaped device, called an analemma, that gives the sun's declination and also the equation of time, which is the amount of time that must be added to solar time to get what is called mean (or medium) time. It is this type of absolute precision that was necessary for the eventual triumph of timekeeping devices in navigation; in fact, standard instruments were eventually maintained by governments for the exact calibration of time.

However, it must not be assumed that accuracy in timekeeping for navigational and astronomical purposes was the major achievement of the mechanical clock. Somehow a new consciousness of time was born, and man began to regulate his life by the clock. To this day, many people still do not pay much attention to time, but the growth of modern capitalism and industrial systems is closely tied to timekeeping. "Time is money," said Benjamin Franklin. Years later the literary champion of imperialism, Rudyard Kipling, was to say, "If you can fill the unforgiving minute with sixty seconds full of distance run. . . . Yours is the world and everything that's in it."

Lewis Mumford has some interesting thoughts on the process by which time consciousness of a new type crept into the Western world.[20] As is generally known, monastic life in the Middle Ages was not only a life dedicated to God but also a life divorced from the chaos of the times. The monastery was a place of extreme regulation and predictability, such as was impossible elsewhere, and monastic vows often included the thoroughly regulated life. Bells were rung at regular intervals to keep people on their schedules. In Mumford's view, the Benedictine order, once including as many as 40,000 monks, was the order

[20]Lewis Mumford, *Technics and Civilization*, Harcourt Brace Jovanovich, Inc., New York, 1934, chap. I, "The Monastery and the Clock."

most dedicated to hard work and regulation and helped to interject the regularity of clockwork into human life. Clocks were developed in the fourteenth century, powered by the downward movement of pendulums hung from high bell towers. It was not until the eighteenth century that coil springs were used for power, so that smaller clocks and eventually watches could be carried around, but the precision of meshing gears had already come about. Not only did the timepieces symbolize an emerging time-driven society, but the making of clocks provided the practice needed for the inventions that were to come.

As Mumford points out, there is nothing precise and timelike about human nature. One of the problems to which anthropologists must become accustomed is that of dealing with people whose lives are regulated merely by sunlight hours and whose days cease when the sun goes down. For Western man, though, the clock set the time pattern, and other devices had to be invented so he could fall in line—better lamps, for example, so that if short sunlight hours in the winter cut down on the time that properly belonged to the workday, the problem could be overcome. By the fourteenth century, the practice of dividing hours into 60 minutes and minutes into 60 seconds became widespread. It took many more years, but the time came when Western man looked upon such divisions as a true measure of natural realities and moral goodness was largely a matter of filling each available second. The time-centered societies began to fit together the vast numbers of inventions that had had their beginnings in the ancient world and suddenly accelerated in the eighteenth century; and the regulation, organization, and timing of these societies led to new sources of energy and productivity.

THE POWER OF THE SUNS   White is one of the strongest proponents of the idea that cultural level is determined basically by technological development. He speaks of four kinds of components of cultural systems—technological, sociological, ideological, and sentimental or attitudinal, but he does not rate these equally as causative forces. "The technological factor is the basic one; all others are dependent upon it. Furthermore, the technological factor determines, in a general way at least, the form and content of the social, philosophic, and sentimental factors."[21] Going a step further, he narrow the technological component into the two factors of energy and tools, admitting, however, that environment helps to determine how effectively energy and tools can be used. The three factors of energy, tools, and environment are reduced to a formula, $E \times T \times V \to P$, in which E = energy, T = tools, V = environment, and P = the total

[21]Leslie A. White, *The Evolution of Culture*, McGraw-Hill Book Company, New York, 1959, p. 19.

product or cultural level. Finally, he summarizes his view in the statement "Culture advances as the amount of energy harnessed per capita per year increases, or as the efficiency or economy of the means of controlling energy is increased, or both."[22]

So far, considerable mention has been made of tools and inventions, but little has been said of energy as such. At first glance, it will seem that White's extreme emphasis on energy makes nearly all cultural progress a recent phenomenon, because we of the modern world are inclined to think of the harnessing of energy as starting at approximately the time of James Watt and his steam engine. Actually, that is an extremely narrow view of the subject of energy, as White makes clear when he subdivides the aspects of energy into biological and technological. The coming of the agricultural revolution, when man first began to settle down to planting and harvesting on a permanent or semipermanent basis, was an important time in the development of human energy, because food supply and the consequent energy of man became more dependable. Not only was the level and consistency of human energy increased, but that energy was converted into more permanent products. Man was able to build more substantial houses and to accumulate products of his labor that had been impossible to accumulate during his untold centuries of a wide-ranging hunting existence. Much more important from the point of view of energy, however, was the organization made possible by some of the increasingly complex agricultural systems—particularly those depending upon irrigation and able to organize people for the control of river systems.

THE FIRST MEGAMACHINES   So great are the implications of the organization of human energy that Mumford applies the word "megamachine" for the first time to the ancient pyramid-building civilization of Egypt. Unaided human energy was able to accomplish feats that seem nearly inexplicable today, and what was true of the pyramids of Egypt was also true of the Great Wall of China, the Hanging Gardens of Babylon, and the Colossus of Rhodes. All were built by massive application of human labor, organized with machinelike precision, long before the age of sophisticated machinery or mechanical energy. The early type of human machinery centered in the institution of divine kingship and the supporting power of the sun god. In Egypt, even before the First Dynasty, the impressment of 120,000 prisoners and 400,000 oxen was recorded.[23] Much more important than the pharaoh's capacity to capture, though, was his capacity to conscript the manpower of his subjects and to rule over a

[22]Ibid., p. 21.
[23]Mumford *The Myth of the Machine*, p. 192.

439

The massive harnessing of human energy into what Mumford calls the "megamachine" was first accomplished by the autocratic rulers of Egypt.

gigantic bureaucracy that was able to control all of Egypt. It was this capacity that produced the giant human machine—the megamachine—that quarried, cut, transported, lifted, and fit nearly 2,500,000 blocks of stone averaging 2 1/2 tons each to build the gigantic pyramid of Cheops. And the organizational skill was achieved with incredible rapidity. A bare 150 years elapsed between the building of the first step pyramid and the construction of the greatest colossus of the pyramid age, the Great Pyramid of Cheops. Similar types of achievements in the organization of human energy were accomplished in the monumental ages of many early civilizations. Men had learned that a major part of the secret of energy is its channelization. At the same time they were taking steps in the development of other sources of energy besides human power.

The power of the god-kings declined and their age passed into oblivion, but before the early civilizations of the ancient river valleys had run their course, they had pointed a way, portentous for both good and evil, for the organization of human populations into human machinery. One special application of this type of organization—the war machine, first developed by the conquerors of Mesopotamia—has remained with us ever since. Both the productive capacity and the destructive capacity of megamachines were to grow through the ages with the implementation of more forms of power and energy.

NONHUMAN ENERGY   On the technological side, energy was harnessed by man in many ways long before the coming of the industrial revolution. The harnessing of animal power began in the fourth millennium B.C., first, as far as is known, with the hitching of oxen to the plow and later, to sledges, carts, and wagons. This was the line of development that would lead to chariots and other conveyances and to teams of horses and mules. Another early development of nonhuman energy has already been dealt with at length—the use of water and wind. The earliest use of logs and rafts was an application of nonhuman energy. The great building blocks of the pyramids were floated down the Nile on rafts. It is believed that the giant stones of Stonehenge were brought by raft all the way from Wales to the south coast of England. Along with the use of floatation power came other inventions connected with the use of water.

The *shadouf* is not worked by waterpower, but it was the first mechanical means of lifting water from the Euphrates and the Nile for agricultural purposes, in use by about 2000 B.C. The *shadouf* was a long beam with a water vessel at one end and a counterweight at the other. The vessel was lowered into the water by hand, but the counterweight made its lifting easy. The principle of leverage was used. Many centuries later a waterwheel was invented, probably first used in Egypt, for lifting water from the river. Such a device, still in use, was turned by animal power. A more important type of waterwheel for powering a mill was probably first used in Greece in the first century B.C., and such mills later became common throughout the Roman Empire, used mainly for grinding grain.[24] Several improvements were made on them. The first waterwheels could operate only where a rapidly flowing river was available; eventually water was impounded in a mill pond and released steadily so that even sluggish streams could be put to use. Mills of such types continued to be used in all parts of Europe until the industrial revolution rendered them obsolete.

Considerable mention has already been made of ships and sails. The harnessing of wind power for the use of ships goes back at least 5,000 years. With the gradual improvement of sails, wind eventually became the primary source of energy for the shipment of the commerce of the world—in Europe and America, in the Arabic world, in India and Southeast Asia, and in the Orient. Wind was cheap and nonpolluting and did not call for the exhaustion of precious resources, but it required great skill and manpower for use and lacked something in dependability and speed. Wind for the turning of windmills was a much later development, being introduced into Europe about the twelfth century A.D. The importance of windmills eventually became con-

[24]Hodges, op. cit., pp. 224–226.

siderable, not only for operating machinery for grinding mills but for pumping water for irrigation and for drainage, as in the Netherlands. Since wind power is cheap, it continues to be used for pumping water in many poorer areas of the world.

STEAM AND RECENT SOURCES OF ENERGY   Several faltering attempts were made to put steam to use before the time of James Watt, but, in 1774, he became the first inventor of a successful steam engine. From then on the mining of coal for power turned into a frantic rush, and the new systems of factory and mine began to organize (and often degrade) labor in new ways. Steam was soon applied to railroad locomotives and to ships, and it began to replace water-power as the energy for factories and mills of all kinds. The principles of the electric dynamo were discovered by Michael Faraday in the 1830s, but the use of electricity lagged behind the use of coal and steam. By the end of the nine-teenth century, just as electricity was finding its practical applications, gasoline and the internal combustion engine were developed, ushering in the age of the automobile and the airplane.

The initial results of the steam engine and the dynamo were tremendous in terms of productive capacity and cultural potential. Historically, these in-ventions have often been thought of first in terms of the international struggle for supremacy. During the nineteenth century, the new sources of energy made England the leading world power, but they were already promoting a great international scramble for the raw materials and the markets of the world.

The results of the sudden unleashing of such volumes of energy and the concomitant productivity had a devastating impact on the very part of the world that has traditionally been of greatest interest to anthropology—the non-industrial world. Old crafts were abandoned in favor of cheap manufactures. The bow, the spear, and the dibble stick that had from time immemorial been the symbol of man's struggle for survival were now but artifacts of a dying world. The baskets, woven with infinite care and skill, and the pottery, dec-orated with the sacred symbols of the people, were now as nothing compared to the floods of Western goods. Missionaries and governments followed the foreign traders, undermining old beliefs and customs and transforming old systems into sociological wreckage.

The energy that produced the goods of commerce also produced the weapons of war, and the fantastic megamachines of the modern industrial powers scoured the earth for industrial minerals and scorched it with flame and bombs. Then, in 1945, the ultimate release of energy was felt in the blast of the first atom bomb, with "the power of the sun." The power of Amen-Ra,

442

the god of the sun, and his pharaohs had never been so great. The power of which Leonardo da Vinci had warned was upon us, the power "to disturb the tranquil stillness of the air, and transform it into the hue of night, to create coruscations and tempests with dreadful thunderclaps and lightning flashes rushing through the darkness, and with impetuous storms to overthrow high buildings and uproot forests, and with these to encounter armies and break and overthrow them."[25]

Over a period of, at most, 7,000 years, stone had turned to copper, to bronze, to iron, and to steel. The muscle of man and beast had been supplemented and nearly replaced by wind and water, by steam, and wondrous new forms of energy. The need for schedule and efficiency, symbolized by the clock, had set a new pace. The productivity and security made possible by all the other changes made man the master of the world—a world that he conceivably could convert into a home more suitable to his nature and needs than he had ever known before, but a world that he now had the power to destroy.

[25]Cited in Mumford, *The Myth of the Machine*, p. 291.

Chapter Eighteen
Man as
Evolutionist

In the long course of human development, increasingly complex levels of culture have generally resulted in an ability to support larger numbers of people, to increase material abundance, and to establish control over larger areas. The more technically advanced societies have enjoyed lavish displays of their technical ability, from the age of the pyramids to the age of skyscrapers, world fairs, and space rockets. They have meted out their surpluses of wealth and energy for such purposes and also to support luxury classes, to beautify their environs, and to further whatever it is that they regard as progress. Many early peoples thought of the Golden Age of Man as something belonging in the past and were therefore not particularly progress oriented; but to the modern world, progress is the deity that has replaced all others, and it is measured almost exclusively in technological terms.

The pursuit of progress brought the world of the technologically advanced states into a position of dominance. Nineteenth-century man looked forward to an ever-expanding economy and the eventual spread of all the blessings of his type of civilization throughout the world. Many thought the age of really devastating wars had come to an end with the downfall of Napoleon and that only minor disturbances would any longer stand in the way of progress.

In America, the West was won and the last Indians were being Christianized, civilized, and culturally sterilized, while overseas Hawaii and the Philippines were receiving the blessings of American rule. England, Germany, and France were spreading their control into Africa, which everyone insisted on calling "the dark continent." The United States had opened Japan to the world, and the great powers were gradually opening all the ports of China, while mother Russia spread her influence eastward into Siberia and southeastward to the Muslim people of Turkestan. Missionaries traveled to all corners of the world, converting the heathen, whose hearts, they thought, had long yearned for the messages of his European and American brothers.

Then there came the shock of two World Wars, the horrors of Hitler, the growth and spread of communist systems, the end of old imperial regimes, restive minorities in all parts of the world, and a revulsion against the inroads of the West. The world no longer appreciated Kipling's advice to Europeans to "take up the white man's burden." The exuberant confidence of the Western world was visibly shaken.

Superficially, it would seem that the world should be a happier place than ever before, because technological progress has brought a vision of freedom from hunger and want to the human species. What, then, are the problems accompanying this increased productivity and the spread of new technologies and products to the entire world? What happens to the old bonds of kinship and tribe, and what new ties attempt to replace them? What happens to the old beliefs that have so long provided meaning, hope, and a sense of cultural rightness? Has culture itself, the very thing that has given man his superiority over the other species, reached some kind of imbalance that compels it to change too fast to be recognizable and to give the security it has provided in the past? Finally, are all the distinctive cultures of the world destined for absorption into one vast supersystem, and if so, with what consequences?

PARADOXES OF PRODUCTION In the third section of this book attention was given to a variety of ways of life, ranging from hunting and gathering to developed agriculture and early civilization. The paradoxes of productivity were becoming apparent in the societies discussed, because improved means of wresting a living from the land did not assure an abundance for all people. It certainly made possible in a variety of ways the support of more people and increased cultural potentials, but it steadily widened the distance between rich and poor. In early civilizations, whole classes of people were degraded into lowly status and were considered easily expendable. One reason was that property was increasingly monopolized by the ruling classes, and the poor were dispossessed. The irreducible minimum required for survival was no longer guaranteed. Another reason may have been that in the most productive areas of the world population was rising to the point of straining means of livelihood, making poverty the inevitable state of many. At the same time, the rich river valleys supported wealthy classes in a standard of luxury never known before, so that such civilizations were watched hungrily by people of the surrounding mountains, steppes, and deserts. The situation has its modern parallels.

INTERNATIONAL IMBALANCE   Just as imbalances in the ancient world arose and caused envy of the agriculturally advanced areas, so the imbalances of the present world lead to envy and resentment. There are two or three portentous differences, however. First, the imbalances are much greater than ever before. Although the underdeveloped countries strive to move forward industrially and many of them actually do, they are plagued by the ever-accelerating rate of growth of the world's most advanced economies. Furthermore, the technologically advanced nations offer greater opportunities to the well-trained industrial technician than do the slowly developing areas of the world, and they often tempt the educated away from their native lands and into the countries of maximum opportunity—a situation that has long been referred to as the "brain drain."

Another problem is that international differences are becoming more apparent. In the ancient world, only those people in direct contact with advanced civilizations knew what there was to envy and possibly to plunder. Now the great advances in communication have made the people of the underdeveloped world highly conscious of the way of life of Europe and the United States. The result is great impatience with their own governments, a growing feeling that they should be able to attain the living standards of the Western world and to do so rapidly. Often they are ruled by regimes that they see as obsolete or exploitative or both, and the appeal of new methods and ideologies grows. The communist promise of an equalitarian paradise is in many ways a delusion and a snare, but it offers rapid organization and change, an end of the old-type exploiters, and economic independence from the former colonial powers. There is, therefore, a third new problem resulting from imbalance

One of the paradoxes of modern
technological progress is the widening of
the gap between the affluent and the
impoverished, as in this contrast between
Palm Beach, Florida, and Calcutta, India.

between the wealthy and the poor lands, and that is the presence of an ideology that attempts to mobilize and unite the latter. However, since old animosities between nations and races and old national ambitions continue, the attempt at unity is not successful. The net result is a world of great unrest and minimal predictability, at the very time when new industrial systems require the greatest possible predictability.

HUMAN SURPLUSES   More than ever before, systems of production result in increasing numbers of surplus people. The untrained, the unskilled, the people of little academic ability were once badly needed for physical labor. Now the industrial systems are finding their labor a surplus commodity. Recently even the educated and well trained are finding themselves in a competitive job market that threatens to make them part of the surplus. The same is often the fate of the aged, who were valuable in many preliterate societies for constituting the tribal memory. In agrarian societies, too, they were able to drift into old age slowly, working less but not entirely useless. Now they must be totally removed from the world of production, and their obsolescence is made obvious.

For many years, however, the much more apparent problem of surplus people has been that of a rising world population. Medical science is one of the factors that has made the burgeoning population possible, but even more important has been the increasing level of productivity. The first essayists on the problem of population, writing at the beginning of the nineteenth century, assumed that famine and disease would do much to hold world population in check. Now the worst plagues are fairly well controlled, and factories and fields manage to turn out enough production to avert, or at least delay, massive starvation. Nearly all students of the problem realize, though, that population increase cannot go on forever without risking the extinction of the earth; one of the paradoxes of the present production system that feeds the 4 billion people of the world is that it might be destroying the very world on which the people feed.

EXHAUSTION AND POLLUTION   For years there has been a rising crescendo of voices protesting the contamination of air in the world's great cities. More recently, attention has turned increasingly to the contamination of the rivers, lakes, and seas and to contamination by pesticides. A number of underdeveloped lands have profited in recent years by new agricultural products that have brought them a "green revolution"—a rapid increase in farm production.

Sometimes the increases in farm production, however, can be brought about only at the price of heavy use of pesticides, and a debate rages as to which is the worse of two evils, inadequate production or eventual contamination of the environment.

The problem of pesticides is only one phase of the great technological dilemma of the modern world. Adequate sources of electricity now seem to be available only with the development of more atomic plants, which increase problems of disposal of deadly atomic wastes. Oil resources are dwindling, and many of the best reserves are along seacoasts. Their development poses a threat of oil leakages and contamination of the ocean; oil transport tankers pose the same threat. If the previously considered problem of relieving the world's great imbalance in wealth is met by bringing the poorer countries of the world up to the productive levels of the wealthiest nations, the effect on the world's environment could be catastrophic. At present, the United States, with approximately 6 percent of the world's population, accounts for about 40 percent of its industrial waste products. If all the masses of China, India, and Southeast Asia were to be equipped with American or European cars and mechanical appliances, the processes of pollution and resource exhaustion would accelerate incalculably.

TECHNOLOGY AS THE MASTER   Another of the disturbing problems of the brilliant technology and productivity of the modern world is basically one of values. As populations become increasingly involved in the scramble to produce more and more wealth and steadily raise the standard of living, it turns out that material desires are insatiable. The old dream of a nation of people well fed, well housed, and able to spend a modest amount on the comforts of life has become outdated. A whole sales technology is created to convince the public that it has basic needs previously undreamed of. The products of industry must be sold so that more can be created, so that more can be sold at an ever-accelerating rate; and the standard of living must become ever more demanding or the goods cannot be sold. Observations about the increasing aspirational level in the United States have been made for many years, but the United States pattern is becoming more and more the model for much of the rest of the world. The same productivity-consumption race is afoot elsewhere.

Technology seems to have set forces in motion that no one can control. A technological compulsion tells us that if capabilities exist, they must be used; and those capabilities increase at a rate that outruns human prediction. A very thoughtful journalist has phrased the dilemma well:

Technology so masters man that he feels compelled to produce whatever is technically possible, whether it be a supersonic jet, hydrogen bomb, or dangerous pesticide.

> Finally, there is a possibility that the technological juggernaut is out of control— rumbling down a mountain while the managers oil its wheels. Nobody really steering it. Nobody able to stop it. Not the Congress or the President or the merit-badge bureaucracies or anyone else.[1]

It is partly thoughts about the machine as controller of the pace of life and, in a sense, master of man that have led to a withdrawal reaction against science and technology. Critics of the antiscience point of view can well point out that we are blaming the machine instead of the driver, the bulldozer rather than the developer, the bomb rather than the bombardier. In a sense this is true, but there is also an awareness that the machine itself compels many decisions on the part of its maker and drastically changes his style of life. It even changes his life style regarding such fundamentals as basic human interaction.

THE HUMAN BOND   The discussion of the human bond in Part Four started with the family and the kinship group. Often the kinship group consisted of those people to whom the individual felt akin, whether they were biological kinsmen or not.

[1]William Braden, *The Age of Aquarius: Technology and the Cultural Revolution*, Quadrangle Books, Inc., Chicago, 1970, p. 18.

The family and kin could be called those people with whom one shares primary-group relations—relationships close enough that each individual is involved in the lives and problems of the others, feelings close enough to preclude indifference and to ensure a sense of belonging. In social and political organization the trend throughout thousands of years has been in the direction of more complex societies that supplement many of the functions of kinship and supersede others. Productive labor is no longer a family function but is carried on, for the most part, in vast, impersonal factories, bureaucracies, and institutions. Education is only partly a family matter; much of the process of education is formalized and bureaucratized. Living arrangements are still centered in the nuclear family but make interaction among more distant kinsmen increasingly difficult.

A number of studies have been done concerning the response of the people of Africa and Asia to the living conditions of the growing cities. It was supposed that the immediate result of urbanization would be the collapse of the extended family. Actually, such families still continue in long-established urban environments in places where extended families for centuries have had the function of taking care of their own members. Several studies of such old cities as Lagos and Timbuktu show a continuation of family cohesion, partly because of a lack of other institutions to rely upon.[2] On the other hand, in many parts of the world, including parts of Africa, the extended family is in a state of decline. Alan Paton's novel *Cry, the Beloved Country* tells a story of dissolution of native mores, traditions, and family structure in South Africa. Edward Shills describes the types of forces that can be expected to undermine old values and old forms of social organization as newly independent countries attempt to become both modern and economically progressive.[3] In countries striving for modernity, extended families, clans, and tribes become obsolete. The developmental model is not the old, traditional lineage head, but the young man who has been educated abroad and understands the ways of modern states. Old bonds become disruptive to modern political development. "Strong attachments to kinship, caste, and territorial groups mean that in administration and adjudication, it will be more difficult to obtain justice, since there will be a tendency for judge and administrator to favor his kinsmen, his caste-fellow,

[2]See, for example, Joan Aldous, "*Urbanization*, The Extended Family and Kinship Ties in West Africa," *Social forces*, vol. 42, pp. 6–12, October 1962. See also Jean Comhaire, "Economic Change and the Extended Family," *Annals of the American Academy of Political and Social Science*, vol. 305, pp. 45–52, May 1956.
[3]Edward A. Shills, "Political Development in the New States: The Will to Be Modern," in S. N. Eisenstadt (ed.), *Readings in Social Evolution and Development*, Pergamon Press, Oxford, 1970, pp. 379–420.

and cobelievers."[4] The fact that many Asian and African people place loyalties to kinsmen ahead of efficiency in administration and impartiality in appointment has been irritating to officials of the West. However, complete impartiality becomes possible only in the context of impersonality, desirable for bureaucratic efficiency, but robbing people of the personal and individual treatment that is an important psychological part of the human bond.

THE FEELING OF NATIONHOOD   Sometimes nationalism has the effect of uniting people into a feeling of kinship, but such feelings develop at the expense of older centers of loyalty, tribal, regional, and associational. Unless nationhood is firmly developed, the state can be torn apart by strong centrifugal forces. The states best able to withstand the pressures of regional and ethnic divisiveness are usually the products of centuries of development, during which their members have shared traditions and heroes, triumphs and defeats. Many of the boundary lines of the energing nations were drawn in such a way that shared traditions were impossible. Instead, boundary lines were determined in the old days of colonialism and were drawn for the convenience of foreign powers. Members of different tribal and linguistic groups with no common heritage were assigned to territories that are now trying to weld themselves into states. The Biafra war in Nigeria in the late 1960s was one consequence. Sometimes the new states have been formed in ways that continue old injustices, as in the case of Burundi, where the dominant Tusi and the subordinated Hutu were constantly at each other's throats. Sometimes states have been formed in such a manner that viability seems impossible. The uncomfortable union of East and West Pakistan was eventually broken. The dismemberment of states is disturbing to the world, but sometimes there is very little to hold them together. It was in recent times, historically speaking, at the end of World War I, that the empires of both Austria and Turkey were dismembered by international treaty.

In spite of the difficulty of the struggle toward nationhood on the part of the emergent nations, and despite occasional failures, the trend of development is clearly in the direction of the nation-state, as it has been for many years in other parts of the world. In many ways the state is to be preferred to disruptive tribalism, but it must not be looked upon as the final integrative achievement of man. Seen from the point of view of meaningful psychological ties, it seems to accomplish its purpose only when faced by the crisis of war or when it keeps up a constant barrage of nationalistic propaganda for its people. In ordinary times, for ordinary people, the great nations of today, with

452   [4]Ibid., p. 385.

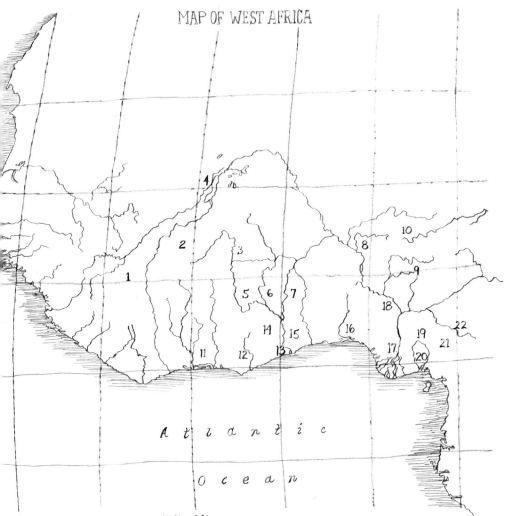

MAP OF WEST AFRICA

TRIBES OF WESTERN SUDAN

1-BAMBARA, 2-DOGON, 3-MOSSI, 4-SONGHAI, 5-DAGABA, 6-TALLENSI, 7-NUPE, 8-FULANI (FULBE, PEUL, incl. TUKULOR), 9-KANURI, 10-HAUSA

TRIBES OF GUINEA COAST

11-ASHANTI, 12-FANTI, 13-GA, 14-EWE, 15-DOHOMEANS (FON), 16-YORUBA, 17-BINI (BENIN) 18-GBARI, 19-IBO (incl. IBIBIO), 20-YAKÖ (EKOI), 21-TIV, 22-JUKUN

Many boundary lines were drawn by European powers for their own convenience, often paying little attention to conflicting tribal territories and the eventual problems of nationhood.

their gigantic cities, industries, and bureaucracies, are commented on far more often in terms of alienation of man from man than from the point of view of the bond of unity. The transition of the emerging states is being accompanied by considerable alienation and disorganization, in spite of the efforts of extended families and associations, as they attempt to adjust to ways disruptive to their old customs and beliefs.

NEW SYSTEMS OF BELIEF   In its purely sociological function, religion can unite people and give them a common focus of ritual and loyalty. In multinational and multireligion societies, religion does not always function in this manner, and some kind of modus vivendi has to be worked out among the religions, with each acknowledging the legitimacy of the state. A few of the world's religions have extended far past their lands of origin and have competed for loyalty in foreign lands. Buddhism and Christianity were among the first prominent religions to spread by missionary activity, and in later years the Muslims competed in the proselytizing effort. In many cases, whole populations have been converted to foreign religions or have partially adopted the foreign religions and blended them with native beliefs of their own. Sometimes the blend has been perfectly satisfying. Particularly in West Africa, a whole series of messiahs has arisen, strongly in the Christian tradition but also promoting feelings of nationalism.[5] In other cases such messianism has been mainly a failure. Recall the cases of the ghost dance and the cargo cults (Chapter Fifteen). Islam and Buddhism have sometimes succeeded in being accepted with considerable fervor by adapting themselves to different cultural areas. Buddhism in particular has sometimes blended sufficiently with preexisting native beliefs to be barely recognizable.

There are problems, though, with the importation of religions. To many Africans and Asians, Christianity is identified more with white foreigners and their ways than with a moral doctrine. If religions cannot be redefined to fit the importing culture and give status to its people, they are not entirely satisfying. In the nationalistic days of Japan, prior to and during World War II, Christianity was strongly discouraged. In China attention has turned to communist ideology rather than religion, native or imported, and the missionary effort has been in retreat. In Russia, religion has long been distinctly unfashionable.

Nearly everyone believes that men need faiths by which to live, but faiths can take a great variety of forms. Ideologies have replaced traditional

<hr>

[5]Georges Balandier, "Messianism and Nationalism in Black Africa," in Pierre L. van den Berghe (ed.), *Africa: Social Problems of Change and Conflict*, Chandler Publishing Company, San Francisco, 1965, pp. 443–460.

religions in a number of countries. In spite of its concordat with the church, Italian fascism in the days of Mussolini preached doctrines inimical to traditional Christianity and could be interpreted as an attempt to make ideology the mystical, unifying force that Christianity had once been. Hitler's nazism was an even more fanatical example of the same trend. Communism also has many of the traits of a material, earthy faith, with its atheistic heroes and saints replacing those of the old orthodox church. Will similar ideologies appeal increasingly to the emerging nations of the world? Arnold Toynbee, in a prophetic article written in the 1940s, compares the situation in the modern world with that which existed in the Graeco-Roman world in the days of the triumph of the Roman Empire.[6] New religions and ideologies arose among the subordinated peoples in response to their subjugation to Rome. People fought back against the material world of Roman power by looking to the mystical world of religion. Toynbee sees a parallel developing in which much of the less industrialized part of the world will embrace new ideologies in an attempt to compensate for the purely material triumphs of the West.

Meantime, in the Western world, it is difficult to assess the state of religion. Russia discourages religion; but Sweden, with a recognized church, has even lower church attendance than Russia.[7] Although the old churches have large numbers of followers, the bent of the modern industrial societies seems to be distinctly materialistic. Desmond Morris speaks of the need for a unifying religion and concludes that "a belief in the validity of the acquisition of knowledge and a scientific understanding of the world we live in . . . is rapidly becoming 'the religion' of our time."[8] If he is right, we have to admit also of a counterreligion. A variety of strange cults have arisen in the last decade or so, centering sometimes in the pseudoscience of astrology, or blending religion and psychology, or drawing on ideas and symbols from the Far East, or looking for drug-induced mystical experiences. Many of the cults are clearly antithetical to the rational-scientific bent of the dominant culture. The weakening of traditional religions may be part of a more general change in the nature of modern culture.

Since culture is a total pattern of learned ways of behavior, expression, and thought, of shared attitudes, ideals and mores, it has been defined as "that

[6] Arnold J. Toynbee, "Encounters between Civilizations," *Harper's Magazine*, April 1947, pp. 289–294.
[7] Richard F. Thomasson, "Religion Is Irrelevant in Sweden," *Transaction*, vol. 6, pp. 46–48, December 1968.
[8] Desmond Morris, "Religion," in Paul B. Weisz (ed.), *The Contemporary Scene: Readings on Human Nature, Race, Behavior, Society, and Environment*, McGraw-Hill Book Company, New York, 1970, p. 244.

which binds men together." Culture is seen also as the unique gift that has made man's supremacy in the world possible. Nevertheless, culture, as well as technology, poses certain problems for modern man.

THE PARADOX
OF CULTURE

The essential virtue of culture is that it is a system that teaches each new member of a society how to meet most of the everyday problems of life, how to make his contribution to his society, and the good things to do and the bad things to avoid. Culture stores the information and knowledge of the past for each generation to use, to add to, and to pass along to the next generation. However, while developing the attitudes that aid in its self-preservation, culture can convey attitudes that are narrow, dangerous, and ethnocentric. "Ethnocentrism" is the point of view that one's own culture is best and those which deviate too far from its model are bad. The attitude spills over to such matters as appearance and dress, as well as to moral values, so that the stranger is shunned by the strongly ethnocentric person. The consequence of the ethnocentric nature of culture is often the development of animosities. Since culture is cumulative, it is very reluctant to allow its carriers to forget the offenses of a foreign country, even after long periods of time. Old wars are remembered and grudges are held.

Not only do cultures cling to the animosities of the past, but they cling to many other ideas and values of the past. Under some circumstances, cultural orientations are very difficult to change, so that the patterned mode of existence can become a straitjacket. Jules Henry has pointed out this characteristic of cultures, especially with reference to education.[9] It is difficult for educational systems to become innovative, because too much change is looked upon as cultural death. The first requirement of any cultural system is self-preservation. The culture, of course, will change over a period of time, but the change must be thought of as one of superficial detail, not of fundamental orientation. Furthermore, the change is most palatable only if it serves the already existing cultural values. Hence, innovations in technology and mechanics are, for the most part, readily accepted, being seen merely as means of serving a culture that is already dedicated to the maximization of production and constant material progress. An innovator taking the opposite view and suggesting reducing the number of cars on the highways or stopping work on new freeways will be looked upon as a crank if not a traitor. Cultural values are things

[9]Jules Henry, *Culture Against Man*, Random House, Inc., New York, 1963.

that must be agreed upon. In the modern case, everyone must believe in progress and must also believe that progress can be measured fairly well by the number of square miles of concrete poured in any one year.

In an age when it seems necessary to make changes in cultural orientations, it is tempting to denigrate the importance of cultural continuity. Yet, in spite of its problems, culture must have a sense of continuity about it. Communication depends as much upon cultural understandings as it does upon linguistic understandings. In Durkheim's view, all societies are primarily moral systems, not in the sense that everything done is justifiable, but in the sense that the members must have a certain measure of agreement about rights and wrongs in order to hold the system together. Advanced and complex societies tolerate more differences of opinion in basic philosophies than do primitive societies, but even they demand agreement in many customs and mores and are intolerant of philosophies that seem to undermine their basic values. At the same time, the pace of change is so great that old values must change. Increasingly with the passage of time, modern societies face the intergenerational shock of changing values. In an old, relatively stable society, culture always seems a sure guide to ways of living, always supplying answers, whether those answers are scientifically valid or not. But retaining such cultural fixity in modern society can limit the ability to adapt; in Henry's phrase, the old traditions can become systems of "learned stupidity." "Creativity is the last thing wanted in any culture because of its potentialities for disruptive thinking." Creativity is encouraged only "after the creative thrust of an idea has been tamed and directed toward socially approved ends."[10]

Clearly, we face a dilemma in an age of rapid change. Too great a deviation from the old ways is proscribed by the society, and he who strays too far is haunted by the specter of failure and ostracism. Success continues to lie in fairly rigid conformity. Yet in spite of a considerable degree of social compulsion toward conformity to traditions, social customs do change, and they have to change. Several of the important changes are well under way, such as changes in attitudes toward minority races and toward runaway human reproduction. There are other attitudes that are even harder to change—the idea that material progress can be equated with human progress, for example, that all cities must continue to grow, that all material desires must be satisfied, that all resources must be exploited at whatever cost, that all countries of the world must be brought into the same common technological system and value system. The last idea is probably the most dangerous of all, seen from the point of view of species survival and of man's future evolution.

[10]Ibid., p. 288.

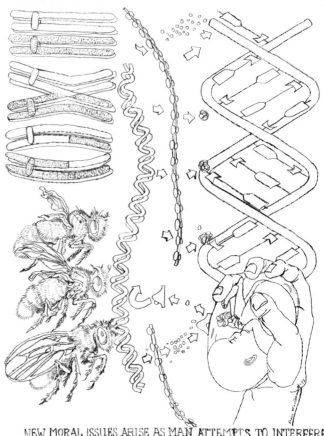

NEW MORAL ISSUES ARISE AS MAN ATTEMPTS TO INTERFERE WITH HIS GENETIC FUTURE.

MAN AS EVOLUTIONIST   To a degree man has been the architect of his own evolution since the first elements of his culture began to protect him. The capacity to use tools became a selective factor, and also the capacity to cooperate and organize and to invent the magic and mythology that held human groups together more effectively than mere force could have done. In the long course of evolutionary development, the human species has evolved production systems that prevent natural selection through hunger, and in recent time it has greatly reduced natural selection through disease. In the course of its development, the species has undermined some of the very characteristics that were vital to its evolutionary triumph—the narrowly exclusive human band, the old magical systems, and even the relative immutability of basic cultural patterns.

Man as evolutionist has learned new ways to deal with the genetic material that is his—how to modify human nature to fit many conditions, how to educate people into specialized occupations that constantly change, how to subdue and channel basic drives, how to crowd greater physical and mental effort out of the same biological machinery. Now, both science fiction writers and scientists are predicting increased interference with the genetic material itself. Genetic counseling is given in an effort to prevent serious defects in offspring, but the rising talk is of genetic engineering to eliminate all defects and to produce better types. Moral issues arise, for who is to say what constitutes "better types"? There is even talk of the possibility of "cloning," a process by which material from the nucleus of an adult cell could be used to make a genetic carbon copy of the donor himself. In an age when control over the growth of human populations becomes ever more necessary, the possibility arises that increasing amounts of human selective breeding will be done. An important Russian biologist is quoted as predicting a type of genetic engineering in which rival countries will compete for the development of superior mentalities in a genetics race.[11]

Meantime, the evolution of cultural systems gradually eliminates many of those cultures that are most unusual, pulling them toward the main currents of modern technology. The isolated areas of the world become part of the whole, and separate breeding populations, or gene pools, lose their distinctiveness as they intermix with others. An increasing danger arises, a danger of the gradual homogenization of the human race into one or a few great megacultures.

THE CRITERIA OF SURVIVAL   Throughout the previous millions of years of primate existence, no one could have predicted which genetic type would be most likely to gain ascendancy over the world. Nature was to experiment with genetic materials and with time in a manner that at first glance seems wasteful, gradually working on new varieties and new mutations, none of which could remain genetically fixed. Cultures, too, have gone through a long process of experimentation, during which no one could have known which of several alternative systems would prove most likely to survive into the future. However, the slow, experimental method of natural and cultural selection has not proved wasteful but undoubtedly has been an important means of survival. If one genetic variant proved unadapted to its environment, it was replaced by others. If one culture succumbed, there were hundreds of others experimenting with different patterns of life. Now the possibility arises that man will no longer be an architect of his evolution by the indirect methods of the past but by human design and plan.

[11]Alvin Toffler, *Future Shock*, Bantam Books, Inc., New York, 1970, p. 204.

Certainly, as Garrett Hardin suggests, there are some characteristics of the old evolutionary course that must be controlled.[12] Since the development of atomic bombs, it has become obvious that unless major wars are controlled, there will be no future to discuss and the whole process of the evolution of man will have come to naught. There also must be enough agreement among mankind to prevent a warfare of populations in which some segment of humanity attempts to crowd others off the planet. And there will have to be an agreement renouncing the right to plunder and pollute the planet and providing for cooperation in the steps necessary for environmental control. Beyond that point, the rush toward a technical-scientific, homogenized world is a frightening prospect, carrying the possibility of megamachine, megaculture, and megadeath.

ANTHROPOLOGY AND THE VIEW OF THE FUTURE   Anthropology, with its insistence on the right of all cultures to be regarded as important parts of the great human experiment, cannot but recoil at some of the descriptions presented by science fiction and by large numbers of scientists as well. The utopias of a mathematically planned and directed world culture have no attraction. Anthropologists have often been taken to task for their fascination with the primitive and with cultures and subcultures that seem far from the great road down which the stupendous juggernaut of modern technology rolls. They have shown, perhaps, a nostalgia for the old grandparents of the race and the quaint rituals and kinship systems and a revulsion for a world in which the only equivalent to kinship is the biologist's gene pool. They are sometimes asked what worlds they will study in the future, as all mankind moves into a great system of urban modernity, becoming increasingly equal and alike.

There are two replies, both factual and in a sense normative. No means has yet been worked out by which all elements of the great cultures of the world can be reduced to patterns of total conformity. New cultures and subcultures arise right in the midst of mass cultures, sometimes in total defiance of mass cultures—little communes, religious sects, radicals, defiant youth, reactionaries, racial and ethnic groups, reformers, fanatics, dreamers of dreams. Even in the advanced societies of the world, scientific-technological trends fall short of stamping out great cultural differences. Educated, technically advanced urban centers of Japan or India are not the same as those of the West, nor are they the same as those of China or Indonesia. Not only do strong cultural differences exist, but it seems vital that they continue to exist. The human

[12]Garrett Hardin, comments on "In Search of an Ethic," in Weisz (ed.), *The Contemporary Scene*, pp. 265–268.

Any attempt to fit all people and all cultures into a common mold runs counter to the basic assumptions of anthropology, whether the controls are accomplished by an all-encompassing technology or by a goose-stepping army.

future will be much more secure if it is not compressed into one great system, but if the variety that has always characterized man continues to flourish. As Hardin points out, the species that puts all its genetic eggs in one basket is vulnerable to ruin under conditions of great change.[13] The species that develops wide genetic and adaptive variety will have a far better chance in the uncertain future.

The human species has survived through the ages largely because of its tremendous cultural variability. Many peoples have followed the long road from stone to steel, borrowing from one another but always contributing something distinctly their own. In the discernible trend toward a more scientific, mechanized future, not enough attention has been given to the need for variety. Instead, the emphasis is on shaping the human being to fit the system; and no one knows, and few people of recent times even ask, what the essential nature of the human being is and how far it can be strained and shaped into a computerized order.

Neither the anthropologist nor the conveyor of any other of the sciences of man can yet define man's nature, despite centuries of effort. All we know, based on the study of a tremendously wide field and an incredible depth of time, is that his nature is not given to any narrow definition. We know, as the Yanomamö know, that there is something fierce about the human; but we also know, as the prophets have known, that there is something kind, altruistic, occasionally even saintly. We know, as the Dugum Dani do, that the human being contains somewhere within him the seeds of singing and that the spirit must be free to soar, even though it must eventually fall again to earth. We know, as the hunters and herders have known, that the spirit of man is closely akin to those of the animals among whom he lives but that there is also something about him that transcends the animal. We know, too, that man does not wish to forget the ancestral spirits who pioneered the way to art, magic, and science, or the myths they told and the gods they created. Like the rainbow, the spirit of man is multicolored, changing throughout its entire cultural range and its millenniums of time. There is a compulsion to create, to leave notations in stone, clay, or ivory, notations that attempt to speak for all time and say that a special type of being has been here. There is a compulsion in man to wonder about his creator and the spirits that move him, to react to the awesome and the dread and the beautiful. Certainly man was not made to be chained to one all-embracing system, but to develop in myriad ways the consciousness that we are psychologically compelled to believe is the ultimate achievement of eternity.

[13]Ibid., p. 267.

GLOSSARY

Aborigine A native or indigenous inhabitant (most frequently used in reference to the indigenous population of Australia).

Age set A tribal association of all males or females of approximately the same age who have undergone initiation rites together and remain in meaningful association.

Affinal marriage Marriage to a relative-in-law (affine), usually the brother or sister of one's deceased spouse.

Angakok An Eskimo shaman or medicine man.

Animatism Belief in an impersonal, supernatural power or force that can be associated with animate or inanimate objects or persons or places.

Animism Belief in spiritual beings; also, the attribution of spirit and consciousness to all animate things.

Anthropoid The suborder of primates including man and the great apes.

Anthropology The science of man and his origins, psychophysical nature, and culture.

Anthropomorphic Having human characteristics, as in the case of gods represented in human form.

Archaeology The study of the material remains of the past—fossils, artifacts, structures, and evidences of ways of life.

Archaic religion A religion of an early, urban civilization, characterized by priestly orders in close association with the state.

Artifact Any object showing human workmanship, such as tools, weapons, and objects of art.

Aryan Pertaining to the Indo-European family of languages and to the early Indo-European speaking invaders of India.

Association A social group organized for specific purposes, usually on a nonkinship basis.

Australopithecine Literally, "southern ape man"; an early Pleistocene hominid, probably an ancestor of modern man.

Avatar The appearance in human form of any of the gods, especially Vishnu.

Band A small, nomadic community of hunting-gathering people.

Barabaig A small cattle-herding tribe of eastern Africa.

Behistun stone   A stone cliff in Persia with inscriptions that provided the key to cuneiform writing.

Bifurcate collateral   Of or pertaining to kinship systems in which separate terms are
used for parents and each class of their siblings, e.g., mother's sister, father's
sister, mother's brother, and father's brother.

Bifurcate merging   Of or pertaining to kinship systems in which mother and mother's
sister, and father and father's brother, are merged (called by the same term).
Other of the parents' siblings are called by separate terms.

Brachiation   Swinging from branch to branch by use of hands and arms, as in the
case of gibbons and orangutans.

Brahman (also spelled Brahmin)   The highest caste of the Hindus, traditionally assigned
to the priesthood.

Bride wealth or *bride price*   Gifts paid to a bride's family at the time of marriage. Sometimes called "progeny price" because the gifts serve to compensate the bride's
family for the fact that her children will be part of the husband's lineage.

Carbon dating   Dating materials by calculating the amount of change from carbon 12 to
carbon 14.

Cargo cult   A native cult in New Guinea that attempts to find magical means to cause
cargoes to come to the people from overseas. Sometimes the term is applied to
other cults of a salvationist type.

Cartouche   An oval-shaped figure surrounding important names in Egyptian hieroglyphics.

Caste   A system of social class based on heredity and precluding individual mobility,
found especially in traditional India.

Caucasian   Of or pertaining to the so-called white race, primarily of Europe, North
Africa, and western Asia.

Chief   The head of a lineage or small tribe, often possessing authority only for limited
purposes, as war chief, peace chief, or chief of a hunt.

Chieftain   The head of an important lineage or of a tribe. He is surrounded by much
more pomp than a mere chief.

Chuckchi   A hunting and reindeer-herding people of eastern Siberia.

Churinga   A sacred stone that represents a spirit center to Australian aborigines.

Circumpolar people   One of the hunting-and-gathering or pastoral peoples of the
northern tundra that possess certain similarities in culture and world view.

Civilization The stage of cultural development characterized by agriculture, urban centers, and usually a written language.

Clan A group claiming descent from a common ancestor, usually remote and mythological.

Class, or social class A collectivity of people of approximately the same status in society, so regarded by themselves and others.

Classificatory kinship system A kinship terminology that lumps many kinsmen under the same term, as in the case of our words "aunt," "uncle," and "cousin."

Collective representation Any symbol that serves to unite a people—a flag, emblem, totem, sacred object, or god.

Consanguine relative A member of one's biologically related group, literally, "of one blood," but in actuality usually calculated through the patrilineage or matrilineage, not both.

Corporate kinship group A kinship group in which all property is held collectively, with authority vested in a single individual.

Couvade The practice whereby a prospective father observes the same ritual taboos as his wife before, during, and immediately after childbirth.

Cro-Magnon A type of *Homo sapiens* common in Europe at the end of the last glacial period.

Cross cousin A cousin whose relationship with ego is traced through parents of opposite sex, e.g., father's sister's child or mother's brother's child.

Crow system A basically matrilineal kinship system, but one that recognizes the father's line by giving a special designation to all males of the father's matrilineage.

Cultural degradation A discredited theory that primitive peoples had regressed from higher levels to their present state because of their sins.

Cultural relativism The idea that both peoples and cultural practices should be understood and judged in the context of the culture that produced them.

Culture The total, historically derived life pattern of a people, including skills, beliefs, attitudes, institutions, and world views.

Culture area A geographical area in which different cultures show considerable similarity.

Culture shock The emotional shock often experienced by a person in contact with a culture possessed of values and customs widely divergent from his own.

Cuneiform   A writing system consisting of wedge-shaped characters, usually imprinted on clay, as in ancient Mesopotamia.

Dendrochronology   The science of dating events and artifacts by a study of the growth rings of trees associated with them.

Dibble stick   A sharpened stick for digging roots, grubs, small burrowing animals, etc.

Diffusion   The process by which cultural traits and ideas spread from one culture to another.

Divination   The practice of foretelling the future or seeking hidden knowledge by omens or with the aid of supernatural powers.

Dryopithecine   A fossil ape of Miocene times that may be ancestral to the anthropoids and man.

Dual descent   Descent traced through both the matrilineage and the patrilineage.

Ecology   The study of species in relation to their environment.

Empiricism   The practice of relying on observation and experiment for knowledge and of drawing conclusions only after examining the pertinent data.

Endogamy   The practice of marrying within a specified group to which one belongs.

Eta   A depressed social caste of Japan, traditionally leather workers.

Ethnography   The branch of anthropology that describes cultures.

Ethnology   The branch of anthropology dealing with comparative and analytical studies of cultures.

Ethnomorphic   Of or pertaining to conceptions of the universe or the gods developed in relation to one's own culture.

Eugenics   The attempt to improve genetic stock through careful breeding.

Evolution, biological or physical   The development of species of plants and animals from simpler forms through modification in successive generations.

Evolution, cultural   The development of cultures from simple forms to increasingly complex forms in ways that display a degree of regularity.

Evolution, general   From a cultural-evolution perspective, the development along similar lines of the entire human species.

Evolution, multilineal   From a cultural-evolution perspective, the evolution of cultures along somewhat divergent lines, dependent largely on environment and diffusion of ideas.

Exogamy   The practice of marrying outside a specified group to which one belongs.

Fictive kinship   A relationship based on the rights, duties, and obligations of kinship but lacking any genetic foundation, as, for example, in godfatherhood.

Functionalism   A theoretical approach to the study of cultures that emphasizes the contribution (function) of each part in the maintenance of the whole.

Gene pool   The sum of the genetic possibilities of an inbred population.

Generational kinship terminology   A system in which no distinction in terms is made between siblings and their first cousins or between parents and their siblings.

Genotype   The genetic or inheritable traits of an individual or group.

Geographical race   A population that has long inhabited the same continent or isolated region and therefore shares certain distinctive genetic traits.

Ghost dance   A group dance for communicating with and receiving help from the spirits of the dead, found especially among Western American Indians in the 1890s.

Ghost-soul   The spirit believed to wander away from the physical being in dreams, illness, and death; in Tylor's analysis, the first step in a belief in the duality of the material and spiritual worlds.

Gikuyu (or Kikuyu)   A large tribe of people of Kenya.

Glotochronology   A system for approximating the date at which two related peoples separated, based on change in their fundamental vocabularies.

God, high   A god supreme over all others.

Hand ax   A Paleolithic stone artifact sharpened at one end and probably held in the hand to strike a blow. (Also called *coup de poing*.)

Harijan   A member of the lowest level in the Hindu caste system, often called an "outcaste" or a "pariah."

Headman   The leader of a small, nomadic band, having influence but no real authority.

Hieroglyphic   A writing system based on highly stylized pictures; most frequently, the writing of the ancient Egyptian priesthood.

Historic religion   As used in the text, one of a series of religions that developed during the early period of written history and were established by religious prophets.

Hominid   A member of the family consisting of human beings and their immediate ancestors, including the australopithecines.

Hominoid   Resembling or related to human beings (the term is applicable to hominids and also the great apes).

Homo erectus   Literally, "upright man," as opposed to modern *Homo sapiens,* or "knowing man." The best-known specimens are popularly referred to as Java man and Peking man—fossil types of the mid-Pleistocene.

Homo habilis   An early fossil Pleistocene hominid found in Olduvai Gorge and, in Leakey's opinion, more advanced than the australopithecines.

Homo sapiens   Modern man; literally, "knowing man."

Horticulture   The growing of fruits, flowers, and vegetables. In anthropology, the word also implies farming with simple tools such as dibble stick and hoe.

Huitzilopochtli   Important Aztec god of war, requiring many human sacrifices.

Human paleontology   The study of the fossil remains of man and his primate forebears.

Ideogram   A picture or symbol used to suggest an idea, not simply the object pictured.

Immunology   The science dealing with chemical and blood factors that cause immunity to disease.

Incest   Sexual relations between two persons who are too closely related genetically for the act to be permitted by their society.

Indo-European   See Aryan.

Infanticide   The killing of babies.

Integrated way of life   A way of life in which most actions and beliefs are consistent with a central philosophy of life.

Jajmani   In India, a system of payment in goods or services for other services rendered.

Jati   In India, a local group of people belonging to the same subcaste.

Joint household   A household composed of related conjugal family units.

Kachina   One of a type of spirits found in Hopi, Zuñi, and some of the other Pueblo cultures and represented in ceremonies by masked men.

Kayak   A light, skin-covered canoe of the Eskimo.

Kibbutz   A collective farm or other collective settlement in Israel, noted for a collective system of rearing children.

Kingdom   A politically organized community headed by a monarch, differing from a chiefdom in that the monarch holds much greater power.

Kiva   An underground ceremonial chamber of the Pueblo Indians.

Koranic law   Law derived from the Koran, holy book of the Muslims.

Kshatriya   The second highest caste of India, traditionally comprised of warriors and princes.

Kula Ring   A trading circle of southwestern Melanesia, dealing in ceremonial arm bands and necklaces and also in economic goods.

Lamasery   A monastery of the Yellow Sect of Buddhism, found in Tibet and other parts of central Asia.

Language area   A geographical area in which peoples speak related languages.

Lapps   A people of northern Scandinavia, Finland, and the Kola Peninsula, traditionally hunters, fishers, and herders of reindeer.

Levirate   The practice whereby a man marries the widow of his deceased brother.

Levirate, anticipatory   The practice of permitting a younger brother to have sexual relations with one's wife in cases where he would be eligible to inherit her.

Lex talionis   The law of revenge (eye for eye and tooth for tooth).

Lineal system   A kinship system in which parents' siblings are called by the same names (in our case, "aunt" and "uncle") and all their children are called by the same term (in our case, "cousin").

Linguistics   The study of languages.

Lochial   Pertaining to birth.

Logogram   A letter or symbol used to represent an entire word.

Magic, contagious   Magic believed to operate because of a spiritual relationship between things that are or have been closely associated.

Magic, holophrastic   Magic believed to operate on the principle that the part can represent the whole, leading to the conclusion that the sacrifice of one can purify the entire group.

Magic, imitative   Magic believed to work because ceremony imitates the desired event.

Mana   A supernatural, impersonal power embodied in an object or person.

Masai   A major cattle-herding tribe of Kenya and Tanzania.

Matrilineal   Pertaining to the tracing of descent through the mother's line.

Megaculture   A giant culture tending to absorb all others.

Megamachine   A giant machine; a society so organized as to resemble a giant machine.

Melanesia   Islands of the southwestern Pacific, mainly east of New Guinea, inhabited by dark-skinned people.

Mesolithic   The Middle Stone Age, period of transition from primarily a hunting way of life to intensive foraging of grains, fruits, and in some cases sea life.

Messianic movement   A religious movement based on promises of otherworldly salvation or delivery from subjugation.

Metallurgy   The science of metals, especially their melting and alloying.

Miscegenation   Biological mixture of races.

Mithraism   Adherence to a religious cult related to Persian Zoroastrianism that spread into the Roman Empire at about the beginning of the Christian era.

Moiety   One of two often intermarrying tribal divisions, each of which has rights and duties relative to the other.

Molimo   A wind instrument played by the Ituri Pygmies; the rites associated with it.

Mongoloid   Of or pertaining to a major racial division of mankind that includes East Asians and, in many classifications, American Indians.

Monogamy   Marriage of one man to one woman.

Monolithic unity   A community or alliance so completely unified as to speak with one voice on any issue.

Mousterian   Pertaining to the culture of Neanderthal man.

Multilineal evolution   See Evolution, multilineal.

Myth   A traditional tale, believed to be historically true, explaining the origin of a people, world view, social order, or rituals and beliefs.

Natural selection   Survival of those individuals best fitted for a particular environment and elimination of the least fit.

Neanderthal   An extinct fossil man dominant in Europe, western Asia, and northern Africa during the last glacial advance.

Neolithic   The New Stone Age, characterized by domestic plants and animals and improved stone tools.

Omaha system   A patrilineal kinship system, unusual in that it gives a common name to all females of the mother's patrilineage.

Ontogenetic growth   The development of an individual organism from the moment of conception.

Paleolithic The Old Stone Age.

Parallel cousin A cousin whose relationship with ego is traced through parents of the same sex, i.e., the child of father's brother or mother's sister.

Particularizing principle in kinship Use of specific terms to differentiate each kind of kinsman, for example, separate words for father's brother and mother's brother.

Pastoralism A way of life centering around the herding of domesticated animals and usually calling for nomadism or transhumance.

Patrilineal Pertaining to the tracing of descent through the father's line.

Peasantry A way of life dependent on small scale, subsistence farming, usually by plow agriculture, but existing in state systems.

Phoneme The smallest unit of sound in a language.

Phratry A group of related or linked clans within a society, each with obligations to the others.

Phytomorphic Plantlike, referring especially to gods conceived as resembling plants.

Pictograph A symbol belonging to a writing system originally based on stylized pictures.

Pithecanthropus erectus Literally, "apelike with erect posture"; the name originally given to Java man, now classified as *Homo erectus*.

Pleistocene The period of the great Ice Ages and of the development of mankind and the other hominids.

Pollen analysis The analysis of pollen found in association with archaeological specimens in order to determine the flora and probable climate of their time.

Polyandry The marriage of a woman to more than one man.

Polygamy The marriage of a man or woman to more than one partner.

Polygyny The marriage of a man to more than one woman.

Polynesia The islands of the Pacific enclosed by a triangle extending from Hawaii to New Zealand to Easter Island.

Pongid An anthropoid ape.

Poro The men's secret fraternity among the Kpelle of Nigeria.

Potlatch A ceremonial feast of the Northwest Coast Indians, marked by lavish giving of gifts.

Prehensile tail A tail that can be used for grasping, found among many New World monkeys.

Prescriptive rules of marriage Rules designating a particular person as one's rightful marriage partner, sometimes a cross cousin.

Primate A member of the order of mammals including man, the apes, monkeys, and a few related species such as tarsiers and lemurs.

Primitive Pertaining to a culture without a written language.

Protohuman Closely approaching *Homo sapiens* in form.

Psychic unity of man, theory of The theory that all races of mankind are sufficiently similar that they will evolve similar cultures under similar circumstances.

Race A human population sharing enough of a common gene pool to result in distinctive physical characteristics.

Rank Social position relative to others. In social systems based on rank, rank is more individualized than social class.

Redistributive mechanism A means, such as lavish gift giving, for preventing the wealth of a society from concentrating in a few hands.

Religion A system of belief relating to supernatural beings or forces, and the rituals and other behavior accompanying such belief.

Revitalization movement A religious or political movement that reawakens in a society confidence in its own traditions and its future.

Role The behavior expected of a person relative to his position or status.

Rosetta stone A basalt stone found at the Rosetta mouth of the Nile and holding the key to the interpretation of Egyptian hieroglyphics.

Sachem A member of the intertribal council of the Iroquois. The term is also applied to members of other Indian councils.

Samoyed A member of a circumpolar tribe relying mainly on herding reindeer for a living and located near the mouths of the Ob and Yenisei Rivers.

Segmentary lineage A small lineage recognized as a segment of a larger lineage or clan but largely independent of the latter.

Senilicide The practice of killing the old and feeble.

Shadouf A long beam with a water vessel at one end for drawing water from the Nile, one of the earliest applications of the principle of leverage.

Shaman A practitioner of magic, religion, and healing in a primitive tribe.

Simpua A little girl adopted into a Chinese household in order later to become the wife of one of the sons.

Slash and burn To clear or partially clear land for gardening by burning lighter brush and girdling larger trees.

Social class See Class.

Social control The enforcement of conformity to a society's standards by such means as teaching and habit, as well as more severe methods.

Social Darwinism Adherence to the theory that a society must be ruthlessly competitive so that only the fit will survive; an application of natural selection theories to society.

Social organization The ways in which people and social groups are organized and interrelated, including such institutions as kinship groups and the state.

Society A group of people, whether band, tribe or nation, who are distinctive from all others and share common institutions for regulating interrelationships.

Solidarity The sense of close social cohesion ("all for one and one for all).

Sororate The practice whereby a man can inherit his wife's sister if his wife dies.

State system A social system with a central authority unquestionably superior to all component parts.

Status The position or positions one holds in society.

Stratification The separation of members of a society into different social classes, statuses, and ranks.

Structural analysis of myth The analytical method of Claude Lévi-Strauss consisting of breaking myths into simple component parts to compare their structures.

Structuralism The study of cultures mainly in terms of their social organization and how aspects of organization are related to the entire culture.

Stylization Any work belonging to a type of art that departs from nature in a fairly consistent manner.

Subculture A group showing cultural variation within a larger cultural pattern.

Sudra The lowest of the four major castes of India, traditionally the servant caste.

Swidden Pertaining to horticulture in which land is cleared and used for a few years until the soil is exhausted and then new territory is developed while the old land recovers. (See Slash and burn.)

Syllabary A writing system in which each character represents a syllable.

Symbiotic relationship A relationship in which two dissimilar organisms or species live together in mutual dependence.

Syncretism   The fusion of ideas from two or more religions into one belief system.

Taboo   A prohibition containing the threat of supernatural sanction.

Taoism   A religion of nature and mysticism founded by Lao-tzu in China during the sixth century B.C.

Taravad   The matrilineal household of the Nayars of India.

Technology   All the means employed for providing the goods needed for human survival and comfort.

Titular chief   A chief whose powers are limited by the presence of subchiefs of almost equal importance.

Totemic plant or animal   A plant or animal symbolizing a particular clan and often believed to have a special spiritual relationship to the clan.

Transhumance   Migration in a seasonal pattern in order to keep cattle or other animals in the best possible pasturage.

Transmigration   The return of the soul after death in another human or animal form.

Tree-ring dating   See Dendrochronology.

Trial by combat   Trial in which guilt or innocence is established by a fight between contestants, in the belief that heaven will bless the arms of the innocent.

Trial by ordeal   Trial in which the accused is found innocent or guilty on the basis of whether he can pass a dangerous or painful test.

Tribe   A group of people who possess a common culture and language and are culturally distinct from other groups. Usually the people consider themselves related to some degree, but the group is not necessarily politically cohesive.

Tuareg   A nomadic, camel-herding people of the Sahara Desert, formerly controlling trade routes across the desert.

Tundra   The Arctic region beyond the northern forests where only mosses and sedges grow; habitat of the Eskimo and other circumpolar people.

Tungus   A pastoral people of Siberia, the southern groups of which herd cattle and horses, the northern groups, reindeer.

Unilineal descent   Descent traced through only one side of the family, so that there is only one significant ancestor in each generation.

Universalistic principles   Religious or political principles with universal appeal, granting equality to all men willing to conform to the religion or ideology.

Urheimat   The original homeland of the speakers of a language or group of languages.

Vaisya   The third caste of Hinduism, including farmers, merchants, and artisans.

Venus of Willendorf   The best known of a number of late Paleolithic figures of pregnant females believed to be goddesses of fertility.

Vigesimal   Of or pertaining to a numerical system using base 20, as in the Mayan system.

Vision quest   The quest of a young man of such tribes as the Great Plains Indians, aimed at seeing an animal spirit that would provide assurance, identity, and a sense of manhood.

Warfare, primitive   Desultory fighting, characterized by raid and counterraid but seldom constituting a sustained operation.

Wergild   Blood money, or the price to be paid for having killed a person.

Wife lending   The custom, common among Eskimo, of lending wives to close friends or honored guests (but always involving some kind of mutual obligation).

Witchcraft   The use of supernatural powers to do harm, usually believed to be with intent but occasionally conceived of as accidental and unintentional, as in the case of Azande witches.

World view   The view of life and of the natural and supernatural worlds held by a society.

Yanomamö   Literally, "true men"; a fierce tribe of people of the Upper Orinoco region of Venezuela and Brazil.

Zinjanthropus bosei   A hominid specimen found by the Leakeys at Olduvai Gorge and dated at 1,750,000 years ago, now generally classified with the australopithecines.

Zoomorphic   Literally, "animal form"; refers to gods and supernatural beings conceived in animal form.

Zoroastrianism   A religion of ancient Persia founded by Zoroaster and characterized by belief in a struggle between the forces of good and evil. It has had strong influence on several later religions.

Index

A

Achaemenid Dynasty, 404
Açunga, 354–355
Afterlife, 350–352
Age sets, 166–167
Agrarian societies, 226–230
Agriculturalists, 277–278, 282
Agriculture:
    development in America, 91–92
    development in Old World, 196–197
    origins, 48
    slash and burn, 147–148
Ainu, 99, 129, 177, 350
Alberuni, 13
Aldous, Joan, 450
Aleuts, 97, 117, 132
Allah, 181
Alphabet:
    Egyptian, 406–407
    Phoenician, 414
    Semitic, 414
Altamira Cave, 81–84
Ambrona Valley, Spain, 48, 49, 79
American Indians, 222, 237, 261, 281, 287
    origins, 89–92
    religions, 377
    revitalization movements, 387–389
    (*See also* specific tribes)
Amish, 34
Ancestor worship, 187, 275–276
Andaman Islanders, 119, 367, 368
Angakok, 323–324
Animatism, 346–347
Animism, 176, 177, 210–211, 344–346
    Tylor's theory of, 344–346
Anthropology:
    applied, 37–39
    current appeal, 7–9
        chart summarizing current appeal, 9
    description of field, 5–6

Anthropology:
  divisions of, 31–53
    chart illustrating divisions, 32
  physical, 50–52
  viewpoints of, 6
Apaches, 157
Arabic decimal system, 408–409
Arabs, 239, 309–310
Arambourg, Camile, 67
Archaeological recording, 45–47
Archaeology, 31, 43–49, 53
Art, 81–86
  and notation, 393–400
  Paleolithic, 393–400
Arunta, 352
Arutam soul, 354
Aryan invasion, 232
Ashanti, 162
  law, 327
  slavery, 237–238
Ashurbanipal, 404, 405
Asiatic nomads, 171, 179, 188
Associations, 301–304
Assyrian writing, 404
Aurignacian, 84
Australian aborigines, 93–94, 119–126, 251,
    257, 352
Australopithecines, 65–69, 77–79, 85, 87
  photograph of skull, 66
Azande, 359–360
Aztecs, 132, 196, 228–229, 281, 300
  religion, 374
  Veracruz dialect, 41

B

Baboons, 71–72, 85
Bachofen, J. K., 21
Baganda, 182
  polygyny among, 262–264
Balandier, Georges, 454
Bantu, 124–126, 363

Banyankole, 182, 234
Barabaig, 182–187, 194, 360
Beals, Alan R., 201, 231
Bear cult, 177
  Paleolithic, 79–80
Bedouin Arabs, 181
  cousin marriage, 256
Behistun stone, 402–403
Bella Coola, 118, 136
Bellah, Robert N., 378–381, 385–386, 390
Benedict, Ruth, 23, 24
Biblical food taboos, 357
"Big man" of Melanesia, 304–305
Bilateral descent, 278–279
Black, Davidson, 64, 99
Boas, Franz, 22–24, 32, 41, 99
Body size, 106
Bohannon, Laura, 33
Bohannon, Paul, 325
Bordes, Francois, 79–81, 91
Bororo, 145, 146
Boucher de Perthes, Jacques, 17, 20, 62
Brace, C. Loring, 67, 101–107
Braden, William, 450
Brahma, 205
Brahmans, 231–233, 235, 270
Brain, C. R., 78
Brain development in primates, 80, 85
"Brain drain," 446
Breuil, Henri, 393–395
Bride price, 139, 175, 183, 185, 192, 205, 246,
    257, 259–261
Broekhuijse, Jan, 152
Broom, Robert, 65
Buddha, 232, 383
Buddhism, 192–193, 210, 232, 267, 378
Bunyoro, 182
Burial rites, 355
  Neanderthal, 79, 81, 85
Bushmen (South African), 96, 100, 117–118,
    162, 257

C

Caduveo, 145, 270–271
Calcutta, 447
Camayurá, 145
Cannibalism:
  among Bororo of Brazil, 146
  among *Homo erectus* types, 64, 81
  in New Guinea, 64, 151, 152
  and witchcraft, 360
Cargo cults, 157, 388
Cartography, 433–434
Caste, 165, 180, 187, 193, 226, 230–235
  in India, 230–233
  and social cohesion, 233
  in United States, 234
Çatal Hüyük, 48
Cattle complex, 183
Ceram, C. W., 46
Cero Chivateros, Peru, 89
Chagga, 270
Chagnon, Napoleon, 145, 147, 150
Chaka, 326
Chamberlain, John Stuart, 98
Champollion, Jean François, 405–406
Chariots (*see* Wheeled transport)
Cherokee, 166
Cheyennes, 317
  law, 337
Child-rearing patterns, 11
Childe, V. Gordon, 27, 28, 228
Chimpanzees, 72–74, 85
Chinese:
  description of Mongols, 13
  medical remedies, 363–364
  religion, 445
  writing system, 408–409
Choukoutien Cave, China, 64–79
Christianity, 176, 189, 192, 351, 354, 360–361,
    370, 372, 378
  beliefs regarding American Indians, 15
  conversion of Mexico, 15

Christianity:
  in India, 204, 216
  and law, 335
  sacrificial idea compared, 212
Chuckchi, 171–172, 250–251
Churinga, 122
Ciesa, Pedro de, 15
Circumcision, 123, 125, 187, 211
Clans, 278–280, 282, 283
Clark, J. Desmond, 91
Class (*see* Social class)
Clay (*see* Pottery)
Cleator, P. E., 403
Clovis points, 89–91
Coe, Michael D., 410
Cohen, Yehudi, 23
Colombia, 428
Common Market, 312
Communication, forms of, 392–393
Communism, 446
Confucius, 378, 383
Coon, Carleton S., 100, 106
Couvade, 367
Cree, 364–365
Creek, 166
Cro-Magnon man, 63, 81–85
Crow Indians, 301
Cultural evolution:
  diversity of theories, 27–28
  L. H. Morgan's theory of, 20
  in New World, 28
Cultural relativity, 23
Culture:
  concept of, 7
  continuity, 457
  discovery of, 16–17
  evolution of (*see* Cultural evolution)
  paradox of, 456
  and personality, 24
Cuneiform writing, 401–404
  illustrations, 402–404

D

Dahomey, religious syncretism in, 386
Dani (*see* Dugum Dani)
Darius I, 402–403
Dart, Raymond, 65, 78
Darwin, Charles, 17–18
Darwinism, compared with cultural
    evolution, 18–19
Darwinists compared with social Darwinists,
    62–63
Dating techniques, 44–45, 67
Deetz, James, 45
De Gobineau, Joseph A., 98
Dentition, 103–106
Devore, Irven, 72
Disenchantment of modern world, 385–386
Divination, 164, 166, 185, 331, 333–334
Divine law, 328–331
Division of labor, 197, 203, 251
Divorce, 181
DNA, 50, 100
Dobu, 24, 347
Dobzhansky, Theodosius, 100, 107
Dodoth, 182
Dollard, John, 234
Domestication:
    of animals, 92, 170
    of plants, 91–92
Douglas, Mary, 357–358
Downs, James F., 126, 129
Dowry, 175, 186, 192, 194, 199, 215
Dreams and animism, 344–345
Drucker, Philip, 140
Drug use:
    Jívaro, 352–354
    and Native American Church, 389
    Yanomamö, 150
Dryopithecus, 68–69
Dubois, Eugene, 63–64
Dugum Dani, 32

Durkheim, Émile, 24–26, 93, 123, 355, 369,
    385
    collective representations, 25
    Elementary Forms of the Religious Life, 25
    influence on functionalism, 26

E

Ecclesiastes, 415
Egyptians, 41–47, 106, 132, 305–308, 351, 352,
    355, 375
    state, 305–308
Eisenstadt, S. N., 301
El Jobo, Venezuela, 89
Endogamy, 256
Eskimos, 11, 34, 40, 91, 97, 103, 106, 117, 173
    law, 321–324
    social organization, 134
    technology, 132–134
    world view and religion, 135–136
Eta (of Japan), 234, 235
Ethnocentrism, 456
    in European views of Africa, 13
Ethnography, 31–34, 52
Ethnology, 31, 34–37, 53
Evans-Pritchard, E. C., 359–360
Evolution, physical: chronology of, 67–68
    and cultural development, 79–86, 88
    hominids: in Africa, 65–67
        in Asia, 63–65
        in Europe, 63
    molecular time scale for, 51, 52
    and race, 97–100
    and tool use, 76–79, 81, 84, 86
Exogamy, 121, 256
Exploration, age of, 13–14

F

Faience, Egyptian, 427
Family and marriage, 249–272
    joint family, 274–278

Family and marriage:
  minimal family, 270-272
  (*See also* Kinship; Marriage; Monogamy;
    Polyandry; Polygyny)
Farb, Peter, 27, 28
Farmers (*see* Peasants and farmers)
Fertility:
  symbols, 84
  Venus figures, 84
Fire, early use of, 49, 64, 79
Food sharing, 121, 128, 135, 143, 176
Food taboos, 232, 357
Forde, Daryll, 280
France, 445
Frazer, Sir James, 21-22, 166, 350, 356
Frazier, E. Franklin, 237
Freud, Sigmund, 35, 93
Friedl, Ernestine, 212
Functionalism, 26-27
Funerals (*see* Burial rites)

G

Gandhi, Mahatma, 230
Gardner, Robert, 32, 152
Garn, Stanley, 100
Geertz, Clifford, 209
Genetics counseling, 459
George, Katherine, 13
Ghost Dance, 346, 387-388
Ghost-soul, 344-345
Ghosts, 131, 135, 154, 156-157, 344-345, 354
Gift exchange, 393-394
Gikuyu, 258-260, 301
Gilgamish, 374
Glottochronology, 42-43
Goddesses of fertility, Paleolithic, 394, 398
Goodall, Jane van Lawick, 72-73
Goode, William J., 351
Gopalpur, India, 201-206, 230, 231
Gorilla, 74, 85
Great Flood, 374

Great Plains Indians, 161, 317, 320, 346
Greek village (Vasilika), 212-217
Green revolution, 448
Gururumba, 152, 154-157, 347
Gutenberg, Johann, 415
Gypsies, 42

H

Haida, 118, 136, 139, 140
Hair form, 103
Hammurabi, Code of, 329-330
Hardin, Garrett, 460
Harijans, 230
Harner, Michael J., 351
Hawaii, 252, 445
Hawkins, Gerald S., 435
Head hunting, 146, 151-152, 352-354
Hebrews, 260, 261, 282, 357
Henry, Jules, 145
Henry the Navigator, 13
Herodotus, 12, 403
Heyerdahl, Thor, 95, 405
Hierneaux, Jean, 101
Hieroglyphics, Egyptian, 405-408
  illustrations, 406, 407
Hinduism, 201, 204, 210, 211, 232-233, 357,
  378
Hittites, 428
  syllabary system, 413 (illus.)
Hodges, Henry, 428-430
Hoebel, E. Adamson, 322
Hoijer, Harry, 414
Holmberg, Alan, 38
Holmes, Lowell D., 17
Homans, George C., 368
Hominid evolution (*see* Evolution, physical)
Homo erectus, 63-64, 68, 79, 85, 87, 99, 100
  Ambrona Valley hunters, 48-49
Homo habilis, 67, 79
Hopi, 158, 160, 274, 281, 287
Horticulture, defined, 144

Horticulturists:
  chart illustrating, 167
  kinship and marriage, 151, 155–156,
    160–161, 164–165
  religion, and world view, 148–150,
    156–157, 161–162, 165–167
  social organization, 151, 154–156,
    164–165, 167–168
  technology, 146–148, 154–155, 158–160,
    163–164
  tribes included: Dugum Dani, 152–154
    Gururumba, 154–157
    Pueblos, 157–162
    Yanomamö, 146–151
    Yoruba, 162–168
  warfare, 146–148, 158–160, 163–164
Hospitals, 349
Hottentots, 99, 100
Howell, F. Clark, 48, 67, 76
Howells, William, 91, 106, 355
Hrdlička, Aleš, 62
Hsu, Francis L. K., 276
Human distribution:
  and adaptability, 96–97
  in America, 89–92
  in Australia, 92–94
  in desert lands, 96–97
  in Pacific Islands, 94–96
  and racial variation, 98, 101–102
Human Relations Area Files, 36
Human surpluses, 448
Hunters and gatherers:
  chart illustrating, 141
  kinship and marriage, 121, 125, 130, 131,
    134, 139
  religion and world view, 122–123, 125–126,
    130–131, 135–136, 141
  social organization, 121–122, 125, 129–130,
    134–135, 139–140
  technologies, 119–121, 124, 129, 132–134,
    137–138

Hunters and gatherers:
  tribes included: Australian aborigines,
    119–123
    Eskimos, 131–136
    Ituri Pygmies, 123–126
    Northwest Coast tribes, 136–141
    Washo, 126–131
  warfare, 121–123, 135, 140–141
Hutterites, 34
Huxley, Aldous, 13

I

Ibn Fadlan, Ahmed, 13
Ibo, 238
Ideograms, 405
Ifugao, 318, 320, 324
Incas, 97, 132, 196, 252
Incest, 192, 274
  taboo, 252–256
  and witchcraft, 360
Indo-European languages, 41
Industrial Revolution, 198–199
Infanticide, 134, 148, 251, 262, 267–268, 271
Initiation rites, 122–123, 125, 301
International imbalance, 446, 447
Inventions:
  nonmaterial, 424
  technical, 424
Iroquois, 166, 281, 371
  dream interpretation, 346
  league of, 296–298
Islam, 181–182, 189, 193, 210, 378
  (*See also* Muslims)
Ituri Pygmies, 123–126, 162, 221

J

Jarmo, 426
Jati, 203–205, 231
"Java man" (see *Homo erectus*)
Jefferson, Thomas:
  as archaeologist, 16

Jefferson, Thomas:
  as cultural relativist, 16
  theories regarding American Indians, 16-17
Jericho, 48
Jesus, 363, 385
Jie, 182, 186
Jivaro, 145, 146, 346, 372
Joint family, 274-278

K

Kaingang, 145
Kalmyk steppes, 430
Kanuri, 238
Kardiner, Abraham, 20
Kenyatta, Jomo, 258-259
Khan, Genghis, 188-192, 194
Kibbutz, 253, 271
Kikuyu (see Gikuyu)
Kinship, 121, 130, 134, 139, 143, 175,
    180-181, 185, 186, 192, 194, 246-249, 255
  and caste systems, 231
  decline of, 451
  extensions of: clans, 278-280, 282-283
    joint families, 274-278
    lineages: bilateral descent, 278-279
      dual descent, 280-281
      matrilineages, 270-274, 278, 280
      patrilineages, 278, 280
      unilineal descent, 278-279
    moieties, 281
    phratries, 282
  recognition by chimpanzee, 72-73
  and slavery, 136-139
  and social class, 223-226, 229, 231
  and status, 289-290
  systems of kinship: bifurcate collateral, 287
    bifurcate merging, 286-289
    Crow, 287-289
    generational, 285
    lineal, 286
    Omaha, 287, 288

Kipling, Rudyard, 437, 445
Kirchhoff, Paul, 250, 282, 283
Kluckhohn, Clyde, 295, 361, 373-375
Knorosov, Yuri, 411-412
Koenigswald, G. H. R. von, 64
Koran, 180, 256, 260, 262
Koryak, 173
Kpelle, 302
Krader, Lawrence, 298-300, 309
Krishna, 383
Kroeber, Alfred L., 23, 41, 99, 284-285
Kromdrai, 65
Kshatriya, 231, 232, 235
Kwakiutl, 24, 118, 136, 139-141, 376

L

Lafitau, Father, 16
Lagos, Nigeria, 451
Landa, Diego de, 410
Lang, Andrew, 371
Language:
  areas, 41-42
  characteristics of, 391-392
  structure of, 40
Lao Tzu, 383
Lapps, 97, 171-173, 175-177
Lascaux Cave, 84
Law, 314-337
  characteristics of, 315-317
  chart illustrating, 319
  and criminal intent, 318
  definition, 315
  divination, 331
  enforcement, 317-318
  rudimentary, 321-326
  trial by combat, 334-335
  trial by ordeal, 331-334
  Wergild, 318-321
Leakey, Louis S. B., 45, 67, 89-90
Legal systems:
  Ashanti, 327-328

Legal systems:
  Barotseland (Lozi), 326-327
  Eskimo, 321-324, 337
  Ifugao, 324
  Tiv, 324-325
  Zulu, 324-326
Lenski, Gerhart, 27, 229
Leopard society, 302-304
Leroi-Gourhan, André, 395-397
Lévi-Strauss, Claude, 25-26, 145, 251, 429
  structural analysis of myth, 376-378
Levirate, 260-261
Leviticus, dietary rules of, 357-359
Lewis, Oscar, 39, 272
Library:
  of Alexandria, 415
  of Nineveh, 404, 415
Lieberman, Leonard, 98
Lineage (see Kinship, extensions of)
Lingayat Brahmans, 204, 205
Linguistics, 40-43, 53
  (See also Language)
Linnaeus, Carolus, 60
Linton, Ralph, 194, 221, 275, 310, 311
Livingston, Frank B., 101
Lowie, Robert, 23, 223, 300-301
Lozi of Barotzeland, 326-327
Lunar notations, Paleolithic, 399
Lyell, Charles, 17

M

Macaque, Japanese, 71, 85
Macedonian Dynasty (of Egypt), 405-406
Magdalenian art, 84, 399
Magic:
  and anxiety, 367-369
  contagious, 349-350
  for crops and herds, 187-188
  functions of, 347
  holophrastic magic, 21
  hunting magic, 124-125, 128
  imitative, 349
Magic:
  origins of, 64-65
  and reassurance value, 367-369
  and religion, 348
  repetitive, 349
  and sacrifice, 350
  and science, 347
  will magic, 349
Maine, Henry, 21
Malinowski, Bronislaw, 22, 26, 35, 253, 294,
  347-349, 365, 367-368, 373, 379
Mallowan, M. E. L., 401
Malthus, Thomas, 18
Mana, 157, 346-347
Manchu Dynasty, 191-192, 276
Manus Islands, 352
Maori, 222-223, 363
Markham, Edwin, 198
Marquesans, 363
Marriage, 175-176, 181, 183, 186, 192, 193
  affinal, 260-261
  and children (Gikuyu), 257-259
  cousins, 255-256, 265
  Indian peasants (Gopalpur), 209-210,
    215-216
  (See also Family; Horticulturists; Hunters
    and gatherers; Incest taboo; Kinship;
    Monogamy; Pastoralists; Peasants;
    Polyandry; Polygyny)
Marshack, Alexander, 375, 397
Marxists, 298, 389
Masai, 182-183, 185-188, 270, 301
Mather, Cotton, 15
Matrilineal descent, 270, 274, 278, 280, 288
Matrilocal residence, 270, 274
Mayans, 132, 350
  numbering system, 409-411
  writing system, 411-413
Mead, Margaret, 23, 24, 35-36, 349
  quotation regarding anthropology, 10
Medicine men, 362
  cures by, 362-366

Melanesia, 94, 244, 304–305
Mesa Verde, 157
Mesolithic art, 400–401
Metallurgy, 163, 187, 427–430
Micronesia, 94
Middleton, John, 37
Middleton, Russell, 277
Mills, C. Wright, 299
Mohammed (*see* Muhammad)
Moieties, 251, 281
Molecular time scale of hominid evolution, 51–52
Mongols, 188–194, 223, 308–309
Monogamy, 134, 143, 249, 268–270
Montagu, Ashley, 101
Morgan, Lewis Henry, 20–21, 93, 99, 249, 284
Morris, Desmond, 455
Mousterian culture, 50, 63, 79
Muhammad, 96–97, 260, 382, 385
Muisik soul, 354
Muller, Max, 375
Mummification, 355
Mundurucú, 145
Murdock, George, 36–37
Murngin, 121
Murphy, Robert, 145, 177, 181, 182
Muslims, 181, 182, 192, 204, 210–211, 233
(*See also* Islam)
Myrdal, Gunnar, 234
Myth:
common themes, 373–374
destruction stories, including the Great Flood, 374
interpretation, 373–374
structural analysis of (Lévi-Strauss), 376–378

N

Naga, 232
Nambikwara, 145
Natchez Indians, 224–226
Nationhood, problems for Africa, 452

Native American Church, 389
Navaho, 40–41, 170, 211, 253
Navigation:
Polynesians, 95–96
techniques, 432–435
Nayar, 270
Taravad, 274
Neanderthal man, 50, 62–63, 68, 79–81, 85, 87, 88
New Guinea:
Highland tribes and cannibalism, 64
(*See also* Dugum Dani; Gururumba)
Newman, Philip, Jr., 152, 154–157
Nigeria, 11
Nimkoff, N. F., 277
Nootka, 132, 136, 137, 139, 141, 356
Northwest Coast Indians, 136–141, 155, 167, 222–224, 283
Nuer, 188, 257
Nyul-Nyul, 121
Nzkara, 333

O

Obsidian trade, 425–426
Oedipus myth, 376–377
Oglala Sioux, 23
Olcott, Mason, 231, 232
Olduvai Gorge, Tanzania, 45, 67, 78
Omo Valley, Ethiopia, 67
Ontogenetic growth of primates, 75
Ordos Mongols, 190–194
Oriental society, theory of, 308
Orwell, George, 313
Osiris, 383

P

Pagan cults and witch belief, 361
Paleontology, 48–49
Palm Beach, 447
Pars pro toto, 400
Parsis, 355
Parsons, Talcott, 27

Pastoralists, 170–195, 277–278, 282
  chart illustrating, 195
  kinship, 175–176, 180–181, 185–186, 192, 194
  religion and world view, 176–177, 181–182, 187–188, 192–193
  social organization, 175–176, 180–181, 185–187, 191–192
  technology, 172–175, 179–180, 183–185, 190–191
  tribes included: Barabaig and Masai, 182–188
    Mongols, 188–194
    reindeer herders (Lapps, Samoyeds, Northern Tungus), 171–177
    Tuareg, 177–182
  warfare, 175–180, 182, 185, 188–190, 193
Paton, Alan, 451
Patrilineal descent, 255, 256, 278, 280, 287–288
Patrilocal residence, 255–256, 275
Peace Corps, 34
Peasants and farmers, 37–38, 197–219
  chart illustrating, 219
  common traits, 217–218
  economics, 199–203, 212–214
  kinship and marriage, 204–205, 209–210, 215–216
  religion and world view, 205–206, 210–211, 216–217
  social organization, 200–201, 203–205, 209–210, 215–216
  societies included: Greece (Vasilika), 212–217
    Gopalpur (India), 201–206
    Java, 207–212
  technology and production, 202–203, 208–209, 212–215
Pei, Weng Chung, 64, 99
Persia, 402–403
Personality studies, 24
Peru, craftsmanship, 428

Peter, Saint, 386
Peyote, 389
Philippines, 445
Phonograms, 405
Phratries, 281–282
Piaget, Jean, 345
Pictographs, 405
"Piltdown man," 62
Pit River Indians, 127
Pitcairn Islanders, 101
Pithecanthropus erectus (see *Homo erectus*)
Plains Indians (*see* Great Plains Indians)
Pollen analysis, 49
Pollution, 448–449
Polyandry, 130, 143, 249–250, 261, 265–268
  in Ladakh, 266–268
  in Toda, 265–266
Polygamy, defined, 261
Polygyny, 130, 143, 164, 246, 250, 258–259, 261–265, 269, 275
  among Baganda, 262–264
Polynesia, 94–96, 222–224, 283, 304–305, 432
  map, 94
Poro society, 302
Pottery, 426–427
Poverty, culture of, 39
Primates:
  behavioral studies of, 71–74
  classification of, 70–71
  common traits of, 74–76
  dominance patterns, 72–75, 77
  evolution of, 68–70
  grooming behavior, 72–74
  posture, 76
  social organization, 71–74, 85
Primatology (*see* Primates)
Printing:
  block, 415
  moveable type, 415–416
Ptolemy, 406
Pueblo Indians, 144, 157–162, 170, 211
Pygmies (*see* Ituri Pygmies)

R

Race, 97-107
  concept of, 98-107
  and hominid distribution, 98
  and hominid evolution, 97-100
  nonracial concepts, 101-107
Radcliffe-Brown, A. R., 22, 26, 367, 369, 394
Radin, Paul, 317
Rama, 205
Ramapithecus, 69, 77, 87
Rank, social, 222-223, 229
Rasmussen, Knud, 132
Rawlinson, George, 403
Redfield, Robert, 316
Reformation, Protestant, 370
Reincarnation, 205-206
Reindeer domestication, 171-175
Reindeer herders, 171-177
  chart of, 174
Religion, 343-390
  contrasted with magic, 348
  crisis in, 386
  eclipse of traditional religion, 455
  evolution of, 378-385
    archaic religion, 379-380
    historic religions, 381-385
      China, 383-384
      Egypt, 382
      Greece, 383-384
      India, 383
      Persia, 382-383
    primitive religion, characteristics, 379
  and ideology, 454-455
  as reflection of society, 369-372
  and social cohesion, 123
  in Sweden and Russia, 455
  syncretism, 386-387
  (*See also* Horticulturalists; Hunters and
    gatherers; Pastoralists; Peasants)
Religious societies, 166
Resources, exhaustion of, 448-449
Revitalization movements, 386-389

Rhodes, 426
Ricardo, David, 18
Rice cultivation, 208-209
Robertson, William, 16
Robinson, John T., 65
Romans, 282, 283, 331
Rosetta stone, 405-406
Russia, 445

S

Sacrifice, 165-166, 176, 187, 194, 205, 224,
  229, 237, 239, 380
  human, explanation of, 350
Sahagún, Bernardo de, 15
Sahlins, Marshall, 188, 293, 296, 304, 305
Samoans, 35
Samoyeds, 97, 171, 173, 175
Sapir, Edward, 23
Sarich, Vincent, 51, 100
Satanism, 361-362
Schliemann, Heinrich, 45
Schmidt, Wilhelm, 371
Schweitzer, Albert, 364
Science, contrasted with magic and religion,
  347
Secret societies, 165-166, 222, 302
  illustration, Poro mask, 303
Semang, 119
Sequoia, 413
Service, Elman, 27, 143, 250, 289-290
Sex:
  premarital, 35-36
  role in social development, 75
  roles, 221-222
  taboos, 39
Shamans, 85-86, 131, 135, 141-143, 148, 150,
  176, 362-364
Shang Dynasty, 408
Shih Huang-ti, 415
Shills, Edward, 451
Ships, of ancient world, 432-433
Shoshone, 118, 127, 131, 356

Siberia, 445
Sikhs, 233
Simpson, Ruth deEtte, 89–90
Sinathropus (see *Homo erectus*)
Sioux, Oglala, 23
Siriono, 118
Siva, 205
Skin color, 101–103
Slametans, 211
Slash and burn agriculture, 147–148
Slavery, 140, 165, 180–182, 220–221, 229,
    235–239, 272
Slotkin, J. S., 389
Smith, Homer, 362
Social change, 420–443
Social class, 197, 203–204, 209–210, 220–241
    and agrarian societies, 226–230
    and slavery, 235–239
    and surplus production, 220–241
Social Darwinists, 18
Song duel, 322–324
Sorcery, 185, 211, 217
Sororate, 26
Soul:
    immanence of, 372
    theories of, 350–354
Speech, characteristics of, 392–393
Spencer, Herbert, 18
State:
    and associations, 301–304
    characteristics of, 298–300
    and conquest, 308–311
    development of, 300, 302–308
    and international organization, 312–315
    and persistence of tribalism, 311–312
    role of "Big man" and chieftains, 304–305
    and theory of Oriental society, 308
Status, 18, 125, 136, 139–140, 143, 167, 181,
    191, 210, 221, 253
    achieved, 221–230
    ascribed, 221, 230

Status:
    and kinship, 289–290
    and sex, 221–222
    and slavery, 235–239
Sterkfontein, 65
Steward, Julian, 27
    multilineal cultural evolution, 28
Stoddard, John Lothrop, 98
Stonehenge, 375, 435–436
Stylization, 400–401
Sudras, 231
Sumeria:
    eye idols, 400
    writing system, 401–402
Supernaturalism:
    and law, 337
    (*See also* Magic; Religion; Sorcery)
Swadesh, Morris, 42–43
Swanson, Guy, 370–372, 378
Swartkranz, 65
Syllabaries, 413
Symbolizing, 391
Symbols:
    language as symbolism, 391
    male and female, 395, 397 (illus.)
    mesolithic, 400–401
Syncretism, religious, 386–387

T

Taboo, 135, 186, 304
    food, 232, 357
    incest, 252–254
    and law, 323
    sexual, 148, 155–156, 234
    and social control, 356
Tanala, 235–236, 275–276
Taoism, 211, 378
Taos Indians, 158
Tapirapé, 145, 354–355
Tasaday, 33
Taung skull, 65

Tax, Sol, 37
Technology:
   as master of man, 449–450
   (*See also* Horticulturists; Hunters and
      gatherers; Pastoralists; Peasants)
Teeth (*see* Dentition)
Teilhard de Chardin, Pierre, 65
Tenochtitlán, 229
Teotihuacán ruins, 14 (illus.)
Tewksbury, William, 333
Thomas, Elizabeth Marshall, 257
Thomasson, Richard F., 455
Tibetans, 265, 267–268
Timbuktu, 451
Time:
   calendrical calculations, 435
   clocks and timepieces, 435–439
   time-centered world, 438–439
Tiv, 33, 251, 347
Tiwi, 251
Tlingit, 118, 136, 140, 281, 287
Toda, 265–268
Toffler, Alvin, 459
Tool use:
   by chimpanzees, 72–73, 85
   development of, 76–79, 81, 84, 86
   stone, 93
Totem animals, 352
Totemism, 122, 126, 160
Toynbee, Arnold, 455
Trade, 293, 312
   origins, 48
Transhumance, 173–175, 191
Transmigration, 351–352
Trepanning, 363
Trial by combat, 334–335
Trial by ordeal, 331–334
Tribalism, 292–298
   and confederacies, 296–298
   development, 296

Tribalism:
   gift exchange and trade, 293–294
   lack of central authority, 294–296
   and state control, 311–312
Trobriand Islanders, 35, 274, 280, 347
Trois Frères Cave, 395
Troy, 45
Tsimshian, 136
Tuareg, 171, 177–182, 360
Tungus, 171–173, 175–176, 194
Turkana, 182
Turkestan, 445
Turnbull, Colin, 123–125
Tylor, Edward B., 13, 19–20, 344–345, 368,
   371, 378

U

Unilineal descent, 278–279
United Nations, 312
Ur, 47–48
Utes, 157

V

Vaisya, 231, 233
Vasilika, Greece, 212–217
Vega, Garcilaso de la, 15
Vegetarian castes, 203–204
Vicos, Peru, 38
Virgin of Guadalupe, 15, 387
Vishnu, 205

W

Wagley, Charles, 145
Warfare, 262
   (*See also* Horticulturists; Hunters and
      gatherers; Pastoralists)
Warner, Esther, 333
Washburn, Sherwood, 72, 75–77
Washo, 126–131, 177, 264
Weber, Max, 367, 385–386, 389–390

Weidenreich, Franz, 62, 64, 99
Wergild, 318–321
Weyer, Edward, Jr., 145
Wheeled transport:
    chariots, 431
    wagons and carts, 430–431
White, Leslie A., 23, 27, 29, 223, 250,
        256–257, 299–300, 311
Whorf, Benjamin Lee, 25
Winnebago Indians, 317
Wissler, Clark, 23
Witchcraft:
    Azande, 359–360
    in Christian belief, 361–362
    explanations of, 360–362
    Navaho, 361
Witchdoctors, 362–363
Wittfogel, Karl, 28, 308, 310
Wolf, Eric, 15, 199, 206

Wooley, Sir Charles Leonard, 47
Würm Ice Age, 80, 81, 88

Y
Yahgan, 97, 118, 321
Yako, 280
Yang and Yin, 373
Yanomanö, 145–152, 167, 168, 221, 255–256,
        292–293
Yoruba, 145, 162–166, 188, 301
Young, Dr. Thomas, 405
Yurok, 136, 141

Z
Zinjanthropus bosei (see Australopithecines)
Zoroaster, 382–383
Zulu, 301
Zuñi, 24, 158–160, 167–168, 222, 272–274,
        376